D0425637

MUSICAL GUMBO
The Music of New Orleans

MUSICAL GUMBO

The Music of New Orleans

Grace Lichtenstein and Laura Dankner

W· W· NORTON & COMPANY
New York · London

Since this page cannot legibly accommodate
all the copyright notices, p. 367 constitutes
an extension of the copyright page.

Copyright © 1993 by Grace Lichtenstein and Laura Dankner
All rights reserved
Printed in the United States of America
First Edition
The text of this book is composed in Antikva Margaret with
the display set in Broadway. Composition and manufacturing
by The Maple-Vail Book Manufacturing Group.
Book design by Charlotte Staub.

Library of Congress Cataloging-in-Publication Data

Lichtenstein, Grace.
Musical gumbo : the music of New Orleans /
Grace Lichtenstein and Laura Dankner.
p.   cm.
Discography: p.
Includes bibliographical references and index.
1. Music—Louisiana—New Orleans—History and criticism.
I. Dankner, Laura.   II. Title.
ML200.8.N48L5   1993
780'.9763'35—dc20   92–30690

ISBN 0-393-03468-2
W. W. Norton & Company, Inc.
500 Fifth Avenue, New York, N.Y. 10110
W. W. Norton & Company Ltd.
10 Coptic Street, London WC1A 1PU

1 2 3 4 5 6 7 8 9 0

To our favorite
New Orleans musician,
Steve Dankner

Contents

CONTENTS •

Acknowledgments

vvvvvvvvvvvvvvvvvvvvvvvvv

This book would have been impossible to produce without the cooperation of the musical community in South Louisiana and its branches in New York and Los Angeles. We particularly would like to thank the following musicians for their help: C. J. Chenier, Tony Dagradi, Michael Doucet, Jacques Gauthé, Victor Goines, Herbert Hardesty, Fred Kemp, Ellis Marsalis, Jason Marsalis, Wynton Marsalis, Steve Masakowski, Cory McCauley, Earl Palmer, George Porter, Jr., John Rankin, Zachary Richard, Mac Rebennack, Kermit Ruffins, Irma Thomas, Wayne Toups, Allen Toussaint, and Sherman Washington.

Concert producers, critics, editors, patrons, managers, record companies, and agents also contributed mightily. We are grateful to Bunny Freidus, formerly of Columbia Records; Allison Miner; Jan Ramsey, publisher of *Offbeat;* Ben Sandmel; Jeff Hannusch; Jason Berry; Quint Davis, Eugenie "E.J." Jones, Rhonda Ford, Anna Zimmerman, Susan Mock, and Louis Edwards of the Jazz and Heritage Festival; Marion Layton Levy of Rounder Records; photographer Rick Olivier; Beverly Gianna and the staff of the Greater New Orleans Tourist and Convention Commission; Kimberly Carbo; Arthur Pulitzer; Kelly Strenge, Alicia Toups, and Jim Black in Lafayette; Helene Greece; John Rockwell of the *New York Times;* Linda Halsey of the *Washington Post;* Leslie Ward and Joyce Miller of the *Los Angeles Times;* Bob Stone; Dr. Joyce Jackson of Louisiana State

University; Nick Marinello; Melody Mineo; Macon Fry; Ara Porter; Dick Waterman; Freddy Pate; Shannon Vale; Floyd Soileau; Chris Strachwitz; Slash Records; Reggie Toussaint; Charlie Bering; Victoria Clark; Adam Block of EMI; B.B.; Ruth Innis of BMG Records; and Reddy Teddy.

From Grace Lichtenstein, special thanks for advice, encouragement, and companionship to my writers' group—Ann Banks, Gwenda Blair, Catherine Breslin, Carol Brightman, Jane Ciabattari, Kathryn Kilgore, Robin Reisig, Anne Summers, and Marilyn Webb, as well as to Elaine Freeman, Jan Goodman, and Sandy Gold.

From Laura Dankner, special thanks for professional and personal assistance to Connie Atkinson formerly editor of *Wavelength;* Rand Speyrer; Bruce Daigrepont and family: George Buck; Bruce Raeburn of the William Ransom Hogan Jazz Archive at Tulane University; Robert Curtis and the staff of the Maxwell Music Library, Tulane; Mark McKnight, University of North Texas Music Library; Vincent Pelote, Rutgers University; Alfred Lemon and Stan Ritchey of the Historic New Orleans Collection; Gary Talarchek of Loyola University for help on grants; Dean David Swanzy, Loyola University College of Music; Jim Hobbs, Darla Rushing, Rosalee McReynolds, and Edith Roy of the Loyola University Library; Rosario Barrios of the Loyola University Music Library; Mike Klein for computer help; Tower Records in New Orleans; Friends of the New Orleans Center for Creative Arts; Roundup Records; Roots & Rhythm; Barbara Bartocci; and Carolyn Bishop.

From both authors, our heartfelt thanks to Steve Dankner; Kay Metelka, Mike Sartisky, and the Louisiana Endowment for the Humanities for a grant supporting our research; to our thoughtful editor at Norton, Hilary Hinzmann; and to Sarah Lazin, a most attentive agent who puts the interests of her authors first.

MUSICAL GUMBO
The Music of New Orleans

1 Introduction: Jambalaya, Crawfish Pie, Filé Gumbo

> Now don't you be no fool, eh
> You let the bons temps rouler
>   —from a classic Louisiana song

"Let the good times roll"—not every city would appreciate being described in so hedonistic a phrase. New Orleans embraces it. And for three centuries, the world has responded by beating a path to its door.

That has been especially true in recent years; New Orleans' irresistible, spicy cultural roux has infiltrated the country's— even the world's—taste as never before in food, literature, and the performing arts.

From New York to New Zealand, Louisiana cuisine heats gourmet palates. Thanks to Paul Prudhomme, the local food has achieved what might be termed a blackened break-through. Restaurants featuring Louisiana cuisine multiply as quickly as crawfish across the country, while redfish disappears from menus only because demand outstrips supply. Theatergoers have long seen the Crescent City through the eyes of Tennessee Williams. Now, in addition, readers revel in its strange and wonderful characters through best-selling novels such as Anne Rice's *Queen of the Damned* and John Kennedy Toole's *A Confederacy of Dunces*. Movies like *The Big Easy* make the city's nickname as instantly recognizable as that of the Big Apple. Bands like the Neville Brothers play venues from Boston to San Diego. Folk heroes once hardly known outside their own parish, like Dewey Balfa, appear on the "Today" show. Long-established Bourbon Street musicians play sold-out tours throughout Europe and Asia. Stars from Paul Simon to Sting to Linda Ronstadt borrow Cajun riffs, zydeco accordions, and New Orleanian sidemen.

The universe, it would seem, is becoming one huge bayou.

Our love affair with this town at once indolent and vivacious, a blend of skyscrapers and swamps, stately mansions and shotgun shacks, is not new. New Orleans culture has cast a spell over the nation and the world for nearly a hundred years.

But it is the music—more than Mardi Gras, more than the French Quarter, more than the streetcar (now a bus) named Desire, more than the beignets for breakfast—that has always been at the heart of our fascination with New Orleans. No other place has contributed a richer heritage of pop music to the rest of the United States, from Dixieland to rock 'n' roll to contemporary jazz, from Louis Armstrong to Wynton Marsalis, from Fats Domino to Dr. John, from Mahalia Jackson to Harry Connick, Jr.

Nor is there a town that matches its vibrant current scene. These days, the good times roll seven nights a week in New Orleans at an astonishing two hundred and fifty clubs, cabarets, and hotels featuring live performers. And 300,000 fans from around the world gather annually to attend its Jazz and Heritage Festival.

This book tells why this phenomenon happened, who the major figures are, and where it is headed. In this chapter, we look briefly at how Louisiana developed over two hundred years. Then we examine what is still its most famous popular music export—traditional jazz and Dixieland. In chapters 3 and 4, we take a backward glance at the evolution of rhythm and blues and eventually rock 'n' roll, New Orleans' longest-lasting product of the postwar period. Chapter 5 explores the growth of country music in the South Louisiana environs in the form of Cajun and zydeco. Chapter 6 is about the rebirth of jazz, this time in a contemporary form, in the Crescent City. The final section describes the clubs, concerts of live music, and festivals for which the region has become famous, gives information on buying New Orleans records, and lists the best available discs, books, and videos.

The origins of the remarkable state at the mouth of the Mississippi are both royal and rowdy, highbrow and humble, exotic and down home. Embedded in its history is the notion of waves of diverse ethnic, religious, and racial groups washing upon its shore, where they percolated in a unique cultural blend, a blend more unusual than perhaps any other city on the North American continent. Along with that blend, despite the periodic waning and waxing of the city's fortunes, there is an undercurrent theme: the dedication of the people of the region to earthly pleasures, especially dancing and music.

The Choctaw Indians were the first humans to inhabit the delta marshland. In 1682, the French explorer La Salle navigated the great river that Indians called the Mississippi, and claimed the entire chunk of land on either side—from the Allegheny Mountains in the east to the Rockies in the west—in the name of his sovereign, the Sun King, Louis XIV. With the territory thus designated Louisiana, two brothers, Pierre le Moyne, sieur d'Iberville, and Jean-Baptiste le Moyne, sieur de Bienville, set sail from France in order to establish colonies. In 1699 d'Iberville planted a cross in the swamp along a bend of the Mississippi where the river takes a jog near Lake Pontchartrain. The cross was the site of their newest settlement, named in honor of the duke of Orleans.

Work began on the town in 1718, but France had a hard time recruiting colonists. A Scottish gambler living in France, John Law, got the contract to exploit the colony in what now seems to have been a major real estate fraud. He lured Europeans to the tiny place by selling shares in a land company that he claimed would yield incredible riches of gold and silver. To bolster its manpower, the French transported convicts to form the core of the work crew that built the town's first huts on the Mississippi's mosquito-infested shores. A shortage of women was solved temporarily shortly thereafter when eighty-eight prostitutes from an infamous Parisian prison were shipped to New Orleans. Then, in 1727, a group of teenaged girls arrived, chaperoned by nuns of the Ursuline Order. These young women, imported as brides for the settlers, became known as the "casket girls" because they carried their dowries in portable trunks.

The town managed to survive floods, hostile Indians, and disease. Soon colonists began importing slaves from both the West Indies and Africa. Germans joined the colonial mix. But New Orleans was more muddy frontier town than budding Versailles when Pierre Cavagnal de Rigaud de Vaudreuil was appointed the territorial governor in 1742.

During his ten years in office, the marquis set the tone for the good times that were to come. Influenced by his wife, he brought to the New World the Latin Catholic custom of holding a series of balls, banquets, and parades in the weeks leading up to Lent. It was just what the growing leisure class needed to take its mind off the hardships of colonial life. The pre-Lenten festivities of Carnival, or Mardi Gras, burst into life.

So it was that music, dancing, and parades became an institution—a way of life—in Louisiana by the time the Spaniards took possession of the territory in 1766. That way of life included a tolerance of sinful fun and games—gambling, drinking, and fornication. New Orleans was on the road to becoming the foremost good-time city in the New World. According to historians, the Spanish occupation did not make too much of a dent in Louisiana except architecturally, but the population soared from 7,500 in 1766 to 50,000 in 1803.

Where were the newcomers from? Nova Scotia primarily. Acadians, descendants of the first French people in the New World, took advantage of land grants available from Spain in Louisiana to flee the British, who had conquered Canada. Settling around St. Martinville, they became the core of a new strain of French Louisianians, the Cajun community. Meanwhile, both whites and free blacks arrived from Cuba and Santo Domingo.

In 1801, Spain, desperate for money, sold the territory back to France. However, Thomas Jefferson, the president of the young United States, felt that owning the flourishing seaport would be of great strategic value. He persuaded Napoleon to sell his vast holdings for fifteen million dollars, and in 1803 Americans began to flood the growing city of New Orleans. As the port became increasingly busy with ships ferrying supplies to the frontier west, the French flavor of the city became seasoned with Spanish, British, West Indian, Cuban, and Protestant American touches. The haughty French looked upon the American intruders as uncouth, and a "battle of the ballrooms" soon broke out over whether to dance French or English quadrilles. Dancing, the new American governor reported to Washington, was not a trivial matter to New Orleanians but a "foremost concern."

Nevertheless, distinctly Latin elements remained. For one thing, African Americans from the beginning were more of a force in the city than anywhere else in the South. The Code Noir, or Black Code, of 1724 required masters to allow slaves to rest on Sundays, permitted marriages, and allowed owners to free slaves. By 1803 there were thus already three thousand free blacks in New Orleans. In addition, a minority of wealthy white men kept up the custom of "placage," which allowed them to take African American girls as mistresses until they were married. After marriage, these men sometimes installed their mistresses in great houses. Often, in their wills, these masters provided that their mistresses and children would be free. The result was the development of a class of Creoles of Color, light-skinned, French-speaking men and women. (The original whites of French descent were also called Creoles, but today the term is increasingly used in reference to Creoles of Color.) Creoles had, as one sociologist notes, a "freedom of movement . . . unprecedented on the North American continent." By the early 1800s, Creoles of Color "occupied a position very near the top of the social order of the city."

Moreover, thanks to its Latin roots, antebellum New Orleans exuded a gaiety and a love of showy splendor unknown in the

Protestant North. The city was filled with music almost from its inception. During La Belle Epoque, the years before the Civil War, the city boasted three theaters. Concerts and opera productions in Italian, French, and English were frequent. Dancing was the passion of the people. Celebrations and festivals abounded. What's more, the "French tendency to parade at the slightest excuse (a Napoleonic legacy) was copied by other groups," according to one account. "Every holiday came replete with parade bands and martial music." As the city grew, so did its reputation for revelry. "Visitors seemed to agree: New Orleans had the best food and the worst sanitation, the longest social calendar and the shortest life span, while supporting more alcoholics, prostitutes and gamblers than any other city in America," as journalist Mel Leavitt put it.

Urban slaves in New Orleans had a long musical tradition. Before the Civil War, besides the descendants of the original French settlers, Spanish families, white Americans, wealthy Creoles of Color, and free blacks from Santo Domingo and elsewhere in the West Indies (who brought the practice of vodun, or voodoo, with them), there were many slaves serving the city's great homes and nearby plantations. Indeed, because of its location, New Orleans had one of the biggest slave markets in the United States. By 1850 the Code Noir had disappeared and slaves here had their rights trampled on, and their families split up, like their counterparts elsewhere.

Nevertheless, the status and lifestyle of the urban slaves were unique. They were "perhaps the most sophisticated group of bondsmen since the days of ancient Rome," according to one historian, because so many were either in domestic service or working at a skilled job such as carpentry or blacksmithing. Moreover, in an urban setting owners were not able to keep such a rigid hold on them as plantation owners kept on their slaves. Some actually were allowed to hold balls in their masters' homes; others were able to save enough to buy their freedom. In addition, they had a recreational outlet their counterparts in nearby states did not. One day a week, they were permitted to get together to dance.

The slaves congregated at a number of places, the most famous being Congo Square, a large open space at the intersection of Rampart and Orleans streets on the border of the Vieux Carré. From the accounts by white observers from that period, it would seem that every Sunday beginning in 1835, drawn to Congo Square by the incessant beat of drums, throngs of slaves would throw off their cares by dancing the Bamboula, the Calinda, and other joyous, exotic dances of African origin. Their stringed instruments and drums were similar to those used in Africa. To white onlookers, they looked primitive, exotic, and uninhibited. It could be that many of the celebrations in Congo Square were disguised voodoo ceremonies, as one book, *Bourbon Street Black*, suggests. But whatever else those slaves were doing, they were, in the authors' words, "reveling in another of the currents that would feed the new jazz."

Among the observers of this entertainment was the young composer Louis Gottschalk. A biographer, who unfortunately uses phrases that sound patronizing to our contemporary ears, describes the scene that Gottschalk supposedly witnessed as a child:

> The visitor finds the multitude packed in groups of close, narrow circles. . . . [In the center] sits the musician, astride a barrel, strong headed, which he beats with two sticks, to a strange measure incessantly, like mad, for hours together. . . . There too labor the dancers male and female, under an inspiration of possession. . . . The head rests upon the breast, or is thrown back upon the shoulders, the eyes closed, or glaring, while the arms, amid cries and shouts and sharp ejaculations, float upon the air, or keep time with the hands patting upon the thighs, to a music which is seemingly eternal. . . .

The Civil War interrupted such merriment, of course. The Congo Square gatherings were resumed by freed slaves after the war. They were ultimately stopped by authorities in 1885 because they were considered disruptive. But by then much had changed in the Crescent City.

As a rollicking port it continued to teem with sailors, settlers, and suppliers from the North, the Caribbean, and beyond. The city's bawdy houses and taverns were as busy following the war as before. But after the radical Republicans were thrown out of office, racism and segregation sprang up here as it did throughout the bitter South. First the churches, then the schools, then every aspect of society was separated by race.

The light-skinned Creoles, once members of the upper crust of society, were suddenly stripped of their trappings of status in 1894 and lumped by law in a category with emancipated slaves and blacks of all hues. However, these Creoles, far better educated and wealthier than others of African descent, considered their darker brethren to be crude and unsophisticated. They developed their own form of society, with fraternal and burial organizations, bands, and balls. The result in New Orleans of separate strata of whites, Creoles, and blacks, the latter group residing "downtown" in the Vieux Carré, the former two "uptown," had a marked influence on popular music.

Since music had been a part of New Orleans life for more than a century, there were many separate white and Creole orchestras in the years after the Civil War that played "refined" music—either classical recitals or sedate dances. The city was stocked with well-schooled musicians, and bands were everywhere. The late nineteenth century was the great era of marching bands throughout the United States—John Philip Sousa was the most famous musician of his day. It was customary for youngsters in New Orleans, as elsewhere, to take lessons from their elders so they, too, could play in the bands of their social clubs or civic organizations.

Blacks also formed organizations that supported marching brass bands. By 1881, thirteen such bands from New Orleans played at the funeral of President Garfield. The bands were integral parts of the social clubs that came to dominate the black community. These, after all, were the days before unions or Medicare. Members paid dues to these clubs in exchange for sick benefits and eventually an elaborate funeral. But in addition the clubs were places where members could gather during their off-hours. There were picnics and dances as well as elaborate funerals during which fellow members, and at least one band, accompanied the horse-drawn hearse to the funeral and sat at large wakes afterward. A roll call of brass bands in the 1880s in the city would include the Excelsior and Onward, considered two of the finest. The Oriental Brass Band was formed around 1886. Not only were the bands active in their own affairs, but they played on such holidays as Labor Day, when the city traditionally had huge public celebrations.

Marching bands did not have to worry about finding instruments. After both the Civil War and the Spanish-American War, military bands frequently were dissolved in New Orleans and their members sold their used instruments to the pawnshops on Rampart Street. Many of these European instruments—cornets, clarinets, trombones, and the like—found their way into the hands of Uptown black families as well as white ones. Long before anyone coined the word "jazz," New Orleanians were accustomed to hearing the sounds of these brass instruments marching through their neighborhoods.

Jelly Roll Morton vividly recalled the parades of his youth in his conversations with folklorist Alan Lomax:

> New Orleans was very organization-minded. I have never seen such beautiful clubs as they had there—the Broadway Swells, the High Arts, the Orleans Aides, the Bulls and Bears, the Tramps, the Iroquois, the Allegroes—that was just a few of them, and those clubs would parade at least once a week. . . .
>
> Those parades were really tremendous things. The drums would start off, the trumpets and trombones rolling into something like *Stars & Stripes* or *The National Anthem,* and everybody would strut off down the street, the bass-drum player twirling his beater in the air, the snare drummer throwing his sticks up and bouncing them off the ground, the kids jumping and hollering, the grand

marshal and his aides in their expensive uniforms moving along dignified, women on top of women strutting along back of the aides and out in front of everybody—the second line. . . .

The men who were to grow up to be jazz giants all reminisced in later years about the bands and parades of their youth in the fading years of the nineteenth century and the early ones of the twentieth. "The most miserable feeling a youngster in New Orleans can experience," said guitarist Danny Barker, "is to be in a classroom in school, studying, and hear a brass band approaching, swinging like crazy, then pass the school and fade off in the distance." Sometimes the parades were so long, lasting well into the night, that it became customary for young players who trailed the band, carrying the instruments for the players, to sit in—to beat the drum or play a few notes on cornet while the older men took a break for a beer. Many, including Louis Armstrong and Sidney Bechet, were still in their early teens, in short pants, when they first became apprentices to the great brass bands.

One more key element helped ignite the explosion of innovative popular music around the turn of this century. In 1897, in an effort to control rampant vice, the city passed an ordinance restricting prostitution to a thirty-eight-block area just below Canal Street. This was soon labeled Storyville by the press, after Alderman Story, author of the ordinance, although denizens always referred to it simply as "the district." It became official on New Year's Day, 1898, a unique red-light district, the only one in the United States established by law, rather than custom. For the next twenty years, Storyville's brothels, sporting houses, and taverns flourished. Their activities practically demanded musical accompaniment, and their customers bankrolled it.

It was here, in the district's barrel houses and bordellos, some of which were multistory mansions tarted up in red velvet upholstery and oriental rugs, that great piano "professors" such as Tony Jackson and Jelly Roll Morton got their start. It was in its dance halls that patrons and musicians alike first heard the subversive syncopation of ragtime, the catchy popular music that was imported from towns like St. Louis. It was in Story-ville, as well as in the parades on the streets of New Orleans, on the riverboats that plied its waters, and at the funerals in its neighborhoods, that the music we now call jazz began.

Storyville has been romanticized in stories and movies over the years, but make no mistake: it was a rough area. The streets, lined with bars and "cribs"—tiny rooms for prostitutes—as well as fancy brothels, were busy twenty-four hours a day. Patrons and police alike carried guns to settle frequent fights. Men gambled away their paychecks at crooked tables. Drug use was widespread. Danny Barker once offered this set of definitions of the different options available:

"Whore house—managed by a larceny-hearted landlady, *strictly* business.

"Brothel—juice joint with rooms, and a bunk or a cot near.

"Sporting house—lots of stimulants, women, music. An old queer or cripple serves.

"Crib—two or three stars venture for themselves, future landladies.

"House of assignation—women pull shifts and report where they are needed.

"Clip joint—while one jives you, another creeps or crawls in and rifles your pockets."

The function of music was to put customers in a mood to spend more of their money on women and liquor. There were about thirty-five truly fancy houses at Storyville's height. While band musicians found work in cabarets and honky-tonks, madams at the classier brothels hired string trios or piano players to serenade their customers. Storyville chronicler Al Rose calculated that the district provided work for twelve thousand people. But it employed perhaps fifty musicians on an average night, with most of them working purely for tips, although some were given minimum guarantees. All in all, about two hundred musicians found work in its twenty-year existence. Nevertheless, Storyville was where such artists as Clarence Williams, Freddy Keppard, Kid Ory, and King Oliver bloomed, bright stars in the fresh firmament of jazz.

Storyville was shut down toward the end of 1917 because the U.S. Navy ordered prostitution banished within five miles of a naval base. By that time, however, the melodies of Bourbon Street and of brass bands had been wedded to old blues and shouts, to older rags and dance music, creating a sound louder, hotter, more immediate, and more emotional than anything ever heard before. As Sidney Bechet wrote in his autobiography, "New Orleans, that was a place where the music was natural as the air. The people were ready for it like it was sun and rain. That music, it was like where you lived. It was like waking up in the morning and eating, it was that regular in your life."

This steamy subtropic port had spent nearly two centuries germinating the new sound. "Something came along there where the Mississippi Delta washes its muddy foot in the blue Gulf, something that bullies us, enchants us, pursues us out of the black throats of a thousand music boxes," Lomax rhapsodized. "This something was jazz, which took shape in New Orleans around 1900 and within a generation was beating upon the hearts of most of the cities of the world."

As with so many analogies in this part of the world, Lomax concluded with a metaphor linking music and food. "Tolerant New Orleans absorbed slowly over the centuries Iberian, African, Cuban, Parisian, Martiniquan, and American musical influences. All these flavors may be found in jazz, for jazz is a sort of musical gumbo."

$\mathcal{2}$ The Cradle of Jazz Still Rocks

THE BIRTH OF JAZZ

There is little left of Congo Square in New Orleans except the name, now adorning one of the stages at the Jazz Festival each spring. The square, once a historic gathering spot for slaves, is part of an urban renewal project, the center of which, ironically, is Armstrong Park, a rather forlorn patch of greenery named in honor of the city's greatest jazzman.

Its vibrant history, however, identifies Congo Square as one of the true cradles of jazz or, more correctly, the African music that became a component of jazz. As mentioned in the previous chapter, slaves first began to gather in Congo Square in 1835, filling the open space each Sunday, their "free" day, in order to dance, sing, and play their instruments. For years after the Civil War, former slaves continued to flock there for dancing and celebrations. Authorities put an end to that in 1885, claiming they were disruptive.

But the tradition refused to die. Soon, the celebrations moved to an open space uptown where a man named Poree kept his animals and wagons. Calling the place Lincoln Park, Poree hired a band in the 1890s to play dance music for the crowds. Its leader, who never recorded a note and who had stopped playing by 1907, was to go down in history as the first great name of New Orleans jazz. He was a cornetist named Charles "Buddy" Bolden.

In the brassy wake of Buddy Bolden's horn, jazz was born in New Orleans. But no one called it that when his orchestra first began making noise among the dancers in Lincoln Park. At the time, popular music consisted of traditional dances such as waltzes and schottishes, brass-band marching music, plus the bluesy spirituals and work songs that rural blacks had made familiar to their urban brothers. A new rhythm, though, was rippling along the Mississippi—ragtime, with music written by such composers as Scott Joplin of Missouri, its syncopated melodies so captivating they spread like wildfire. Both musically educated Creoles and less-schooled blacks began to pick up ragtime, giving it a more uptempo beat.

The earliest "jazz"—the origins of the word are obscure but had a sexual connotation—took dance music and blues and rags and, in a magical alchemy of improvisation, transformed them. As critic Martin Williams wrote, this "rhythmic evolution" began "with a phrasing, a melodic rhythm, rather close to ragtime but looser, and using rhythms ragtime only hinted at. It ends with a percussion of four evenly spaced beats to a bar."

Bolden was the first legend in jazz, as well as its first tragic figure. He was the archetypal young man with a horn, irresistible to women, who rose to the height of fame only to be struck down in his prime, in his case by madness. Nevertheless, according to everyone who heard him, Buddy Bolden, a product of the rough "Uptown" ghetto, blew a horn that punctured the status quo.

Born Charles Joseph Bolden in 1877, he came out of a social environment in the waning years of the last century that was fertile soil for innovative music. From his earliest years, Bolden had heard the brass bands that were at the heart of the social clubs in black neighborhoods, bands that played parades and picnics and especially the large, elaborate funerals that gave the dead a rousing send-off. He undoubtedly heard string bands played by educated Creoles, as well as the mournful field songs and shouts of the rural plantation workers who flocked to the city.

Legend had it that Bolden was a barber, but his biographer, Don Marquis, assures us that bit of misinformation probably came about because it was typical for young musicians to hang around their local barbershops. Perhaps Buddy got his hands on a cast-off horn from some other player, or perhaps he picked up one left behind by a military-band cornetist in a Rampart Street pawnshop. Marquis thinks he developed his personal style of playing in a small string band, rather than from parade bands. Wherever he played, though, by 1895 or so he was experimenting with a louder, bolder style. Just as brass bands began playing rags, or ragging older tunes—that is, playing them with a bright new syncopation—Bolden did the same with dance bands. He changed the tempo of street songs and popular dance tunes to a more swinging beat, a sound the refined Creoles put down as "honky-tonk."

Soon, Bolden was booking his own group for gigs such as the Lincoln Park get-togethers. Unfamiliar though his tunes might sound, blacks and Creoles alike began to catch the beat. A young Creole who would make his own mark and who would himself claim to have invented jazz, Jelly Roll Morton, remembered how compelling it was. "We'd be hanging around some corner, wouldn't know that there was going to be a dance out at Lincoln Park. Then we'd hear old Buddy's trumpet start." If there were other famous bands playing nearby, Bolden would overpower them, pointing his horn toward the city several miles away to "call the children home." By 1905 or so he was famous throughout the city. Boys like Louis Armstrong and Sidney Bechet, who recalled Bolden as a "showman," listened to him in the park or by peeking through the spaces in the walls of dance halls.

Bolden's rivals were the Creole orchestras of John Robichaux and Emmanuel Perez, among others. Most of these players did not make enough to play music full time. In their "day jobs" they were carpenters, barbers, and the like. Many more-educated Creoles, including the fathers of such pioneers as Bechet, Freddie Keppard, Jelly Roll, Louis Nelson, and Johnny St. Cyr, played music for a hobby. But those who did not react to Bolden's new "hot" sound were soon left behind. Paul Dominguez, for one, was resentful at what he felt was a loss of status for the reading musicians who were forced to play the new jazz. "Bolden cause all that," he said with bitterness. "He cause these younger Creoles, men like Bechet and Keppard, to have a different style altogether from the old heads like [clarinetist Lorenzo] Tio and Perez."

By 1906, Bolden was the "King" of the cornet players, famous throughout the black and tan communities. His band played for numerous social clubs, but his home base probably was the Union Sons Hall, renamed Funky Butt by its sporting crowd. Bolden's theme song was a blues called "Funky Butt"; soon it was sung up and down the Mississippi. Tragically, Buddy himself was beginning to experience severe mood changes and headaches, perhaps, Marquis has suggested, because he felt threatened by other musicians picking up his ideas and feared his own limitations. He drank more and more; he grew violent; he missed jobs. In 1907, Buddy Bolden was committed to a state mental institution, where he spent the final twenty-four years of his life, never to hear the flowering of rhythm and melody for which he had sown the seeds.

By the time Bolden left the scene, numerous bands had taken up his powerful challenge. Other cornetists such as Buddy Petit and Bunk Johnson competed for his crown. Bands would advertise themselves by setting up on the flatbeds of wagons and playing tunes as the wagons were pulled through the streets. When two bands intersected, they would have "cutting" or "bucking" contests to see which could dominate. Among the pretenders to Bolden's throne, critics feel that Freddie Keppard might have come closest to Bolden's style. His sound was more polished but rhythmically closer to ragtime than to later jazz.

A powerful cornetist born in 1890, Keppard put together the Olympia Orchestra around 1905. Featuring Alphonse Picou on clarinet, it played legitimate society jobs but could swing at the dance halls. Then he joined an ensemble billed as the Original Creole Orchestra, which was the first to play out of town, bringing the New Orleans style to San Francisco in 1913, Chicago in 1914. Keppard was such a suspicious man that he played with a handkerchief over his hand so no one could see his fingering. Apparently it was this attitude that led him to turn down an offer to make a recording of the new hot music. It was an unfortunate decision, because a group of white imitators got the chance instead.

Jazz was sweeping black New Orleans by the time the U.S. entered World War I. It could be heard day and night in the social clubs, on street corners, as well as in the rather dangerous halls that sprang up both in the black section of town and in Storyville. The King's mantle was picked up by a succession of melodic cornet players, first Keppard, then Joe Oliver, and ultimately Oliver's protégé, Louis Armstrong. Future legends such as Armstrong and Sidney Bechet, then still in their teens, trailed after their idols like Oliver, waiting for a chance to sit in with a band when a player got exhausted or simply took a break.

Joe Oliver, a physically imposing man who was blind in one eye, became the lead trumpet for the Olympia Orchestra. Born in 1885 in Donaldville, not far from New Orleans, he, too, played loudly and rhythmically like Bolden. But Oliver practiced long hours to coax a beautiful tone out of his horn. Contemporaries loved to tell anecdotes about him. According to one, Oliver took care to walk on the sidewalk during marching band performances, rather than in the gutter, because he didn't want to take the chance of hurting his lip by stepping in one of the many potholes while playing. Another declared Oliver would taunt a defeated rival in a cutting contest by "talking" with his cornet and mute, telling the rival to go away. Louis Armstrong used to say that Oliver was so powerful he would blow a cornet out of tune every two or three months. One incident grew to the status of myth: it began when Oliver and Keppard were playing across the street from one another in Storyville cabarets. Determined to seize the crown, Oliver strode over to his piano player and commanded him, "Get in B-flat." As the pianist, Richard M. Jones, later recounted, "I did, and Joe walked out on the sidewalk, lifted his horn to his lips and blew the most beautiful stuff I have ever heard. People started pouring out of other spots along the street. . . . Before long our place was full."

By 1914, installed in Pete Lala's Café by songwriter Clarence Williams, Oliver, featured in a band led by trombonist Kid Ory, was the undisputed leader of New Orleans jazz. He had developed a unique style, muting and bending notes by inserting a variety of cups, glasses, and bottles into his horn. "He was the best gut-bucket man I ever heard," Mutt Carey, a colleague, once said. Appearing in tough venues like the Storyville or Uptown dance halls, Oliver took no chances; he carried a gun in his coat to rehearsals and would threaten band members who showed up late.

As word spread north and west of the hot new style, more and more blacks began to travel outside the city limits. Many, including Bechet and Morton, played gigs in neighboring states—Texas, Mississippi, Florida. Keppard and Morton both spread the news on visits to the West Coast. But it was Chicago that was the great magnet for the best musicians.

Two events conspired to make Chicago thrive as the torrid epicenter of jazz. First, bowing to demands of the Navy, whose ranks filled the streets of New Orleans, the city fathers closed down Storyville as an official red-light district in 1917. Although the city still hummed with music, many of the places that had given Oliver and the rest steady work shut down. Second, as the war fueled the factories and mills of the north creating thousands of jobs for decent wages, huge numbers of southern agricultural workers, including impoverished blacks, deserted their plows to earn a better living up north, swelling the population of cities like Chicago. They were hungry for entertainment, and they had the money to spend to hear it.

The first wave of New Orleans expatriates were almost instantly successful. A steady stream of newspaper clippings about their welcome made its way south; as Sidney Bechet wrote later, "there was a real excitement there."

What did their bands sound like? This explanation, from the liner notes of the *Smithsonian Collection of Classic Jazz,* outlines the New Orleans music succinctly:

> New Orleans jazz is played in a kind of counterpoint or polyphony in which a trumpet (or trumpets) . . . states a melody, with such embellishment and departures as the trumpeter may feel during a performance. Simultaneously, a clarinet improvises a counter-melody or a kind of obbligato, a trombone improvises a version of a ground bass, and a rhythm section, consisting of drums, a plucked string bass (occasionally a tuba), a guitar (occasionally a banjo), and a piano, provides an interplaying harmonic rhythmic accompaniment.

Words, however, hardly convey the revolution these musicians caused. Nightclubbers in Chicago, then New York were thrilled. The soulful, spirited, toe-tapping solos and ensemble playing were like nothing they had ever heard before. Inspired by the acceptance of men like Keppard, others—Bill Johnson, George Baquet, Kid Ory, Mutt Carey, and Tig Chambers, and eventually, in 1917, Joe Oliver—followed. The exodus had begun.

Thanks to Storyville, the music of the black and Creole communities reached the ears of white listeners and players as well. Almost from the beginning, the new music began to waft through the red-light district, where piano "professors" were hired by madams like Lulu White to entertain customers, who were exclusively white. Tony Jackson, the most acclaimed "professor" of his day and composer of the song "Pretty Baby," and Jelly Roll Morton could make quite a few dollars a night in tips from whites, thanks to their ability to switch from blues tunes with dirty lyrics to classical and operatic numbers to rags like "Tiger Rag" and "Maple Leaf Rag."

Meanwhile, white bands, playing versions of popular tunes that imitated the new African American sound, sprang up among musicians who played for white society's dances and picnics. White groups as well as blacks began to travel north to play, with Chicago, once again, being the frequent destination. Thus, a band led by trumpeter Tom Brown was invited in 1915, after traveling vaudevillians in Chicago had sung its praises. Brown and his men found themselves accused of playing "jass," meaning whorehouse, music. Rather than reject the notion, the band welcomed it. By calling itself Brown's Dixieland Jazz Band, it became the first to use the actual word "jazz" in its name. More important, it scored enough of a hit that a Chicago promoter brought a second New Orleans band north. This one, led by cornetist Nick LaRocca, was destined to secure a place for itself in American cultural history as the first musicians to record jazz.

Listeners who hear the LaRocca-led group today might well wonder why this band, whose sound was a bit stilted and ordinary in comparison to the Keppards and Olivers of the day, should have made what became the recording heard round the world. The best answer seems to be that it was the first. Keppard supposedly got offers to make one of the early wax recordings but refused. Meanwhile, along came the group forever known as the "Original Dixieland Jazz Band."

LaRocca was the son of an immigrant shoemaker from the Irish Channel section of New Orleans. The elder LaRocca, an amateur player himself, once smashed young Nick's horn because he did not want him to become a professional musician. LaRocca was born in 1889. He arrived in Chicago in 1916 with a band that included clarinetist Larry Shields, a young man who had taken lessons from Sidney Bechet. After a well-received appearance in the Windy City, the band followed Brown's to New York, where, billed as the "Dixie Jasz Band," it opened in the Paradise Club on the third floor of the Reisen-weber Building in midtown.

Gradually, more and more fans flocked to Reisenweber's to listen to the group that had started this craze for jazz. In 1917, Victor Talking Machine Company, a.k.a. Victor Records, still in its infancy, brought them into a studio. There, the group recorded two songs: a corny version of "Livery Stable Blues," complete with Shields's clarinet imitating a rooster and other barnyard noises, and the "Dixie Jass Band One-Step." The platter, the first jazz record ever, was an instant hit; jazz was on its way to international fame.

There was no question but that the Original Dixieland Jazz Band and other white groups, such as the New Orleans Rhythm Kings, played blander, toned-down versions of tunes borrowed from black bands. In time, the music of the traditional white bands became known as Dixieland, to distinguish it from the looser, more original traditional jazz played by the original core of New Orleans black and Creole musicians. Still, the white Dixieland bands probably helped pave the way for the surge of the best black and Creole players who were deserting New Orleans for the big time up north. In halls such as the Royal Gardens, the Deluxe, the Dreamland in Chicago, early jazz greats like Oliver, Kid Ory, Johnny Dodds, Paul Barbarin, Zutty Singleton, and, most important, Louis Armstrong—New Orleanians all—developed the full flowering of the music that we know today as New Orleans jazz.

THE PIONEER—JELLY ROLL MORTON

In Louis Malle's 1978 film *Pretty Baby,* a fictionalized look at Storyville, a dapper, light-skinned piano professor acts as a kind of Greek chorus, commenting musically on the movie action, yet standing somewhat apart from the other characters, all of whom are white. The piano man is clearly modeled on Ferdinand La Menthe, the jazz pioneer we know by the name of Jelly Roll Morton. Actually, the real Jelly Roll was colorful enough to deserve an entire movie based on his life, and there has recently been a Broadway musical, *Jelly's Last Jam*, starring Gregory Hines.

Morton was probably the first full-fledged jazz composer and arranger. Mo·eover, he had the good fortune to have been recorded live by folklorist Alan Lomax in the 1938 in one of the earliest oral-history projects. Working at the Library of Congress, Lomax, a sympathetic listener, provided Morton, a man with an extremely healthy ego, with a forum to expound on the early days of jazz in New Orleans. As a result of his evocative tales, punctuated with musical examples, Morton claimed a place at the forefront of jazz history.

Does he deserve it? Absolutely, although contemporaries insisted he was prone to embellishing stories and inflating his personal contributions. Duke Ellington once said, "Jelly Roll Morton's greatest talent is in talking about Jelly Roll Morton." Lomax, on the other hand, regarded him as the "first and most influential composer of jazz," a "Creole Benvenuto Cellini." Whether he really was as innovative as he says he was, or whether his contribution simply was better documented than others, Jelly Roll today stands tall in the pantheon of New Orleans jazzmen.

Morton was present at the creation of jazz in the Crescent City and, like so many musicians who were crucial to its formative years, was a Creole. Born on October 20, 1890, he claimed that his family was of old French stock and throughout his life clung to a sense of superiority based on his Creole blood. There is some doubt about just how well-born he really was, but it is known that his father, F. P. La Menthe, was an occasional trombone player. (His mother's second husband was named Morton; Jelly Roll chose to go by that name, he said, because he didn't want to be called "Frenchy.") The house he grew up in was filled with musical instruments, and young Ferdy took formal guitar lessons from a Spanish teacher at the tender age of six. But his parents never wanted him to play professionally.

"They always had it in their minds that a musician was a tramp
. . . with the exception of the French opera house players."
Indeed, it was a recital at the opera house that first piqued his
curiosity about the piano. By the time he was ten, he had taken
lessons from a variety of professors and had quit the guitar in
favor of the keyboard. Nor were his pre-teen activities limited
to instruments; he also sang in a quartet, which avidly sought
out wakes at which they could perform.

New Orleans brass bands marched through the streets regularly, social clubs were forever holding picnics and dances
that included musical accompaniment, and the sound of piano
and string music poured out of Storyville's fancy bordellos every
night. So it is easy to understand how the boy wound up playing for money despite the family's attitude.

Morton's mother died when he was fourteen, and he moved
in with his grandmother. At that time he was, in his own words,
"considered one of the best junior pianists in the whole city."
While he worked at making barrels in a cooperage during the
day, he roamed the forbidden red-light district at night. "I liked
the freedom of standing at a saloon bar, passing along the streets
crowded with men of all nationalities and descriptions . . .
women standing in their cribs," he recalled. Taking advantage
of the fact that he was allowed to stay out late on weekends,
the adventurous adolescent found himself a piano gig in Storyville. What a life it was for a fellow who had to steal long
pants for his work! The money was terrific (he was paid one
dollar a night but he could make twenty dollars a night from
tips). The girls were friendly. Pretty soon Ferdy was dressing
up like the other flashy dudes—new suit, Stetson hat, and "St.
Louis flats," shoes that must have been the Air Jordans of their
day. The outfit gave him away. When his grandmother spotted
him one day coming home from the district in those fancy
clothes, she turned him out of her house. A musician, she
scolded in French, was "nothing but a bum and a scalawag."

For the next two years, he played sporting houses in Biloxi,
Mississippi, a job dangerous enough for him to carry a pistol

at all times. Then it was back to Storyville in 1902, the heyday of the district, a period when Buddy Bolden's powerful new music was sounding a clarion call to all the city's young players. Within the sporting houses and cabarets, dozens of clever pianists were also transforming the old popular tunes. Uninhibited goings-on included the so-called naked dances performed by prostitutes and their johns, a dance described by some as fornication standing up. These required piano professors (who sometimes would play behind screens that were supposed to shield the dancers from the pianists' racially inappropriate gaze) to dress up rags and introduce new, slow blues numbers.

Jelly Roll reveled in this musically innovative, sensual world. The easy money brought him more great clothes and, more important, diamonds, one of which he had set in a front tooth. As Lomax wrote, "Piano keys opened doors into a white world where the other boys in the bands could not follow. . . . His notoriety set him apart from the common musicians of Storyville." He acquired a nickname, Winding Boy, that suggests sexual prowess and perhaps hinted at pimping. On a musical level, he was especially adept at barrelhouse music, making up filthy lyrics to songs that Bunk Johnson described as "the music the whores liked."

Morton, though, was only one of a dozen wonderful keyboard men in those first years of the new century in New Orleans. The city, he told Lomax, was "the stomping grounds for all the greatest pianists in the country. We had Spanish, we had colored, we had white, we had Frenchmens, we had Americans." There were so many jobs in the district that men such as Sammy Davis (no relation to the later dancer and actor), Alfred Wilson, Albert Cahill, and Kid Ross, all major talents, played steadily.

"All these men were hard to beat," Jelly Roll declared, but there was one so universally respected that "any one of them would get up from the piano stool" when he walked into a room. That man, whom even Jelly Roll hailed as the greatest single entertainer of his day, was Tony Jackson.

Jackson, born in 1876, and thus several years older than Morton, set the standard for a long line of versatile, crowd-pleasing New Orleans keyboard players that stretches from Morton to Tuts Washington, Professor Longhair, James Booker, Mac Rebennack, and Harry Connick, Jr. Since he made no recordings, he never achieved the international recognition granted other pioneers, and critics have had to guess at how he sounded from the recollections of those who heard him. The verdict, however, is unanimous: he was the best.

What's more, he overcame enormous odds. Growing up poor, he had no instrument on which to learn, so at the age of seven, he built one—a contraption that resembled a harpsichord. Later, he was able to practice on a neighbor's organ. It was not until he was thirteen that Tony played an actual piano, located in a bar in his neighborhood.

He made up quickly for lost time. By his fifteenth birthday, he was regarded as the king of the keyboard in the sporting houses of the city. Once Storyville became official, Jackson worked steadily, treating the patrons of Lulu White, Countess Willie Piazza, Antonia Gonzales the "female cornetist," and other top madams to all kinds of music. They said he had a repertoire of a thousand songs; opera, marches, and his own originals, such as "Pretty Baby," were among them. His singing voice was as distinctive as his playing, with a "wild earnestness" to it, in the words of one admirer. Clarence Williams summed up Jackson's genius this way: "We all copied him. He was so original and a great instrumentalist. I know I copied Tony, and Jelly Roll too." Jackson, he concluded, speaking in the 1950s, "was on the order of how King Cole is now, only much better."

In the early 1900s, Jackson moved on to Chicago, where he had a hugely successful run. By the time he died in 1921, the piano styles he had pioneered had influenced dozens of younger musicians. Taking over his lead was Jelly Roll Morton, who carried jazz piano to further heights.

Morton must have learned much at the Frenchman's, an after-hours spot at the corner of Villere and Bienville where musicians gathered to jam after they got off their regular jobs at four or so in the morning. "It was only a back room," he noted, but "there would be everything in the line of hilarity there. They would have even millionaires to come to listen to different great pianists. . . . All the girls that could get out of the house, they were there." People from all over the country, he remembered, would crowd the Frenchman's until well past noon.

In places like these the "society music" of the better-educated Creoles was absorbed and transmuted. "When the settled Creole folks first heard this jazz," Leonard Bechet, the clarinetist's brother, said, "they passed the opinion that it sounded like the rough Negro element. In other words, they had the same kind of feeling that some white people have. . . . But after they heard it so long, they began to creep right close to it and enjoy it."

Morton became one of the new music's premier messengers. He made New Orleans his base in the first years of the century while venturing as far away as California, paying his way in some places not so much as a musician as a pool hustler. On a sojourn in Memphis in 1908, he met W. C. Handy, composer of many classic early blues. He appeared in vaudeville and minstrel shows, and claimed to have introduced scat singing as a novelty long before Armstrong took it up.

Early on, he had begun to write down his own compositions—primarily blues and stomps—and soon he also began to gather men for pickup bands needed in parades. He joined these talents in what he called "this peculiar form of mathematics and harmonics that was strange to all the world," the art of arranging music for ensembles and leading them. The genesis of his original music was varied. For instance, one of his most famous tunes, "The Pearls," was written to please a "pretty little waitress" at the Kansas City Bar in Tiajuana. He chose the title because each section of the piece was designed to match the other, "contributing to the total effect of a beautiful pearl necklace."

Morton gravitated to Chicago for an extended stay in 1923. His five years out west had distanced him from the growing colony of brilliant New Orleans instrumentalists who were developing such a distinctive sound, and some of them felt he behaved like the haughty, class-conscious Creole he was. Nevertheless, they recognized great music when they heard it. Lil Hardin, the pianist in King Oliver's band who later married Louis Armstrong, told of how Jelly Roll showed up at a Chicago booking agency where everyone used to congregate. Once Morton sat down at a piano, Lil knew she was in the presence of a master. "The piano rocked, the floor swayed while he ferociously attacked the keyboard with his long skinny hands, beating out a double rhythm with his feet on the loud pedal. I was thrilled, amazed and scared," she said.

In Chicago, Morton found both a publisher for his music and recording companies for the bands he led. Some of his early pieces had been issued on piano rolls. However, the Melrose Brothers, a Chicago firm that was banking heavily on the new sheet music, had offered him money for "Wolverine Blues" while he was still on the West Coast. As soon as he returned to Chicago, he visited their store. A banner outside proclaimed, "Wolverine Blues Sold here." Inside, Jelly Roll, resplendent in cowboy hat and big red bandanna, introduced himself and in a typically grandiose gesture talked about his music for the next two hours.

His first recordings, which he made the next year, were mostly piano solos, as well as a historic version of "Mr. Jelly Lord," with the New Orleans Rhythm Kings, the first racially mixed band ever put on wax. Then in 1926, he organized a group that he called the Red Hot Peppers. Included in the lineup over the next two years were top New Orleanians such as Kid Ory on trombone, Johnny St. Cyr on banjo, and Baby Dodds on drums. Their leader showed himself to be disciplined yet open-minded, according to the players, requiring the band to rehearse for several nights and providing its members with their parts written out. Still, St. Cyr said later that the "reason his records are so full of tricks and changes is the liberty he gave his men. He was always open for suggestions."

"Smokehouse Blues," "Black Bottom Stomp," "Dead Man Blues," "Grandpa's Spells," "Beale Street Blues," "The Pearls"— these were among the classics they produced for Victor, records that have been enshrined over the decades as being among the very greatest traditional jazz studio work. "One of the most remarkable series of recordings in jazz history," declared Martin Williams. "Probably no jazz records before or since have received more preparation and care." The publicity surrounding them was novel too; upon the release of "Jackass Blues," the Melrose Brothers outfitted a mule with signs advertising the record and Jelly Roll himself sat atop it as it trotted down State Street.

Jelly Roll stayed on top of the jazz world in general in Chicago during those middle twenties, collecting royalties and playing club dates throughout the Midwest. Nevertheless, other names from his hometown and elsewhere—such as Louis Armstrong and band leader Fletcher Henderson—playing in new venues in places like New York, were taking jazz beyond the limits of the diamond-studded piano professor. It was not long before Jelly Roll Morton's style turned stale; by the time big bands became the rage in the thirties, he was nearly forgotten.

His big ego, though, was never deflated. Morton at first blamed his decline on voodoo. When he read one day in the Baltimore *Afro-American* that W. C. Handy was being called the originator of jazz and blues, he wrote a stinging letter of protest claiming the title for himself: "W. C. Handy is a liar," the letter proclaimed. While recognizing his delusions, new, younger listeners in the Washington area, where he had settled, began to discover him again in small clubs. The Library of Congress sessions were a boost to his self-confidence and they helped the French rediscover him. Eventually, he even made some new records for Victor in New York. His sidemen once again were among the most eminent New Orleans pioneers, Sidney Bechet, playing soprano sax, and Zutty Singleton among them.

His spirit was revived, but his health was not good. After moving to Los Angeles in 1940—in part because he thought the mild climate would benefit him—Jelly Roll Morton, self-proclaimed "Originator of Jazz and Stomps, Victor Artist, World's Greatest Hot Tune Writer," died in July, 1941. His final royalty check from Melrose, which he hoped would relieve his financial straits, amounted to just fifty-two dollars.

SIDNEY BECHET—REED POET

If Jelly Roll was the first major jazz composer to come out of New Orleans, Sidney Bechet was its premier Pied Piper. A soaring soloist on both the clarinet and the soprano sax, he was the most talented of the well-traveled pioneers who left the Crescent City very early to spread the sound of jazz to every corner of the Western world. More than three decades after his death, critics continue to enhance his reputation. Whitney Balliett, who called Bechet "the first jazz romantic," enshrined him as "probably the most lyrical and dramatic of all American jazz musicians."

Bechet was a Creole like Morton. However, he was anything but ashamed of his slave ancestry. His autobiography, *Treat It Gentle,* is a remarkable testament, taken from a series of tape-recorded reminiscences, which captures Bechet's poetic use of language. In it, he begins by telling of his rebel grandfather, a slave named Omar, who beat out rhythms in Congo Square and risked his life to be with the woman he loved. The saga of Omar reads like a Louisiana *Roots.* It also echoes the story of a historic slave leader named Bras Coupe, who got his name when he lost an arm. Historians suspect Bechet's actual grandfather was born too late to have been the actual Bras Coupe, but the story sets the stage for much of what was to follow: the Bechet familial love of music, Sidney's own rebellious, prickly nature, and his understanding of the African rhythms that underpin jazz.

Sidney was born in 1897 into a middle-class New Orleans family. He was the youngest of five brothers, all of them musically inclined. His father, Omar, was a shoemaker who played the flute and cornet as a hobby. There were all kinds of instruments in the household, and as a child Sidney wasted no time in fooling around with them.

An oft-told tale concerned his discovery of the clarinet at the age of six. His brothers had formed the Silver Bells Band, with one of them, Leonard, on the clarinet. Leonard kept his clarinet locked up but, as Bechet noted, "I wasn't ready to be kept out of anything." Once he found the key to his brother's dresser, he would borrow the instrument often and practice with it under the porch of the family's house. His mother caught him one day. The minute she heard her youngest play, she realized that Sidney should be encouraged rather than punished. "Instead of making me put the clarinet back," he wrote, "she made me play some more for her." That evening, Sidney's budding talent was put on display in the living room. His brothers, although surprised at their precocious little reed man, were delighted.

Word spread fast through the community. One player used to see Sidney as a child hanging around a barbershop where there were many instruments. "What is that?" he asked Piron, the barber, picking up one of them. "That is a flute, Sidney," replied the barber. The boy began playing it on the spot. Next he picked up an instrument that reminded him of a pipe. "That's a new something they call a saxophone, son," said the barber. "I see if this pipe will make a tune," said the boy, and sure enough, he coaxed a melody out of the saxophone as well. There probably was some exaggeration in these tales, but there is little doubt he was a prodigy.

The leaders of the new music who were jazzing up ragtime in those years actually played in the Bechet household. For someone's birthday party, Freddie Keppard's band was hired, but the clarinetist did not show up on time. The sound of the band set the little prodigy afire. "I knew I was too young for them, but I sure wanted to play along," Bechet wrote. So he told himself, "If I can't play with them, I'll just play along with their music." He plunked himself down in Leonard's dentist chair (the older brother was in the process of becoming a dentist) and, without being seen, began to join in. Hearing the clarinet, the band figured their missing man had shown up. Instead, after prowling around the house, they discovered to their astonishment that it was six-year-old Sidney.

"I was just having myself a hell of a good time, improvising," he remembered. "It was just entirely natural to me, just a whole lot of happiness. I'll never forget that feeling." Keppard's men, he knew, "were masters. Ragtime didn't have to look for a home when they were playing it." When the evening was over, Bechet felt like "the richest kid in New Orleans. You couldn't have bought me for a sky full of moons." He understood that he wouldn't be happy until he could become a regular member of their musical fraternity.

Bechet did not have to learn everything on his own. George Baquet, the Keppard Band's clarinetist, gave him his first lessons. As he grew older, he played with, and learned a lot from, Big Eye Louis Nelson and Lorenzo Tio, two of the best clarinetists of the period, as well as cornetists Buddy Petit and Bunk Johnson. He even formed a trio with a drummer and Louis Armstrong, who was a few years younger. One of their main gigs was to play in the streets on the back of a wagon in order to help advertise Saturday night boxing matches. Sidney's family was often not happy about the company he found himself in. Leonard Bechet remarked that fellows like Bunk were "rough and ready," drank too much, and didn't have the "prestige" accorded more soothing Creole music makers.

However, by the time he was fourteen, Sidney was considered by some to be the finest hot clarinet player in a city that was full of them, and he defied his upbringing so he could perform as much as possible. He played regularly at Pete Lala's in Storyville, plus famous cabarets like Economy Hall and Perseverance Hall. Having been a major truant, he moved out of his parents' house on Marais Street at sixteen to become a full-time musician. From there, it was on to gigs in Texas, then back home, where, by 1914 or so, Keppard and others were sending back clippings of their triumphs in Chicago and New York. Bechet could hardly wait to see those faraway places. He got the chance in 1917, when he joined the Bruce and Bruce Stock Company. The group toured through the South, with Bechet learning a great deal about being a showman, not just an instrumentalist. The company finally wound up in the place the youngster thought of as heaven: Chicago. He was a sensation there with his sweet, bluesy clarinet soaring above bands that included Roy Palmer, the trombonist, and Lil Hardin on piano. After hours, he was among the musicians who gathered at the Pekin to hear the legendary Tony Jackson.

By 1918, Bechet, at the urging of a talent scout and organizer named Will Marion Cook, moved on to New York. It was a momentous decision, because as the leader of the Southern Syncopated Orchestra, Cook was determined to introduce jazz to a new continent. In 1919, Cook put Bechet and the thirty-five other musicians on a cattle boat bound across the Atlantic. Their first stop: the Royal Philharmonic Hall in London.

If ever a population was ready for New Orleans music, it was the Europeans. World War I had slowed the arrival of jazz, and they were eager to make up for lost time. The anticipation was intense when the first Americans began appearing on London and Paris stages. In the audience for the premier engagement of the Southern Syncopated Orchestra was no less a musical authority than Ernest Ansermet, the Swiss conductor who also wrote reviews for the popular press. Ansermet, not one to look down his nose at non-classical music, was astounded by the "extraordinary clarinet virtuoso" he heard that first night. "I wish to set down the name of this artist of genius; as for myself, I shall never forget it—it is Sidney Bechet, . . . the first of his race to have composed perfectly formed blues on the clarinet," he raved. It was the start of a lifelong love affair between the Creole from New Orleans and his Continental fans. Indeed, soon all of Europe—ordinary folk and intellectuals alike—was infatuated with this American music. Jazz elements crept into the compositions of such leading classical composers as Stravinsky, and, later, Ravel and Milhaud.

What was it that moved the Europeans so? There was an ecstatic quality to early jazz, a freedom from the constraints of written music, a passion and a poetry, that rang incredibly fresh in the ears of listeners used to the solemn majesty of classical music. Bechet, equipped with both the joy of jazz and technical skill, was able to deliver that earthy quality in solos that came straight from his heart to others. Bechet himself was clear about the innate emotional source he tapped: "You tell it to the music, and the music tells it to you," he said in *Treat It Gentle*. Many years later, British critic Max Harrison noted that "even at that early stage he had securely located his own rich vein of expression."

The band made such an impression on England that it was invited to play a command performance in Buckingham Palace garden before King George V. Bechet was tickled: "It was the first time I ever got to recognize somebody from having seen his picture on my money." The orchestra then broke into smaller groups and Bechet and several others soon were playing across the Channel in Paris.

Two other incidents occurred on that first trip abroad, one a high point, the other quite the opposite. Back in Chicago, Sidney had been introduced to the soprano saxophone. The instrument is closely related to the clarinet (straight, rather than curved at the bell end like other saxes) but with a more powerful, dominating tone. It is also notoriously difficult to stay in tune playing it. Bechet picked up one in a pawnshop but could never get the right sound out of it. Then, in London, he saw one in the window of an instrument maker. After trying out just one chorus of "Whispering," he knew he had in his hand the horn that would obey his personal lyric commands.

The second event, even with its dire consequences, might have saved Bechet's life. He and a friend were walking down a London street one day when they encountered a prostitute Bechet knew. They went to the friend's apartment and began "fooling around," as Bechet later wrote. A scuffle ensued and the prostitute wound up filing a complaint against him. Bechet was arrested and deported. Meanwhile, the Southern Syncopated Orchestra boarded a ship without him. The ship sank at sea after a tragic collision, taking eight orchestra members to a watery grave.

Upon returning to the U.S., Bechet won a leading role in the all-black cast of the musical *How Come*. His character was a saxophone-playing Chinese laundryman. As the show went on tour, it added a new cast member, whom Bechet himself had scouted. It was none other than the woman later crowned "empress of the blues," Bessie Smith. By the time *How Come* reached Broadway, the two were a couple, in between their battles.

What a pair they must have made! He was a roly-poly fellow who had already gotten into his share of scrapes; she was as large and physical as her talent, a dynamo originally from Chattanooga known for her two-fisted drinking, swearing, and general outrageousness. The show lasted just a month. The Bessie and Sidney show split at about the same time as the Broadway show.

It was in this period that Bechet finally began to record, thanks to the efforts of New Orleans band leader and promoter Clarence Williams, who got contracts for both Sidney and Bessie. His first record with Williams, the 1923 "Wild Cat Blues," was for Okeh, one of the burgeoning "race" labels that specialized in black jazz. It made a stunning impression on younger reed men back home in New Orleans, such as Barney Bigard. The following year, Williams teamed Bechet and his soprano sax up with Louis Armstrong in the Red Onion Jazz Babies, a band named for a New Orleans bar. On tunes like "Cake Walking Babies," the two men traded leads and threw themselves into solos that demonstrated to a wider public the genius of the mature New Orleans style.

Bechet went on to other triumphs, including a short stint with Duke Ellington's band and the opening of his own night spot in Harlem, the Club Basha, bankrolled by royalties from the sale of sheet music for several songs he had written.

By 1925, though, Bechet was ready to hit the road again. This time, the destination was Paris; the vehicle was a show called *Revue Negre*. Its lead dancer, a chorus girl, brought down the house at the Théâtre de Champs-Elysées with a new American sensation, the Charleston. Her name was Josephine Baker and, like Bechet, she was destined to become an institution in France.

For five years Bechet toured Europe, bringing jazz to such far-flung capitals as Moscow. Unfortunately, his violent temper could mean trouble. In 1928 he got into a gunfight on the streets of Paris with some other musicians. Two innocent bystanders were wounded and Bechet went to jail for eleven months. Afterward he was deported. Rather than head back to the U.S., he went to Berlin. His wanderings during the early Depression years took him back and forth between Europe and the U.S. He appeared in bands led by Noble Sissle and Ellington once again, and made memorable recordings with the New Orleans Feetwarmers, a group featuring his friend Tommy Ladnier on the trumpet. Although he went through hard times like all musicians (at one point he opened a tailor's shop in Harlem to make ends meet), Bechet found steady work at Nick Rongetti's club in Greenwich Village.

By the time World War II broke out, Bechet had come to be recognized as a jazzman in a class by himself, even though swing had replaced New Orleans jazz as the music of the moment. He settled into a big house in Brooklyn, where he opened the Sidney Bechet School of Music. It might sound strange for such a famous musician, but he apparently did it both to make additional money and to instill a jazz heritage in younger players.

Bechet made few visits to his hometown, but one was historic—a star-studded engagement at the Municipal Auditorium featuring the reunion of Bechet and Armstrong. "I had a lot of pleasure playing with Louis again," Bechet wrote in what must have been a gross understatement.

Bechet's wanderlust, however, never left him. By the early 1950s he was back in Paris, perhaps because the French culture was closer to his New Orleans roots than anything he could experience on U.S. soil. According to Martin Williams, Bechet became, in his final years, as big a musical celebrity in France as Armstrong was around the world, with his performances at French music halls "as avidly attended as those of Maurice Chevalier, his appearances in clubs as fashionable as those of Edith Piaf." He traveled around the world to give concerts that were enthusiastically received by fans on the Continent, in South America, and in the U.S. His domestic life was equally happy if unconventional. He was comfortably ensconced on an estate in a Paris suburb with his German-born wife, and had a young French mistress and son in the city itself.

Bechet died at the age of sixty-two of lung cancer, his place in the history of music secure. Nor was it only for the jazz he had helped give birth to in the early years of the century. "When he discovered his real instrument, the soprano saxophone, he developed a style that was a combination of a trumpetlike lead plus elements from a clarinetlike obbligato, fused together in a single melodic part," Williams wrote. No one since has been able to match his tone. Bechet set a standard that every great soprano-sax player who came after him, from Johnny Hodges to John Coltrane, has had to come to terms with. To every succeeding generation of listeners who hear his work on repackaged albums and compact-disc sets, Sidney Bechet soars anew.

SATCHMO

New Orleans jazz reached its high C of creativity in the person of a black man born among the poorest of the poor, raised in the roughest streets, shuttled among relatives, and taught to play the cornet in a home for juvenile delinquents. By the time Louis Armstrong died in 1971, he was Satchmo, the world's foremost jazz ambassador, whose grin and gravelly voice were recognized from Australia to Zaire. Yet although many people still know Armstrong mainly for his hit version of "Hello Dolly," he was far more than just a celebrated entertainer. In the unanimous view of musicians and critics, he was the most revolutionary, most influential jazz master of the century.

Today's listeners sometimes have trouble grasping the breadth of his contribution. For one thing, traditional jazz is by now so familiar that we rarely think about what techniques transformed it into an art form. Also, Armstrong became such a popular, beloved figure after World War II that his crossover success overshadowed his pure jazz creations.

If anything, however, his genius is underrated by the general public. The *New Grove Dictionary of Jazz*, a bible of music history, says, "His approach was so remarkable that Armstrong became the model for virtually all jazz musicians of his time." His imprint was felt beyond the bounds of jazz or pop. One biographer thinks a case can be made that Armstrong was the most important figure in twentieth-century music, because in "single-handedly" remodeling jazz he "had a critical effect" on every kind of subsequent music from rock to the classical work of modernists like Copland, Milhaud, Poulenc, and Honegger. It may not be overstating his influence to say, as one observer has, that his trumpeting "affected the brass technique of almost every horn player in the Western world."

Given the strikes against him from birth, it is amazing that Louis Armstrong survived, let alone became the most acclaimed performer New Orleans ever produced. He was born, most likely in 1901, in Back O'Town, a crowded slum whose shanties were without indoor plumbing. It was called The Battlefield because, as Armstrong explained, "the toughest characters in town used to live there." His mother, Mayann, may or may not have been a prostitute. His father, Willie, a laborer in a turpentine plant, abandoned Mayann soon after his birth. As a baby he lived with his grandmother, Josephine, who could not afford to dress him in anything more than rags and could not feed him past the subsistence level. "I did not know a fork from a comb," he recalled. (Armstrong maintained a lifelong attachment to the standard New Orleans dish of his youth, signing his letters "red beans and ricely yours.") After a few years he moved back in with his mother on Perdido Street in "Black Storyville," a dilap-idated neighborhood filled with honky-tonks and women's "cribs." As deprived as his childhood may have been, however, there was one constant from the start—music.

From the beginning he sang in church, soaked up the sounds of the new hot music pouring out of nearby dance halls, strut-ted along with the second line behind brass-band parades. Per-haps, as one scholar suggests, "the very first positive image" of black men that made an impression on young Louis was the uniformed musicians in those smart-stepping ensembles. By the time he was five years old, the cornet, a shorter, more mellow cousin of the trumpet, was the instrument that had caught his ear. It was the horn most brass-band players of the time preferred.

On the corner of his block was Funky Butt Hall. Although he was not allowed inside, from the sidewalk young Louis could hear the clarion call of Buddy Bolden's cornet. The man played so hard the little boy wondered if he "would ever have enough lung power to fill one of those cornets." Still, Bolden's tone had more decibels than delicacy; from the first, the boy preferred the more moving, melodic lines of players like Bunk Johnson.

Dipper, as Armstrong was nicknamed then, managed to get through the second grade in a nearby school. But he was out in the mean streets a lot, selling newspapers to support his mother, singing tenor in a barbershop quartet, and running a little wild. He was with his singing pals on Rampart Street on New Year's Day, either 1912 or 1913, when, in his version of the story, the altercation occurred that was to irrevocably change his life.

It was customary to celebrate the holiday by shooting off fireworks and guns. Little Louis (another nickname), blasting blanks in the air from a borrowed .38, had the bad luck to be collared by a policeman. Whether for this minor offense or, as biographers have suggested, for more serious delinquency, he was sentenced to a term at the Colored Waifs' Home, a reform school with some apparently socially progressive aims. Different teachers instructed their charges in various trades. Louis gravitated toward the school band. At first the teacher in charge rebuffed him; troublemakers from Armstrong's neighborhood were considered incorrigible. Then, after six months, the man relented, allowing little Louis to play the tambourine first, then the drum, then the alto horn. When the school bugler was released from the home, Armstrong took over his job. Soon, he was given his first, rudimentary lessons on the cornet, the instrument of his dreams. What little training he got was technically useful, but it might have been ultimately destructive. Never having been taught correct embouchure—the position of the mouthpiece on the lips—Armstrong was to be plagued throughout his career with lip problems.

All Louis cared about, though, was having the chance to play. This was how he described the payoff:

> The first day we paraded through my old neighborhood everybody was gathered on the sidewalks to see us pass. All the whores, pimps, gamblers, thieves, and beggars were waiting for the band because they knew that Dipper, Mayann's son, would be in it. But they had never dreamed that I would be playing the cornet, blowing it as good as I did.

The neighborhood folks were so tickled they filled up several hats with small donations. By the time Armstrong was let out of the Waifs' Home as a young teenager, about two years later, he was ready to become a musician.

He could not even afford to buy his own secondhand cornet when he began working in street parades and sitting in with early blues combos in the tonks, the drinking and gambling establishments that dotted his Perdido Street neighborhood. Little Louis would follow King Oliver or Bunk Johnson on parade, pleading with the cornetists to teach him the instrument's secrets. Bunk occasionally let him carry his horn, and the boy practiced whenever he could get his hands on it. At fifteen, he finally got a job at Henry Ponce's tonk. A friend, Cocaine Buddy, advised him, "All you have to do is put on your long pants and play the blues for the whores that hustle all night." The women were generous with their money, Buddy assured him: "They will call you sweet names and buy you drinks and give you tips."

He worked incredibly hard. During the week he would play far into the night in order to collect $1.25 plus tips, grab a few hours' sleep, then trundle off to his day job hauling coal for ten hours to make another 75 cents. But he was never too tired to make the rounds of tonks with friends to hear the latest piano player, especially those from the levee work camps, who "beat out some of the damnedest blues you ever heard."

The player he was most attached to was Joe Oliver. It was a strange match—Armstrong, ingratiating and open, Oliver fierce and dominating—but the big man took little Louis under his wing, even going out of his way not to embarrass him at cutting contests. These confrontations took place when two bands trying to advertise themselves by riding the tailgates of trucks wound up facing one another. Usually, as soon as Armstrong realized the other band was Oliver's, he would stand up so Oliver could see him and take it easy. The one time he forgot to stand, Oliver's band gave Armstrong's a thorough licking. The next time the older player saw him, he bought Armstrong a beer to laugh it off. And it was a thrilling day indeed when King Oliver finally handed Louis one of his used cornets to replace the poor one the teenager had managed to find in a secondhand store.

By 1917, Armstrong had made enormous strides. Although the demise of Storyville had accelerated the musical migration to Chicago, there still were plenty of accomplished players in the Crescent City; Armstrong was soon counted among them. Playing with the Kid Ory band in Lincoln Park one day, cornetist Mutt Carey, the "Blues King" of the moment, let the Dipper sit in for him for a while. The youngster astonished him. "He played more blues than I ever heard in my life," Carey recalled. "It never did strike my mind that blues could be interpreted so many different ways."

The day Joe Oliver left Kid Ory's band and headed for Chicago in 1918, Louis was at the train station to see him off. He was climbing back on his coal wagon when Ory spotted him. "You still blowing that cornet?" asked the band leader. He hired Armstrong on the spot; it was everyone's opinion that he alone could replace the King. Once he took Oliver's place on the bandstand, he deliberately aped the King musically and physically, going so far as to drape a towel around his neck as Joe had. He did not have to imitate anyone for long, however. His own swinging style soon earned him the cornet crown.

Armstrong got another big break in 1918 when band leader Fate Marable hired him to join a permanent band that played on the Streckfus riverboats. The boats plied the Mississippi year round, entertaining tourists on board and at various stops. It was a valuable job, first because it meant permanent employment, second because Marable's outfit was a sight-reading group that played a wide range of material. Anyone invited to play with Marable was "going to the conservatory"— getting a degree in advanced jazz. Louis was excited. "I wanted to do more than fake the music all the time." During his three seasons on the boats he played regularly with drummer Baby Dodds, bassist Pops Foster, and guitarist Johnny St. Cyr, men themselves destined to become among New Orleans' finest musical exports.

After he quit the boats in 1921, Armstrong had several opportunities to head for greener pastures outside New Orleans. Not yet sure enough of himself, he resisted, even when Fletcher Henderson, soon to become a pioneering band leader, asked him to join a traveling troupe that starred Ethel Waters. Instead, he perfected his technique in the dance halls and got even more valuable experience in ensemble playing as a member of Papa Celestin's Tuxedo Brass Band.

Finally, he got the offer he could not refuse—Joe Oliver beckoned from Chicago. On August 8, 1922, Armstrong played a funeral job with the Tuxedo Band, the last appearance he was to make in New Orleans for many, many years. Then, "I rushed home, threw my few glad rags together and hurried over to the Illinois Central Station." It seemed to Louis that the entire city was there to see him off, including Mayann, who handed him a fish sandwich, his one meal for the entire journey. In Chicago, on the other hand, there was not a soul on hand when his train pulled in. Bewildered, Louis Armstrong, shortly to become the toast of the town, stood there like a hick for a half hour until a policeman approached. "Oh, you're the young man who's to join King Oliver's Band!" he exclaimed. It turned out Oliver had to go to work, but had left word for Armstrong to take a cab there.

That first night on the Lincoln Gardens bandstand was the high point of Louis's life. "I had hit the big time. I was up north with the greats. I was playing with my idol," he later recalled. "My boyhood dream had come true at last."

Never in his wildest dreams would he have imagined that this was only the beginning.

Pioneers like Tony Jackson, Keppard, and Oliver, as well as white bands like the Original Dixieland Jazz Band, had already established the beachhead in Chicago for New Orleans' music. However, while New Orleans played the role of "America's Florence" (in Alan Lomax's phrase), the city from which flowed "the most original thing America has contributed to the arts of mankind," Chicago was the metropolis where the renaissance of New Orleans music reached its explosive climax. And Armstrong was its Michelangelo.

All the elements had come together upon his arrival: groups like Oliver's Creole Jazz Band, its playing by now tight and confident; budding independent record companies eager to press the excitement onto hot wax; clubs (some of them backed by gangsters) like the Royal Garden, Dreamland, and the Elite, whose stages seemed glitzy compared to the bare-bones aura of the tonks down South; and most of all, listeners who embraced and supported the men who made the music. The town was teeming with both black and white jazz buffs. Chicago was the capital of the decade eventually dubbed the Jazz Age.

Here is how Lomax characterized the scene:

Negroes with cash money in their jeans . . . Negroes who were called Mister . . . when these folk heard the triumphant and happy New Orleans marches leap out of the trumpet of King Oliver, when they heard their own deep song, the blues, voiced in gold by a big band, they began to shout. From that moment jazz was no longer a New Orleans specialty; it became the music of the whole Negro people.

Into this overheated, increasingly sophisticated atmosphere stepped Louis Armstrong. "Oh, those cats were glowing!" he exclaimed on first hearing Oliver's band. Nervous as he was about being able to keep up, the fact was he was supremely prepared. Hardly a year passed before Armstrong was being recognized by aficionados as the catalyst for an entire leap forward in the music's progression. He made his first recordings as a member of the Oliver band in 1923. In those earliest Gennett discs, made with the band playing together into one mike, long before multi-track, overdubbed recordings, Armstrong was careful not to upstage his mentor; he was, after all, the second cornetist, not the lead. Supposedly he stood twenty feet behind the rest of the band to make sure his horn did not overpower Oliver's. Still his clean attack, his sense of rhythm, and his energy were apparent to all on numbers like "Froggie Moore" (a Jelly Roll Morton tune) and "Snake Rag."

Most important, he was "doing something he would eventually make into a whole system," as biographer James Lincoln Collier mentions, "playing away from the beat" so that many notes were "attached only very loosely to the ground beat." How elementary it sounds to those of us who have grown up with the embroidery of time changes that makes jazz such a compelling fabric of sound. Yet in 1923, it was revolutionary. The sides Armstrong cut with Oliver's Creole Jazz Band have stood the test of time; they are not just historic, they are ageless.

Nor was that all. By 1924, Armstrong had begun to sing as well as solo on cornet, something he had not done since his boyhood quartet days. His audiences loved his infectious rasp

from the start and Louis, as ebullient and emotional an entertainer as ever stood onstage, loved to please them. Over the
course of his career, he was acknowledged as a vocalist of
such unprecedented inventiveness that every subsequent singer
who ever improvised a phrase was paying homage to Armstrong.

Lil Hardin deserved some credit for propelling Armstrong
further into the limelight than he might have gone otherwise
at this point in his career. The Oliver band's pianist, she had
studied classical music at the Fisk University prep school before
coming to Chicago. Lil began taking a personal as well as professional interest in the shy new fellow. She encouraged him
to shed excess pounds along with his countrified clothes. As
their relationship deepened she not only helped Louis buy more
up-to-date duds, she convinced him to leave Oliver in order to
become a star in Fletcher Henderson's band. Armstrong joined
Henderson in New York in 1924. By that time, both Louis and
Lil had divorced their spouses (Armstrong had wed a young
woman back in Gretna, Louisiana) and were married.

Armstrong's successes were numerous and varied from that
time on. With the Henderson band, he had a showcase in the
most important city in the country. Musicians, critics, and jazz
buffs, white as well as black, came to his club dates in the
manner of acolytes to a temple—to worship and to study. It
was with Henderson that he first began to do vocal solos. In
1925, he accompanied Bessie Smith on a series of recordings,
including "St. Louis Blues" and "You've Been a Good Ole Wagon,"
that have come to be regarded as the most perfect blend of
two towering talents ever captured on record.

However, the most sensational sessions were still to come.
From 1925 through 1928 back in Chicago as leader of his own
Hot Five and Hot Seven combos, he made a series of recordings, all done quickly and under primitive conditions for the
small Okeh label. His earliest solos in this collection were on
cornet, but it was during this period that he switched to the
trumpet, a change he never reversed. The Okeh recordings
marked the pinnacle of his career as an artist and are revered

as the works that transformed jazz into a mature art.

The Hot Five consisted of Armstrong, Kid Ory, Johnny Dodds, Lil Hardin Armstrong, and Johnny St. Cyr. On the Hot Sevens, John Thomas replaced Ory on trombone, Pete Briggs was added on tuba, and Baby Dodds joined as the drummer. (There were other changes on some sessions, including Earl Hines on piano and Zutty Singleton on drums.) Amazingly, these were strictly studio groups. They never played live dates, and the musicians looked upon the recording experience as nothing more than an enjoyable and profitable sideline. (They were paid fifty dollars each per session.) In addition, Armstrong accidentally introduced scat singing in the course of these sessions. According to legend, the Hot Five was in the middle of "Heebie Jeebies" when Louis dropped the lyric sheet, forcing him to make up nonsense words until someone picked it up.

In the end, what matters is that on these matchless sides Louis Armstrong invented, improvised, and perfected the classic jazz solo. Numbers like "Struttin' with Some Barbecue," "Potato Head Blues," "Hotter Than That," and "West End Blues" are to the Jazz Age what the Sistine Chapel is to the Renaissance.

The marital collaboration of Louis and Lil collapsed in the 1920s, but Armstrong found others to prod him into new endeavors and manage his career. Returning to New York, he appeared in the Broadway musical *Hot Chocolates*, in which he first sang the Fats Waller tune "Ain't Misbehavin'." A tough white promoter named Joe Glaser took over the handling of Armstrong in 1935, and he moved Armstrong further away from jazz, more into the larger realm of show business. Through movies, big-band groups, and world tours over the next thirty-five years, Louis Armstrong grew into an international superstar.

He never forgot his roots in New Orleans, but neither was he sentimental about the city, either. Asked in 1959 why he had not played his hometown in a long time, he answered, "I'm accepted all over the world and when New Orleans accepts me, I'll go home." His feelings had not stopped him from welcoming an invitation from the city's oldest, most famous black Mardi Gras organization to grace their parade in 1949 as king of the Zulus. However, he was well aware of the segregationist practices (including a ban on racially mixed bands) that existed in New Orleans as late as the mid-1960s. Attacked late in life by some activists who saw him as an Uncle Tom, Armstrong nevertheless was idolized by young African Americans on the New Orleans music scene. "Within Bourbon Street Black, he was, and is, the human most admired," wrote the authors of the book of the same name, "the personification of all they loved, hoped for, and strived to attain." One of the most recent and most honored of Louis's spiritual children, Wynton Marsalis, invoked "Pops" as the Thomas Edison of jazz. "All we can do," he told one group, "is be glad we live in the same century as Louis Armstrong."

At the time of his death in 1971, Louis Armstrong was mourned and eulogized not only by blacks but by people of every color the world over. Few legends have worn that mantle with more humor and grace. His contributions to popular entertainment were so enormous that even now, it is hard to write about Louis Armstrong without sounding hyperbolic. Still, those contributions are as real today as they were fifty years ago. "Americans, unknowingly, live part of every day in the house that Satch built," wrote critic Leonard Feather. It is fitting to leave the last observation to a fellow musician. "I'm proud to acknowledge my debt to the Reverend Satchelmouth," Bing Crosby once said. "He is the beginning and the end of music in America."

APRÈS LOUIS

For the first two decades of the new century, New Orleans was the fertile soil from which burst forth a new American art form. But with the migration of its brilliant instrumentalists and composers to the greener pastures of the north, the city retrenched as a music capital.

Not that music disappeared in the twenties and thirties. According to guitarist Danny Barker, there remained a core of fine players, including Buddy Petit, Kid Rena, Sidney Desvigne, and others.

"A lot of them would play roadhouses and vaudeville shows and circuses and riverboats and lake boats," recalled Barker, whose remarkable career spanned more than sixty years. He explained that although the biggest stars had departed, "we in New Orleans in the twenties were aware of what was happening in jazz. We'd hear records by other bands. . . . We'd pass a house and hear a piano roll." Barker himself, born in 1908, honed his own skills in the early twenties before heading north, where he was a sideman in Cab Calloway's band, among others. Meanwhile, band leaders such as Lee Collins made New Orleans their base for forays all across the South. Younger New Orleans players found work in everything from minstrel shows to department store openings, which typically would feature live music.

The last major talent to emerge from the Crescent City's pool of early jazz instrumentalists was cornetist Henry "Red" Allen. Born in 1908, he grew up in Algiers, on the west bank of the Mississippi across from New Orleans. His father, Henry Allen, Sr., was also a horn man and the leader of an important brass band. His father's friends helped the young boy get work in dance halls while he was a teenager, and, like Louis Armstrong, he learned still more in bands organized by Fate Marable on the riverboats. Once Armstrong left for Chicago, Allen was considered the best cornetist in town. When band leaders Luis Russell and Paul Barbarin joined the exodus to Chicago, they spoke highly of the junior Allen, whose nickname came from the way his light-skinned face colored as he blew his horn. Soon, he, too, was invited to join Joe Oliver in Chicago.

He built his reputation in New York, however. In the late twenties and early thirties, his inventive solos and flexible tone made him a huge favorite among nightclubbers and band leaders alike. He became the featured soloist in Luis Russell's big band that fronted for Armstrong in the thirties, but he reached the height of his fame playing alongside such big-band giants as Coleman Hawkins in Fletcher Henderson's ensemble. Among his numerous recordings, his solo on "Shakin' the African," a tune recorded with composer Don Redman, was later hailed as a preview of bebop.

While great black soloists like Allen grew scarce in New Orleans in the thirties, what had come to be known as the New Orleans style itself fell out of favor. The white variation of the style, Dixieland, helped to keep the traditional sound alive. Front and center were the New Orleans Rhythm Kings.

The Rhythm Kings' leaders, Paul Mares on trumpet, George Brunis on trombone, and Leon Rappolo on clarinet, were childhood buddies from New Orleans who organized the New Orleans Rhythm Kings in Chicago in the early twenties. Through a series of recordings, made while the group was in residence at a gangster hangout, Friar's Inn, their fame spread. Their versions of tunes such as "Farewell Blues" mesmerized an entire generation of young, white Chicagoans such as Bud Freeman and Jimmy McPartland, at least until those young men got to hear Oliver and Armstrong. (They later eclipsed the New Orleans Rhythm Kings with their raucous "Chicago style" sound.)

The Rhythm Kings never did reach the peak of popularity achieved by the Original Dixieland Jazz Band. But their playing infused Dixieland with a smoother, more elastic set of signatures, especially Brunis's "tailgate" patterns (as his vigorous style, with its heavy use of the slide, came to be known) at the end of tunes, that were absent from the earlier white band's presentation.

Paul Mares was modest about his band's contributions. "We had only two tempos, slow drag and the two-four one-step. We did our best to copy the colored music we'd heard at home. We did the best we could, but naturally we couldn't play real colored style," he said. Brunis had an extended career after his

Rhythm King days, first with Ted Lewis, then as a regular on Fifty-second Street in New York in the fifties. Always a clown onstage, he might have been the musician who started the routine, at the end of a set, of leading a parade through the audience to the tune of "When the Saints Go Marching In."

Men like Sidney Bechet were scornful of Dixieland's white performers. "They tried to write the music down and kind of freeze it," he wrote. "Even when they didn't arrange it to death, they didn't have any place to send it; that's why they lost it." But for two New Orleanians who grew up in the thirties and forties, Dixieland was the road to a vibrant revival of the original jazz spirit. Their names were Pete Fountain and Al Hirt.

January 25, 1964, is enshrined in music history as the start of a new era. On that date, the Beatles hit the *Billboard* pop charts with their first American single, "I Want to Hold Your Hand." However, another catchy tune, this one an instrumental with a much older pedigree, also began its meteoric rise that day: Al Hirt's "Java." Unfortunately, "Java" (written by Allen Toussaint) would turn out to be the high point in a bizarre, roller-coaster career for the trumpet virtuoso who at one time was christened "the greatest horn in the world."

Alois Maxwell Hirt, the son of a New Orleans policeman, was raised on the big-band sound of Harry James and Roy Eldridge but originally started out to be a classical musician. Born on November 7, 1922, he was fascinated as a child by a band his parents had hired for a private party. Soon he was taking trumpet lessons. He graduated from Fortier High School, and then spent three years at the Cincinnati Conservatory of Music, but dropped out to capitalize on the jazz recognition he got by winning a Horace Heidt radio talent show. Before long, he was in the Army, where he played in bands that welcomed homecoming troops. At the war's end, he sat in with some of the most stellar bands of the day, including those of Tommy and Jimmy Dorsey.

The longing for home cooking, however, lured him home. Playing in California in 1950, he got a package one day from a friend—frozen crawfish. Hirt, a man the size of a nose tackle whose weight topped three hundred pounds, turned to his wife and said, "What the heck are we doing here?"

The Hirts returned to his native city, where he toiled for years as a disc jockey and soloist in a radio house band in order to support his burgeoning family, which eventually included nine children. He had no trouble finding kindred spirits back home who, like Hirt, were interested in breathing a new urgency into traditional jazz. In 1955, Hirt put together a six-piece combo featuring another home boy, Pete Fountain, on clarinet.

Hirt's big break came in 1960, when Monique van Vooren, the movie star, happened to catch his act at a Bourbon Street club. What she saw was a bearded giant who not only was technically dazzling, with a penetrating tone and a style that updated Dixie with elements from the Swing Era, but who charmed his audience with little dance steps and other nuggets of showmanship. Impressed, she sent her husband and manager, Gerard W. Purcell, to New Orleans and he signed Hirt to a contract. He was a natural for television; his first appearance on Dinah Shore's show captivated an audience of millions. By the start of 1961, Hirt was flying high and solo, with an album on RCA and a performance at President John F. Kennedy's inaugural ball.

For a while, Hirt was the toast of both his town and everyone else's. His mass audience lapped up the music he referred to as "roving Dixieland," a brand of Dixie laced with pop and occasionally overlaid with lush string arrangements. *Time* magazine waxed ecstatic over his group: "Snarling, growling, shivering into a remarkably clean vibrato or soaring through long, liquid phrases," Hirt's trumpet "slices through the group's sound like a blade," it said. Critic Leonard Feather put the jazz world's stamp of approval on Hirt's hybrid idiom, noting that "regardless of the arguments of whether or not he is basically a jazzman (and obviously some of his work is not intended to be even remotely related to jazz) it is beyond dispute that Al Hirt, in an amazingly short space of time, has earned the respect of innumerable fellow-musicians, as well as the American public at large."

Hirt was aware of fame's capriciousness. "We try to satisfy everyone's tastes," he said, "but I know that in this business you're hot for a while and then you cool off. I got eight (soon to be nine) kids to put through college. I want to make it while I'm hot." He tried, touring incessantly, recording one album after another, making a splash on the Las Vegas scene. After "Java" rose to Number 4 on the charts, he opened his own club on Bourbon Street. His pianist was a local keyboard man just beginning his own family, Ellis Marsalis.

Even at the peak of his renown, Hirt had his detractors. Critic Nat Hentoff belittled him, suggesting that Hirt was popular in part because he was "cute" in the manner of Yogi Berra. Hirt further distanced himself from the jazz world by turning down the chance to appear at either the Newport Jazz Festival or the fledgling New Orleans festival. "Al is no longer a jazz musician," said Purcell, his manager. "It would be similarly illogical for him to play in an opera house." He also battled personal problems. His first marriage collapsed and there were rumors of drugs and alcohol.

Still, he was a local icon when near-tragedy stuck in February, 1970. Greeting crowds from a float in the Bacchus parade during Carnival, Hirt suddenly staggered. A brick thrown from the crowd had hit him squarely in the mouth. He needed stitches across his entire lip. "It sure takes all the fun out of Mardi Gras," he said wryly. Although he recovered, Hirt never regained the stature he held in the early sixties. His club on Bourbon Street closed. He played fewer and fewer engagements. He seemed to have a love/hate relationship with New Orleans, knocking it in interviews, yet always returning. His booking agent said Hirt was paranoid about the press and would do interviews only if he was paid for them. Occasionally, appearing in a club or a concert hall, he could still pour out a few of the lovely phrases that made him a link (albeit a tarnished one) in the great chain of New Orleans trumpeters.

While his onetime band mate foundered, Pete Fountain flourished. Eight years younger than Hirt, Peter Dewey Fountain, Jr., has for years been the genial standard bearer for Dixieland, pounding out warhorses from "Wolverine Blues" to "Avalon" to the inevitable "Saints" with a cool professionalism, if little urgency. Like Hirt, he won a nationwide following thanks to television, but unlike him, did not seem to have squandered it. Like Hirt, he strayed quite far from the music purists would regard as jazz, but unlike him, he managed to walk the fine line between commercialism and sentimentality.

The son of an amateur musician who drove a Dixie beer truck for a living, Fountain grew up in the city's seventh ward, hearing the good local bands of the thirties, including those of Sharkey Bonano, Leon and Louis Prima, and Raymond Burke. His first love was the drums, but he switched at age twelve when a physician told his family that playing a wind instrument would build up his weak lungs. For a dollar down and a dollar a week, his father got him a fifty-dollar clarinet.

By the time Pete, Jr. was fourteen, he played well enough to be recruited by Warren Easton High School, which collected good players for its marching band. When he wasn't practicing, he would continue his musical education in the French Quarter. "I went to Bourbon Street every night and stood outside the clubs," he recalled. He not only got to hear men like Louis Armstrong, Barney Bigard, and Jack Teagarden, he got to sit in with some of the best bands, black and white, in the city. But the most important impression was made by a clarinetist whose name would become inexorably linked with his, Irving Fazola.

"Faz" was a player of great promise whose idol had been Leon Rappolo of the New Orleans Rhythm Kings. After a rocky beginning (Fountain requested a tune Faz hated, and Faz replied, "Get lost, kid"), their friendship blossomed. Determined to emulate Fazola, Fountain at sixteen formed a group with two brothers who would later be the nucleus of the Dukes of Dixieland, trombonist Freddie and trumpet player Frank Assunto.

The youngsters got their union cards and immediately started playing local gigs for scale, $125 a week. It was enough of a start for Pete, who quit high school two months before graduation. He was thrilled when Faz came to hear them. Then one night Fountain got an emergency call from a burlesque theater. A substitute clarinetist was needed; Irving Fazola had died that day at the age of thirty-six. When a grieving Fountain joined the band that evening, he recalled, "It was Faz pushing the rings and Leon Rappolo blowing the breath into me." Later, Faz's mother gave young Pete his idol's clarinet.

By 1950, Fountain had formed his own group, the Basin Street Six. It was a tight group that "swung out on all of the old Dixie standards," he remembered fondly. "Our only problem was that by that time Dixieland was dead"—killed, he thought, by bebop and difficult economic times. At one point, the group, which did manage to cut a record, was reduced to accepting a spot on a banana boat in Central America. By 1954, however, Dixieland was dancing back into the hearts of New Orleanians. Leading the parade was the New Orleans Jazz Club. Organized a few years earlier, it was winning converts with a Sunday afternoon jam session on radio station WWL that soon introduced Fountain to a wide new audience. The Assuntos' group, the Dukes of Dixieland, was attracting major attention nationally. Fountain and his newest group, a quartet, played the Famous Door for a year until Pete himself became a member of the Dukes. When he wasn't playing with his regular band, Fountain jammed with other gifted young Dixie players, especially the man everyone called "Jumbo," Al Hirt.

In this productive climate, Fountain matured as a player. He found the "fat" sound he had been searching for, an original approach that he felt blended the big voice of Fazola with the drive of Benny Goodman, all of it embroidered with Fountain's own quivering vibrato. But life on the road was taking its toll. "On the bandstand, I was really making a name for myself," Fountain recalled, "but I was drinking my way out of everything else." By 1956, with his house about to be foreclosed and his marriage in jeopardy, Fountain left the Dukes, returned to New Orleans to dry out. He quit the music business and got his first "straight" job, working for the same exterminator who had hired Hirt. Once he straightened his personal life out, Fountain joined a band fronted by Hirt at Pier 600, a well-known club. It was there he got the call for a guest appearance in California that shifted his career into a new gear.

Band leader Lawrence Welk had turned his corny popular arrangements into a national phenomenon on television. After Fountain's first guest shot, Welk realized that the Dixie reed man could add New Orleans spice to his band's bland diet. Fountain accepted Welk's invitation to become a regular solo-ist, reasoning that it was steady work and would not damage his career. At the end of his two-year stint with Welk's troupe, Fountain was as famous a musician as anyone on the American scene. Whether he still was a jazz man was open to question.

Fountain himself acknowledged that he grew fed up with Welk's strict rules and chafed under the leader's narrow musical taste. The end came when Fountain phrased a solo "just as Satchmo would have" on a Christmas special and Welk proclaimed it "sacrilegious." Pete was ready to go home again. The city welcomed him with open arms, proclaiming the occasion Pete Fountain Day.

He never left again, except for short trips to appear on such high-profile programs as the Johnny Carson show. In New Orleans, he formed a new band that played an appealing blend of styles that Fountain dubbed "swinging Dixie"—an updated Dixieland with plenty of pop standards in the mix of tunes. Critics enjoyed Fountain's return to his roots so much that they voted him Downbeat's New Artist of the Year in 1960. Soon, he formed the Half Fast Walking Club, a group that stages its informal parade shortly after dawn each Mardi Gras day.

In order to cut down on his seven-nights-a-week playing time, Fountain soon opened his own club on Bourbon Street. It quickly became an express stop on the tourist circuit. He later moved his club to the New Orleans Hilton, where he enjoyed a relaxed schedule of one set a night four nights a week. Replying to critics who felt that he no longer played true jazz, Fountain said: "I'm not sure what genuine jazz is. What I do is play what the people want to hear. Too many performers think they have to educate their public, play over the heads of their public, and those performers get forgotten pretty quick."

He acknowledged that there was a time some years ago when "the well ran dry." For "almost ten, fifteen years we didn't have that fire going all the time. People would come to see me at my club," he said, "but it wasn't the same." To jump-start his creativity, he asked for a spot on Carson's show, which he had not done in a long while. Playing with Doc Severinsen that night, everything suddenly clicked, and Dixieland's most enduring star was back on track. He admitted that in recent years he would not change the tunes in his show often. "My solos change— from reed to reed. They change personality from what I eat, from my day. I try to keep the improvisation alive, and not get stale."

Pete Fountain may not have taken Dixieland beyond where it stood as a jazz idiom in the heyday of its revival thirty-five years ago. But there is a stability to his life that must be the envy of many top musicians. He and his wife Beverly, who comes to hear many of his shows, have been married for over forty years; they own a big spread outside town, and are mentioned frequently in the New Orleans society columns. The seventh ward is proud of Pete. The bottom line, as the New Orleans Jazz Club's magazine *Second Line* wrote, is that "with all his 'commercial' background, Pete Fountain remains a solid jazz player. He is too rooted in the New Orleans atmosphere to be otherwise and too good a musician to give a slipshod performance."

GRAND OLD MEN

When Alan Lomax recorded Jelly Roll Morton in 1938, he touched off a revival of traditional jazz that has continued—

with some ups and downs—to thrive to this day in clubs from the French Quarter to suburban Metairie. The movement gathered momentum in 1939 when two intrepid researchers, Frederick Ramsey, Jr., and William Russell, acting on a tip from Louis Armstrong, tracked down Bunk Johnson in New Iberia, a Cajun town in South Louisiana. They arranged for him to play live dates nationwide. Meanwhile, Heywood Broun rediscovered Kid Rena and recorded him. Together with the informed writings of Russell, Rudi Blesh, and others, these artists helped traditional jazz claim its rightful place atop the summit of American art forms.

By mid-century, aging musicians from the old school did not lack for gigs, regardless of the competition from other musical styles from swing to rhythm and blues. Papa Celestin, until his death in 1954, was "the band leader of choice at debutante parties and other social functions," according to a local paper. Interest did diminish in the early sixties, but a new revival began when Allan Jaffe, a jazz buff, founded Preservation Hall in 1961.

As guitarist Danny Barker and sociologist Jack V. Buerkle wrote in their book *Bourbon Street Black* in 1973,

> One of the unique facts of the New Orleans scene is that a premium is placed on older, black musicians. Regardless of the inaccuracy of the stereotype, many tourists walking up Bourbon Street or down St. Peter to Preservation Hall expect to hear an older black man, white shirt open at the collar, suspenders, simply cut trousers, plain black shoes, and legs crossed. . . . The jazzmen who set the streets and halls of New Orleans "afire" in the days of Buddy Bolden, Freddie Keppard and Chris Kelly were young men. Now the image is reversed; hot jazz is associated with old men. . . . The old cats are expected to be able to recapture the golden days.

A courtly gentleman who did fit the stereotype was one of the last of the grand old piano men, Tuts Washington, whose career took him from the honky-tonks of the post-Storyville era to the genteel lounges of the Fairmont and Pontchartrain hotels. Almost until the day of his death in 1984 at the age of seventy-six, Washington conducted what amounted to a public seminar in the New Orleans keyboard style, a style with links all the way back to Morton and Jackson.

Isidore "Tuts" (as in Tootsie Roll) Washington was born in New Orleans in 1907. He was raised by his aunt in the Uptown section after his mother died when he was six. He learned the piano on his own, listening to players in Storyville as a child. When he wanted to remember a song he had heard he would whistle it until he could get home to his piano, and it has been suggested that Professor Longhair, whose whistling made the Mardi Gras song "Big Chief" a classic, got the idea from Tuts.

Soon he was staying out until all hours of the night. His aunt, he later recalled, "tried to run me off the piano. She'd get me a job in a hardware store, or washing dishes." Sometimes, angry because he neglected his chores, she would beat him and send him to bed without dinner. However, Washington found a mentor in Joseph Louis "Red" Cayou, whom he described as "the best piano player we had in New Orleans before he left in '25 (to live in California). His hands were like lightning." Cayou took the young man under his wing. Washington put in stints with various bands on Bourbon Street led by such stalwarts as Kid Rena, Papa Celestin, John Handy, and others. He also performed solo at the "joints" that once lined South Rampart Street. Women, he bragged, used to throw money on his piano and fight over him in his heyday.

Except for some years in California, Tuts did not travel, choosing to stick with the clubs he knew in New Orleans. He never recorded during his prime because, he said, he was so well known he didn't have to. (Recording dates often paid less than club gigs back then.) Jeff Hannusch, who produced Washington's only solo album, released a year before he died, suggested that pride might have been a factor. It was possible that no one approached Tuts in his younger days about recording, especially since companies were always more interested in pianists who also sang.

While appearing at a local spot called the Cotton Club, he

befriended a teenager who hung out there, charcoal smeared on his upper lip to disguise the fact that he was underage. The youngster was Henry Roeland Byrd, later to be known as Professor Longhair. Byrd admired Washington's ability, especially his clean fingering; with his unerring touch, Tuts was able to reach the difficult chords of two-handed stride and boogie-woogie styles.

Washington's playing transcended styles, however. Like the "professors" before him, he could play whatever was required—blues, stride, boogie woogie, standards, "sentimental" tunes. Critics heard what Jelly Roll Morton called the "Spanish tinge"—rumba and Calypso swirls—in his playing, along with hints of ragtime, all driven by Washington's own eccentric rhythms. Although he said he didn't play rock 'n' roll, he appeared with singer Smiley Lewis (of "I Hear You Knockin' " fame) in the late forties or early fifties, and recorded "Tee Naa-Nah," a regional hit, with him. For the remainder of his life, Tuts became a fixture at clubs and lounges all over New Orleans, watching as local boys such as Fats Domino and James Booker, both of whom had come to watch and listen to the grand old man while they were learning their craft, absorbed his influence and came into their own as pianists.

Washington's final years were spent playing in the pleasant surroundings of luxury hotels. Meanwhile, in other hotels, in the raucous tourist joints along Bourbon Street, and elsewhere in the French Quarter, his contemporaries kept the sound of traditional jazz resounding through the city of its birth. Many elderly jazzmen, including trombonist Louis Nelson, trumpeter Kid Thomas Valentine, clarinetist George Lewis, and cornetist George "Kid Sheik" Colar found steady employment at Preservation Hall on St. Peter Street, an austere, dark box with a few rows of folding chairs and plenty of standing room, that became a landmark of sorts.

Preservation Hall, with its wooden sign and its musicians lined up with their backs to the front windows, looked as if it dated back to the glory days of jazz. In fact, it was an art gallery in the mid-fifties when traditional jazz artists got together regularly there for jam sessions. Since segregation was the law of the day, racially mixed groups would occasionally get arrested for playing together. Still, the jams were so popular they attracted dedicated fans. In 1961 Allen and Sandra Jaffe, jazz archivists, subleased the room from its owner and scheduled regular shows, passing the hat to pay the musicians. (Eventually, they got union wages.) Dubbing the place Preservation Hall, they gave older players a regular forum for their art. It took a few years, but word got around to jazz buffs nationwide, especially when Hall bands began touring and recording. Today, with lines outside seven nights a week, Preservation Hall flourishes.

Contributing to the resurgence of traditional music was Danny Barker, who with his wife, singer Blue Lu Barker, returned to his native city in 1965. Noticing that there were only one or two brass bands still playing, he organized one of young people, including members of old-timers' families such as his cousins, the Barbarins. The twenty-five years since then have seen a flowering of brass bands, both traditional and more contemporary, where younger instrumentalists could learn their trade at the side of their forerunners.

At clubs such as the Palm Court Jazz Café and the Louis Armstrong Foundation Jazz Club, as well as Preservation Hall, traditional jazz continues to weave its spell, played now not only by the "old cats," almost all of them over eighty years old, but also by skilled revivalists a half-century younger, such as clarinetist Michael White and trumpeter Wendell Brunious, and European transplants such as French-born band leader Jacques Gauthé. Night after night, groups devoted to the old ways, plus singers such as Banu Gibson, who specializes in standards from periods all the way up through the Big Band Era, remind New Orleans and its visitors that the "cradle" of jazz still sways to the beat of its birth.

③ Rebirth —
The First Wave of R&B

BEGINNINGS—
FESS, FATS, AND THE FIFTIES
••

The most popular music in New Orleans in the years immediately after World War II consisted of boogie-woogie piano à la Tuts Washington, big bands, and jump blues, the raucous sound produced by little combo spinoffs of the big bands. As the forties progressed, all these strains contributed to a new phenomenon in which the Crescent City would again play a leading role: rhythm and blues, R&B for short, a euphemistic phrase for what the music business called "race" music—meaning music intended exclusively for black listeners.

R&B arose out of the factionalism of jazz. Nationally, the traditional jazz of the pioneering New Orleanian instrumentalists had splintered before the war, when the Swing Era took hold. In its wake, jazz, to reduce it to the simplest terms, had divided into two branches: big band and bebop. Both the big bands that catered to black audiences (those of Count Basie and Lionel Hampton, for instance) and smaller combos, especially the jump-blues band led by Arkansas-born Louis Jordan, played music bouncier and more raunchy than the polished white big bands of the era—Tommy Dorsey, Benny Goodman, and their ilk. In clubs and halls that dotted the black districts of cities from Los Angeles to Kansas City to New Orleans to Washington, D.C., these bands offered their energetic audiences tunes that were eminently more danceable than the abstractions of bebop. As Nelson George wrote in *The Death of Rhythm and Blues,* "For the masses of blacks, after bebop's emergence, jazz was respected but in times of leisure and relaxation they turned to Louis Jordan and a blend of blues, jump blues, ballads, gospel and a slew of sax-led instruments and fading black swing orchestras." The hallmark of R&B was the beat, but the other key element, besides the honking sax, was a singer who could shout or moan the blues like Wynonie Harris and Joe Turner.

The first wave of R&B broke over the levee via both records and live appearances by acts such as Harris and Louis Jordan. As in many cities directly after the war, its sound was also infiltrating the airwaves through new radio shows and stations aimed specifically at black listeners. Soon, local players such as Dave Bartholomew and Paul Gayten began forming their own combos to lay down the new beat. "We were jazz musicians" at first, explained Earl Palmer, a member of the Bartholomew band and the preeminent New Orleans drummer of the postwar years. "The younger ones were trying to play bebop; the older ones were trying to play like the best Dixieland. R&B was more basic, more primitive," he continued, but it was also more commercial. Thus, leaders like Bartholomew gravitated toward that sound because it enabled him to get more varied bookings.

Segregation, of course, was very much in force in postwar New Orleans, and thus R&B was initially a black musical phenomenon. It reached only those whites curious enough to venture into black clubs or to tune into black radio. Night spots that brought the best R&B acts to New Orleans, such as the Dew Drop Inn, the Tiajuana, the Caldonia Inn, and the Robin Hood catered to black patrons, although whites were permitted, by law, as long as the races did not "mix." There were also rooms for whites only that featured black musicians, such as the Brass Rail, where Gayten's orchestra played, but they were tame by comparison.

The concept of keeping the races separate was not only bizarre, it was difficult to "enforce." Typically, it meant that whites and blacks sat at separate tables in clubs, or separate sections in theaters. When someone went table-hopping, it could lead to a police raid. In the rural South, barns were sometimes set up as primitive, temporary dance halls. A rope would be strung to divide the areas where members of each race could dance. The stars of the so-called chitlin' circuit, such as the singer Ruth Brown, recalled with wry amusement that once the music got hot and the adventurous young blacks and whites began to dance, the ropes sometimes would get trampled on. It was not uncommon for the police to be called to restore the social order.

The first star to bubble up out of this cauldron of sounds in New Orleans was a gospel-trained vocalist named Roy Brown. Born in New Orleans in 1925, Brown had his biggest hit, "Good Rockin' Tonight," in 1947, and his soulful style had a major impact on numerous young singers, including Elvis Presley, who made the most famous cover of it.

Brown's mother had been a church choir soloist. At the age of twelve, Roy started his own spirituals quartet, but his fervent singing soon got him in trouble at his family's Eunice, Louisiana, church. He and his companions had some wine beforehand and they "jazzed up" a spiritual until everyone in church was rocking. When he got home his mother administered a beating. "That wasn't a spiritual you were singing. I don't know what it was but it wasn't a spiritual." she said.

How his signature song, considered by many a direct precedent for rock 'n' roll, came to be performed and waxed is the stuff of which legends are made. Brown started out his career in Los Angeles as a crooner imitating Bing Crosby, his favorite singer. He migrated to Texas, where his band had its own radio slot, an unusual accomplishment for a black act in that period. Brown himself wrote "Good Rockin' Tonight" for his trumpet player to sing. Then one night in 1946, just as the tune was being announced on the radio, the trumpet player was felled by indigestion. Brown jumped in, shouting the prescient lyrics: "Have you heard the news / there's good rockin' tonight," much to the astonishment of his band, which had never heard him sing like that.

A few months later, Brown had to escape from Texas because of his involvement with a white woman. He headed for his hometown, arriving with nothing but the clothes on his back and shoes so worn he had to line the bottoms with cardboard. But the dynamic entertainer was determined to climb back into the spotlight. He wrote the words of "Good Rockin' Tonight" on a paper bag and set out to impress the biggest acts in town. On his first night, he talked his way into a club where Wynonie Harris was performing. During intermission, Brown pitched the tune to Harris. No dice. Harris's band did let Brown sing it himself, but Harris, a notoriously contemptuous man, still brushed him off. Brown's next stop was the Dew Drop Inn, where Cecil Gant, another popular singer of the time, was appearing. Gant's reaction could not have been more upbeat. Upon hearing the song, he got so excited he called Jules Braun, the president of Deluxe, a new record company in New Jersey, and even though it was the middle of the night, he had Brown sing "Good Rockin' " over the phone. It might not have been his usual business practice to audition unknown vocalists thousands of miles away, but Braun recognized a great tune when he heard one. He was bowled over. He promised to catch a plane to New Orleans right away—and he did. (He had been planning a trip anyway to record Paul Gayten and Gayten's fine vocalist, Annie Laurie.) Within days, Braun took Brown to a tiny studio owned by an engineer just beginning to get involved in the field, Cosimo Matassa, and recorded him.

The musicians hired for the date were as amazed at Brown's powerful delivery as Braun was. "He had a religious, kicked-off style, like a deacon or a preacher," Bob Ogden, a drummer who played behind Brown, said. Inspired, the band gave Brown an appropriately gospel-style backing, "like the sisters are shoutin' in church when everything gets happy," Ogden said. When "Good Rockin' " was released as a single that summer, with its honking sax at the beginning, it was a local sensation, and so was Brown, in person. "You should have seen Roy sing," the leading local black deejay of the era, Dr. Daddy-O, raved. "The words. The daring. The drums. The horns and him standing up there six feet tall and hollering it and shaking his body. He was just a big salesperson who was selling sex."

On the strength of "Good Rockin' Tonight" and other hits such as "Boogie at Midnight" and "Hard Luck Blues," Brown went on tour, playing such top theaters as the Fox in Brooklyn and the Apollo in Manhattan. However, he discovered that he was being cheated by his manager, and he lodged complaints with the musicians' union. Brown charged that people in the music business retaliated; he soon found bookings hard to come by.

Roy Brown experienced a small revival in 1956 thanks to Dave Bartholomew, a neighbor in New Orleans, who produced several sides for Imperial with the same band that backed Fats Domino. But the label dropped him after he ran afoul of the Internal Revenue Service. Brown wound up serving time for tax fraud. For the remainder of his life, he got by on small club dates, by selling encyclopedias door to door, and by pressing shirts. According to Mac Rebennack (Dr. John), Brown was a very sensitive man whose attempted comeback might have been thwarted by nervous breakdowns. Even though his voice was a powerfully emotional one, influencing such stars as Bobby "Blue" Bland, Little Richard, and Jackie Wilson, even though Wynonie Harris and a half-dozen other singers recorded "Good Rockin' Tonight," Brown got only a small fraction of royalties due him. He never attained true stardom.

Brown did get help once, though, from the man whose early career owed so much to his hit tune. Short of money, he tried to crash a birthday party for Elvis Presley in 1959 or 1960 in Little Rock. As Roy told the story, "I slipped the porter five dollars [and said] 'Tell Elvis Good Rockin' Brown is out here.' Elvis came to the door and I told him I was in trouble." The King wrote "$1600," his bank-account number, and signature on the back of a piece of paper. Brown took it to the bank the next day and got his money.

Roy Brown died in 1981 at the age of sixty-five. Just a few months before, he had made a triumphant return to his roots—appearing onstage at the New Orleans Jazz and Heritage Festival in a coveted "star" slot, right after Ernie K-Doe and right before Dr. John.

However sad the personal story of Roy Brown, "Good Rockin' Tonight" launched the golden age of R&B in New Orleans. Matassa, the record's engineer, and Dr. Daddy-O, the enthusiastic deejay, were on the crest of the R&B wave.

Matassa, a bespectacled Tulane dropout whose father ran a jukebox business, became part of the music scene by opening a combination record store and radio repair operation with a friend, Joe Mancuso. At first J & M Record Shop, located at the corner of Rampart and Dumaine streets, specialized in blues records that Matassa got from a source on the West Coast, conveyed cross-country to New Orleans by a railroad Pullman-porter friend. By 1947, he realized that music was once again generating excitement in the Crescent City, yet there was no place for the independent labels that were in the vanguard of R&B to record it. So Matassa set up a studio, J & M Recording, in a tiny space the size of a residential living room, behind the record shop. (It later was moved to a larger site nearby.) Along with Sam Phillips's Sun Studio in Memphis, J & M was to become one of the two most productive studios in early rock 'n' roll.

Deluxe, Braun's label, started the R&B parade to Matassa by having Roy Brown make "Good Rockin' Tonight" in that studio. Braun also recorded singer Annie Laurie and singer/pianist Paul Gayten doing "Since I Fell for You," another R&B hit. In the next decade, J & M microphones captured on wax the magic of Fats Domino, Little Richard, Shirley and Lee, Huey Smith, Art Neville, and numerous other talents.

Around the same period, Vernon Winslow was an art teacher at Dillard University in New Orleans, among the leading black institutions in the country. A northerner and a jazz buff, Winslow wondered why there was not more black music on local radio stations. When he began talking to the stations about greater programming for what was then called the Negro market, he got one "positive" response. The station WJMR, run by whites, told Winslow that because of his color he couldn't be on the air (in 1948 segregation affected both visible and nonvisible job opportunities in New Orleans), but they did ask him to write scripts in Negro lingo for the white disc jockey of a show called "Jam, Jive and Gumbo." A sophisticated academician, Winslow himself did not speak the dialect of the streets, so he took himself to the Dew Drop Inn to pick up the hip new phrases. He chose the records for the show, wrote the scripts, and christened the deejay "Poppa Stoppa." There was a procession of Poppa Stoppas, all white. The show drew a large black following.

Winslow's tenure at WJMR ended when he committed the racial gaff of reading his script himself during a moment when the white announcer was away from the mike. Even though it was radio, not television, and even though there was nothing "black" in his speech, the station fired him on the spot. However, he was hired by another station the next year to start the first show done by blacks. Combining his college background with street jive, he renamed himself Dr. Daddy-O. It did not take long before the voice of Dr. Daddy-O was spreading the news about R&B throughout New Orleans.

Early on, Winslow broadcast live shows directly from Matassa's studio, featuring Dave Bartholomew's band. Recordings, though, were his mainstay. " 'Good Rockin' Tonight' was our ace," Dr. Daddy-O recalled. "We would just play it loud and long." Since it got far more response than the smoother records of the national stars like Nat Cole, and since white stations ignored such records, listeners of both races tuned in to his show to hear "that racy black music." Under the sponsorship of Jax Beer, his "Jivin' with Jax" show soon captivated New Orleans' budding audience of R&B fans. By the early fifties, Dr. Daddy-O was such a fixture on WMRY, a station that could be heard throughout South Louisiana and East Texas, that Jax appointed additional Dr. Daddy-Os on stations in Houston, Baton Rouge, and elsewhere to pattern themselves after the original. Winslow also spawned imitators on other stations with names like Jack the Cat and Okey Dokey.

By now, word was spreading that New Orleans was a hotbed of R&B activity, with both talented performers as well as plenty of outlets for recording, broadcasting, and publicizing their work. Northern and West Coast labels began sending scouts to the city. Thus, paradoxically, at a time when segregation ruled the South, there existed the combination of adventurous white independent record company owners and black artists who would collaborate on a flowering of New Orleans music for the second time in the century.

However, honking saxes and blues shouters never drowned out the piano, the instrument that, along with the cornet, had underlaid New Orleans music from the turn of the century onward. Tuts Washington and other players, such as barrelhouse pianists Sullivan Rock and Archibald, kept the boogie-woogie flame alive. As the forties ended, two dynamic keyboard performers were creating tunes that hammered home the thumping foundation for the Crescent City's distinctive R&B style. One was to become a legend after his death, the other the biggest star the city had given music since Louis Armstrong. Their names were Professor Longhair and Fats Domino.

THE LEGEND—PROFESSOR LONGHAIR

Out of a background of dire poverty and almost no schooling came the artist Allen Toussaint dubbed "the Bach of rock 'n' roll," a pianist and singer who toiled in relative obscurity at a time when the New Orleans version of African American dance music was gaining its greatest recognition. The life of Henry Roeland "Roy" Byrd, known to everyone as Professor Longhair, or just plain Fess, was so full of contradictions perhaps only a novel or play could do it justice. His recordings are much more available today than they were during his lifetime. His likeness graces both the entrance to Tipitina's, New Orleans' foremost music club, and the banner atop one of the two main stages at the Jazz and Heritage Festival. His originality is attested to in scholarly books and critiques. Heard today, his music, more than that of any R&B performer of the fifties, echoes all the blues, jazz, and Latin elements that give the city such a cosmopolitan pedigree. Why then wasn't he more popular while he was in his prime? Could it have been at least partially his own fault?

Byrd was born in 1918 in Bogalusa, a small town fifty miles north of New Orleans. His parents split up while he was a baby and his mother moved with Henry, as she called him, and his older brother Robert into a New Orleans tenement house near Rampart Street. Little is known about his formal schooling. He was less than ten years old when he began to tap-dance with friends in the street, collecting loose change tossed by passersby. His dancing was highly regarded; friends nicknamed him "the Whirlwind." His mother apparently taught him to play several instruments, including a guitar she bought for him. But it made his fingers sore, and by the time he was a young teen, Roy was hanging out around "joints" in his neighborhood, where he learned piano techniques by watching some of the town's stride and boogie-woogie masters such as Kid Stormy Weather, Sullivan Rock, and Tuts Washington.

Washington, just ten years his senior, liked the boy and took him under his wing. What impressed him most, Byrd said, was how accurate Washington's fingering was. But Washington tried in vain to teach the youngster the stride left hand; Byrd's fingers were not long enough to reach the chords. "Fess had to roll his left hand to cover what I can," Tuts explained. "Fact is, that's how he came up with his style."

Not entirely. He was equally fascinated with Sullivan Rock's style; Rock showed him how to play "Pinetop's Boogie Woogie," a tune recorded in 1928 by Pinetop Smith, one of the most famous of the boogie-woogie pianists. Boogie woogie, with its powerful rolling bass lines, was a piano style that went back to the turn of the century. It was extremely popular as dance music both in the urban ghettos of Chicago and in industrial camps in the South, where barrelhouses (so called because they featured barrels of beer) were set up to entertain workers.

While working as a tap dancer and pianist in the joints and gin mills of the thirties, Byrd was also exposed to the blues, the favorite folk music of those recently arrived workers who grew up in rural areas. (Champion Jack Dupree, soon to become a well-known blues pianist, took lessons from Byrd in exchange for singing lessons.) Add to these blues influences the pervasive second-lining of New Orleans behind brass bands, and the antics of the black Mardi Gras Indian groups who danced through the streets at Carnival, and one can hear the layers of sound that the young man's ear collected and assimilated.

Perhaps the most important was the "Spanish tinge," the all-important Latin flavor that was crucial to early jazz. Byrd told one interviewer he took note of the Latin bands who played, as he did, in the recreation hall of the Civilian Conservation Corps, which he joined in 1937, doing construction work. He told another that he adored the records of Perez Prado, the Cuban-born band leader. In any event, as his playing evolved it incorporated a distinctive rhythm that crossed the blues with the Calypso and rumba beats.

Byrd was drafted in 1942, then spent eight months recuperating from a burst appendix before being discharged in 1944. During those months he played a lot of piano in the hospital recreation room. By the time he began finding odd piano gigs in postwar New Orleans, he had crafted a unique style from all these materials.

Byrd had to give up tap dancing before the war because of a bad knee. Like Jelly Roll Morton before him, he turned to gambling as a steady source of income. He was a card shark who made a living at the card tables from time to time, primarily playing "coon cat." Directly after the war, he was married briefly to a woman named Beulah Walker and worked for a short time as a cook.

But many of the wilder aspects of postwar New Orleans were more attractive to him than a quiet job and home life. The musical scene was bursting with activity and Byrd was part of it. Although by all accounts he never had a manager until near the end of his life and was ignorant about contracts, he would roam from club to club, play anywhere he could all night long, night after night, drinking up a storm. Like other musicians, he would mingle with the pimps, prostitutes, drug dealers, and night owls at the Dew Drop and the Tiajuana. R&B was hot, providing young ex-servicemen and their dates with supercharged dance music at these places and others, such as the Caldonia Inn. It was there that Byrd got what seemed like his first break, at the expense of an ambitious band leader named Dave Bartholomew.

According to Byrd, the year was 1948. Bartholomew was the headliner at the club, a joint favored by black transvestites in which fights often broke out. One night Byrd sat in at intermission for the regular pianist. He was such a hit that the owner, Mike Tessitore, fired Bartholomew and hired the new pianist along with three sidemen—Apeman Black on saxophone, Big Slick on drums, and Walter "Papoose" Nelson on guitar. Noting that Byrd had not been to a barber for what appeared to be some time, Tessitore anointed his new star with an inspired stage name—Professor Longhair. (Unlike the piano professors of earlier times, he was not a schooled musician.) Soon a local paper was referring to the group as the "Four Hair Combo, featuring Professors Longhair, Shorthair, Mohair and Needs

Some Hair." Byrd was very hair-conscious. He deliberately let his wavy, heavily processed hair grow down to his collar until he recorded a song about a bald-headed woman. At that point, he shaved the top of his head.

The newly nicknamed Professor Longhair was a huge hit both at the Caldonia and elsewhere. Not only was his keyboard work unusual, he had a habit of kicking the piano with his right foot to mark the beat. (At one party, Fess was forced to wear long-toed shoes so he wouldn't damage the upright.) The Star Talent label recorded him for the first time in 1949, using a saloon as a makeshift studio. One of the tunes released was "She Ain't Got No Hair," a Byrd novelty number, with credits going to Professor Longhair and his Shuffling Hungarians, so named because one band member apparently was of Hungarian descent.

The records did not get very far; the union forced the label to withdraw them because they had been non-union sessions. "They said I was ten years ahead of my time in 1949 because nobody wanted to give me credit for what I was doing," Longhair said later. "It was something new . . . all mixed in with Calypso . . . doubles and triples." But he was definitely attracting attention. Ahmet Ertegun and Herb Abramson, scouting for their fledgling Atlantic label, thought they had first dibs on an unknown when they came to New Orleans in 1949 to track him down. It took them a while; he was playing in an obscure club in a black section of Algiers, a town on the opposite side of the Mississippi River from the French Quarter. A white cabdriver refused to carry them the entire way, so they were forced to walk across an open field toward a joint seemingly in the middle of nowhere. Ertegun recalled Longhair playing an upright piano with a drumhead attached to it that he would kick. "It really was the most incredible-sounding thing," he said. "I thought, 'My God, we've really found an original. No white person has ever seen this man.' "

Imagine how stunned Ertegun was when Longhair informed him that he was already signed with another label. A scout for

Mercury had reached him first. In fact, his Mercury version of "Baldhead" (a remake of the earlier song) briefly climbed to Number 5 on the national R&B charts.

During the next several years, he recorded for a variety of labels, including Atlantic, sometimes as Roy Byrd, other times as Professor Longhair. At one Atlantic session, he did several sides at the J & M studio for the princely sum of one hundred dollars—"plenty money at that time," said Fess. Singles such as "Mardi Gras in New Orleans" got local airplay, but did not reach national audiences. Some music historians feel that Longhair's unwillingness to leave New Orleans to seek wider recognition on tour hurt him. Great musician though he was, he simply was not organized enough to join a tour. Besides, he felt card games were more lucrative to him than road gigs. However, in 1952 he did sign on as the opening act for Fats Domino on a brief tour. "Fess stole the show," declared Earl Palmer, Fats's drummer, "except in Kansas City, where the club owner wanted to hold back our pay because Fess had kicked a hole in his piano."

Fats Domino and others were making big waves at the time. His less subtle piano style and better singing voice captured the ear of listeners everywhere. With his more complex playing and marginal voice, Longhair never achieved that breakout hit he was seeking. As sax player Red Tyler told one interviewer, "To a trained musician what he was doing was so unorthodox that you had to listen, because it was something different." But "different," Tyler made clear, was not synonymous with chart-topping. Longhair, he continued, "never had enough money to buy a [new] Cadillac," the surest sign of a musician's success.

Nevertheless, he was composing and recording a body of songs that time would prove to be classics. Among them, "Tipitina"—which Tuts Washington claimed was a reworking of the one song he taught Fess, "Junker Blues"—was a regional hit in 1954. His versions of Hank Williams's "Jambalaya" and of Earl King's "Big Chief," with Fess doing the much-imitated whistling, were also definitive. His rendering of Huey Smith's hit "Rockin' Pneumonia and the Boogie Woogie Flu" was even more jaunty than the original. Many of these records made their way across the ocean to Europe, where Longhair became a cult figure. Unfortunately, he had to stop performing for a while in the mid-fifties because of a mild stroke.

After that, the jobs grew fewer and further between. The woman Byrd lived with (eventually his second wife), Alice Walton, took in laundry to support the two of them. On Mardi Gras Day, 1960, he was arrested on charges of marijuana possession while onstage at the San Jacinto Club. It was close to the last straw. Byrd, like Louis Armstrong, never hid his taste for weed; the bust, coming on a day when even white, racist police were busy protecting the city-wide party, smacked of unwarranted harassment. By the time English blues writer Mike Leadbitter sought out Fess in 1970, "he was down and out and very sad, as neglect, frustration and poor health had taken their toll."

What Leadbitter had no way of knowing was that a resurrection of sorts was just around the corner. Promoter George Wein heard a Longhair record on a jukebox that year and urged the two young jazz buffs scouting for him, Quint Davis and Allison Miner, to find him for the new Jazz and Heritage Festival he was staging. It took Davis a year. Hearing that Fess would come into Joe Assunto's One Stop on South Rampart Street each year around Carnival time to borrow money, Davis finally found his man in the record store. It was not unlike Ramsey and Russell finding Bunk Johnson in New Iberia years before—Fess was run down, broke, and toothless. Still, Davis set him up for a featured spot in the second annual Jazz Festival, arranging for guitar wizard Snooks Eaglin to accompany him. His performance turned out to be mesmerizing. "When Fess got up to play that upright piano" in Congo Square that day, Davis recalled, "everything literally stopped. All the musicians and all of the people came over to the stage."

Davis and Miner agreed to become Longhair's managers.

While they were seeking gigs for him they also got him medical attention and a pair of eyeglasses. Thanks to Jerry Wexler of Atlantic Records, Longhair appeared at the 1972 Montreux Festival in Switzerland with Allen Toussaint and the Meters. He also began recording again with such illustrious sidemen as Eaglin and another premier blues guitarist, Clarence "Gatemouth" Brown, although the circumstances were often bizarre. Two sessions cut in Baton Rouge and Memphis were not released until after his death. Another involved a trip to the frozen north during the winter; Bob Dylan's manager, Albert Grossman, brought Longhair and Eaglin to his compound near Woodstock, New York. The blind Eaglin was unnerved by the sounds of snow falling on the roof. Once again, the master tapes were packed away until years later, although the fees paid by Grossman enabled Fess to buy a piano. Happily, Atlantic reissued some of Longhair's fifties recordings and the French label Barclay gave him some money for the album with Brown, "Rock 'n' Roll Gumbo." More than twenty years after he became a force on the R&B scene, Professor Longhair was productive again.

Listeners became fans not only in the United States but abroad. In 1975, Paul McCartney hired Longhair to play for a party he threw aboard the former cruise ship, the Queen Mary, even though Fess had never heard of the Beatles. In fact, despite McCartney's appreciation of Byrd's artistry, Professor Longhair did not quite respond in kind. He kept referring to Liverpool's most famous left-handed bassist as "McCarthy."

To Allison Miner, who accompanied him on numerous trips, Byrd was a fun-loving, sweet man who adored children and animals. When they were abroad, he liked to go to museums and zoos. He was quite sociable with people he trusted, but he had an intuitive feel for those who did not have his interests at heart. For instance, according to Miner, a certain British record executive made a big fuss over Byrd in London in 1978. Yet when he invited the Professor and his party to dinner at his home, Byrd told Miner, "I don't like this guy," and refused to go. Later, it was discovered that the executive had secretly taped a Longhair London concert and issued a bootleg album of it.

In his final decade, Professor Longhair's life was full of achievements as well as setbacks. His performance became one of the most anticipated moments of each successive Jazz Festival. However, during the 1974 event, the house that Fess and his entire family were living in on South Rampart Street burned down, leaving him temporarily destitute again. A benefit concert featuring two acknowledged piano heirs, Toussaint and Dr. John, helped him get back on his feet. Then, in 1977, a group of his fans dedicated their new nightclub to him. Called Tipitina's, it gave him a permanent stage on which to perform. To hear Henry Roeland Byrd, closing in on sixty but looking older, yet as agile a pianist as ever, hammering away at the piano on the Monday night before Mardi Gras, while acolytes filled the huge floor in front of him, his strangely affecting voice yodeling about waiting for a glimpse of the Zulu King, must have been memorable indeed.

Professor Longhair unquestionably received his due in those last years. With Miner's careful management, he was able to save enough to buy a house and at least a used Cadillac. In 1979 he recorded his finest album at Toussaint's Sea Saint Studios with backing from the cream of younger New Orleans musicians who viewed him as their patron saint. These included Dr. John in the unusual position of playing his original instrument, guitar, John Vidacovich on drums, and Tony Dagradi on sax. The musicians got a kick out of his unconventional band leadership. Dagradi recalled that on one song, Fess declared, "I want the tempo somewhere between nine and fourteen." Nobody had a clue to what he meant until he showed them the old metronome he used, with its numbers missing. In their place, Byrd had scratched his own numbers, and sure enough, right between "9" and "14" was the tempo he sought. On another tune, "Fess and Mac were on either side of Vidacovich playing a rhythm on his chest, trying to show him what to play," Dagradi remembered, laughing. Indeed, those closest to him in his final years talked lovingly about Fess as if he were a genius, certainly, but an extraterrestrial one. He was in his own private universe when he was onstage, said Miner. "The piano was a physical experience for him, and he rode it like it was a spaceship."

Sadly, his return to the limelight turned out to be much too short. He was having a fine time starring with Allen Toussaint and Tuts Washington in a video documentary, "Piano Players Rarely Play Together." Then, on January 30, 1980, he died at home in his sleep. There followed an unruly jazz funeral, at which Aaron Neville, Allen Toussaint, Willie Tee and his brother Earl Turbinton, Ernie K-Doe, the Olympia and the Tuxedo Brass Bands performed. It was attended by more than three thousand people and filmed by the video documentary crew. "As jazz funerals go," Jason Berry and coauthors wrote in *Up From the Cradle of Jazz*, "it was one of the worst managed and most exciting ever, a fitting tribute to an artist whose idiosyncratic music almost defies description."

Actually, critics have done a pretty good job of describing the Professor Longhair sound. According to Robert Palmer, it was a mixture of "standard 8- and 12-bar blues" and "Afro-Caribbean polyrhythms" unique to New Orleans. Gary Giddins wrote that the "power and constancy with which he plays those left-hand patterns suggest pistons instead of fingers." Whatever musical planet Professor Longhair came from, he brought with him an inexhaustible variety of thumping riffs. He harnessed those riffs to the melodic, shuffling second-line struts of New Orleans parade music and the result was a galloping hybrid dance music that could turn any crowd of people, of any color or ethnic background, into a congregation of giddy marionettes.

Professor Longhair's legacy is many sided. His records are as original today as they were when they were made, imbued with a joy and a party spirit that is as intrinsically New Orleanian as the sight of Zulu revelers tossing coconuts from their parade floats on Mardi Gras morning. Elements from his work have been carried forward by the likes of Huey Smith, Toussaint, Dr. John, and James Booker in the late fifties, sixties, seventies, and eighties, and on into the nineties in the rollicking piano and stomping feet of Jon Cleary, an Englishman living in New Orleans. His records may not have been mainstream enough to soar on commercial radio or *Billboard* charts, but since his death, Professor Longhair has ascended to a far loftier position: alongside Tony Jackson and Jelly Roll Morton in the pantheon of New Orleans piano Ph.D.s.

THE STAR—FATS DOMINO

Around the same time that Professor Longhair recorded "Bald Head" in a saloon, twenty-one-year-old Fats Domino made his first recording, backed by Dave Bartholomew's tight band, at J & M. "The Fat Man" began with a boogie-woogie piano introduction, followed by a higher-pitched version of a voice that was to become familiar to millions of American teenagers. "They call, they call me the fat man / 'cause I weigh two hundred pounds," he sang. The piano beat was fresh, urgent, toe-tapping; it almost sounded as if Tuts Washington had latched onto the harder sounds of jump blues. The Creole-accented vocals were unusual yet assured and inviting. "The Fat Man" had hooks that grabbed hold of listeners in an instant and wouldn't let them sit still. It was a sound that with a little modification would soon sweep the nation, whites as well as blacks, under the banner of rock 'n' roll, laid down by an artist who ultimately would outsell every founding father except Elvis Presley.

If ever there was an unlikely candidate for such lasting fame, it was Domino. Neither dynamic nor demented nor dangerous onstage (think of Elvis, or Little Richard, or Chuck Berry), he was instead a pudgy little guy with a great smile beaming out beyond the keyboard who won his audience over with a catchy rolling bass line, not swiveling hips. Aided by a terrific arranger and sharp sidemen, he became, over the next decade, one of the first and finest masters of the two-and-a-half minute hit. Before his reign at the top of the charts was over, he had ushered in the golden age of New Orleans R&B.

Born in 1928 in the ninth ward, Antoine "Fats" Domino was the youngest of nine children. His was not one of the prominent New Orleans musical families, but his uncle, Harrison Verret, a guitar player, played with Kid Ory and Papa Celestin. "He just about raised me," Fats said of his uncle. "He showed me the first note I played on the piano." At an early age he quit school to help earn money for his family. By his teens he was playing literally for pennies in local joints while holding down a factory job during the day.

Tuts Washington told an interviewer that when Domino was still "just a li'l ole fat boy" he would hang around the Club Desire and beg Tuts to play "The Honeydripper." Other major influences on Fats were the classic boogie-woogie pianists Amos Milburn, Pete Johnson, Meade Lux Lewis, and Albert Ammons. Directly after World War II, the teenager started making a name for himself as a member of Billy Diamond's band, a popular local group whose home base was the Hideaway Club in the ninth ward. Patrons liked Domino's rousing version of Ammon's "Swanee River Boogie." He kept his day job at a bedspring factory until a pile of springs fell on him and accidentally cut his hand, temporarily threatening to nip a promising career in the bud. Then one night he went to hear the hottest band in town, under the leadership of Dave Bartholomew. The stage was set for one of the most fruitful musical partnerships of the R&B and rock 'n' roll eras.

Bartholomew, the son of a tuba player well known in local music circles, was born in Edgard, Louisiana, in 1920. As a youngster interested in the trumpet, he took lessons from Peter Davis, the same man who had taught Louis Armstrong when he was in the waifs' home. Before he was out of his teens, Dave was playing with a "reading" band at night while cutting sugarcane by day. He also put in a four-year apprenticeship with Fats Pichon's band playing on the riverboats that plied the Mississippi much as they had done since Armstrong's day. It was an important experience, he explained later, because they "played all types of music . . . jazz, swing, waltzes, you name it. We had rehearsal every morning and if you couldn't read, you'd be in bad shape." Bartholomew's early years also included a stint with Duke Ellington's band.

Discharged from military service after World War II, Bartholomew returned to New Orleans and formed a band that could play jazz, standards, and the new R&B. By 1947, the group—anchored by Herbert Hardesty, Red Tyler, and Clarence Hall on tenor sax, Salvador Doucette on piano, Frank Fields on bass, and Earl Palmer on drums—had jobs all over the city, in clubs such as the Dew Drop and the Robin Hood and numerous Catholic church halls. The band even cut some records for Jules Braun's Deluxe label (Braun was the New Jerseyan who first recorded Roy Brown) and had a local hit with "Country Boy."

Fats Domino's introduction to the band was not auspicious. It was engineered by Earl Palmer. The drummer, who had tap-danced with his mother's vaudeville troupe as a boy, became a sort of deputy band leader for Bartholomew. On breaks during a club date, Dave "would go socialize and solicit more gigs," Palmer recalled, leaving the band in Palmer's hands onstage to play a bit of bebop. It was during one such break at Al's Starlight Inn that Earl invited Fats to sit in. At the time, according to Palmer, the only thing Fats could play was boogie woogie. He was considered talented but crude. After his short appearance, Bartholomew was cross. "I thought I told you not to let that fat dude up there," he said to Palmer.

Nevertheless, the seed was planted. Dave had previously met Lew Chudd, owner of the Los Angeles–based Imperial record label, who wanted to expand from his Mexican music base into R&B. He came to New Orleans in search of talent and hired Bartholomew as a scout. One evening in 1949, Chudd and Bartholomew went to hear the young piano player appearing at the Hideaway. As Dave recalled, Fats "was killing them" that night. Chudd immediately signed Domino and arranged for Bartholomew's band to back him at a recording session at Matassa's studio. The first side was "The Fat Man," yet another reworking of "Junker Blues," the same tune that was the basis for Professor Longhair's "Tipitina."

"The Fat Man," with Domino and Bartholomew sharing writing credits, soared to Number 6 on the national R&B charts in 1950. During the next two years, the band backed Fats on several more sides that did well. The early tunes were recorded at J & M with just a small combo—bass, drums, guitar, a couple of saxes (either Herbert Hardesty or Lee Allen contributed the honking tenor solos), and Fats on the piano. As Palmer explained, the recording sessions meant extra money (they were done during the day while the musicians continued to play clubs at night) and the band strove to capture the same "infectious excitement" that punctuated their live appearances. What Fats had that most of his contemporaries did not, however, was a good contract. His brother-in-law convinced him to get a clause paying him royalties based on sales of records, rather than a single flat payment for the right to the song. A common practice today, it was anything but common in those R&B days. The absence of such a clause left numerous artists destitute after their moment in the limelight passed; its inclusion made Fats Domino a millionaire.

Domino was gaining confidence both as a featured performer and as a singer. Finally, in 1952, he reached the Number 1 R&B slot with the tune "Goin' Home." Fats and the band began to go out on tour, promoting their records with successful live shows. Meanwhile, each time they went into the studio, Bartholomew sought to achieve new effects, despite the primitive conditions. Matassa at first recorded directly on vinyl, not tape, with only one microphone. To change the balance on the lone microphone they would turn a drum over or move musicians to the far side of the room. Songs had to be less than three minutes long; sometimes Cosimo would yell, "I'm running out of vinyl!"

As an arranger, Bartholomew was searching for a sound that was new yet uncomplicated. "It had to be simple so people could understand it right away. It had to be the kind of thing that a seven-year-old kid could start whistling." And it had to have the big beat—a beat Palmer perfected to such an extent his band mates thought the Palmer-brand metronome had been named for him.

By the time Fats and Bartholomew wrote a mid-tempo ditty called "Ain't It a Shame," they had the formula down cold. The record had an irresistible beat, a memorable rolling left-hand riff, and a sing-along chorus. It was hardly surprising that white audiences began dancing to it. For the first time, a New Orleans R&B hit crossed over to the *Billboard* pop charts, where it reached Number 10 in July 1955. Before Pat Boone had time to surpass its success with his lumbering cover, "Ain't It a Shame" had made Fats Domino a rock 'n' roll star.

Domino was hurt by Boone's version. "It took me two months to write 'Ain't It a Shame' and his record comes out around the same time mine did," he commented years later. On the other hand, Pat Boone collected no royalties on it. Nor did Boone have Domino's B-side, "La La." The tune was so catchy, according to Bartholomew, that the Stanford University football team did their warm-up drills to it.

Within a few months, another Domino record, "I'm in Love Again," started to climb the charts. It was followed by "My Blue Heaven," "Blueberry Hill," "I'm Walkin'," "Blue Monday," "Walkin' to New Orleans," and others. The Fats Domino hit parade, depending on which music history you accept, totaled some 43 chart records, at least 18 gold records, and between 30 million and 65 million discs sold over a twenty-year period. Beginning in 1955, Domino shared the glory days of rock 'n' roll with the likes of Elvis, Little Richard, Jerry Lee Lewis, the Drifters, Chuck Berry, Bill Haley, and Buddy Holly.

Those days have been sanitized and romanticized; they were rough on performers' stamina and their personal relationships because touring was the one constant in a frenetic existence. A member of Allen Freed's revolutionary package shows, Fats played all over the United States and Canada. Herbert Hardesty, his tenor-sax companion for thirty-five years, noted that even at such legendary halls as the Apollo Theater in Harlem, conditions were far from perfect. The dressing rooms in the Apollo were eight floors above the stage level, so that after each of the five or more shows a day, everyone would have to hike up flight after flight. In addition, the crowds were so critical you could be stoned off the stage. "If you could make it at the Apollo, you could make it anywhere," said Hardesty. "Pleasing that audience made your career."

Domino was a headliner, but that simply meant he and his band took the stage later than other acts. He was just one of the guys, according to Hardesty. Everyone, stars and sidemen alike, traveled together week after week in buses, with the single exception of Chuck Berry, who preferred to drive his own car. Fats did become the first black star on national television, performing on the Steve Allen Show. That led to dates with Perry Como and Dick Clark's "American Bandstand," two of the mainstays of early television. It was a period in which black artists as well as white could be heard on the biggest radio stations, seen live at the biggest downtown theaters, and even appeared on screen in movies like *The Girl Can't Help It.*

White audiences got to hear Fats's lilting vocals all over the country, from New York's Paramount to casinos in Las Vegas. Fats himself was hardly an incendiary performer compared to fellow pianists Jerry Lee Lewis or Little Richard; he was cuddly, warm, safe. Still, he had his fill of exciting moments. In San Jose, California, Domino was on stage when toughs in the audience at Palomar Gardens threw beer bottles and started a riot. The singer and the band "grabbed their instruments and ran for their lives," according to one account. "The police panicked and lobbed tear gas," Hardesty recalled. Otherwise, the most exciting moments for Domino on the road were those spent gambling. He enjoyed betting on anything; one day he lost all the money in his pockets shooting pool. In Las Vegas, his major activity was craps. The problem was, his luck was bad and he did not know when to quit. "Nobody could tell him that, though," Hardesty noted. Even pit bosses would warn band members: "Get him away from the tables; he's losing too much money."

Fats kept a down-home flavor on tour by packing big pots in which he would cook his own gumbo. "Actually, we all cooked in our rooms. The pay wasn't great, so that was how we survived," said Hardesty. When the band spent one Thanksgiving on the road, Fats and Dave Bartholomew traveled with a huge turkey in their car that Fats roasted following their performance.

In the studio, at first in New Orleans, later in Los Angeles, Domino and Bartholomew strove for new twists to keep their big-beat formula from getting stale. The singer caused Cosimo Matassa grief more than once. "He'd stop right in the middle of the only good tape we had going and say 'how do I sound?' " Matassa said. "It drove you crazy." It did not upset the band members, who lent what one historian called an "off-the-cuff, house-party atmosphere" to the Domino hits. On occasion, Bartholomew would tell Palmer, "Look, just try a different beat." What do you want? Palmer would ask. "I don't know what I want. I want to hear something different," Bartholomew would reply. One result of such improvising was the zippy shuffle of "I'm Walkin'."

In the sixties, with his sound not quite the stuff of surefire Top 40 that it once was, Fats branched out. He was a regular at the biggest Las Vegas rooms, even though he later admitted that his gambling losses totaled over two million dollars. "I was a country boy who didn't know no better," he shrugged. At least he was in good company. During his many Vegas dates, he became friendly with Elvis Presley. Just before Presley's second appearance at a major Vegas hotel, he confessed to Domino that he was nervous because his first date there had not gone over well. "Man, that night he went out and tore the place down," laughed Fats.

He made his first overseas appearance at a jazz festival in France in 1962, but French critics were appalled because he didn't know who Thelonious Monk was. For all his fame, Domino was never a venturesome listener or performer. Rather, he was an uncomplicated, even complacent man who replicated his hits onstage, collected his pay, and went home to Rose Mary and their eight children, all of whose names began with A, including Antoine, Jr., Anatole. . . . In the early days, he was lucky enough to have Bartholomew at his side, handling musical and sometimes financial arrangements. Later, relatives handled those chores. He was shrewd enough to know what music fit his band and his fans. Thus, he made more forays into country music, doing well with "Your Cheatin' Heart" and Hank Williams's "Jambalaya" and "You Win Again."

He finally deserted Imperial for ABC records in 1963, then moved on to other labels, but he was never able to duplicate his huge hits of the fifties. In the midst of the psychedelic era, however, he made a comeback with his 1968 album, *Fats Is Back*. An all-star combo played behind him—King Curtis on tenor sax, James Booker on piano, Chuck Rainey on bass, Earl Palmer on drums. One cut in particular—the Beatles' "Lady Madonna"—was a modest hit. It was noblesse oblige; the Beatles loved his music and acknowledged that songs such as "Birthday" on *The White Album* were based on assorted riffs from Fats's records.

An auto accident in Natchitoches in 1970 was the event that really curbed Domino's output. One band member was killed and two were injured; friends said the band was never the same again. Herb Hardesty and Dave Bartholomew continued to work with Fats but his schedule grew quite leisurely. His last big hit was "Whiskey Heaven" in 1980, heard in the movie *Any Which Way You Can*. (He also was among the multitudes who put out a version of the zydeco novelty song "My Toot Toot" in 1985.)

Millions of radio listeners in New Orleans did get a taste of the old sound, however, when he did a widely aired jingle for Popeye's Fried Chicken.

During the late eighties and early nineties, he appeared in concert, at private parties, and at festivals less frequently. He always put on a solid show (he would fly in Herbert Hardesty, his trusty tenor alter ego, for every important date), reprising his hits in a voice that had hardly lost any of its resonance. He remained a low-key celebrity who made few waves in New Orleans. Friends described him as contented. (There were, however, whispers about his drinking.) He did his only interview in thirty years in connection with a boxed CD set of his Imperial records. For years Domino has lived in a palatial white brick house on Marais Street in his old neighborhood with his wife, their children, and a collection of luxury cars. Some time ago, he apparently decided on the spot to pick up two new Cadillacs and a Rolls-Royce at a local dealership. The salesman suggested calling his bank. "I am the bank," replied Fats, who paid cash.

New Orleans musicians knew how much they owed the fat man. Allen Toussaint helped present a big cake to Fats at a show on the occasion of his sixtieth birthday, and the ReBirth Brass Band, most of whose members were not yet born when Domino was at his zenith, released a wonderfully rowdy cover of "I'm Walkin'." Asked how Domino spent his days, Jazz Festival promoter Quint Davis said, "He's probably at home baking cakes."

What accounted for his enormous popularity? One theory is that in an era of sexually threatening rebels—James Dean and Marlon Brando, as well as Elvis and other rockers—Fats was reassuring and non-threatening. Perhaps, although one could make the same claim for groups like the Platters, who never equaled his popularity. Another theory is that his unusual accent made him sound exotic. That might account for one or two hits, but not for a dozen. As a black performer, he certainly had a manner that whites found comfortable, which helped his crossover appeal. But above all, Fats was a consistently excellent singer who made great Top 40 records. His singles featured tunes from a great variety of sources—standards like "My Blue Heaven," country and western, blues—yet they always sounded like no one else. As Cosimo Matassa told one writer, "He could be singing the national anthem, you'd still know by the time he said two words it was him, obviously, unmistakably and pleasurably him."

In producing Fats Domino's hits, Dave Bartholomew tapped into a rich vein of New Orleans–based R&B that made him a sought-after arranger. (Allen Toussaint, who came into Bartholomew's orbit as a teenager around 1957, was terribly impressed by the fact that the producer operated out of an actual office.) After "Blueberry Hill" had been cut, Lew Chudd informed him that Imperial had shipped an unheard-of three million copies. He instructed Dave to go to an auto dealer and pick out a car as his bonus. "I went out and got the biggest Eldorado Cadillac I could find," Bartholomew said later. Meanwhile, other independent label owners were eager to have Bartholomew repeat his success with other local artists.

They didn't have to wait long. Art Rupe, another Los Angeles independent who ran Specialty Records, was so impressed with Domino's success that he followed Lew Chudd to New Orleans in 1952. He auditioned one performer after another. The last one, Lloyd Price, was just seventeen years old and very nervous. Finally, Rupe told him, "Look, kid, if you don't get yourself together, I'm splitting." Price, Rupe continued, began crying . . . and singing "Lawdy Miss Clawdy" at the same time. Rupe, knowing he had found a winner, canceled his plane back to Los Angeles, hired Dave Bartholomew to get his band together plus Fats Domino to provide piano accompaniment, and escorted Price into the J & M Studio to record the tune. With its strong vocal by Price and Domino's unmistakable piano rolling behind him, "Lawdy Miss Clawdy" rocketed to Number 1 on the R&B charts. Price was voted the best new R&B singer that year by *Cash Box*. He eventually moved to Washington, D.C., and enjoyed a long career, although his later successes, such as "Personality," owed little to New Orleans.

Another Domino disciple, with a delivery that was less warm but more raspy than the master's, was Smiley Lewis, whose biggest hit was "I Hear You Knockin' " (co-written by Dave Bartholomew), released in 1955. Born Overton Lemons in DeQuincy, Louisiana, in 1920, he was part of a group that included Tuts Washington and was a regular at the Dew Drop and the Hideaway. The nickname was ironic; when he first came on the scene he was missing his front teeth. (He soon got a bridge.) He died in 1966 of stomach cancer.

Even though Lloyd Price and Smiley Lewis could not match the Domino effect, Fats's remarkable sojourn on the charts convinced independent labels from coast to coast that New Orleans was the place to find and record hot young talent. Not only did the city have a studio with a track record, but it had an arranger (Bartholomew) and a terrific house band that could play behind anyone. As more and more aspiring R&B musicians and producers made their way to Cosimo's little studio from such places as California, Florida, Mississippi, and Georgia, New Orleans began turning out some of the most widely played—and covered—singles ever to hit the airwaves. An extraordinary number of these artists would make the charts; a handful would make rock 'n' roll history.

THE FIFTIES CHART-TOPPERS
••

Much has been written about the transition of rhythm and blues into rock 'n' roll, the term coined by disc jockey Allen Freed to describe the irrepressible music that caught the fancy of white teenagers in the middle fifties. But the transition was summed up best during a session at the J & M studio, when a flamboyant gay black pianist from Georgia sang ten syllables that shook the world: "A WOP BOP ALOOBOP A WOP BAM BOOM."

Little Richard recorded "Tutti Frutti" with the J & M house band in September 1955, and in the process altered the course of popular music. But even before "Tutti Frutti" hit jukeboxes and radio stations in January of 1956, J & M was becoming a rollicking incubator for the big beat.

First, of course, there had been Fats, then Lloyd Price and Smiley Lewis. Next came another product of the Dew Drop Inn named Eddie Jones, whose cool good looks and sizzling chords had earned him the stage name Guitar Slim.

Slim was born in 1926 in Greenwood, Mississippi. Not much is known about his early years. He grew up in the Delta blues environment, although his playing owed more to the Texas electrified style of Clarence "Gatemouth" Brown. In 1949, he formed a trio with teenager Huey Smith on piano and Willie Nettles on drums. Slim quickly gained notoriety for his no-holds-barred live shows. Dressed in brightly colored suits— red, green, blue—sometimes with hair dyed to match, he commanded the stage like a past-life Jimi Hendrix.

"He flailed a low-slung guitar, sounding for all the world as though it were being played through a broken car radio speaker [and sang in a] semi-shout delivery," wrote one historian. "He strutted, pranced, and danced. He did wild splits and deep knee bends. . . . He attacked his guitar as though it were a mistreatin' woman." What's more, Slim liked to turn the treble volume control on his amp as high as it would go, creating a distorted fuzz tone that was years ahead of its time. As a finale, Slim would leave the stage while still playing and singing, using hundreds of feet of microphone wire to wind up his act in the street, while listeners, still hearing his guitar inside a club, screamed and hollered for more.

By 1953 Slim was a headliner throughout the chitlin' circuit, with a lifestyle as flashy as his act. He had a bevy of girlfriends, his own valet, and a thirst so big that his booking agent had the valet ration his alcohol. In October of that year, Art Rupe of Specialty Records brought him to J & M to record under the direction of a young pianist from Florida who was spending a lot of time in New Orleans clubs. The most important single they recorded was a blues tune, "The Things I Used to Do," with the Floridian playing a boogie line that helped make the tune the R&B sensation of 1954. The piano player's career soon outstripped that of Guitar Slim and just about every other singer and keyboardist of his day. His name was Ray Charles.

Today, the record is less interesting for its own sake than it is as a stepping-stone from R&B to rock 'n' roll. The sound of "Things" owed more to that of electric bluesmen like Brown and T-Bone Walker than to New Orleans, and Ray Charles was hardly recognizable in the background. Though Charles himself denied that Slim influenced him much, critics think that Charles incorporated the sounds of Slim and other Crescent City vocalists into what became his gospel style of singing. It's a reasonable interpretation; Charles spent the better part of two years in New Orleans clubs like the Dew Drop.

Building on the success of his one hit, Slim toured—and drank—incessantly. He was so popular that when an auto accident temporarily grounded him, singer/songwriter Earl King, who hardly resembled Slim, was nevertheless enlisted to impersonate him on the road. Slim played the biggest venues open to an African American artist, such as the Apollo, but his follow-up single, "The Story of My Life," was a failure. Those who saw him felt Slim had the talent to be a superstar on a par with James Brown or B. B. King, but he didn't get the chance. He collapsed after a show in Newark in 1959 and died at the age of thirty-two.

"The Things I Used to Do" was another example of the magic act performed by musicians at J & M. As the record climbed to the top of *Billboard's* R&B Top 10 in February 1954, it was accompanied by no fewer than three additional tracks recorded in the same place—a Joe Turner number on Atlantic, "Something's Wrong" by Fats Domino, and "I Didn't Want to Do It" by the Spiders, a popular local group. Nevertheless, even then, when the R&B world was flooded with New Orleans sounds, the much larger white audience in New Orleans as elsewhere was listening to Hit Paraders like Eddie Fisher and Rosemary Clooney, or, a bit later, Bill Haley and the Comets. The year 1955 was a crucial turning point, as R&B hits like the Penguins' "Earth Angel," Chuck Berry's "Maybelline," and Fats's "Ain't It a Shame" made the leap to the pop charts. Still, with Elvis Presley just beginning to make platters for Sun, and Jerry Lee Lewis only a figment of his own imagination, no performer as explosive as Guitar Slim had yet detonated on the mainstream pop scene.

In New Orleans, Little Richard was about to change all that.

He was born Richard Penniman in Macon, Georgia, in the early 1930s, one of twelve children. Although his father sold bootleg whiskey, two of his uncles were preachers, and he grew up singing gospel in a devout Seventh Day Adventist atmosphere.

Richard's parents kicked him out of their house at thirteen, either because of his boisterous music, his homosexual inclinations, or both. He moved in with a white couple who ran a local nightclub, where he first began performing. Soon he graduated to black clubs throughout the South. He was appearing in New Orleans with a group called the Tempo Toppers when Art Rupe of Specialty heard a demo tape Richard had sent him in Los Angeles. Richard had already cut sides for other labels, but they went nowhere. Undoubtedly, that was because Richard had not found his own style yet; he was still a blues shouter who also did ballads in the manner of Dinah Washington.

However, Robert "Bumps" Blackwell, a young, hip gospel producer for Rupe, saw the glimmer of a star in the reel of tape that, as he recalled years afterward, came "wrapped in a piece of paper looking as though someone had eaten off it." Despite misgivings, Rupe let Blackwell send Richard money to extricate himself from a contract with Don Robey, the owner of Houston's Peacock label. Blackwell then went to New Orleans to oversee sessions at the J & M studio with Little Richard in September 1955.

It was almost a disaster. The first day and most of the second went by with Richard laying down several very tame R&B tunes, backed by the studio mainstays, including Allen and Tyler on sax, Earl Palmer on drums, and Huey Smith on piano. The musicians didn't know what to make of Richard. They certainly had seen flaming queens before, but this singer, with his mascara and a pomaded-process 'do that defied gravity, was something else. They didn't know whether to call the performer "he" or "she."

As Blackwell remembered the scene, Richard was inordinately more inhibited in the studio than he was onstage. "There's this cat in this loud shirt, talking wild," Blackwell said, yet Richard could not project that persona in the studio. In Blackwell's phrases, it was a case of a guy who looked like Tarzan but sounded like Mickey Mouse. In order to loosen him up, Blackwell suspended the session and brought Richard over to the Dew Drop. Play that risqué number you have in your act, he commanded. Feeling at home on the club's stage, with an audience, the real, crazed Little Richard complied. Pounding on the piano, he shrieked, "A wop bop aloobop / a good god damn! / Tutti Frutti / good booty . . ." A group of aspiring teenaged musicians who were hanging around outside the studio, including Mac Rebennack, recognized the rhymes immediately. "It was flat out the 'dozens,' real street stuff. "Yo mama turn tricks and yo' daddy sucks dicks'. . . . Kids used to tease each other with that stuff," said Rebennack.

Blackwell had to think fast; he was running out of money and time, but he could not use Richard's words. A local lyricist, Dorothy La Bostrie, had come over to see about selling some of her own songs. Could she clean up the lyrics, Blackwell asked, so Richard could wind up the recording session with the tune? Richard himself was embarrassed to recite the original ones until he turned and faced the wall. La Bostrie listened and left.

Fifteen minutes before the session was to end, La Bostrie walked into the studio with a set of silly, inoffensive new lyrics. [La Bostrie claimed the entire concept of the song was hers alone.] By this time, Richard was afraid he had no voice left, and there was no time for Huey Smith to learn the song, so Richard took over the piano, too. In three takes, they had "Tutti Frutti" down.

But what in the world did "A wop bop aloobop a wop bam boom / Tutti Frutti / aw rooty" mean? Palmer recalled that after the first take, he turned and asked Tyler, "What's he saying?" Tyler shrugged. "What does it matter? He won't be able to explain it anyway." To many, the dirty street-talk origin of the lyrics was obvious, beginning with the title. Rebennack and his friends realized, as he commented later, "This is not about ice cream."

Today, there still isn't much to explain. "Tutti Frutti" was a cannon shot among the first volleys that heralded a new age, a 150-proof nonsense song that distilled the essence of rock 'n' roll. Writers have tried to describe its impact in various ways: as "a kind of comic madness . . . a gleeful, bombastic voice, chaotic piano playing and hard charging drums, guitars and saxophones," as "an eruption of gleeful manic intensity [that captured the song's] sensual dementia," as the Big Bang from which everything since has emanated. Whatever it was, "Tutti Frutti" hit ground zero with a bang, selling 500,000 copies and scaling *Billboard's* R&B ladder to the Number 2 slot.

Richard's follow-ups were recorded with many of the same musicians; indeed, he called Palmer "probably the greatest session drummer of all time" and Lee Allen the greatest tenor sax. "Long Tall Sally" and "Slippin' and Slidin'," "Rip It Up" and "Ready Teddy," "The Girl Can't Help It," "Miss Ann," "Keep A-knockin'," and "Good Golly Miss Molly," all charged toward the top of the charts. "He was playing a Gert Town ratty boogie," said Rebennack, referring to a black New Orleans neighborhood, "and there wasn't no band nowhere that could touch that groove."

The records were promoted immeasurably by Richard's riotous stage and movie appearances. Richard preferred his own band, the Upsetters, on tour, because he and the instrumentalists presented themselves as a complete act, with everyone in makeup. "Richard and them used to work real hard, man, I mean, *real* hard," said Earl King. "He used to dance with the group and Richard was a *wild man*." As he batted his eyelashes, leaped on the piano, and segued from primal scream to falsetto, he confirmed the worst nightmares of parents across the country.

In the years that followed, Little Richard's life gyrated as wildly as his tunes. First, he quit at the height of success, renouncing rock for the ministry. He emerged again in the sixties, attempted a comeback in the seventies, made a spectacle of himself running through the aisles of television talk shows (high on cocaine, he later acknowledged), vamping about how he was "the most beautiful thing in show business," and became a movie star of sorts in such pictures as *Down and Out in Beverly Hills* in the eighties. But none of this activity matters nearly as much as the fact that along with a few contemporaries, Little Richard Penniman put the rock in rock 'n' roll.

Specialty Records was eager to clone Little Richard. To that end, they signed Larry Williams, another New Orleans singer and pianist, who came through with "Short Fat Fanny," "Bony Moronie," and "Dizzy Miss Lizzy." All were hits, and "Fanny" itself paid tribute to Richard's hits and others, mentioning "Tutti Frutti," "Slippin' and Slidin'," "Heartbreak Hotel," and other tunes in its lyrics. But Williams' records, all done on the West Coast, had no special New Orleans feel to them. (Williams ran afoul of the law some time later, served time, and committed suicide in 1980.) More important in the city's musical growth were chart-toppers like Shirley and Lee, Huey Smith and the Clowns, and Frankie Ford.

Shirley and Lee were local kids who actually had their first hit in 1950—before they were out of high school. Cosimo Matassa, in that innocent era, allowed anyone to make a record at his studio for two dollars. Shirley Goodman, Leonard Lee, and some high school friends collected spare change in order to cut their own demo. The song was "I'm Gone." Some months later, Eddie Mesner, the owner of Aladdin Records, yet another Los Angeles label, heard it while visiting Cosimo and insisted that Matassa find Shirley. At first, Shirley's grandmother did not want the underaged girl to have anything to do with Aladdin. Mesner finally pressed a thousand-dollar bribe into the grandmother's hand. Like many older, churchgoing folks, she believed R&B and the blues were "the devil's music," but only a saint would have resisted such a huge sum. Mesner had the two youngsters re-cut the song, and put it on the market in 1952. "I'm Gone" was a surprise hit.

Just fifteen and sixteen years old, Shirley and Lee were billed as "The Sweethearts of the Blues." They were never an actual romantic couple, however, and they never even sang together in harmony because their keys were too far apart. But they were interesting enough for a booking agent to put them onstage as the opening act for Big Mama Thornton. Once again, at the mention of a road tour, the grandmother was appalled. Shrewd by now, and understanding the ways of show-biz sharpies, the grandmother demanded and got both an additional thousand-dollar payment and a salary as the girl's chaperon. The duo continued to make sweet records and appear in shows, with one voice answering the other. They were so young that clubs had to stop serving drinks when they performed. It was a testament to their popularity that counterfeit "Shirley and Lee" pairs cropped up in various stage shows.

In 1955 and 1956, the two hit their stride with two huge singles, "Feel So Good" and "Let the Good Times Roll." Both were done with the J & M house band and both had the exact same introduction as a hook: a two-note downbeat—wom BOM—followed by a piano triplet. "Let the Good Times Roll" was actually a fortuitous afterthought; they needed a B-side for a record, so they fooled around with the title of an old Louis Jordan song. The infectious, rolling beat (very much in the Fats Domino mold), combined with Shirley's strangely compelling, high, little-girl voice, made the tunes perfect crossovers from R&B to pop. The duo left high school to join big rock 'n' roll shows from New York to Los Angeles. Their road shows gave New Orleans musicians plenty of employment; among them were two fantastic keyboard players, both protégés of Professor Longhair, Huey "Piano" Smith and Allen Toussaint. It was not exactly a luxury gig: the band traveled in a station wagon, while Shirley and Lee rode in a Cadillac. Toussaint had vivid memories of the finances of those 1957 and 1958 tours. Each band member was paid $22.50 a night, in dollar bills, out of which they had to pay for their own food and lodging.

Shirley and Lee broke up in 1962, with Shirley settling in Los Angeles and doing occasional session work while Lee went to college and became a social worker. They were reunited briefly, in 1972, for a rock 'n' roll revival show, but felt awkward. Lee died unexpectedly in 1976, but Shirley resurfaced once in an amazingly big way on the 1974 disco hit "Shame Shame Shame." She eventually moved back to New Orleans. Meanwhile, Toussaint, as we shall see, developed into a legendary Crescent City hit-maker. Huey Smith, on the other hand, was a premier session man whose career was a series of near-misses.

A native New Orleanian, Smith was born in 1934 and raised in the Garden District. Even though his instrument was the piano, his early inspiration came from Louis Jordan. Huey was only fifteen when he joined a trio featuring Guitar Slim. In the next few years, he became known at local musicians' hangouts and began playing with an aspiring singer/songwriter, Earl King. By 1955, the Specialty label's man in New Orleans, Johnny Vincent, had started his own label, Ace. Together, Smith and King made Ace's first recording, "Those Lonely Lonely Nights." It was a modest hit, but Huey got no credit for it; to cash in on Fats Domino's fame, Vincent had "piano by Fats" stenciled on the label, even though Fats had nothing to do with the record.

Happily, Smith got to make a modest hit that did carry his name, the classic "Rockin' Pneumonia and the Boogie Woogie Flu." With its rave-up piano derived directly from Fess, it brought to the fore a syncopated keyboard style quite different from that of Domino, and made the charts in 1957. By then, Huey had formed a group, the Clowns, who shared vocal duties (Smith realized his own singing limitations) and fooled around onstage. His lead singer was Bobby Marchan, a female impersonator. Among the Clowns at one time or another were Gerri Hall, Willie Nettles, James Rivers, Robert Parker, and Jessie Hill, all of them well known on the local R&B scene. Huey "Piano" Smith and the Clowns soon had a national hit with a song whose title was taken from a phrase the band's driver used all the time: "Don't You Just Know It." When Smith grew tired of touring, Marchan became, in effect, the group's leader, and James Booker, another piano wizard-in-training, took Smith's place at the keyboard.

Smith's biggest song was "Sea Cruise," recorded by the Clowns with a background of foghorns and catchy effects. An enormous hit in 1959 for Frankie Ford, one of the very few local white singers who made R&B records, it was originally sung by Smith, but Ford's voice was later dubbed over his. Smith claimed that Johnny Vincent stole the tune, turning it over to Ford behind his back. (Vincent had already tried to capture the white teen market with a youngster named Jimmy Clanton.) In Ford, he felt he had at last discovered Ace's own "teen idol," in the Frankie Avalon mold. He wasn't, although "Sea Cruise" reached Number 14 on the pop charts.

Frankie Ford subsequently toured in rock 'n' roll shows with the likes of Avalon, Paul Anka, and Chuck Berry. (In the nineties, he was still making appearances in the New Orleans area.) Meanwhile, a disillusioned Huey Smith drifted. He recorded for several other labels without much success, fought Johnny Vincent for royalties, and finally gave up show business entirely to devote more time to Bible studies. Huey "Piano" Smith served his instrument faithfully and deserved more recognition than he got.

The fifties were such fertile years for R&B in New Orleans that the J & M house band was kept totally booked by hungry producers eager to have that special sound inspire their own stars. According to Rebennack, there were so many round-the-clock sessions that even kids like himself "could slide in the picture." Many local artists had regional or national hits still fondly remembered by oldies lovers. Among them were James "Sugar Boy" Crawford, whose "Jock-A-Mo" (1954) was one of the earliest records to introduce listeners to the rhythms and chants of Mardi Gras Indians (see chapter 7); Al Johnson, whose "Carnival Time" (1956) was another jaunty single that capitalized on the Mardi Gras theme; Lee Allen ("Walkin' with Mr. Lee," 1958); Bobby Charles, who wrote and recorded "See You Later Alligator" in 1955; Bobby Mitchell ("Try Rock and Roll" and "I'm Gonna Be a Wheel Someday"); and Clarence "Frog-man" Henry ("Ain't Got No Home").

A local favorite, Tommy Ridgley, summed up the naiveté of many of these fifties artists in reminiscing about a business deal with Dave Bartholomew and a music lawyer. "I must have signed fifty papers," he said. "I didn't know what in the world I was signing. I just signed. Because you know, it's an honor for people to think enough of you to want to record you." This attitude persisted despite the growing sophistication of the rock 'n' roll music business. By the sixties, some of the old guard had retired, while other pioneers, like Earl Palmer, joined the music migration to Los Angeles. Meanwhile, a new crop of artists was sprouting in the Crescent City, led by a multi-talented pianist and songwriter, Allen Toussaint, who learned to grasp creative control of New Orleans' most entertaining export.

THE STARMAKER—ALLEN TOUSSAINT

Allen Toussaint was another link in the chain of distinctive New Orleans keyboard artists. He grew up worshiping Professor Longhair and began his career sitting in for Fats Domino. But he went beyond his substantial piano talents to become a near-legendary producer, arranger, and songwriter, who in the early sixties had a hand in an astounding variety of chart records. Toussaint commercialized the rumba-cum-blues beat of Professor Longhair, married it to jaunty tunes arranged with plenty of hooks, and matched the tunes with a variety of fine singers. His reign marked another peak in the creative output of New Orleans.

ALLEN TOUSSAINT'S HIT PARADE

Jessie Hill—"Ooh Poo Pah Doo," May 1960

Aaron Neville—"Over You," Oct. 1960

Clarence "Frogman" Henry—"But I Do," March 1961

Ernie K-Doe—"Mother-in-Law," Apr. 1961

Clarence "Frogman" Henry—"You Always Hurt the One You Love," May 1961

Chris Kenner—"I Like It like That," July 1961

Lee Dorsey—"Ya Ya," Sept. 1961

The Showmen—"It Will Stand," Nov. 1961

Barbara George—"I Know," Dec. 1961

Lee Dorsey—"Do Re Mi," Jan. 1962

Benny Spellman—"Lipstick Traces," May 1962

Irma Thomas—"I Wish Someone Would Care," Apr. 1964

Lee Dorsey—"Ride Your Pony," July 1965

Lee Dorsey—"Working in the Coal Mine," Aug. 1966

Lee Dorsey—"Holy Cow," Nov. 1966

Toussaint was born on January 14, 1938, and grew up in Gert Town, a neighborhood on the uptown side of New Orleans. His sister Joyce taught him to read music and play the piano. As a boy, his heroes were Professor Longhair and other R&B pianists including Lloyd Glenn, Albert Ammons, and Ray Charles. But he owed the biggest debt to an obscure musician named Ernest Pinn.

An old-timer whose primary instrument was the banjo, Pinn could play anything from violin to piano. By the time he came to live with his mother, across the street from the Toussaint home, he was "down and out, a wino, with no teeth, a very puny but a happy, jovial man," recalled Toussaint. Most important, "he was excited about music, still." When twelve-year-old Allen took an interest in his playing, the older man began to seek him out nearly every day and gave him lessons in various styles of popular playing. The boy knew boogie woogie, but the older man divulged the secrets of the butterfly piano, the stride piano, and especially the concept of tenths—chords that cover ten notes, two more than an octave, in the left hand. The young man was thrilled at the ways in which Pinn "enlarged my thoughts about the piano. It was all quite sophisticated from where I was," said Toussaint years later, his eyes shining at the wonder of those discoveries as his hands roved over the piano keys, demonstrating Pinn's variations.

"My parents didn't want him around because he was an outcast," Toussaint acknowledged. But he paid them no mind. He and Pinn had a daily routine: "When it wasn't a school day, I would go out on my porch and wait for him to show his face. I would latch onto him and spend the day with him. He'd come over to my house and play all these fantastic things on the piano," Toussaint said. There would be breaks when the boy would follow the man to the liquor store to buy a new pint. The boy happened to find a half-ruined banjo that had been lying around the Toussaint household. Pinn fashioned a new back for it from a beer tray, bought string from a drugstore, and made a serviceable instrument. "He once again played the banjo and was very, very happy," said Toussaint, smiling. Years afterward, Toussaint returned from an extended gig and learned that Pinn had committed suicide with a gun, sitting on his bed at home. "I always felt that if I hadn't been out of town he wouldn't have shot himself," Toussaint said sorrowfully.

While still a teenager, Toussaint joined a band called the Flamingos, featuring an equally young guitarist, Snooks Eaglin. The Flamingos (named for a bird in imitation of the great male R&B groups like the Orioles, Cardinals, and Robins) played numerous high school dances and vied with Art Neville's group, the Hawketts, as the favorite local combo. Toussaint's keyboard skill was soon recognized. By his senior year at Booker T. Washington High School, he was already working with Earl King. King introduced him to the Dew Drop Inn crowd; he would stay up so late at the club that it was increasingly hard to keep up with school, so he dropped out. Soon, he felt very guilty. He returned to school some months later, but his career would not wait. When he got the chance to take Huey Smith's place on a tour with Shirley and Lee, he left school for good.

At the Dew Drop, Dave Bartholomew heard him one night and offered him an opportunity that was almost too good to be true. Fats Domino was on the road; Bartholomew needed someone to lay down his piano track for an upcoming recording on which Fats would dub the vocals later. Toussaint obliged and the tune, "I Want You to Know," made the charts in due course. "I played precisely like Fats Domino would have played it," he noted, not a difficult job for him since he regularly practiced note-for-note covers of piano parts by masters like Domino and Ray Charles. Once he got the nod from Bartholomew, the biggest producer in town, Toussaint said, "People considered me someone to be reckoned with."

By 1958, Toussaint was a major player in New Orleans R&B, acting as house pianist for many sides recorded at J & M. He got his first chance to do an arrangement when he helped out on Lee Allen's "Walkin' with Mr. Lee." Then, an RCA producer decided to stage several days' worth of public auditions and hired Toussaint as the accompanist. After hearing scores of hopefuls, the producers realized that the pianist was more accomplished than the people he was assisting. They asked Toussaint to record an album's worth of his own tunes—in two days. He complied, and the tracks were later released as *Wild Sounds of New Orleans* by "Al Tousan." Although it was rush job, the album did yield one tune, "Java," co-written with Red Tyler, that was later transformed into an instrumental hit by trumpet player Al Hirt.

Toussaint's attempt at solo work was disillusioning. Furthermore, the same year he got his first taste of producing, working on a single by an up-and-coming singer, Lee Dorsey. The two experiences convinced the twenty-year-old Toussaint that his future lay in being "the man behind the artist," rather than in being a star himself. His plans meshed perfectly with that of a white distribution and promotion man, Joe Banashak. Banashak was about to launch the Minit label in partnership with a popular black deejay at WMRY, Larry McKinley, who also managed a local singer, Ernie K-Doe. They needed more than a single artist or the label, so Banashak scheduled an audition in the early part of 1960. Toussaint once again was tapped as the accompanist.

Minit struck gold. That single evening at the WYLD auditorium rewarded Minit with appearances by no fewer than five gifted performers: Jessie Hill, who brought a coarse, homemade tape of a novelty song, "Ooh Poo Pah Doo"; Benny Spellman; Joe Tex; Irma Thomas; and Aaron Neville. It turned out that Joe Tex had previously signed with another label, but Minit was able to sign Hill and Spellman immediately. Moreover, the whole group of performers, plus Ernie K-Doe and Lee Dorsey, became the nucleus of what might have been called the Allen Toussaint Repertory Company. In the next few years, everyone but Tex was to have at least one hit in collaboration with their young piano player.

Minit hired Toussaint to be an in-house producer and arranger. And even though record making in New Orleans had grown more sophisticated since the one-microphone days of J & M, in Toussaint's hands it became very much a down-home affair.

Still living at home with his parents on College Court, he would write tunes in the back of the house. The artists made a habit of hanging out daily in the front room. Allen would bring a newly composed song from the back of the house, and the singers would tinker with it, and then everyone would go to the studio to record them. "I'd write a song for Irma, and the rest would sing background behind her. Then I'd write one for Aaron, and Irma and the rest would sing behind Aaron, and so on," he said. "We were just having a good time, and it happened to bring in money."

Banashak got himself quite a bargain. He paid Toussaint $107, double union scale, for acting as arranger and leader of each session. (Toussaint also got royalties on songs he wrote.) The other players got $55 each per session (four songs), and the background singers $30 each. Under Toussaint's canny direction, what Banashak got for his money was a string of singles that captured the nation's ear.

The years 1961–65 were Toussaint's most creative. The records he produced for Minit, its sister label Instant, and other small labels were more complex than the fifties tunes of Fats Domino and others, yet eminently danceable. Almost every one was marked by the distinctive, Fess-accented rhythm, a good horn section (as opposed to a single honking sax), strong lead singers, and the use of a chorus to give them a gospel call-and-response feel. By this time, nearly every African American male vocalist in the pop world had absorbed the hoarse, emotion-charged gospel style of Ray Charles, so that even lesser singers like Jessie Hill, Benny Spellman, and Ernie K-Doe knew how to bend a note or elongate a syllable for emphasis. In the background, Toussaint's piano laced these singles with unmistakable New Orleans riffs, while a collection of fine instrumentalists such as Nat Perrilliat on tenor sax, Chuck Badie on bass, and John Boudreaux rounded out the band.

Toussaint's skill paid off within a few months, when his arrangement of "Ooh Poo Pah Doo" transformed Jessie Hill's demo song into Minit's first national hit, much to Toussaint's surprise. "Ooh Poo Pah Doo" was a single featuring nonsense syllables like "Tutti Frutti" minus the saving grace of Little Richard's frenzied falsetto flourishes. Toussaint admitted he didn't like it, yet that didn't stop him from making a hit out of it. The record had a loose, one-take feel; the chorus on the call and response at the beginning was ragged while Hill's caterwauling voice rose above it. Somehow, its shuffling rhythm appealed to listeners and the song climbed to Number 28 on the pop chart in May 1960. Minit was off and running. Hill himself never had another hit.

Toussaint's early work with Minit also involved Ernie K-Doe, a sparkling stage performer with a voice that had been honed in church. He was born Ernest Kador in 1936 in New Orleans, the son of a preacher. Young Ernie grew up singing gospel and attending the big gospel shows that came to town. His idol was Archie Brownlee, the dynamic lead singer of the Five Blind Boys of Mississippi.

Kador made his first recording as a member of a gospel group. Then, while living in Chicago for a few years with his mother, he was exposed to some of the great R&B doo-wop groups like the Moonglows and the Flamingos. Upon returning to New Orleans in 1954, he became a regular at the Dew Drop and the Club Tiajuana. With a group called the Blue Diamonds, he attracted interest from small record labels. The sides he cut didn't go anywhere, but he gained recognition as an exciting club performer who wore loud suits and did splits.

Ernie found a home with Minit. His first two sides for Toussaint were modest sellers; he hit pay dirt with the third. It was a song called "Mother-in-Law." Toussaint had written it but was unhappy with the result. He crumpled it up and threw it away, as he did with many of his half-baked ideas. K-Doe (Banashak decided to spell his last name that way) retrieved it from the trash and insisted on giving it a try, over the composer's objections. "K-Doe began to want to do too many vocal calisthenics," Toussaint said. However, the group came up with an arrangement that had Benny Spellman, one of the back-up voices, chime in with deep bass accents on the "mutha-in-LO' " chorus. (Bass accents were very much in vogue, having been popularized by such groups as the Silhouettes and the Coasters.) Thanks either to that hook or to the subject matter, the song ascended in April 1961 to the Number 1 spot on *Billboard's* Hot 100, the pop chart, something no other record from New Orleans had done, not even any by Domino.

K-Doe's follow-up records, "Te-Ta-Te-Ta-Ta," "I Cried My Last Tear," and "A Certain Girl," managed only brief appearances on the charts. However, by then K-Doe had established himself as a banner act on rock 'n' roll and R&B package tours. (He later bragged about more than holding his own while opening for James Brown.) In 1962, he had another minor seller with "Popeye Joe." He continued recording for other labels and became the host of a popular radio show. In later years, Ernie blamed Toussaint and his partner, Marshall Sehorn, for stalling his career by not issuing enough of his sides. Not so, Toussaint protested. Banashak and McKinley were in control of K-Doe's releases, not he.

The truth was that Toussaint had a lot of good performers in his stable. Among them were Irma Thomas and Aaron Neville, who did their best work some years later, and an East Coast group, the Showmen, who had a hit on Minit with their rock 'n' roll anthem "It Will Stand." Toussaint also oversaw hits by Benny Spellman, Chris Kenner, and Clarence "Frogman" Henry.

Henry was less a Toussaint creation than a throwback to early R&B. His biggest hit, "Ain't Got No Home," came out in 1956. It was his own composition, a protest over his long hours at a black club in Algiers where he just couldn't seem to get off the stage. But never was a protest song more cleverly disguised—Henry sang both in falsetto ("I can sing like a girl") and in a deep bass voice ("I can sing like a frog") to illustrate the lyrics. In 1960, Toussaint was hired to arrange two songs, "(I Don't Know Why I Love You) But I Do," a tune by Bobby Charles, a local white songwriter who had also done the original "See You Later Alligator," and "You Always Hurt the One

You Love." On both sides, which were solid hits, Toussaint showed his versatility by coming up with arrangements that are almost in the big-band style—quite different from those he was doing for the Minit stable.

Benny Spellman, a native of Pensacola, Florida, won a brief moment in the limelight with a Toussaint song that had the same hook to the refrain as K-Doe's "Mother-in-Law," except the words were "Don't leave me no MO'." The title was "Lipstick Traces." The flip side was a novelty ballad, "Fortune Teller," which was a first cousin to the Coasters' "Little Egypt." In 1962 "Lipstick Traces" made a bit of a ripple on the charts, "Fortune Teller" none. However, both songs became underground favorites and were covered over and over again in years to come.

Chris Kenner, a former longshoreman, was a talented songwriter, but he needed the clever production of Toussaint to give him his one big hit, "I Like It like That," in 1961. The piano introduction was straight out of the Longhair or Huey Smith fake book. Then, in his lazy, insinuating tenor, Kenner invited listeners: "Come ooon, let me show you where it's at . . . the name of the place . . . I Like It like That." The song climbed to Number 2 on the pop charts. Kenner managed a second huge hit, "Land of 1,000 Dances," a number about dance crazes like the Twist and the Mashed Potatoes that was recorded by many other artists, most notably Wilson Pickett, and became a favorite of bar bands everywhere. Another Kenner tune, "Something You Got," was also a modest hit for Alvin "Shine" Robinson. But Kenner was eventually felled by heavy drinking and in 1968 landed in Angola, the Louisiana penitentiary, for three years on a statutory-rape conviction. He died in 1977.

As Toussaint's reputation for creating hits spread, he was receptive to the idea that he should own a piece of a label, rather than work just for wages and royalties. With local arranger Harold Battiste and members of the Minit house band, Toussaint thus briefly became a partner in a cooperative label dubbed AFO, which stood for "All For One." It was in 1961, during AFO's brief business life, that Barbara George, a song-writer barely out of high school, recorded "I Know (You Don't Love Me No More)" under Toussaint's direction. The single promptly took off, and AFO sold distribution rights to a New York independent label. Shortly thereafter, AFO, at that point the only black-owned label in New Orleans, collapsed.

Toussaint remembered the Minit years with great warmth. "It was the real thing," he said. "It wasn't just a concoction of correctly played sounds. When we were recording, sometimes we'd make a 'human fade'—we would just play softer and softer. We didn't have any overdubbing. When one guy took a solo, the other guys would stand up and snap their fingers and dance around in the studio. We were having a wonderful time. It wasn't business. No clock watching." Irma Thomas later described it as "a family."

Toussaint's remarkable hit streak was interrupted in 1963 when he was drafted. While in the Army, he formed a band with some buddies at Fort Hood, Texas. The group, called the Stokes, managed to cut some sides for another of Banashak's labels, ALON (a backward acronym based on New Orleans, LA). One number, "Whipped Cream," became a hit for Herb Alpert. Meanwhile, "Java" percolated on the charts in its Al Hirt incarnation. But by the time Toussaint got out of the service in 1965, Minit and its subsidiaries were foundering.

In the midst of this environment, Toussaint formed a fruitful new business partnership with Marshall Sehorn, a white record entrepreneur originally from North Carolina. Simultaneously, he began his most synergistic musical collaboration with Sehorn's discovery, vocalist Lee Dorsey.

Dorsey was born in New Orleans in 1926 and was a friend of Fats Domino when both were children. At the age of ten, his parents moved to Portland, Oregon; it was not until after serv-ing in World War II that Dorsey returned to his native city. A bantam-sized fellow with a friendly air about him, he had already had a decent career as a lightweight boxer, but gave it up to pursue music. While seeking a break in show business, he held down a day job as a body and fender man.

Dorsey had a classic R&B voice, with a crying quality not unlike that of Otis Redding and phrasing borrowed from Ray Charles. Sehorn signed Dorsey to a contract for the small label Fury in 1960. The label was eager to get a record out right away, and Dorsey obliged with a slim little ditty that he wrote after hearing children near his house chanting, "Yo' mama's sittin' on the slop jar / waitin' for her bowels to move." Rarely has a hit tune evolved from such unpromising material! Dorsey turned the lyric into "Sittin' here in la la / waitin' for my ya ya." Sehorn hired Toussaint to arrange it, and the resulting song, "Ya Ya," ballooned into one of the biggest pop hits of 1961.

Now, in 1965, Sehorn approached Toussaint again to produce a Dorsey single. For the only time in his life, Toussaint recalled, he deliberately tried to create a hit song. Having spent two years in the service, he felt "everyone else was way around the track" and he had been left behind. So he wrote "Ride Your Pony" in hopes that it would be the smash hit that would put him up front with the winners again. Sehorn knew a chart-topper when he heard one; he sold the single to a small label, Amy/Bell, and it galloped across the country, rising to Number 28 on the Hot 100.

Afterward, Sehorn and Toussaint put together their own production company, with a handshake their only contract. Sehorn handled the business end while Toussaint took charge of the musical side. The partnership reaped immediate benefits, with Dorsey turning out three more big hits in 1966. The biggest was "Working in a Coal Mine," as fetching a single as Toussaint ever produced. The song had multiple hooks, including an insistent bass line and a beat literally hammered home with the sound of an anvil. It didn't hurt that the southern soul vocalizing of masters like Redding was ascendant that year. Dorsey's singing on "Coal Mine," "Get Out of My Life Woman," and "Holy Cow" was very much in that vein. But he did not do the aching love ballads that Redding put across so effectively. "Lee Dorsey was a guy full of life, and his voice had a smile in it," Toussaint commented. "So the song didn't have to be a big romantic subject." Dorsey had "a lighthearted side" made to order for "Coal Mine" or "Holy Cow," with what Toussaint termed its "soft-shoe feel."

"Coal Mine" got Dorsey enough recognition to warrant an overseas tour. Ironically, the American music business was at that moment under fire from the "British invasion"; Dorsey made the reverse trip, appearing in England with the Rolling Stones and the Beatles. But after a few minor singles, including "Everything I Do Gonna Be Funky" in 1969, his star waned. He appeared regularly at the Jazz Festival until his death from emphysema in 1986.

Although Dorsey was Toussaint's last act to achieve smash hits, Toussaint was growing all the while, with assistance from Sehorn, from songwriter/producer into a musical mini-conglomerate. The two men started Sansu Enterprises in 1965 and set up a cluster of small labels—Sansu, Kansus, DeeSu, and TouSea—on which they recorded numerous local acts. In addition, they built their own studio, Sea Saint, in the Gentilly section of New Orleans and installed the quartet soon to be known as the Meters as its house band (they backed Dorsey on "Funky").

During the same period, two other companies, Stax in Memphis and Motown in Detroit, were establishing themselves as major outposts for soul, the music that succeeded R&B. Soul music—the Motown version, particularly—turned R&B from a small, haphazard industry into big business, with large ambitions, Toussaint pointed out. He admired the way Motown prepared artists for tours, albums, and whole careers, not just for next month's hit single. "They kept videotape of auditions. They had real foresight," he said. Despite high hopes, however, Sansu never became a powerhouse nationally as the other two did.

Toussaint himself was enough of a drawing card as a producer to attract many important acts to his Sea Saint facilities. Paul Simon and Paul McCartney both recorded there. McCartney moved his family and band to the city for the duration of work on "Venus and Mars," the album he made at Sea Saint in 1975. "He wanted to have the whole New Orleans experience," Toussaint said. "It is hard to hear a Crescent City flavor in such numbers as "Listen to What the Man Said," although McCartney and his entourage really did make the rounds, visiting clubs from the best known to the most obscure, and making friends with many of the town's artists. The friendship was cemented when Sehorn threw a grand party for McCartney and friends on a riverboat, and McCartney reciprocated by flying dozens of leading New Orleans musicians to Los Angeles for his own shindig aboard the *Queen Mary.*

Throughout the seventies, Toussaint continued to be in demand, doing work for the Band, Joe Cocker, and Gladys Knight, among others. Such hits as the Pointer Sisters' version of the Toussaint song "Yes We Can Can," and "Lady Marmalade" by LaBelle were recorded at Sea Saint under his direction.

Toussaint himself returned to the microphone as singer-songwriter on several albums, most notably "Southern Nights" in 1965, but his contributions as a performer never approached his achievements as a writer or producer. He never had a charted hit under his own name, while such stars as Glen Campbell turned songs like "Southern Nights" into classics. Not too much was heard from Toussaint in the early eighties, but he surfaced in 1987 as musical director of an ambitious musical, "Staggerlee," based on the rogue who is a folk hero among southern African Americans. It ran for 150 performances off Broadway.

Toussaint, a shy, reserved man, remained an enigmatic personality over the years. An introvert in an industry dominated by extroverts, he never achieved the status of an empire builder like Berry Gordy or the "creative genius" title accorded Phil Spector, both of whom were contemporaries of his. No one had juicy Allen Toussaint gossip to dish. Moreover, Toussaint never seemed to be as much at home fronting a band as he was manipulating one. "I'm a producer, musician, studio side-man, and not a star performer," he said. Stars, he said, wake up in the morning with one thing on their minds—a perfor-mance. It is "the primary desire of their heart," he continued. "When they're on, and the lights go on, everything that they've ever been and wanted to be is here and now." He identified Ernie K-Doe and LaBelle as two such performers. He clearly was at his best serving such egos, rather than competing with them. Even when he was front and center onstage, he said, he was concerned with arrangements, harmonies, instruments being in tune, sound balance, and so on. "I don't think an artist should be doing that. An artist should be free to fly," he said.

One could sense his schizophrenia at his annual perfor-mances at the Jazz Festival, where he wore star-spangled suits that contrasted sharply with his softly spoken introductions. By the nineties, he realized that many young Festival listeners had not been born when his biggest hits charted. "Some of you think I'm just a cat gigging up here. I'm a songwriter," he said, pointing out that he had written every song he sang. Later he said that after years of performing "sparingly" he had reached a point where it was "fun, sometimes." But the spotlight was never his natural habitat.

Whatever his limitations as a performer, Allen Toussaint continued to be a highly respected figure in New Orleans, although his image was a bit tarnished by lawsuits over the Meters material. His accomplishments in the narrow world of two-and-a-half-minute pop hits were indeed major. Yet under-neath, everything stemmed from those keyboard lessons with Ernest Pinn. When the "real" Allen Toussaint wanted to let loose, he was known to drop by a hotel lounge and play an impromptu set of piano pieces ranging from Beethoven to Fats Waller to Thelonious Monk. He seemed to take refuge behind the expanse of a baby grand. A Rolls-Royce that he drove displayed his identity in a one-word vanity license plate. It read: "SONGS."

Independent of Toussaint, a few acts emerged from the six-ties with major hits. One was Joe Jones, who had a smash hit with "You Talk Too Much." In 1964, the city's only girl group, the Dixie Cups, had a hit with a pop tune, "Chapel of Love." The following year, they redid the old Sugar Boy Crawford tune "Jockamo," called it "Iko Iko," and succeeded in getting the old Mardi Gras tune on the national charts. Finally, Robert Parker, a saxophonist who had been among Professor Longhair's Shuffling Hungarians and who had also played with Huey Smith, danced his way onto the charts with an infectious tune called "Barefootin' " in 1966. Indeed, Parker represented the end of the line for New Orleans as a capital city of R&B hits. The next wave of headliners nourished by the city for the most part gained recognition slowly, and not for hit singles but for albums and live shows. Thanks to Fats Domino, Little Richard, and the others, the city was present at the dawn of the rock 'n' roll era. From this point on, however, its musical lights would be a good deal more diffuse.

GOSPEL AND BLUES

Both gospel and blues music flourished in New Orleans on lines parallel with jazz and R&B. Some of the great pioneers of these genres, including Mahalia Jackson in gospel and Champion Jack Dupree in blues, were natives of the city, while others, like Clarence "Gatemouth" Brown, chose to reside there.

There does not seem to be a particular style of gospel that came specifically out of New Orleans. Originally, African American religious hymns consisted of spirituals—folk songs based on tales from the Bible. However, after the turn of the century composers began to write new songs for church choirs and soloists in city congregations, songs based more on personal concerns. These new gospel songs were sung both in old-line African Methodist Episcopal and Baptist churches, as well as the newer Pentecostal or sanctified churches. The latter became known for a more emotional quality of services and singing, featuring evangelical preachers who encouraged their parishioners not just to lift their voices but to feel the holy spirit and shout, shake, and speak in tongues.

Out of this background came the woman who was to define the sound of gospel for half a century. Mahalia Jackson was born on October 26, 1911, in New Orleans, but like so many musicians of her era, she headed north while still a girl to make her reputation in Chicago, her home base for the next forty-five years. Nevertheless, as Anthony Heilbut wrote in *The Gospel Sound*, "Everything about Mahalia, her diction, build, manner, bespeak New Orleans."

Mahalia's mother was a Baptist, but her father preached in the Holiness (sanctified) church. In addition, she had relatives in show business on her father's side and she grew up next door to a sanctified church. Thus, although she joined the Baptist church as a girl, she was deeply influenced as a youngster by both the roof-lifting style of evangelical services and by the early jazz that was such a part of her hometown.

Her mother died when she was still a girl, and Mahalia went to live with an aunt, who taught her how to cook and clean. She was not allowed to listen to blues music at home, but she couldn't help hearing neighbors playing Ma Rainey and other singers on their record players. She grew to love the music of blues pioneer Bessie Smith. As a church soloist, Jackson was credited with injecting blues into gospel.

She left school after the eighth grade and for three years she worked as a laundress, saving her earnings. Finally, in 1927, she went to Chicago to live with her Aunt Hannah. There, she found work as a domestic. When she tried out for the Greater Salem Baptist Church, it was the first time she had ever sung with a piano accompaniment. Still, her expressive voice, which had not yet deepened into the contralto instrument heard on her most famous records, won her a role as soloist. Jackson soon became one of a number of powerful voices that were transforming church music in Chicago in the thirties. In 1932, the son of her church's pastor, Robert Johnson, founded a group called the Johnson Gospel Singers. For the next several years,

Jackson toured with the group, spreading the new, more the-atrical, more southern style of gospel throughout churches in the Midwest. By the time the group broke up, Mahalia was an exciting soloist with a dramatic voice, who swayed to the beat and who punctuated a song with shouts of "Lord have mercy!"

Jackson's singing at first did not support her financially, however. She continued to work, becoming a hotel maid when she was fired from her laundry job. Working on the road forced her to miss some work time in that job as well, and she was let go. Having married an equally poor part-time postal clerk, Isaac Hockenhull, she began to take the cosmetics and oint-ments that Hockenhull concocted and sell them out of her suit-case during intermission of her group's shows. But eventually her traveling and his gambling led to the breakup of their mar-riage.

She made her first recording in 1937, but her fame did not really spread until the forties, when she teamed up with another gospel pioneer, the songwriter Thomas A. Dorsey, composer of "Precious Lord Take My Hand" and other now-classic gospel hymns. A former blues singer and pianist from Georgia, Dor-sey wrote songs tinged with blues that dovetailed perfectly with Jackson's blues-accented singing style. She toured the country with Dorsey promoting his songs; she sometimes sang as many as twenty in a row without a break. The two would perform at churches, Dorsey accompanying her at the piano. At the end of each performance, they would split the donations, with the host church getting 60 percent, the duo getting 40 percent. They were called "fish-and-bread" singers, she later explained, because they would remain long enough afterward to be fed. "We sang for our supper as well as for the Lord," she said.

Gradually, as Dorsey began to write more songs tailored to Jackson's dynamic style, listeners, especially in the South, began to follow them from town to town. After five years of nearly constant touring, she had put aside enough money to open her own beauty shop and flower shop. The latter bloomed, patron-ized by numerous Chicago ministers and undertakers who knew of her and were eager to get her to sing at their services.

Although Mahalia remained a Baptist throughout her life, she adopted and popularized the more intense melismatic vocalizing of the sanctified church, singing multiple notes while drawing out a single syllable. On stage, she brought a rocking dynamism to gospel, sometimes moaning or interrupting a song with shouts as the spirit moved her. In 1946, according to one of the multiple versions of the story of her breakthrough, she was warming up her voice for a concert at the Golden Gate ballroom by singing an old spiritual. A gospel song-plugger happened to hear her. "What's that you're singing, Mahalia?" he asked.

"Why, it's just an old song. I've always sung it—since I was a little child down in New Orleans," she replied. Why don't you record it? he suggested. And so she did. The song, of course, was "Move On Up a Little Higher." Although she had already done two 78s for the Apollo record label, this recording carried the power of R&B into the gospel world. "Move On Up" sold like an R&B platter, too; it became the first gospel single to sell over a million copies.

Jackson's celebrity coincided with the growth of gospel as a music experience heard in concert halls and theaters instead of just in churches. By the fifties, she was known nationwide as the gospel queen. She refused to appear in nightclubs, but her audiences never seemed to notice. At first, her fans were almost all black. As she began to appear in more expensive concert dates, her audiences grew whiter, although African Americans continued to buy her records and listen to her at church dates and civil rights rallies. In 1963, she sang for an ocean of marchers, black and white, at Dr. Martin Luther King's March on Washington. As experienced as she was, Jackson was moved by the size and fervor of that crowd; she took out her own camera and snapped photos of the momentous occasion.

In those later years, Jackson disappointed some fans by sweetening her appearances with strings and inferior pop-inflected songs. Nevertheless, by the time of her death in 1972, historians regarded her as the most important performer in introducing gospel to a mass audience as a distinct art form.

Even though Jackson returned to New Orleans only occasionally, the city claimed her as one of its most beloved exports. She was undoubtedly the greatest female voice ever to come out of the Crescent City. Among those she influenced was another New Orleanian, Linda Hopkins, whom she discovered. Hopkins soloed for years as "Baby Helen" with the Southern Harp Spiritual Singers before moving into the secular world of nightclubs and musical theater. Her most notable stage performance was her one-woman show, *Bessie and Me*.

While Mahalia Jackson and large church choirs were teaching the nation to clap hands and sing the praises of the Lord, smaller groups of singers were on the rise in every community, blending harmony with ecstasy in gospel songs. Just as barbershop quartets singing close harmony developed into popular acts like the Ink Spots and the Mills Brothers in secular music, so, in the years just before World War II, gospel ensembles gained prominence in the religious area. The gospel quartets, in turn, were the religious model for secular "doo-wop" groups of the fifties. Among the acclaimed gospel groups were several from New Orleans, including the Southern Harps, the Delta Southernaires, and the Zion Harmonizers.

The Southern Harps, a female group, were perhaps the city's earliest traditional group to gain recognition. Dressed in robes and accompanied by a single piano, they featured Bessie Griffin, a vocalist in the Mahalia Jackson style, and Alberta Johnson, who took turns singing lead. The Delta Southernaires were led by a pair of brothers, Chuck and Chick Carbo. In the early fifties, they crossed over into R&B, recording as the popular group The Spiders.

The Zion Harmonizers, formed in 1939 by the Reverend Benjamin Maxon, Jr., were still going strong in the early nineties, making them the only gospel group in New Orleans that was over half a century old. Maxon was the nephew of Alberta Johnson. Her Southern Harps gave the Harmonizers good exposure in their first years by taking the male group along on various engagements. By 1955 they began to get an occasional paid date of their own at a school or theater. According to Sherman Washington, the leader of the eight-member group, the Harmonizers have evolved so they now sing a variety of religious melodies, "barbershop chords, old Negro spirituals, a little contemporary, biblical numbers, straight harmony, and quite a few uptempo numbers." The group appears on stage nattily attired in matching suits, accompanied by guitar, organ, and drums. Although they do not do much "contemporary" gospel with the frenzied screams that are a high point in younger quartets, the Harmonizers use theatrical, choreographed hand movements and dance steps. Nationally, in recent years, Take Six, an a capella group, was among those whose style showed an appreciation of the older tradition of the Harmonizers and others.

As gospel music spread, thanks to recordings, radio broadcasts, and exposure at all-gospel shows, the Zion Harmonizers, like other professional groups such as the Dixie Hummingbirds, were booked all over the United States and in Europe. According to Washington, the Zion Harmonizers have received more recognition in places like Umbria, Italy, and Rotterdam than they have in New Orleans, where their biggest audience shows up at the Jazz and Heritage Festival gospel tent.

In recent years, the Harmonizers have been joined there by guest soloist Aaron Neville. Neville first joined the group when he and its members discovered a mutual admiration for the gospel work of the late Sam Cooke, when he was lead singer for the Soul Stirrers. A Harmonizers set, with Neville singing lead, is likely to reach its climax with Aaron singing falsetto in a joyous version of "When the Saints Go Marching In." One expert, Dr. Joyce Jackson of Louisiana State University, hears in the Southern Louisiana groups like the Harmonizers the same distinctive influence of Caribbean rhythms as can be heard in the secular music of Aaron's main group, the Neville Brothers.

The gospel tent, the largest at the Jazz Festival, might well be the most important contribution of New Orleans to gospel music since Mahalia Jackson. With as many as ten acts performing daily over two weekends, from those affiliated with local churches to nationally known professional ones, the tent has presented gospel of all styles to a huge, responsive audience year after year. Its growth was the work of Quint Davis, the head of the Jazz Festival, who invited the Zion Harmonizers to appear at the very first event in Congo Square in 1970, and Washington, whom Davis hired to manage the gospel tent at each succeeding festival. The size of the tent itself has more than tripled since the early days at the Fairgrounds, and even now, on the final Sunday, it is too small.

Washington said that at first he had to go out in search of the best gospel performers. "I had to almost get on my knees with some of the ministers to let their choirs sing in the festival," he added, since the ministers worried about the fact that beer was sold on the grounds. Now ministers and group managers come to him asking for a spot on the program. The tent has become, in effect, a mammoth audition stage for groups who wish to tour Europe, since numerous producers now scout acts there.

"If it hadn't been for the festival," Washington concluded, "groups would be still just singing around a few miles out of New Orleans."

Because New Orleans was regarded as a birthplace of jazz, the blues that came out of the city often received short shrift. However, early performers like Buddy Bolden were just as much bluesmen as jazzmen, and jazz of all kinds continually renews itself in the blues. As a city, New Orleans was host to a much more urban—and urbane—piano-based blues tradition than the rural guitar-based blues of the Mississippi Delta. Jelly Roll Morton certainly infused his music with both blues and ragtime riffs. The pianists who played the city's speakeasies and dives in the twenties and thirties then added yet another, cruder strain—that of boogie woogie. Some keyboard men of the pre–World War II era, like Tuts Washington, could play in many styles. Others, however, stuck to the older, simpler tradition of the blues, pounding out personal laments in 8- or 12-bar tunes.

Perhaps the piano blues man most representative of this style was Champion Jack Dupree. Born in 1910, he was orphaned at the age of one. He said his parents were killed by the Klu Klux Klan, and he was raised in the same waifs' home as Louis Armstrong, ten years his senior. "I have a lot of memories of Louis Armstrong, 'cause he used to wake us up in the morning with the bugle—and we hated him for that." Dupree learned the piano at the age of six, but he got no instruction at the home in reading music. By the time he got out of the home at age seventeen, he was embittered by his treatment as a black boy and by being kept away from his brothers and sisters so long. It was a bitterness that would find him content to be an expatriate for a good portion of his adult life.

As a young man, he scratched out a living in honky-tonks. He attributed much of his blues learning to the unrecorded barrelhouse pianist Willie Hall, known (for obscure reasons) as Drive 'Em Down. Before long, Jack too was playing around town. He told one interviewer that he and other barrelhouse players would hold an audience captive, following one another to the piano in a joint all night long, with a glass for tips on top. At the end of the evening, they might split as much as eighty dollars among them. During cane-cutting season they would go to Plaquemine Parish and play on the plantations. "We could live for a month on the money we made up there," he said.

Dupree made his living mostly as a cook, but he also took up boxing at the Rampart Street gym, hence his nickname. After Drive 'Em Down died in 1930, Jack hit the road, hoboing his way first to Chicago, where he met Tampa Red and Leroy

Carr, among the reigning blues players there. He had the urge to wander, though, and his next stop was Detroit. Once there, as Dupree tells it, he ran into Joe Louis and told him he had no place to stay. Louis gave him twenty dollars and recommended a cheap rooming house. "You could get a room for a dollar. If you played the radio it was another quarter, and if you brought a woman it was another quarter." He sparred with lightweights in Detroit at ten dollars for four rounds, becoming proficient enough to be on the card of the first Louis–Schmeling fight.

The boxing trade lost its luster for Dupree after too many punches in the mouth. In 1940 he moved on to Indianapolis, and returned to the club scene, becoming master of ceremonies and performer at the local Cotton Club. He also recorded his first records for Okeh and began writing his own lyrics. Many of his songs contained social commentary on subjects such as the New Deal.

Dupree was drafted and served in the Army as a cook. After his discharge, he hung around New Orleans and then New York, playing at night while plying his culinary skills during the day at Yeshiva University. As he tells it, he went to Europe in 1958 because he was shipped there, together with Judy Garland, by organized-crime figures who ran the clubs they worked in. Dupree opened his own club there and as it became clear that Europeans were very receptive to the blues, he decided to cash in his return ticket. He spent the next fifteen years in England, then moved to Hannover, Germany, after a divorce. In 1990, at the age of eighty, he made a nostalgic trip back to New Orleans for the first time in forty years to play the Jazz Festival.

Champion Jack's blues were salty and rough. He played a solid-stride piano behind his serviceable voice, singing about love and loss as well as issues like freedom and poverty. "Blues is life," he explained. "If you love a woman and she leave you, that make you feel bad. So many white people shoot their brains out. But black people don't shoot their brains out, see? They drink and play the piano." He died in Germany of cancer in January 1992.

Another New Orleanian who drank prodigiously and played piano with some renown was Pleasant "Cousin Joe" Joseph. Born in 1907 in Wallace, Louisiana, he began his music experiments on a $1.75 ukelele and went on to study piano. By his late teens he was a street-corner tap dancer, working for tips with two other adults and a child, none other than drummer Earl Palmer. The group was called Hats, Coats, Pants (Joe), and Buttons (Palmer). In the thirties, Joseph played guitar in local clubs like the Kingfish, and also sang on tours throughout the South with Paul Barbarin and Joe Robicheaux.

Cousin Joe went on to a good career in New York in the bebop years, recording with people like Sidney Bechet. Back in New Orleans in the fifties, he became the first black man to play in an integrated band—Sharkey Bonano and his Dixielanders—in his home city. He nearly drank himself to death, but he reformed in time to enjoy a solid final twenty years singing in Bourbon Street clubs with blues pianist Roosevelt Sykes and others. He was also enormously popular throughout Europe, which he toured several times. (Another nearly unknown New Orleans blues man, guitarist Boogie Bill Webb, also benefited from European exposure.) Cousin Joe had a full-bodied Ray Charles–tinged voice and a winning manner. Though not among the great blues players, he was still an authentic New Orleans artist who was mourned by many fans when he died in 1990.

Although blues guitarists tend to be from the rural South and Southwest, New Orleans became the home of one genuine giant in the field, Clarence "Gatemouth" Brown. Gate, as he is affectionately called, was a product of both Louisiana and Texas, since he was born on April 18, 1924, in Vinton, Louisiana, but raised across the border in Orange, Texas. His father, a railroad man who played all kinds of stringed instruments plus the accordion, was his first teacher. As a youngster who listened to country music before he ever heard the blues, young Clarence was given his nickname because he had a big voice.

Gate served his apprenticeship before World War II as a singing drummer in a road show called Brown Skin Models. Then, after the war, he settled in San Antonio and played with a swing band. The year 1947 found him hitting the clubs in both New Orleans and Houston. The young electric guitarist got his big break in the Texas city when he substituted on short notice for T-Bone Walker, who was already sending a ripple of guitar electricity through the music world. "I played his guitar when he was sick," Gate noted. "He got well in a hurry! That was the first time I played professionally for six hundred people watching."

Gate settled in for a long stay in Houston, a capital of the new electric blues, where he was discovered by Don Robey, a black entrepreneur who owned the Blue Peacock Club. Robey installed Gate in his club and arranged for him to make his first recordings on Aladdin Records. Soon, Robey started his own label. It was on Peacock that Brown made a series of historic records, the first electric guitarist to play blues in front of a big band. As demand for appearances grew, Gate traveled throughout the Southwest with a twenty-three-piece band, spreading the blues gospel, filtered through a Lionel Hampton—like hard swing-band sound. In the fifties he was considered the only real challenger T-Bone Walker had.

During the fifties, he released a number of wonderful, driving records showing off his fluid style and his excellent vocal skills. Among them was the classic "Okie Dokie Stomp," an instrumental that got its name because the New Orleans disc jockey whose radio name was Okie Dokie had dropped by the studio while the band was rehearsing. Unfortunately, Gate barely got more than a session fee for the Peacock sides; Robey gave himself songwriting credits and ensuing royalties. It was not until 1964 that the guitarist extricated himself from Robey's clutches.

By then, he was a guitar hero not just in the U.S. among

blues buffs but in Europe, which he toured for the first time in 1955. He had been sent around the world as a blues ambassador by the State Department, wowing audiences from Nicaragua to Kenya, where he played for several hundred thousand listeners and had to be carried above the throng by seven-foot tribesmen.

For the past thirty years, Brown has amazed listeners with his versatility of style as well as instruments. He played the fiddle as a sideman on a Professor Longhair record, put out two albums of Cajun tunes, and has sprinkled his live performances with everything from straight-ahead blues to country to R&B material. But he continues to be best known as the keeper of the Southwest electric blues tradition. (The difference between his songs and those of the Delta guitarists, he has pointed out sharply, is that too many of the Delta songs have "negative, backward, and ignorant" lyrics about killing women.) Brown's most recent albums on Rounder, one of which captured a Grammy, spotlighted his voice as well as his guitar. A longtime resident of Slidell, near New Orleans, he is in his late sixties, still a sinewy, ebony-skinned figure with an ever-present cowboy hat on, still singing with authority in a raspy voice that has darkened but not faltered.

If Gatemouth Brown was the most acclaimed blues guitarist living in the New Orleans area in recent years, then Snooks Eaglin, who played with Professor Longhair, among others, was his heir apparent. A decade younger than Gate, Fird Eaglin, Jr., was born in 1936, and about the only thing the two guitarists had in common was the ability to play in any style imaginable, including classical. As a baby, Snooks had a brain tumor; an operation saved his life but cost him his sight. Apparently that didn't stop him from being a mischievous youngster. He got his nickname from the equally frolicsome radio character Baby Snooks.

He was a self-taught guitarist who learned tunes by listening to all kinds of records from the age of six. In 1949, he had a brief moment in the limelight when he won top prize in the

Negro Talent Hour on radio station WNOE. Within a few years he was getting studio dates for records, playing on Sugarboy Crawford's hit "Jockomo," among others. In addition, as a member of the Flamingos (as was Allen Toussaint) he was heard at numerous local school gigs. Snooks was the lead singer and star of the group, a situation that he said led to Toussaint's departure. "He was crying about 'cause I was making more money," Snooks said. Not so, said Toussaint; he just had too many other gigs outside the group. Toussaint agreed, though, that Snooks was the indisputable star among them.

The strangest development in Eaglin's early career happened in 1958. A professor and folklorist from Louisiana State University, Harry Oster, decided that Snooks was a folk bluesman and arranged to record him for the Folkways label. "He wanted me to get some stuff from old records," Snooks recalled. "I went home and dug up all the old 78s—'Rock Island Line' by Leadbelly and all that stuff." The album was memorable for his version of "High Society," in which Snooks's guitar played all parts of a brass band.

After doing some R&B sides for Dave Bartholomew on Imperial, he toured as part of a package that included such headliners as Sam Cooke. On some dates, Eaglin was billed as "Lil' Ray Charles." But whoever had the idea to try to capitalize on his blindness, it didn't work, and he never quite caught fire. In 1969 he and his wife, Doretha, moved to the little town of St. Rose. Not much was heard from him for the next decade.

Things began turning around in 1971, when Quint Davis put him together with Professor Longhair at the Jazz Festival. He not only began to make a name for himself as a Fess sideman, he also did a recording for a Swedish label that included his classical send-up, "Funky Malaguena." For three years he labored as the featured act at the New Orleans Playboy Club, but his talents were not fully realized until 1987, when Black Top, a local label with ties to the well-known Rounder Records, brought him into the studio with first-rate sidemen and truly professional production. The result, his album "Baby, You Can

Get Your Gun," and the follow-up "Out of Nowhere," proved what fans of Eaglin at the Jazz Festival dates and elsewhere already knew—that he was a fine vocalist and muscular guitarist who was as at home on a blues classic like "Boogie Chillen" as he was on soul hits like "It's Your Thing" or R&B like "Lipstick Traces." Like Gatemouth Brown, as well as the Neville Brothers and Irma Thomas, Snooks, the one-time bluesman, discovered that audiences in the nineties were ready to appreciate a mature entertainer with New Orleans roots whose branches reached out into R&B, ballads, soul, and pop.

4 The Second Wave of R&B

RIGHT PLACE, RIGHT TIME

Out of the first R&B boom came a constellation of singers, songwriters, arrangers, instrumentalists, and label owners imbued with the special music traditions of New Orleans— Professor Longhair, Fats Domino, Cosimo Matassa, Dave Bartholomew, Allen Toussaint, Marshall Sehorn, and Earl King, among others. Many of these people, in turn, served as mentors, employers, and teachers for the next generation of rock and soul performers. It was this second wave, which included Dr. John and the Neville Brothers, who introduced the second line to fans across the nation and the world.

A few artists who had begun their careers in the fifties and early sixties, such as Mac Rebennack (Dr. John), Art and Aaron Neville, and Irma Thomas, were able to build a devoted following in the seventies, eighties, and into the nineties. Others, such as Earl King, Eddie Bo, and Clarence "Frogman" Henry, took roller-coaster rides from obscurity to modest fame and back to small clubs, finding rejuvenation at least once a year at the Jazz and Heritage Festival. Although New Orleans was no longer the magnet for recording or for independent labels that it had been at the height of the Fats Domino or Toussaint eras, it remained an important capital of pop music and an incubator of world-class talent.

Perhaps the least-known important figure of this second wave was James Booker. An eccentric, intellectual man who battled drug abuse most of his life, he was called by his peers the piano prince of New Orleans. To this day his stature among other keyboard artists is close to that of Professor Longhair. He had only one minor hit record, yet he influenced his fellow artists profoundly. His brilliant playing, undercut by his mental instability, made for a career that was an eerie mirror of the first king of jazz, Buddy Bolden.

James Carroll Booker III was born on December 17, 1939. He liked to point out that he was born in the same year Jelly Roll Morton died, and in later years enjoyed comparing himself with composers of the past. "You might say Jelly Roll Morton, Mozart, and W. C. Handy are all resurrected in the form of Little Chopin in Living Color," he once said. His father was a preacher who had a secular career as a dancer. His mother and his older sister were gospel singers. Before he was ten years old, "Little Chopin in Living Color" was considered a piano prodigy, but the first instrument he could call his own was a saxophone, a Christmas present from his mother. He liked to tell people later that he had really yearned for a trumpet but "I was appreciative enough and elated enough over blowing any instrument to stand in front of the mirror and teach myself the scales."

James had been born blind in one eye; fate dealt him a second physical blow when, in 1949 he was hit by a speeding ambulance. He survived, but his leg was broken and he walked thereafter with a limp. During his recuperation he was given morphine, an occurrence he later described as "probably the first experience of euphoria." Painkillers became a lifelong addiction.

In 1953 he enrolled in Xavier Preparatory School. His first group, Booker Boy and the Rhythmaires, included a school pal who would also become a star, Art Neville. By then his sister was a regular on a gospel radio show and James would tag along on her visits to the station. Soon he, too, was a regular

on radio, playing blues and gospel. That was not all he could play. Allen Toussaint, who knew him as a "hyper" kid then, would listen in amazement as Booker played Bach Two- and Three-Part Inventions or a Rachmaninoff sonata "while holding a conversation with you."

The city's musical community began to take notice of the young keyboard whiz. Edward Frank, a well-known local pianist, dated Booker's sister and got him an audition with Dave Bartholomew. Thus, at fourteen, the youngster made his first record for Imperial. It did not make him a schoolboy wonder, but it got him work as a session man at J & M, where he filled in Fats Domino's piano parts on records when Domino was on the road. He was still practically a child when he made singles for Chess under Paul Gayten's direction.

"He was the first one in our little clique that hung around J & M that started playing sessions regularly," recalled Mac Rebennack. When sessions were over, Rebennack continued, "Booker would walk in there and play Bach fugues. Then he would entertain us by throwing in 'Malaguena,' boogie woogie, some really tough things." Before the fifties were over, Booker was doing road shows with Shirley and Lee, subbing for Huey Smith when the Clowns went on tour, and playing behind Joe Tex.

Through Tex, Booker met Johnny Vincent of Ace Records, who was eager to take advantage of the new popularity of the organ sound on R&B records. Booker, easily the best organist in the city, cut several sides for Ace, including "Teenage Rock" and "Open the Door." Unfortunately, they went nowhere, and Booker was hurt when Tex's voice was dubbed over his on a third side. He turned his back on the music business and enrolled in Southern University in Baton Rouge to study for a music degree.

Booker could not stay away from the recording scene for long, however. In Houston in 1960, he recorded several singles for Peacock, Don Robey's label. One of them, "Gonzo," became Booker's first and only regional hit. When he landed back in

New Orleans, his talent brought him plenty of gigs and his fellow musicians liked him personally, but as the decade progressed his drug abuse became notorious. Rebennack said he would make the rounds of producers and performers, collecting two weeks' pay from each of them, then buy dope and disappear. On other occasions, he could be a charming raconteur and player. An evening with him, wrote cartoonist Bunny Matthews, "could be a little like having the entire Bacchus parade march through your living room." [The krewe of Bacchus stages one of the largest, most raucous Mardi Gras parades.] On occasion he would bowl over other musicians during jam sessions at Papa Joe's, the after-hours spot in the French Quarter where they all gathered, by creating musical puns on the spot and doing take-offs of jazz and pop stars.

His reputation as an organist caught the attention of a local club owner, who opened three "organ clubs" for Booker to perform in. The way Booker told the story, he couldn't handle all the work, so he taught Mac Rebennack how to play the instrument and made him his understudy. The way Rebennack told the story, Booker gave him organ lessons with the idea that the two of them would split up the jobs—Booker would play with black bands, Rebennack with white ones. In any event, Booker worked the organ gigs in the sixties, along with numerous jobs with Lloyd Price, Wilson Pickett, Little Richard, and others. He also lived in New York for two years, and sat in with the band that played for Aretha Franklin, among others. (She recorded his tune "So Swell When You're Well.")

His career as a sideman came to a screeching halt in 1970, however, when he was arrested at the Dew Drop for possession of heroin and spent a month in the parish prison. When he was released, Rebennack sensed his friend had grown bitter, pointing to a song Booker wrote called "You've Got a Hell of a Nerve." He even tried to outdo Rebennack by writing a song called "Classified" in response to Rebennack's "Qualified." "Booker was a very trying guy," added Rebennack. "There were times I shied away from Booker, and I loved him to death."

The man was indeed eccentric, Rebennack continued, but "in the early days he was eccentrically hip. The stuff that happened later was eccentrically pathetic." In his hip phase, he once pulled a disappearing act when the two men were playing with a band at the Aragon ballroom. Then, as the band kicked into its first song, Mac looked down into the orchestra pit, and realized James was playing away on the theater's huge pipe organ. Another time, he literally frightened a saxophone player away from a gig. The player was showing a brand-new alto sax to Booker when James took the instrument and began playing it flawlessly. Saying that he couldn't play in a band where the organist was a better saxophone player than he was, the player fled.

Weird though he was, Booker found plenty to keep him occupied throughout the seventies, doing session work for Ringo Starr, the Doobie Brothers, and the Grateful Dead, among others. He also recorded an album for Jerry Wexler of Atlantic Records that was never released. However, Wexler did get Booker the job of doing vocals in the movie *Pretty Baby*. But his heroin habit got in the way of any major career moves. In one attempt to get clean, he played for an entire year in a cocktail lounge in Downington, Pennsylvania, a town not far from Philadelphia. In 1976, when he managed to kick a methadone habit, he became so paranoid that he was committed to the mental ward of Charity Hospital.

James Booker's solo career seemed permanently stalled, although exciting appearances at the Jazz Festival led to an agent booking him on a European tour, during which he recorded an album in Zurich, "New Orleans Piano Wizard: Live!" The album showed that the Ivory Emperor, as someone dubbed him, could play from any period of music in a variety of styles. His version of "Sunny Side of the Street," for example, was a florid tribute to the Tuts Washington school of the thirties, with a swinging left hand and ornate flourishes of triplets. It was followed by a gospel rendition of "Black Night" that owed a lot to Aretha, a stride "Keep on Gwine," and a pure pop number,

"Something Stupid," that was undoubtedly a staple of his Downington days. The album won the Grand Prix de Disque de Jazz for best live album of the year. Even so, it did not necessarily show off the complete Booker. With a rhythm section behind him, Booker could dive into an R&B or funk number like his signature song, "Junco Partner," with the authority of a manic, updated Professor Longhair. Those who heard his live performances in his last years playing at the Maple Leaf in New Orleans, with crack sidemen like Red Tyler on sax and John Vidacovich on drums, were amazed at his virtuosity. One critic, Tom McDermott, argued that Booker "was the New Orleans pianist who best synthesized the traditional jazz and R&B schools" and was in the same class as Art Tatum. "Both utilized a very personalized stride style," wrote McDermott. "Both had an affinity for paraphrasing classical music," and both could transform different styles into "something personal and breathtaking."

At the start of the eighties, Booker's mood swings began to get out of control. When lucid, he would act like a misunderstood genius, rambling about the perfidy of record companies and friends. In a conversation with Bunny Matthews, he concluded: "If you're qualified to be an exception [to the world's rules], that's something that's quite natural to draw resentments. It's very difficult to deal with. I've been just about on the brink of insanity three or four times. My brain gets certain signals just like heart trouble."

When fans came to hear him, they never knew what to expect. On one night he might respond with a fantastic performance, then return for a second night and vomit on the piano. At live shows he was known to walk off in the middle of a song. When the Rounder label set up a date to record him, he showed up the first day and then refused to play anything. The next day, he played brilliantly. Yet despite his troubles, he went out of his way to help others. He took a liking to the son of the local district attorney, something of a child prodigy himself, giving Harry Connick, Jr., informal lessons and even inviting him onstage during one Jazz Festival performance.

But his bright periods were interrupted by more and more bizarre incidents apparently linked to drugs and alcohol. In 1981, according to Jeff Hannusch, he played a luminous set aboard the riverboat *President* one night, then had to be committed to a mental institution two days later after being found, incoherent, wandering the streets. In death as in life, his anthem was "Junco Partner." He died at the age of forty-three on November 8, 1983.

Was James Booker the genius so many thought he was? Until more of his recorded output is released, it seems impossible to answer the question. He did not invent a style, like Fess did, nor was he a winning vocalist, the way Fats was. But he could update everyone else's style in amazing ways. There are tantalizing glimpses of that genius in the two Rounder albums and a few European releases that have gone out of print. On "Mr. Mystery" he galloped through "That's What the People Say" in a driving yet more melodic Domino style. On "Classified," he did a haunting jazz rendition of "Angel Eyes." At the same time, his choice of material could be atrocious—"Something Stupid" and "King of the Road," for example. Friends such as Rebennack said it was entirely possible that the material he cut for Peacock and Atlantic was superior to anything else by Booker that was actually issued.

Perhaps that is true. Nevertheless, Booker remained only a cult figure. Even while the "ivory emperor" was alive, his music was not heard by a broad national audience. Instead, the man who truly synthesized earlier New Orleans piano styles into something new and who kept himself together enough to put the city's sound on the huge international rock music map was his one-time protégé and admirer, Mac Rebennack, a.k.a. Dr. John.

THE CONDUIT—DR. JOHN

Dr. John, he of the rippling nouveau boogie-woogie piano and the voice that cackled as if he were singing with a mouth full of crawfish, was the most important white artist to emerge from New Orleans R&B. Building on the fame he won in the psychedelic era, he merged the Crescent City keyboard sound into the mainstream of rock and thus introduced it to a vast new audience on both sides of the Atlantic, much as Fats Domino had done in the previous era.

What's more, he made his contribution on his own terms, singing in a patois borrowed from black slang and building on the legends of his hometown. Who could have predicted that what one rock history called his "funk, glitter and voodoo charm" would be commercial? But it was. Furthermore, when the charm was no longer in favor, he eased into a more mature style that got him bookings for every venue from jazz clubs to radio jingles. While other stars of the sixties found themselves over the hill, Dr. John, genially singing pop standards, became timeless.

He was born Malcolm John Rebennack, Jr., sometime around 1940. (Every biographical note seems to give a different birth date, and he refuses to disclose the correct one.) He was such a cute kid that he was a model for Ivory soap ads. His introduction to music came by way of his family, which included several pianists. "My aunt Andree showed me how to play the Texas boogie," he said. "I used to like to hear her play stuff like 'Everybody Loves My Baby.' " Other uncles and aunts, as well as his mother and his sister Bobbie, also played. The first music he could recall hearing were minstrel songs sung by his grandfather, tunes such as "Didn't He Ramble" and "I've Been Hoodooed."

His entrée into show business was his father, who had an appliance store and record shop. Mac Sr. also visited clubs and hotels on South Rampart Street regularly, stocking their jukeboxes with what at the time were still known as "race" records. Mac Jr. accompanied his father and soon learned to work a turntable himself, playing King Oliver, Louis Armstrong, Big Bill Broonzy, Horace Silver, and whatever else he could find, over and over. As a student at Jesuit High School (an institution favored by the city's most society-oriented Catholic families) he began hanging out at the J & M studio of Cosimo Matassa, a friend of his father's. Thus, barely into his teens, he was present at the birth of rock 'n' roll, listening in while such historic records as those of Guitar Slim and Little Richard were cut.

Of course, young Rebennack did not know then that they were historic. He simply loved hearing the great house band and individual players. "Whether it was Huey Smith or Edward Frank, all the piano players used to just kill me," he recalled.

He was still very young when his father allowed him to come along on a trip to Gretna to fix the public-address system at a black club called the Pepper Pot. Junior was supposed to stay in the car, but he saw an older man banging away on a piano despite the lack of amplification. It was Professor Longhair. The boy was filled with curiosity over the pianist's strange fingering. "Man, what is that you're doing?" he asked. "That's overs and unders," replied Fess, demonstrating how he struck certain chords. "And what do you call that stuff?" asked the boy about another figure. "That's double-note crossovers," he said. The youngster, never having heard the terminology, thought the older man's playing was "off the wall" but incredibly original.

He got started as a professional not on the piano but on the guitar. First A. J. Goma, who worked at Werlein's music store, was his teacher, then the great session guitarist Roy Montrell. Another teacher, when he had the time, was Papoose Nelson, a sideman who toured with Fats Domino. He was so eager to play that in high school he joined two bands, one of which played a lot of Fats Domino covers at high school dances, and another started by a fellow named Leonard James. In addition, he was getting an education at J & M. Most of the time he and his young friends, like Leonard James or James Booker, were shooed away. But later, one of his teachers sent him in as a substitute, even though he did not have a union card yet. (Rebennack guessed that the contract listed the regular guitarist, not him.) Gradually, he got the call to sit in on recordings led by Paul Gayten.

Rebennack developed his playing style in part by watching Booker "like a hawk." They were friends, and James gave Mac informal lessons in styles such as that of Pinetop Smith, the great boogie-woogie artist, and Lloyd Glenn, a big name in R&B. He also soaked up snatches of lessons offered by Huey Smith and Al Johnson. The New Orleans sound was in its R&B heyday, with sessions scheduled practically around the clock at J & M. There were more bookings than the regulars could handle, so Rebennack got his share of gigs. It was quite a finishing school. At first, he could hardly sight-read and had to have the tenor-sax player repeat a phrase in order to play it himself. One leader was so annoyed he said he wouldn't use the youngster again on a session until he could read. (Rebennack applied himself and learned.) Sometimes, he was ribbed by the other musicians for trying too hard to play guitar like his idol, T-Bone Walker. "Producers and arrangers could get really lethal with us," he remembered. Red Tyler, when he was tenor man on a session, gave the other musicians their marching orders. "Red sat down and said, 'These are the chords we're gonna play,' and he dictated something to the horns, and maybe something to the rhythm section. There was never any argument, it was 'just do it!' "

Rebennack left high school in his junior year, taking correspondence courses to get his diploma. Meanwhile, after several years of session work and tours with stars like Jimmy Clanton and Frankie Ford, his unofficial apprenticeship ended. One day Lee Allen, the tenor player, and Hungry Williams, the drummer, said to him, "Okay, kid, you're in the funk clique now." He had been accepted as a regular. It meant more to him than his union card. He went on to do A & R work for Ace Records, and began writing songs for acts such as Johnny Adams. He even made his own solo debut, cutting "Storm Warning" on Rex Records.

Segregation was still very much enforced in New Orleans

and the Gulf states in the early sixties. Since Rebennack played with black as well as white bands, he had to be very careful. "When I traveled with black acts, I was, like, put in the back and passed off (as black). You did what you had to do to survive." Unfortunately, as he recalled, "this was real ixnay stuff. When you left parts of Orleans Parish and hit Jefferson or St. Bernard Parish, if I sat in with a black band, I could cost them their gig." Actually, what it cost him was his membership in good standing with the white branch of the musicians' union. Rebennack, among others, was harassed, fined, and generally given a hard time for crossing the color line.

It was neither the union nor segregation but a fellow musician who nearly cost him his playing ability. On tour in Jacksonville, Florida, he tried to intervene in a fight over a woman between Ronnie Barron, a singer in his band, and an enraged man who was pistol-whipping him. Rebennack lunged at the gun, trying to wrestle it out of the man's hand. The gun went off, hitting Rebennack in the index finger and nearly severing it. The finger was sewn back on but Rebennack could not play the guitar for a long time. He tried to get by on bass and drums until Booker, seeking help in the various organ clubs, showed him how to play the Hammond B-3 organ.

Rebennack's career was interrupted again in 1964 when his marriage to Lidia Crow hit the rocks and he found himself in deep trouble over heroin. Although he will talk about his drug problem and subsequent incarceration only obliquely, he apparently was arrested and then offered a deal by authorities. In exchange for doing "time" in a mental ward of a U.S. Public Health Service Hospital rather than someplace worse, he was forced to sign away the rights to a lot of his songs. (He'd not say to whom, nor in whose name they were placed.) "It wasn't exactly like I was volunteering," he said, noting that he was forced to detox with the powerful and numbing tranquilizer Thorazine. When he got out of the hospital, a shaken Rebennack moved to California, where his mother and sister were living, to rebuild his life.

California in the mid-sixties was one of the prime centers of the new rock music that was flowering in the wake of the Beatles and the Beach Boys. Through New Orleanian Harold Battiste, who had become an important part of the Sonny and Cher band, he got session work with various acts and played in groups such as the Zu Zu Band (with Jessie Hill of "Ooh Poo Pah Doo" fame) and Morgus and the Three Ghouls. Then, prompted by Battiste's suggestion and by his own interest in voodoo, Rebennack assembled a new persona for himself that was perfectly in tune with the psychedelic era. He became Dr. John, the Night Tripper.

In the 1840s in New Orleans, there had indeed been a real Dr. John Montaine, a black man who claimed to be an African potentate. For three decades, Dr. John reigned as the King of Voodoo, a master of the occult who mixed potions and wove a spell over rich white folks of his day. Harold Battiste said that the idea behind the modern character was to make Dr. John "the new guru." According to Rebennack, he chose the name "specifically because my sister knew some stuff" about the original Nigerian Dr. John. "I felt a spiritual kinship," he added. However, his original plan was for Ronnie Barron, his lead singer, to adopt that persona. But band leader Don Costa, who managed Barron, convinced him it would be a bad career move. So an annoyed Rebennack, faced with preparing a new album but lacking a lead singer, decided to do it himself, despite misgivings about his voice.

While making his first "voodoo rock" album, "Gris-Gris," Rebennack also conceived a show that would tour in support of it, based on old-time minstrel shows. But the whole thing was done in the spirit of respect, he said, not merely as a showbiz gimmick. "I'd even talked to the reverend mothers and some of those old gris-gris scientists in New Orleans about whether it was cool to do this," he said. "I'm too superstitious to be doing something that would jeopardize anyone. Music is too much of a spiritual thing to have bad come of it."

As Rebennack developed the album and the stage act behind

it, he sincerely felt he was introducing a unique aspect of his home city's culture to young listeners. Perhaps that helped make Dr. John the huge success he was. "Gris-Gris," which appeared in 1968, presented Dr. John as a seer with "prescriptions," "medicine" to cure all ills, and "remedies of every description," surely an appropriate sage for the period, when millions of Americans began to experiment with psychedelic drugs. The images from songs like "Walk on Gilded Splinters," and the hypnotic beat behind the chorus's chants were intriguing. Onstage, Rebennack was Dr. John himself, draped in a long robe and a feathered headdress, playing a piano lit with candelabra. The show also featured singers and dancers in costume, led by Colinda, a sinuous dancer who performed with a snake. Rebennack was being too modest when he said years later that he had a "cult following"; he was, in fact, one of the great acts of the period. Rock historian Charlie Gillett described his vocals as "growled" and "gravelly" and "almost buried in a murky, mysterious mush of piano, guitar, bass, and drums—like Booker T and the MGs having a nightmare. Instead of virtuoso solos, Dr. John presented textures, moods, atmospheres."

With Dr. John, Rebennack consciously assumed the role of a musical Johnny Appleseed, spreading the pollen of a little-known aspect of New Orleans culture among the masses almost twenty years before "world beat" music from Africa and the Caribbean became a major pop influence. The follow-up albums, "Babylon" and "Remedies," were less successful, but Rebennack had by then adopted Dr. John as a permanent stage name and personality. The tours also gave him on-the-job training in being a lead vocalist. "I knew I wasn't no singer, but I wasn't worried about it," he insisted. In fact, one could hear a lot of James Booker phrasing both in his piano playing and vocal phrasing. (He eventually stopped doing the "voodoo show" when Colinda got married and retired from the stage.)

A difficult 1970 tour of Europe led to the presence on his next album of British megastars Eric Clapton and Mick Jagger.

Working without several regular band members who could not get passports, Dr. John wound up firing their replacements soon after reaching the Continent. By the time he reached England, he had only his drummer and background singers with him. In addition, he had a bitter fight with his manager, Charlie Green. Amid this chaos, he was scheduled to lay down tracks for "The Sun," the first in what he conceived of as a three-record set called "The Sun, the Moon and the Herbs." Stuck without players, he was able to get in touch with Clapton, Jagger, and others who admired his work. On the first day, Trident Studio was filled with more musicians than he could use, including African and Jamaican percussionists, and, he recalled, it "smelled like the original hashish or opium dens of the Orient."

Back in the United States, Dr. John's recording schedule was in shambles. When finally he got his hands on the master tapes made in England, many of the tracks were missing, apparently as part of his dispute with his manager. Dr. John and Atlantic engineer Tom Dowd made a new mix, and they were able to put together enough songs for a single album, but Dr. John felt it was of poor quality. To cap the disaster, Green and partner Brian Stone had Rebennack, who had returned to drugs, put in a psychiatric ward for a while. They said they were trying to get him clean; he maintained they were trying to get their hands on his money by having him declared incompetent.

Dr. John did break free of Green and Stone. Perhaps harking back to happier, simpler times, he then devoted himself to a new album based on his New Orleans R&B roots called "Gumbo." It was not his best-selling work, but it was among his finest. Along with "Treacherous" by the Neville Brothers and "The New Orleans Album" by the Dirty Dozen Brass Band, "Gumbo" stands as a tribute to the Crescent City in ¾ time, a summing up of the many Afro-Caribbean, blues, and jazz influences that made the city's music unique.

"This album is like a picture of the music New Orleans people listen to, a combination of Dixieland, Rock and Roll, and

Funk," Rebennack said, describing it as "basic good-time New Orleans blues and stomp music with a little Dixieland jazz and some Spanish rumba blues." It began with "Iko, Iko" (actually a redoing of Sugar Boy Crawford's "Jockomo"). Rebennack also waded into a powerful version of "Blow Wind Blow," originally recorded by Junior "Izzycoo" Gordon of the Spiders, and offered a fascinating "Big Chief," with Ronnie Barron playing a lick on the organ that Fess originally did on piano. Rebennack imitated Archibald (a New Orleans–born traditional pianist whose real name was Leon T. Gross) on "Stack-a-Lee," Huey Smith on a medley of tunes, and even threw in a nice Dixieland version of "Somebody Changed the Lock." On "Mess Around," he adapted the piano style of Ray Charles. "Gumbo" wound up with a rousing version of "Little Liza Jane." Among his background singers, he enlisted Shirley Goodman, Ronnie Barron, and Alvin "Shine" Robinson, among others. Dr. John himself sang with a happy energy that was occasionally lacking on his other albums.

With the issuing of "Gumbo," Dr. John left his voodoo period behind, although he kept the stage name. Continuing to mine the New Orleans vein, he scored major album sales in 1973 with "In the Right Place," produced by Allen Toussaint. It had a great funky sound, thanks to the Meters behind him, and included two singles that became hits, "Right Place, Wrong Time" (which reached Number 9 on the pop charts) and "Such a Night." Where "Gumbo" had looked backward, "In the Right Place" looked both backward and forward, showing that an updated New Orleans sound had a place on the rock scene. Indeed, "Such a Night," an appealing mixture of honky-tonk piano, brass-band trombone, and contemporary lyrics, became Dr. John's personal anthem. Although the follow-up album, "Desitively Bonnaroo," also done with Toussaint, was a flop, Dr. John was carving out a permanent place for white funk. Whether as an arranger (Aretha Franklin's "Spanish Harlem," Carly Simon and James Taylor's "Mockingbird") or as a role model (the singer and pianist Leon Russell was probably his closest imitator), he showed that New Orleans stylings could still be commercial.

In the eighties, Dr. John, working out of New York as his home base, continued to put out interesting albums of his own and to work as an arranger and producer for others. "Dr. John Plays Mac Rebennack," a solo piano effort, was among the most praised critically. A blues album with Mike Bloomfield and John Hammond, Jr., and a jazz album with Fathead Newman were also well received. He attributed a lot of his success to the examples of his predecessors in the New Orleans tradition, especially Toussaint and Red Tyler. "He was always very consistent," he said of Tyler. "If he couldn't find the right background singers, or if he couldn't get strings to do it right in New Orleans, he'd [go elsewhere]. Both them guys left big impressions in my head."

Dr. John showed a longevity that other rock artists might envy. In 1989, his album of pop standards, "In a Sentimental Mood," was a surprise hit and won a Grammy. His engaging vocals, especially his duet with Rickey Lee Jones on "Making Woopee" demonstrated his ability to segue into a post-rock career. As he entered his fourth decade as a performer, Mac Rebennack, along with Wynton Marsalis in jazz and a few others, assumed the mantle of caretaker of his hometown's musical heritage. He continued to play with and produce local artists he admired, even though he obviously made much more money on his jingles for advertisers like Radisson Hotels and Popeye's Chicken.

Why did he spend time working with someone like the underrated soul singer Johnny Adams, who stood little chance of making his long-overdue national breakthrough? Rebennack felt it was the least he could do. "New Orleans musicians consistently gave of themselves to help other guys at the cost of making a decent living," he noted. "They give so much that we're looked at as a bunch of chumps in the record industry. People figure well, these guys work cheap, they don't deserve [success]. It's really been a backwards thing. but if we don't do it, these guys who are great artists get buried."

THE METERS AND THE BIRTH OF FUNK

While Dr. John was funking up white rock music in the late sixties and early seventies, the Meters were doing much the same for the emerging black mainstream sound of southern soul music. Along with James Brown and Booker T and the MGs, the Meters were among the most active groups propelling funk into the front rank of musical styles.

But what exactly did the word mean? In New Orleans lingo going back to the early days of the century, "funky" meant either literally stinky or reeking of the sweat of sex. (Funky Butt Hall, remember, was the name of an important joint in Louis Armstrong's youth.) As years went by, the word came to assume a more varied set of meanings. According to songwriter Earl King, it implied "a concentrated rhythm and stiffness." To Meters bassist George Porter, Jr., it defined the more sophisticated syncopation that groups were adopting in the late sixties.

It is safe to say that in contemporary New Orleans, funk has been synonymous with the jams of the Meters, the thirteenth-ward quartet that sharpened its chops in the dives on Bourbon Street and was nurtured to professional maturity under the baton of Allen Toussaint.

The group's leader was Art Neville, who had scored his first hit as a teenager in 1954 with "Mardi Gras Mambo." The eldest son in what would become the city's most famous funk family, Art was born on December 17, 1937. He studied piano as a child and absorbed the R&B keyboard styles of the day, especially those of Lloyd Glenn and Professor Longhair. While still in high school, he joined a group, the Hawketts. They became friends with a local disc jockey, Ken Elliott. Known as Jack the Cat, Elliott helped the group turn a country song into "Mardi

Gras Mambo." The group recorded the tune in a radio studio and the single was sold to the Chess label. Released in time for the Carnival season, it became a local hit. The Hawketts never made another record, but they got local bookings thanks to their "Mambo" exposure, and toured with Larry Williams (of "Bony Maronie" fame).

Art played fairly regularly in New Orleans for the next several years before joining the Navy. Then, in 1961, Allen Toussaint, in the midst of his prolific hit phase, wrote "All These Things" specifically for Art's smooth baritone voice. A pleasant ballad, it, too, did well locally. Nevertheless, it was his younger brother, Aaron, who had the biggest smash of all, "Tell It like It Is," in 1966. Art wound up leading a band that backed Aaron on a tour that followed. When the tour was over, Art formed a group he called the Neville Sounds to play New Orleans clubs such as the Nitecap. At first, brothers Aaron and Cyril were members, but they soon split off to do other work. Meanwhile, Art had assembled three sidemen who provided the perfect balance for his muscular organ playing: guitarist Leo Nocentelli, bassist George Porter, Jr., and drummer Joseph "Zigaboo" Modeliste.

Nocentelli, born in 1946, was the son of a part-Sicilian warehouse worker and amateur banjo player. Starting on the guitar at the age of twelve, Leo became accomplished enough by age seventeen to become a session man at Motown in Detroit, where he played on such hits as the Supremes' "Where Did Our Love Go?" Although Nocentelli was not from the thirteenth ward, he was known even in his teen years as a virtuoso. George Porter, who was a year younger, was an aspiring guitarist in those days, and whenever he or a friend needed advice they would telephone Leo for his expertise. "Man, we're stuck on this chord. How do we finger it?" George would ask, and Leo would invariably have the answer. By the time they met face to face around 1964, they felt almost like old friends.

By the mid-sixties, George had switched to bass. There were fewer and fewer good bassists around because so many had been drafted as part of the Vietnam War military buildup. When Art lost his regular bassist to the Army, he hired Porter. George was modest about his talent at that point; he had a feeling Art wasn't crazy about his guitar work, and he wasn't particular well known yet on the bass, but he "was hanging out with the right guys" when Neville put together his band.

Drummer Modeliste was an old colleague of the Nevilles, as well as Porter's cousin. The youngest of the bunch (he was born on December 28, 1948), he had grown up in the thirteenth ward with the Neville brothers and had put in some time playing with the Hawketts.

The foursome got a chance to hone their sound by playing together week after week, first at the Nitecap, then at the Ivanhoe, a French Quarter club where they were a fixture for a year and a half. Their bread and butter was R&B, but whenever Art took a break, the other three would "swing" out into jazz. On Sunday nights Nocentelli, Porter, and Modeliste would extend their range to bebop, teaming up at another club with a saxophone player. It was a musical apprenticeship that would serve them well in the coming years.

One evening, Toussaint, whose fame as a producer was spreading nationwide, dropped by to hear his old friend Art. He liked the sound of the entire group, and promptly hired them to be the house band for Sansu, the company he had formed with Sehorn. In the studio, the foursome made their mark almost immediately, ably backing Lee Dorsey, Earl King, Benny Spellman, and other Toussaint regulars, as well as outsiders who came to the studio hoping for Toussaint's magic touch. The Pointer Sisters' "Yes We Can Can" was only one of many singles whose exclamation-point riffs came from Neville, Nocentelli, Porter, and Modeliste. "We never knew who the artist was going to be," Porter said. "Allen would spell the music out, then he'd find the artists and make the artists fit the track."

It was inevitable that the house band would garner its share of attention. The group did two singles under Art's name, "Bo Diddley Parts 1 & 2" and "I'm Gonna Put Some Hurt on You."

Finally, in 1967, they recorded their own instrumental number, along the lines of the material they had been playing at the Ivanhoe. The tune, "Sophisticated Cissy," had all the earmarks of a soul sensation. Sehorn, acting as their manager, quickly made a deal to put it and other tracks on an album for the Josie label. But there was one problem. The record company thought "Art Neville and the Neville Sounds" was much too long a name. What catchy title could they substitute? Everyone gave it some thought and put their suggestions in a hat. The winner was Toussaint's; "the Meters" were now officially ticking.

Their first album, "Cissy Strut," was released in 1969. Not only was the band tight and solidly rhythmic, it was right in step with the more adventurous soul sounds coming out of other southern-based acts like Booker T and the MGs. "Cissy Strut" quickly found admirers, and the Meters recorded two more albums, "Look-Ka Py Py" and "Struttin'," in the next fourteen months.

The single "Cissy Strut" was especially successful, reaching Number 4 on *Billboard*'s R&B chart. But according to Art, the group never had a clue about its popularity, because neither Sehorn nor Toussaint informed them about sales. "We played six nights a week from six o'clock to five o'clock in the morning for almost two years and we didn't know we had a hit record," he said. They remained in the dark about such matters as contracts and royalties, partly because they were not inquisitive enough and partly because that was the attitude record companies preferred artists to have. "In those days, musicians weren't being encouraged to be aware of the business. It was like, it would take away from your creative output," Porter commented. What's more, as Porter put it, "Allen Toussaint was famous. We thought we had no reason not to trust him."

The Meters' reputation burgeoned as the group toured and recorded over the next several years. In 1970, they were named the "best rhythm and blues instrumental group" by both *Billboard* and *Record World.* Moving over to a major label, Reprise, they issued "Cabbage Alley" and "Rejuvenation," the latter with white rock artists Robert Palmer and Lowell George as guest stars. "Rejuvenation" won rave reviews; "honest and natural, unstained by high-powered commerciality," declared *Stereo Review*.

One of the highlights of the seventies for the Meters and other local musicians was Paul McCartney's stay in New Orleans while making "Venus and Mars." The Meters were the featured entertainment when Marshall Sehorn threw his riverboat party honoring McCartney. When McCartney returned the favor by flying 125 of his New Orleans pals to California for his own boat bash aboard the *Queen Mary*, the Meters were on board. "McCartney just wanted to give back to all these people in New Orleans that he has a lot of love for," said Porter. The guest list glittered—the Jackson Five, Cher, Greg Allman, Paul Williams, and more, with a row of waiting limousines from Newport practically to Marina del Ray. "Everybody who was anybody was sitting in and jamming that day," recalled Porter, who shared a mike with the former Beatle and his wife, Linda.

It was not the last of the Meters' involvement with British rockers. The Rolling Stones, having heard about the Meters via McCartney, hired them to open several of their 1975 "Tour of the Americas" dates. There were other memorable moments in the seventies, including a date in Chicago backing Professor Longhair. Toussaint and Dr. John were also on the bill, and the show was recorded for public television. ("Actually, Fess didn't like the Meters as a band," confessed Porter. "As a keyboard player, he and Art would run into each other a lot and he thought that Leo played too much. But most of the time in order to get me and Zig, he had to take the whole band.")

In 1975, the Meters put out a new album for Reprise, "Fiyo on the Bayou," that captured some of their greasiest funk. It was a heady period. "Some of the attitudes changed," said Art. "You know, heads went to swelling up." All four original Meters wanted more of a say in the direction of the band. In addition, Porter, by his own admission, was heavily into drugs.

Their growing popularity did nothing to solve their money problems. The band was under contract to Toussaint and Sehorn, who made deals for them with record companies. Toussaint and Sehorn also owned the company that published their music and the studio where they booked time to record. The financial arrangements made with artists by record companies, then and now, were structured to benefit the publishers and studio owners before the artists saw any real money.

Typically, record companies would give groups an advance to make an album, but charge all recording costs and touring costs against their royalties. Thus, Toussaint and Sehorn could make a nice profit by signing a deal for a Meters album with Reprise, a subsidiary of Warner Brothers, and then pocketing the cost of managing, publishing, and recording them. Artists in such a situation (and that includes all but the biggest) wind up with what is known in the record business as a "shortfall." Because their bills are larger than their advance, they owe the label money until they collect enough royalties from album sales to offset their shortfall. "Fiyo" sold 88,000 copies, a respectable number for a local band in New Orleans, but a meager number in comparison with the likes of James Brown, and certainly not enough to erase the shortfall owed to Warner's.

The Meters' success carried with it the seeds of the band's destruction. The group's next album, "Trick Bag," was released while the Meters toured Europe with the Stones, but it did not sell any better than their previous releases. At this point, the group, which had added Cyril Neville on percussion, left Toussaint and Sehorn behind. It chose to make its "New Directions" album in San Francisco with producer David Rubinson, who had worked with the Pointer Sisters and Herbie Hancock, among others. With the participation of the Tower of Power horn section, "New Directions" merged powerful West Coast riffs and Meters rhythmic soul into a fine, pulsating hybrid.

But what some believed was the Meters' best album was destined to be its last. The band was still deeply in debt to Warner Brothers and was squabbling with Toussaint and Sehorn over alleged cost overruns. The band then had a disastrous experience with "Saturday Night Live." The show was scheduled to take place live in San Francisco at Mardi Gras time in 1977. The Meters were scheduled to appear first, but when several members were missing at the dress rehearsal, the producers pushed back their slot to the final minutes. The show ran overtime, and the band never did appear on camera.

The "Saturday Night Live" fiasco was the breaking point. Art, the core of the Meters, quit first, followed by Cyril. Soon the performers, Toussaint, and Sehorn were mired in a variety of lawsuits over money and ownership of the name "Meters."

How could things go so wrong? Mostly, it was a matter of money. "We were probably one of the most successful [New Orleans] groups of our time, and every time we played we got deeper in debt. We were the most famous broke band that ever was!" laughed Porter. In the late seventies and early eighties, Nocentelli and Modeliste moved to Los Angeles, and Porter did a lot of session work.

There was never a question of their influence, even when funk, as practiced by bands like Booker T and the MGs and James Brown, nearly drowned in the tide of disco. Acts as diverse as the Jackson Five, George Clinton and his Funkadelic colleagues, and Prince clearly listened well to the sinuous syncopations of the Meters. As rhythm, rather than melody, became more and more central to soul music, the reputation of the Meters soared. Furthermore, the group was just too good to disappear. Seven years after the breakup, the foursome was persuaded to play a "reunion" date to kick off the New Orleans World's Fair. There were several more reunions until Neville, Nocentelli, and Porter finally settled their suits with Toussaint and Sehorn. The terms allowed the three to use the band's name again. By 1989 they were playing regularly once more as the Meters. (Modeliste, who did not settle, was replaced by David Russell Baptiste on drums.) After their torrid "official" return performance, *Times-Picayune* reviewer Scott Aiges raved, " 'Fire on the Bayou' came roaring from the stage in a version that went from being refined to fire breathing to relentless." The group still sounded a lot like the "old" Meters but with new twists. Besides favorites like "Fiyo" they did blistering covers such as "Thank You Falettinme Be Mice Elf Again" that made listeners swear that the Meters, not Sly and the Family Stone, had done the original version. "We've all matured a lot musically," said Nocentelli. "The people who hear the Meters now will hear more than any audience has before."

In fact, they could hear individual Meters, considered masterful studio musicians, in other configurations. Porter, by now clean and sober, did session work with people like David Byrne, fronted his own band, Running Pardners, and was invited onstage when he came to hear such headliners as Harry Connick, Jr. Nocentelli was in demand as ever on records by stars like Etta James.

As for Art, the Meters' breakup led to an even more exciting development. He created a new band by teaming up with all three of his brothers.

FIRST FAMILY—THE NEVILLE BROTHERS

The Neville Brothers came together as a formal musical group in 1977, but in a larger sense the family had been part of the city's R&B heritage since the fifties. As mentioned before, Art, the eldest (born in 1937), had his first hit with the Hawketts in 1954, while Aaron (born in 1941) began singing with a group called the Avalons in 1956. Charles, the second oldest (born 1938), got his musical feet wet playing saxophone in the Dew Drop Inn house band.

But it was Cyril, the youngest brother (born in 1948), who articulated most forcefully the historical connections between the Nevilles and New Orleans culture, Cyril who made it a point to steep himself in the city's diverse musical antecedents.

"The essence of our music is like the essence of New Orleans," Cyril said. "It's African, American Indian, French. It's military, because there was a lot of military stuff happening here with parades, and the military drum cadences got mixed with African cadences." The result, he liked to emphasize with a mixture of amusement and annoyance, was "this thing the record industry can't put a label on."

The Neville Brothers toiled for many years in the music business, dealing with physically punishing day jobs, grinding tours, hit singles that provided only fleeting fame, drug problems, and prison terms. Thus, the Nevilles represent not just the amalgam of musical styles that have converged on New Orleans, but the struggle of the African American working-class family in the post–World War II South.

Art described the Nevilles as both a family and a "tribe," one that included their uncle, George Landry, who was Big Chief Jolly in a Mardi Gras Indian group called Wild Tchoupitoulas. The family originally lived on Valence Street in the thirteenth ward, a working-class, racially mixed "Uptown" neighborhood not far from Tipitina's. Then, during World War II, they moved to the Calliope housing project. The clan eventually moved back Uptown; Art's house on Valence Street was to become the tribe's informal headquarters.

From the beginning, the brothers (along with their sister, Athelgra) were surrounded by music. "When people came to visit, they brought a harmonica or guitar or a record," recalled Charles. "If people were playing cards, somebody was singing or playing something." Before she married Arthur Neville, Sr., their mother, Amelia, and George Landry, her brother, formed a dance team. Apparently they had a shot at a professional career with Louis Prima, a white New Orleans band leader who later made a name for himself in Las Vegas. But the parents of Amelia and George vetoed their plans because they didn't want them to go on the road at a young age. Arthur Neville, Sr., was a Pullman porter and also worked as a cab driver and as a merchant mariner.

Art was the first of the brothers to become a performer. In high school, he and brother Charles, along with friends, formed a group called Turquoise. Art moved on, though, when another band, the Hawketts, invited him to become their lead singer. Not surprisingly, since the Hawketts were based in the ninth ward, home of Fats Domino, a fair distance away, the group, which was much in demand for proms and high school dances, specialized in Domino tunes. "I used to eat, sleep, and drink Fats Domino," said Art.

After the Hawketts' "Mardi Gras Mambo" became a hit (it is still played on the radio at Carnival time) Art's voice caught the attention of Specialty Records chief Art Rupe. Rupe brought Art into the studio as a soloist, where he made several singles, including "Cha Dooky Doo," produced by Harold Battiste, and "Ooh Whee Baby," neither of which made much of an impression on record buyers. Then, in 1958, Art signed on for a three-year hitch in the Navy, and brother Aaron took his place for a time in the Hawketts, who were still playing local gigs. Art's biggest solo hit, as mentioned before, was the 1961 Allen Toussaint ballad "All These Things."

Meanwhile, Charles, whose instrument was the tenor sax, went on the road at the age of fifteen, playing in a band that was part of the Rabbit's Foot Minstrel Show. Although he performed behind such blues and R&B headliners as B. B. King, Bobby "Blue" Bland, Ray Charles, and Johnny Ace, he also picked up a heroin habit. Needing money constantly, he stole. "All the people I knew who were using, they were shoplifters, so they taught me the trade," Charles said. He was caught and served time in 1958 and again in 1960. Despite his drug episodes, Charles was the most adventurous Neville, intellectually and physically. He liked to read, was curious about faraway places (he lived for a long period as a jazz musician in New York as well as in Oregon), and served the most complete musical apprenticeship, playing R&B, swing, and cool jazz during his career.

Aaron, on the other hand, was the yodeling Neville. Asked

when he knew he had a special voice, he laughed and replied, "When the doctor slapped me and I said 'aaa-aaaaaah-an-aah,' " at which point he sang a typical melismatic Aaron Neville floating falsetto note. Only a year old when the family moved to the projects, Aaron grew up listening to a strange mélange of doo-wop, gospel, and cowboy music. As a child, he loved both Pookie Hudson, lead singer of the R&B group the Spaniels, and Sam Cooke. "I got turned on to him the first song he made with the Soul Stirrers," he said of Cooke. "It was a thing called 'Any Day Now' and I've been singing it ever since."

At the same time, young Aaron loved to play cowboy with friends and absorbed music from country/western artists ranging from the Sons of the Pioneers to Gene Autry and Roy Rogers, complete with yodeling. Next came his doo-wop phase, when he joined brother Art and other youngsters harmonizing on street corners, imitating the likes of the Spaniels, Orioles, and Clovers, whose sound so permeated the airwaves in the fifties.

Art and Aaron both learned early that singing could get them somewhere. Art won local talent contests, and Aaron could sing his way into basketball games without paying. "My favorite song was 'The Wheel of Fortune.' I used to sing it to whoever was on the door, and they'd let me in," he recalled. Once the family moved back uptown, Aaron attended Cohen High School and joined the Avalons, a group that performed locally at an amusement park. He also began appearing at the Driftwood Lounge on Bourbon Street with a band that included Snooks Eaglin on guitar.

By 1959, Aaron was a high school graduate, a married man (he had met Joel, his wife, in high school), and a convicted felon. He had fallen in with a fast crowd and wound up serving the first of several jail terms. This one was six months for auto theft in the parish prison. It was there that he acquired a dagger tattoo on his cheek, as well as experiences that he utilized in songs such as "Jailhouse," which he recorded in 1967:

They come up here skippin' and jumpin'
But you know that they won't last long
One day they gonna wish they was a baby boy
In their mother's arms.

The prisoners, he explained, protected one another. "I always have been big, and I had a partner named Melvin. We would stop the older cats from messing with the youngsters coming in. There was nothing to do but sing and fight."

Once he was released, Aaron was steered toward Joe Banashak's Minit Records by his friend Larry Williams. (Some New Orleanians claim that Williams, who later committed suicide, was involved in a burglary ring, and that its activities landed Aaron in jail.) In 1960, as the label got rolling, Aaron recorded Toussaint's song "Over You," as well as "Every Day," a tune that, like "Jailhouse," he wrote behind bars. "Over You" was a regional hit. Unfortunately, subsequent releases, several of them quite wonderful, such as "Get Out of My Life," "Let's Live," and "Waiting at the Station," did nothing. In between gigs, Aaron put food on the table by working as a truck driver and dock worker. For Art, too, a hit single like "All These Things" (1961) was not enough to support a family, so Art put in his daytime hours on the docks.

Even Aaron's biggest solo did not signal a permanent change in fortune. In 1966, he made a single for Parlo, a local label owned by saxophonist Red Tyler, among others. It shot like a rocket up to Number 2 on the R&B charts, perhaps because the lyrics, ostensibly about love, also conveyed a Black Power theme thoroughly in sync with the civil rights movement. The song was "Tell It like It Is."

As popular as "Tell It like It Is" was, it did not make anyone rich. In fact, Cosimo Matassa went into hock to promote Parlo's parent company and the label soon collapsed. Aaron got ten thousand dollars for a quickie LP built around the song and toured major halls like the Apollo Theater in New York. Yet once the tour was over, the money stopped coming in. "Tell It like It Is" is now revered by sixties soul fans, but the fact is that everyone connected with the hit emerged quite disgruntled. To make matters worse, Aaron and Art, who was in the "Tell It like It Is" touring band, learned while on the road that their father had died.

Back in New Orleans, Art Neville regrouped. He formed the Neville Sounds, soon to become the Meters. (Leo Nocentelli had also been in Aaron's touring band.) At first, Aaron and Cyril, still a teenager, were among the group's vocalists. But after a while Aaron and Cyril, who developed a close relationship, broke away to form their own act, the Soul Machine.

Seven years younger than Aaron, Cyril approached music from a new generation's vantage point. His instrument was the conga drum and he absorbed the Afro-Caribbean stylings of the Mardi Gras Indians through his attachment to his uncle, Big Chief Jolly. As he matured, Cyril infused his own music with reggae and Latin rhythms. He also developed an acute political sense of the injustices perpetrated against African Americans.

Instead of charging ahead, though, the various Nevilles seemed to be dancing in place for the next several years. Art had the most success with the Meters. But Aaron, whose producer was the magic man Toussaint, endured a frustrating period. His ethereal voice made banal songs like "Where Is My Baby" and "She's on My Mind" sound good, and good songs like "Hercules" sound terrific. Yet in an era that saw the rise of so many great male soul singers (Otis Redding, Sam and Dave, Smokey Robinson, Marvin Gaye), Aaron Neville temporarily faded from view.

The Soul Machine tried its luck both in Nashville for a few months and in New York, where Aaron and Cyril teamed up briefly with brother Charles. They called themselves the Wild Tchoupitoulas. As Cyril described this new permutation of Nevilles, "We did a thing with the Indian songs—Charles on sax, me on congas, Aaron on piano. Charles had his horn cases and we had a shopping bag with the tambourines and cowbells and a washboard sticking out of it. We would catch the subways like that." But the tribulations of the Nevilles continued. In the sixties, Charles had skipped town after being arrested in New Orleans for possession of two joints of marijuana. In 1972, he returned to serve his time. He spent three years in Angola.

By the mid-seventies, the personal and collective future of the Neville Brothers looked bleak. The Meters broke up. Aaron was a one-hit wonder, who became a part-time longshoreman with a heroin habit; he performed occasional dates at the Club Alhambra. Charles was an inmate in one of the most notorious state prisons in the country.

The death of their mother, killed in 1975 by a hit-and-run driver, could have been the last straw for the Nevilles. Instead, it was the catalyst for a new beginning.

According to Charles, Big Chief Jolly wanted his nephews to carry on the Mardi Gras Indian tradition by making a record of traditional tunes. He also reminded the brothers that their parents had always wished they would work together as a band. "So the next year everybody came together," said Charles. They went into a studio in 1976, with the Meters backing them, and put out an album on the Island label called "The Wild Tchoupitoulas." It did not sell a lot of copies but it was a revelation to the Nevilles. As Cyril told one writer, "It was like a family reunion. To play in a band with all my brothers and my uncle too was like heaven."

Whether viewed as an interpretation of Mardi Gras Indian folk tradition or as a soul / funk album, "Wild Tchoupitoulas" (pronounced chop-ah-TOO-las) was a remarkable testament to New Orleans' varied musical strands. There was R&B, doo-wop, reggae, and Caribbean drumming in the compositions, but a distinct Indian-chant bent to the lyrics. It had a beat and you could dance to it. Songs like "Hey Pocky Way" were also perfect for audience participation. The Nevilles were on their way.

However, they were still under contract to Toussaint and Sehorn, who produced the album and who held publishing rights to a number of "Wild Tchoupitoulas" songs. The Nevilles had to threaten lawsuits, but they soon won their recording freedom. Out on their own, they made their first album under the name "The Neville Brothers" on Capitol in 1978. Already a favorite of other musicians, the brothers opened shows for the Rolling Stones in Europe.

A rousing effort produced by rock veteran songwriter and arranger Jack Nitzche, who had a hand in many of Phil Spector's hits in the sixties, "The Neville Brothers" got little promotion, and did not make a dent on the national scene. Nor did the best of their early albums, "Fiyo on the Bayou," released on A & M in 1981. "Fiyo" was made possible in part by Bette Midler, who raved about the band after hearing the brothers at Tipitina's. (The album was produced by Joel Dorn, who also produced Midler.) By way of a thank you, Aaron's version of the old Nat Cole hit "Mona Lisa" was dedicated to her. The song's lush arrangement included the New York Philharmonic strings, and Aaron sang the tune in a booth that was dark except for a single spotlight beamed on a photo of Cole himself. About the only criticism leveled against "Fiyo" was that it, like "The Wild Tchoupitoulas," sounded more Metric than Nevillish, especially on such Meters numbers as "Hey Pocky Way" and the title song. The hottest tune on the album, "Fiyo" featured a chorus that included Cissy Houston and her teenaged daughter, Whitney. Leo Nocentelli's guitar also distinctively greased the melodies.

With this album, the Nevilles came into their own musically, if not commercially. Aaron and Cyril brought their unique dual presence to the harmony on "Brother John." The brothers' Caribbean tinge was never illuminated more beautifully than on Jimmy Cliff's "Sitting in Limbo." And Aaron's doo-wop roots were well displayed on "The Ten Commandments of Love." All the elements were there—they simply were not noticed at the time. Indeed, in 1989, *Rolling Stone* paid the album belated homage by naming it one of the hundred "greatest LPs of the eighties."

Disappointed by the mediocre sales of the record, the Nevilles stayed active by playing clubs like Tipitina's, where they drew a loyal, growing, and increasingly white audience. Their appearances at Tipitina's have become legendary. Each performance was an eclectic mix—Aaron's inevitable "Tell It like It Is," Indian chants, reggae, even Stephen Still's "Love the One You're With." Sometimes they would do a spiritual medley, sometimes old R&B, and occasionally Aaron would throw in his favorite novelty, the "Mickey Mouse Club" theme song! Purple T-shirts with a crown and the band's name on it sprouted on students throughout the Tulane and Loyola campuses.

The band again appeared as the opening act for two Rolling Stones shows in the United States in 1982. In 1984 a live album, "Neville-ization," was released by Blacktop, a local label. By 1985 the band had a cult following that went beyond New Orleans, but breakout success eluded them, possibly because of what one magazine described as "the band's unsavory reputation and tough look." Another magazine declared bluntly, "Before they cleaned themselves up, the Nevilles were thieves, thugs and junkies," a characterization the brothers did not dispute. Aaron, Charles, and Cyril did indeed battle drug addiction. Art was philosophical about the band's negative image. "Hey, man, we couldn't help it if we looked like we were gonna take you out," he shrugged.

When they got a deal from EMI, they put out an album, "Uptown," deliberately designed for middle-of-the-road airplay. Among the guest artists who appeared on it was Keith Richards. Although spiced with material like the Jimmy Buffett rocker "Midnight Key" and sugared with a cover of "Drift Away" by Aaron which eclipsed Dobie Gray's original, the 1987 release went nowhere.

Still, the brothers kept showing up—at Tipitina's, on soundtracks, in cameos of films like *The Big Easy*, and especially at the Jazz and Heritage Festival, where they were headliners. What finally put the brothers over the top, in terms of national recognition, was the timely combination of a finely crafted album, "Yellow Moon," in the spring of 1989, and Aaron's smash duet with Linda Ronstadt, "Don't Know Much," released late the same year.

The group had begun work on "Yellow Moon" in 1988. At the helm was Daniel Lanois, the heralded producer of albums like U2's "Joshua Tree," who had his New Orleans studio draped in Spanish moss to make the Nevilles feel totally at home. A & M Records captured attention for the album by releasing one of the songs, "Sister Rosa," as a single, along with a video that was a surprise hit on MTV. Written by Cyril, the most political of the brothers, it was a rap-influenced tribute to Rosa Parks, the civil rights pioneer. As Cyril explained, "I have children who are eighteen, sixteen, and seven, and they all listen to rap music. When I found it was hard for them to remember their homework but easy for them to learn rap songs, Daryl (Johnson) and I decided to take our African-American history, put it to a beat, and rap it out. It's desperately important for kids today to have a better outlook on themselves than we had when we were growing up."

"Yellow Moon" also contained shimmering solos by Aaron— the lead on "Will the Circle Be Unbroken," Dylan's "God on Our Side," the reggae-flavored title cut "Voodoo," and a version of "A Change Is Gonna Come" to rival that of Sam Cooke's. Some fans might have felt cheated of the dance-fever drive that powered the Nevilles' live performances, but it had other virtues, particularly its social and political statements on ghetto life. Former jailbirds, doo-woppers, and show-biz veterans they might be. Nevertheless, as the brothers gained popularity, they brought their social consciousness to the fore and were active in charities for the poor and the homeless. Here, they were asking to be thought of not only as New Orleans' best classic R&B band but as serious anti-war black nationalists.

More important, in terms of the music business, "Yellow Moon" made a marketing statement: it reached the *Billboard* pop charts and sold 800,000 copies worldwide. The breakthrough was capped by Aaron and Linda, who reprised their duet during the Grammy show on prime-time TV and collected the award to boot.

The Nevilles' 1990 follow-up album, "Brother's Keeper," was the culmination of the union of the four brothers on record. From the first bars of "Brother Blood," they sounded supremely confident in their ability to project funky music that was also socially conscious. Almost all the songs were written or co-written by family members. Aaron once again weighed in with his otherworldly sound and spirit on "Steer Me Right" and "Fearless," while Art contributed "Sons and Daughters," a brooding ghetto morality play. Cyril took a major leap forward in songwriting with "Jah Love," composed in collaboration with U2's Bono.

The album did not really break new musical ground but, like "Yellow Moon," it sold well, and the band's bookings grew dramatically around the U.S. Although some fans might have been disappointed when the Nevilles showcased only a few of its tunes in their live shows, preferring to stick with a predictable play list of safely rehearsed older numbers, the Neville Brothers clearly had surpassed their cult status.

Meanwhile, Aaron recorded a new solo album, "Warm Your Heart," with Linda Ronstadt and George Massenburg as his producers. "My heart is with the innocence of the fifties," he said, and it was this innocence, as much as the tasteful production, that made the album a huge success. With it, Aaron staked his claim to a place among the greatest sweet soul crooners—singers like Clyde McPhatter, Smokey Robinson, and his early idol, Sam Cooke. The carefully chosen songs, including his favorite hymn, "Ave Maria," made for a stirring reentry into the mass market sweepstakes. One cut, a remake of the Main Ingredient's pop-soul hit "Everybody Plays the Fool," floated to the Number 2 slot on *Billboard*'s Adult Contemporary singles chart. An astonishing twenty-five years after "Tell It like It Is," Aaron Neville had finally shed the stigma of being a one-hit wonder.

His brothers branched out too. Art was reunited with the Meters. Charles had a jazz group, Diversity. The group featured a classical harp, cello, and violin along with sax and other jazz instruments playing everything from bebop to funk. Cyril formed the Uptown All-Stars, which played more reggae and world beat—oriented music. In addition, the next generation of Nevilles was in the process of stamping its imprint on the city. Charmaine, Charles's daughter, began appearing regularly at clubs, doing a unique imitation of Louis Armstrong plus lovely, jazzy vocal adaptations of all kinds of other material. Ivan, Aaron's son, became a polished songwriter and keyboardist. He contributed to the brothers' albums, did a great deal of session work in Los Angeles and toured with Keith Richards. A rap group, Def Generation, was formed in the late eighties, featuring various grandchildren and their friends.

For Art, Charles, Aaron, and Cyril, family came first. In the wake of "Warm Your Heart," Aaron chose to continue to tour with the Neville Brothers, not as a solo act. "Success to me is being together as brothers and still looking out for each other," he said. "We lived together as kids and now we're taking care of each other as men. I may get more attention than them but it's still Neville, the Neville name."

Were these mushy sentiments just hype, coming as they did from an improbable source, a menacing ex-con with an angelic voice? Not to his fans, much less his brothers. "There are things that happen with a family that would break another organization up. We wouldn't let it happen," avowed Cyril.

"Yellow Moon" and "Brother's Keeper" ordained the Nevilles indisputably as the leaders of the New Orleans pop renaissance. The stardom won by Aaron courtesy of Ronstadt was simply an extra help in introducing the band, live and on record, to a much broader national audience. The words to "Brother Blood," written by local poet Ron Cuccia, defined as well as anything what Art has called the "voodoo music" of New Orleans synthesized by these committed siblings:

> I've got drums of the jungle, drums of the street
> Drums of the Indian chief
> I've got the fire of the gospel, a river of blues
> And I got the soul of belief
> And I keep trying for everything
> It's been a long, long road
> I've got a song that's about to explode
> I was born to the beat that pounds like the heat
> And I've got the drums of the spirit.

IRMA THOMAS AND LESSER SOUL QUEENS

Irma Thomas is the paradigm of a talented artist who is not a household name nationally, but who is revered regionally as the finest female vocalist of the bayous. With just one national hit, "Wish Someone Would Care," in 1964, she was one of the southern soul women who "sang big and charted small," to borrow writer Gerri Hirshey's phrase. A singer with the pipes and punch of Etta James and Esther Phillips, Thomas was never able to equal their success. She spent years in California, waiting for the break that never came.

Like most of the R&B singers of her generation, Thomas came to singing via church. She was born on February 18, 1941, in Ponchatoula, Louisiana, but her family moved to New Orleans when she was still an infant. Her mother belonged to the Sanctified church, while her father was a Methodist. Irma herself attended many churches. "The church was a social gathering for blacks during segregation," she said. "That was your focal point, your form of entertainment."

The music of her childhood, however, was much broader than just gospel. She spent a lot of time with her grandmother, who lived in a rural area, and she grew up initially with the country and western "hillbilly" music that she caught on the radio. Once she was back in New Orleans as a schoolgirl, she heard everything, from brass bands at Mardi Gras to John Lee

Hooker (a favorite of her father's) to Mahalia Jackson to Clyde McPhatter and Ruth Brown. A local movie house featured a vaudeville show once a month, where she was enthralled by such acts as the Coasters. "My mother said I was always drawn to music. I was so independent I would leave the house and she'd find me at the corner bar, playing records and dancing," she recalled.

Her own performing began in school choral groups in the sixth grade. A teacher convinced her to enter a local talent show, and she came in second. She was taking piano lessons, but her teacher informed her mother that her money was being wasted because all little Irma wanted to do was sing. She never consciously made it a career choice; her ambition was to become a schoolteacher. But her formal education ended abruptly after the eighth grade. She was fifteen years old and pregnant.

Thomas has never been coy about her early years. "I was sexually promiscuous," she said straightforwardly. Her parents insisted on a shotgun wedding with a young man who may or may not have been the baby's father. After a second child, the couple separated, and Irma moved back with her parents, living at home until her third child was born.

At eighteen, the young mother of three got a job as a waitress at a club where Tommy Ridgley and his band played. One night she asked to sing a few numbers. Ridgley obliged, and Irma sang, among other songs, one called "Teenage Love." The club owner was less than thrilled, and fired her for neglecting her tables. Ridgley then hired her to sing with the band, but her debut was not exactly a financial windfall. "I made two dollars the first night and had to give it back to put gas in the car to get home," she said with a smile as wide as the Mississippi.

Soon she joined another band and toured throughout the Gulf area, playing one-nighters at small black clubs from Baton Rouge through the Florida Keys, getting fifty dollars a night and thinking it was big money. Meanwhile, Ridgley introduced

Mardi Gras, 1885. *Credit: The Historic New Orleans Collection*

Jelly Roll Morton. *Credit: New York Public Library*

Louis Armstrong and his Hot Five. *Credit: New York Public Library*

Sidney Bechet, Claude Jones, and Armstrong. Credit: New York Public Library

New Orleans Rhythm Kings. *Credit: Hogan Jazz Archive*

Tuts Washington. *Credit: Rick Olivier*

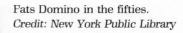

Fats Domino in the fifties.
Credit: New York Public Library

Fats Domino with Doug Kershaw.
Credit: Rick Olivier

Professor Longhair.
Credit: Hogan Jazz Archive

Little Richard.

Allen Toussaint and Lee Dorsey. *Credit: Rick Olivier*

One of Allen Toussaint's autos. *Credit: Rick Olivier*

James Booker. *Credit: Harriet Blum*

Mac Rebennack as Dr. John, the night tripper. *Credit: New York Public Library*

The Meters. *Credit: Rick Olivier*

The Neville Brothers.

Irma Thomas. *Credit: Rick Olivier*

Dewey Balfa. *Credit: Rick Olivier*

Beausoleil. *Credit: Rick Olivier*

Zachary Richard. *Credit: Rick Olivier*

Clifton Chenier. *Credit: Harriet Blum*

Buckwheat Zydeco. *Credit: Rick Olivier*

Harry Connick, Jr.

Wynton Marsalis.

her to the owner of a local label, Ron Records, and she cut a single, written by Dorothy La Bostrie (the "Tutti Frutti" lyricist), called "(You Can Have My Husband But Please) Don't Mess with My Man." The naughty tune turned into a regional hit in 1959. It looked as if young Irma Thomas was on board the express train to R&B success.

Somehow, though, her career got stalled. While she tried to stay close to home to tend to her children, she spent her share of time on the chitlin' circuit, playing gigs that coincided with payday for hard-working sharecroppers and laborers. "They were weekend jobs, and we had good turnouts, because to get in the door was only a couple of bucks," Irma recalled. The bands she sang with often could not afford the fancier black hotels; they sometimes stayed in transient houses that the band gave the name "whip shacks."

In 1961, she joined forces with Allen Toussaint and Minit. Although he wrote a number of wonderful songs for her, she was never able to latch onto the same kind of breakaway hit that Ernie K-Doe and Lee Dorsey had. Nevertheless, songs like "It's Raining," "Ruler of My Heart," and "I Done Got Over" became staples of her repertoire. Thomas liked the camaraderie that existed in those days among her fellow artists, like Aaron Neville. But it was Minit, not Thomas, who made the money off her singles. She never got a dime in royalties until she co-wrote "Wish Someone Would Care."

That plaintive ballad, recorded on Imperial, made Thomas a charted artist at last. It crept up to Number 17 on the singles chart in early 1964, and kept Irma in business, playing small clubs and more fraternity parties than she would care to count. In 1966, she went to England on a punishing three-week tour. It was in this period that an original of hers, "Time Is on My Side," was covered by a group of British boys who were so devoted to black music they called themselves the Rolling Stones, after a Muddy Waters song. The Stones' version was a hit; Irma's original was forgotten. Meanwhile, the English tour was so strenuous she lost her voice completely. "My throat specialist told me that I had a choice of doing one of two things," she recalled. "I could shut up for three months or I could get an operation." She decided on the rest cure. Afterward, she learned how to sing correctly, projecting from her diaphragm.

By this time the Beatles, Rolling Stones, and others had captured the airwaves of American radio, making the Toussaint-inspired New Orleans tracks of that era sound dated. Soul music, on the other hand, was making great leaps forward, with southern singers such as Otis Redding (who covered Irma's "Ruler of My Heart"), southern studios in Memphis and Muscle Shoals, and northern record companies such as Motown and Chess leading the way. In late 1967, Chess offered Irma Thomas a contract and brought her to Muscle Shoals for a three-day recording session.

"Of course, I was a bit excited. Who wouldn't be? Chess was a hot label at that time," she said, pointing out that such soul singers as Etta James, whose "Tell Mama" was a huge seller, were on the label. Unfortunately, Irma discovered that once she went into the studio, Chess had total control over her material. The Chess producers picked the musicians (some of the most illustrious players of their day, including Spooner Oldham on keyboards and the Muscle Shoals horn section), the songs, and the arrangements. Irma was pushed into doing "Security," an Otis Redding tune that Etta James was recording at just about the same time, as well as other songs she felt she was not suited to.

To make matters more complicated, Chess wanted Irma to sign an exclusive agency contract that would have granted the label 25 percent of her earnings. She balked. After the one album got a so-so response, her relationship with Chess came to an end.

Artists are not always objective judges of their work. Thomas believed she did a "lousy job" on some of the Chess sides. Yet, as a recent CD reissue of that album demonstrates, her performances recorded in Muscle Shoals were fabulous. "Cheater Man," an uptempo soul classic, was among the tunes longtime fans of Irma Thomas still request at concerts. But as far as Thomas was concerned, her encounter with Chess was merely another bruising battle with greedy businessmen.

She returned to New Orleans and continued to play the regional club circuit. In terms of the record industry, she seemed doomed to be forever the bridesmaid, never the bride. When Hurricane Camille smashed onto the Gulf Coast in 1970 and wiped out a number of the clubs she regularly appeared at, Irma took it as a sign. Leaving two of her children with their grandmother, and sending the other two ahead to an aunt, she packed her belongings in a U-Haul and moved to Los Angeles.

For a year and a half, she worked her day job selling auto parts at Montgomery Ward, and sang only at a few weekend gigs. As she viewed it, she had a responsibility to raise her four children; "I didn't have time to worry about a career," she said. When she did venture into the West Coast recording scene, she found that it was a culture permeated by drugs. When a producer friend brought her to a lavish party filled with "the in-crowd," she was there "thirty minutes and I was ready to go." What's the problem? her friend asked. "I don't like what's going on," she said, referring to the open use of drugs. "He thought I was a bit strange," she remembered.

Irma never seemed to have any luck with men. The next phase of her life began, as she put it, when she "met another crook." She was getting bookings in Anchorage, of all places, and especially in the Bay area, thanks to a small agency. She soon moved to Oakland, although she was careful to arrange a job transfer from Montgomery Ward to another one of its stores. After an unsatisfactory and short alliance with Atlantic Records, the "crook," a homeboy from New Orleans, began to arrange engagements for her in her hometown. He made some unethical deals with places like the Marriott Hotel, and Irma found herself playing several weeks there for nothing in order to satisfy the man's debts. However, almost before she realized it, she was returning to New Orleans for as long as five months at a time. "My poor kids were literally raising themselves back in Oakland. I didn't think it was fair to them," she said. More important, she finally met a good man named Emile Jackson, a New Orleanian who did not want to live in California.

Thus, in 1976, Irma Thomas returned from exile to the Crescent City. Although she was getting plenty of gigs, including a spot at the Jazz and Heritage Festival, she was still nervous about giving up her day job. The only reason she did not ask for a transfer from Montgomery Ward, she noted with a laugh, was because they did not have a branch in New Orleans.

Thomas was able to make a living from music, however, thanks to steady club bookings and private parties. Jackson became her manager. She made several albums with small labels, including the disco-flavored "Safe with Me" for RCS and "Soul Queen of New Orleans" for Maison de Soul. The latter album was notable for, among other things, one of Irma's humorous monologues, spoken in the middle of "Wish Someone Would Care," which were a highlight of her live shows.

A typical monologue would begin with the band playing softly in the background as Irma began musing out loud. "I've had the opportunity to talk to a lot of ladies," she might start. "And I've discovered that we women have a lot in common. We've also discovered that a man is a *hell* of a thing. Ah, but we women are a hell of a thing too. . . ." She reminds male two-timers that "yours is a non-profit item and ours is a profit-making item." As a strategy for women to strike back at a man who is cheating, she suggests "you meet him at the door with nothing on. And have your clothes lying on the bed. And just for a wee bit of color, have a rose in your teeth. . . . He won't know whether that man just left or you were just coming in. Guaranteed, he won't hang out again!"

The first time she did one of these risqué "raps," she said, was when she had to kill time during a Baltimore performance in the sixties until James Brown, the headliner, showed up. However, touches like this made her a cherished commodity on stage.

Until the late eighties, it seemed as though New Orleans was keeping Irma as its own special secret. Eventually, fans and other singers, such as white soul singer Rita Coolidge, managed to put the word out. Like the Neville Brothers, Thomas began to capture a larger white audience, without changing her soul-oriented persona. Indeed, many of Thomas's memorable shows, such as those on the riverboat *President,* were totally integrated. She brought a down-home, house-party atmosphere to her appearances, as young and old, black and white, danced in front of the bandstand and waved white handkerchiefs to the beat. Afterward, Jackson would sell T-shirts to fans and Thomas, a star without any pretensions whatsoever, would inscribe each one personally in indelible ink.

Thomas's first Rounder album, "The New Rules," in 1986 signaled a small breakthrough. Writer Jeff Hannusch had touted her to the Massachusetts label, which until then had not recorded a single New Orleans black female vocalist. Out-of-town bookings and trips to Japan and Europe followed, including one overseas tour with Solomon Burke's band that she would be happy to forget. (Burke, she said, bullied everyone, "and he's supposed to be a preacher!") Her European fans not only knew every cut on all her records, they could name the sidemen on fifteen-year old discs. By the time her second Rounder album, "The Way I Feel," was released in 1988, Irma was getting bookings regularly at clubs like the Blue Note in New York and Johnny B's in Cambridge, Massachusetts, and at Benson and Hedges blues shows in major cities.

Thomas marked her fiftieth birthday in 1991 with a typically warmhearted gesture—a benefit for the homeless. She had every reason to celebrate; after nearly three decades, Irma Thomas was a survivor and a star. She reigned in her hometown as "the Soul Queen of New Orleans." Streamlined and fit, her personal life stable, she had found a secure niche among new, young, white audiences, who appreciated ethnic music, she believed, because they realized that in her material (and in that of other revitalized performers, such as Ruth Brown) "there are stories being told, not just sounds being made to music."

In the Crescent City, the affection she generated was palpable. Invited to appear at everything from Christmas tree lightings to the Super Bowl, she was treated like a beloved neighbor, not just a local celebrity. There was an approachable quality to Thomas, both on and off stage, and she cultivated it, inspired by one of her idols, Pearl Bailey. "She showed me you could be a star and still be human," said Thomas. Those qualities were especially apparent at every South Louisiana performance. When she launched into a favorite tune like "I Done Got Over," and her fans started singing along with hankies aloft, Irma Thomas elicited over and again the joyous spirit of the second line.

In Thomas's wake came several other powerful female voices. One was Leigh Harris, a white woman who used the stage name "Lil Queenie," whose distinctively hoarse voice was heavily influenced by soul music. Next there was a former gospel singer, Marva Wright, with a sanctified sound and a hip-shaking, full-figured "Big Mama" presence.

Perhaps the most enjoyable of the female singers whose popularity rose in New Orleans after Thomas was Marcia Ball, a white blues belter with roots in both Louisiana and Texas. As she loved to tell fans, she lived in Austin but ate in New Orleans.

Ball was born in Orange, Texas, and grew up just over the board in Vinton, Louisiana. (The exact opposite, she pointed out, of Clarence "Gatemouth" Brown.) Taking after her grandmother, who played ragtime and Tin Pan Alley songs on the piano, Marcia began taking piano lessons at age five. She grew up on a steady diet of local music, including Fats Domino and Clifton Chenier, although when she attended Louisiana State University in the late sixties, it was already the psychedelic era. Irma Thomas, whom she first heard when she was thirteen and Thomas "wasn't that much older," was one of her idols. The soul singer made a huge impression on young Marcia because she was very pregnant at the time. Years later, Ball said, the image of Irma singing while pregnant helped her face surprised audiences when she herself performed in the same condition.

Ball made her first appearances as a singer in those college years when a friend asked her to sing harmony with her. That led to her joining her first band, Gum, as well as to many trips to New Orleans from Baton Rouge to soak up the various music genres.

After college, she settled in Austin, a town that was quite a bit more liberal toward "hippies" than Baton Rouge. But as her career took shape she was obviously more of a Louisiana artist than a Texas one. "New Orleans is a piano town and a horn town," she once explained, "Austin definitely is a guitar town." During the seventies and eighties, she became the queen of what she termed the Crawfish Circuit—the clubs not only in New Orleans but in Lafayette and other off-ramps of Interstate 10 between the Crescent City and Houston. Her first album, the 1977 "Circuit Queen" recorded in Nashville, billed her as "Freida and the Firedogs." But she soon reverted to her real name and more comfortable Louisiana stylings. In 1984, Rounder released its first Marcia Ball album, "Soulful Dress." Still, she insisted that the highlight of that year for her was finally getting to meet Irma.

In concert and on record, Ball drew heavily on Louisiana material. Her piano style contained hints of Fess, Fats, and Huey Smith, while her choice of songs included works by Mac Rebennack, Red Tyler, and Chenier. (Her second Rounder album was "Hot Tamale Baby," the title song being a Chenier cover.) As she began writing more of her own tunes, Ball paid tribute to her favorite New Orleans performers. The song "That's Enough of That Stuff," for example, was written as a "video" of a surreal Tipitina's scene played in her mind:

> We got Fess down playin' on a jukebox
> We got Fats on the radio
> We got Tuts on piano in the living room

With the Nevilles singin' Iko Iko
Queenie in the kitchen
Rads in the hall
Everybody havin' a ball
Irma and Smiley, Shirley and Lee
Ain't no body tellin' me that—
—That's enough of that stuff
I'm gonna tear the whole place up
I gotta little too little
Got a lot too much
That's enough of that stuff

One silky-voiced male singer in the New Orleans R&B vein whose longevity—and lack of national recognition—challenged that of Irma Thomas was Johnny Adams. A locally acclaimed vocalist with an enormous range, Adams's popularity rarely crossed the Louisiana border. Nevertheless, for more than three decades he has entertained hometown audiences with his gospel-tinged renditions of songs like "Reconsider Me."

Born in 1932, Adams was a member of the gospel group the Soul Revivers when songwriter Dorothy La Bostrie convinced him to try an R&B song she had written. She steered him to Ric Records, a local label, which released his version of her song "I Won't Cry" in 1959. That single, produced by Mac Rebennack, and follow-up ballads were regional hits. Another single, "Losing Battle," which was written by Rebennack, reached Number 278 on the national R&B charts in 1962. It was about then that Adams, along with several other New Orleans artists, decided to seek greener pastures up north.

Berry Gordy's Motown label was just gearing up what was to become the country's most successful black hit factory. The artists drove to Detroit and auditioned for Gordy. The entrepreneur was impressed by Adams's supple tenor and graceful falsetto. But on the verge of a deal, Gordy got word from New Orleans that Adams was already contractually obligated to Ric. Years later, Adams declared that Ric's owner, Joe Ruffino, had "tried to hold on too tight." The deal with Motown was scotched.

A disappointed Adams returned to New Orleans, Throughout the sixties he moved around from label to label without much success until 1968. That year, his version of the ballad "Release Me" was picked up by Nashville recording mogul Shelby Singleton and turned into a major R&B hit. A second effort, "Reconsider Me," which was a country song performed by Adams with a soul twist in the manner of Ray Charles, was even bigger. Despite these accomplishments, Adams was never able to turn his hits into a lasting national identity.

"No voice coach, ever!" he bragged. Adams was able to show off his three-octave power to audiences in local clubs, at the Jazz Festival, and, in the eighties, to ecstatic listeners in Europe. Always nattily dressed, never giving less than his all, he delivered a repertoire ranging from soul standards like "Stand by Me" to his own hits to blues like "Garbageman," which he co-wrote with Muddy Waters. In the eighties, like Thomas and other New Orleans favorites, he got a new lease on his recording life from Rounder Records. Both "Room with a View of the Blues" and "Walking a Tightrope" were CDs of such smooth vocalizing they would be used as models for younger urban bluesmen like Robert Cray.

Approaching the age of sixty, Adams was still going strong, with his only competition as a soulful balladeer coming, at least in the eyes of many New Orleans R&B buffs, from Aaron Neville. Once Neville hit the charts again with Linda Ronstadt, Johnny Adams was probably the finest talent that still remained relatively undiscovered on the New Orleans R&B scene.

5 Ragin' Cajuns

CHANKY CHANK—
FOLK MUSIC OF SOUTHERN LOUISIANA

Cajun music is as American as sweet potato pie—even though it consists of songs sung in French by the descendants of Acadians from Canada, using, among other instruments, the accordion, introduced to Louisiana by German settlers. It is a rural folk music as rich in tradition as the hillbilly music from the hollows of Tennessee and West Virginia or the blues of the Mississippi Delta. Like its black cousin, zydeco, Cajun music originated far from New Orleans, in the flat farmlands and swamps of South Louisiana east of the Texas border. The Cajun people were not really assimilated into American society until this century. But they boast a longer history on this continent than every North American ethnic group outside of Indians and the original French colonials of Louisiana. It is amazing that this mostly poor, shabbily treated minority group has been able to keep its melodies alive; what's even more exciting is that a fair share of the music has a beat and you can dance to it.

The word "Cajun" is derived from Acadie, as their first settlement in the New World was called. The Acadians came from France to Canada in 1604, three years before the first settlers established Jamestown in what would become the United States.

In 1713, the English gained permanent possession of the territory and renamed it Nova Scotia. Then in 1755, the French were expelled from Canada. Families were split apart, children were separated from parents, and thousands were herded onto ships bound for American locales where they weren't wanted. After a decade of heartbreak and wandering, as described in Longfellow's poem "Evangeline," many of them migrated to South Louisiana, which was still under French rule.

There, on the bayous Lafourche, Teche, and other waterways, their culture flourished again. The Anglos, Spanish, German, Afro-Caribbeans, and others in their region adopted French as their primary language. Some settlers thought of the town of St. Martinsville as "le petit Paris." The most adventurous settlers then pushed into the western cattle-ranching and sugarcane "prairies" of South Louisiana where, in the early 1800s, they established farms and commercial centers not unlike American western towns.

Cajun music first took hold in these isolated outposts. After long days of work in the fields, families would gather to sing "complaintes," which were long, unaccompanied story songs of their French heritage. These ballads, along with drinking songs, love songs, and lullabies, dealt with the old life and the new frontier, with wars and heroes, holidays and work, and the battle of the sexes in much the way early country music did. Dancing was as popular here as it was in urban French Louisiana.

Gradually the Cajuns integrated Anglo and black material into their music. Their dances began to include jigs, reels, and hoedowns, as well as the waltz and other traditional dances. Once the violin was introduced in their region, they typically played their tunes on two fiddles, one playing lead, the other a more rhythmic bass line. In the nineteenth century, the music came into its own at dances held in homes, which were the leading recreation among Cajuns. Nicknamed "fais do dos," the gatherings got their name from the phrase that means "make sleep." The premise was that once children were asleep, the adults could start having fun.

The distinctive Cajun fiddle sound developed, according to folklorist Barry Jean Ancelet, because "the most popular musicians were those who were heard." Thus "fiddlers bore down hard with their bows and singers sang in shrill, strident voices to pierce through the din of the dancers." The accordion, which came via German settlers about 1840, was picked up by the Cajuns because it was so much louder than the fiddle. By the time the first recordings of Cajun music were made in the late 1920s, dance bands consisted of accordion as the lead instrument, fiddle, and triangle, known as the "ti fer," short for "petite fer," or little iron. Sometimes a guitar was added for rhythm. The washboard was used for extra percussion and this was adopted by blacks in the region as the frottoir, or rubboard, worn on the chest and played with spoons or bottle openers.

Until late in this century, almost all Cajun musicians were part-timers who farmed or plied a trade for a living while collecting a few dollars for dance-hall gigs or records. The first ones to gain a following were those who made the earliest records. Recording companies such as Columbia and Victor began scouring South Louisiana in the late 1920s, looking for musicians who could make discs that would help them sell record players. Usually they would set up shop in a New Orleans hotel, bring in a bunch of musicians and pay them twenty-five dollars per song.

The earliest Cajun record—"Allons à Lafayette" and "The Waltz That Carried Me to My Grave"—was made by Joe Falcon on accordion and his wife, the former Cleoma Breaux, on rhythm guitar. This unique duo (Cajun women rarely took part in any activity outside the home) was popular in the simple dance halls that had sprung up outside towns from Lafayette to Beaumont and Port Arthur in East Texas. Around the same time, Cleoma and two brothers recorded the first version of another classic, "Jolie Blonde."

Besides Joe and Cleoma Falcon, Dennis McGee and Sady

Courville were among the best-known practitioners of the older, traditional Cajun styles. McGee, a farmer and barber born in 1893, and Courville, a furniture salesman born in 1905, were twin fiddlers and brothers-in-law. In their spare time they would play various country dances. Then, in 1927, a local booster arranged for them to make their radio debut on a Shreveport station, and the next year set up a recording date in New Orleans.

The recording session meant a big leap not just in their celebrity but in their means of transportation. Dennis later explained that the two men originally traveled from place to place via horse and buggy. But New Orleans was far away, so Courville bought a Model T to get them to the city. Unfortunately, some time later, however, that very auto almost cost him his job. They were returning home to Eunice from a dance when the car ran out of gas, leaving them stranded. By the time Courville arrived late in the morning at the furniture store where he worked, his boss was so angry he demanded that the young man make a choice: sell furniture or play music. Courville, with a family to support, quit making music for a while.

Meanwhile, McGee had become a barber. As his own boss, he could continue to make time for music. He made many appearances and several records with a black Creole accordion player and singer named Amédé Ardoin. They met when they were both sharecroppers for the same farmer, who encouraged the white fiddler and the black accordionist to play side by side. Later, both wound up living in Eunice. Although segregation was in force, the two played together at dances, some restricted to whites, some for blacks only. Ardoin, who apparently succumbed to alcoholism, died in 1941. But McGee rejoined Courville late in life to make a handful of albums and to appear at the Washington, D.C., national folk festival, when both the century and the men were in their seventh decade. Courville died in 1987. McGee played right up until his death in 1989 at the age of ninety-six.

The isolation and cohesiveness of Cajun society was shaken at the start of the twentieth century by nonmusical developments. The discovery of oil near Jennings in Southwest Louisiana brought an influx of jobs, industrial installations, and strangers to the area. Then World War I introduced local boys to the cities and countries beyond the bayous. Perhaps the most pernicious change came in 1916, when French was banned in public schools and students were forced to learn English. Poorer Cajuns and black Creoles of the region, many of whom spoke nothing but French, were looked down on as backward hayseeds by the moneyed Anglos, not to mention by their own more cosmopolitan offspring. "Being French became a stigma," in Ancelet's words.

The result was a steady push toward assimilation in the years before World War II, even as Cajun music was getting wider exposure on vinyl. The period between the wars saw Cajun culture diluted as musicians left the accordion behind, added English to their songs, and mixed in large measures of infectious Texas swing music.

Cajun music of the thirties was dominated by string bands, many of which jumped on the western or "Texas swing" bandwagon. The kings of Cajun swing for decades was a group from the oil patch known as the Hackberry Ramblers. Luderin Darbone on fiddle and Edwin Duhon on guitar were the core members of the group from the time they teamed up in 1933.

Darbone grew up in East Texas but met Duhon after his family moved to Hackberry, a Louisiana oil town. Both their fathers were oil workers. At the insistence of his mother, Darbone had learned to play the violin "by notes," although he said he threw his reading skills away in order to become a freer dance-hall player. The two young men, along with a second guitarist, began playing dances near home for the important extra money—three to five dollars a night, "big money then," as Darbone recalled.

Soon a Beaumont, Texas, radio station, which had remote

broadcasting facilities in Lake Charles, gave them a regular slot. At first, they played 80 percent "English" tunes, in a swing style that owed much to the hugely popular Bob Wills, the leading swing fiddler of his day. (On a few of their records, they even punctuated verses with a Wills trademark, the cry "Aaah hah!") Just a few numbers in the Hackberry repertoire were traditional Cajun songs. "We didn't know if people would like us or not, because in those days we were sort of replacing the accordion bands," noted Darbone.

As it turned out, people loved them, and after they moved to Crowley, Louisiana, they made their first recordings for RCA's Blue Bird label. As they caught on with listeners, the local Montgomery Ward outlet in Lafayette hired them to play in the store three times a week. The store renamed them the Riverside Ramblers after a brand of tires they sold. Back in the studio, they cut a few Cajun sides in French for Blue Bird as the Hackberry Ramblers, then a few hillbilly numbers as the Riverside Ramblers. Over an incredible fifty-plus years, Darbone and Duhon, along with various sidemen, were among the foremost cultural ambassadors, introducing Cajun music to millions of country fans in the Southwest and beyond. They were still going strong in the nineties.

Another fiddler who made an immense contribution to the spread of Cajun music was Harry Choates. In the same hybrid tradition as the Hackberry Ramblers, Choates merged traditional songs with a lively brand of swing that caught on quickly throughout the oil patch. Born in Louisiana but raised in Port Arthur, he was among the first to intersperse English phrases in French songs. He also started a whole body of work that one folklorist summed up in the sentence "You left me to go away to Texas." Choates was perhaps most famous for recording what was to be the hit version of "Jolie Blonde" in the forties. The song, first recorded by the Breaux family in 1928, came to be regarded as the Cajun national anthem.

Choates, like other southwestern performers right after World War II, rode the honky-tonk circuit en route to regional, if not national, fame. His life was cut short at the age of twenty-nine after he was arrested for nonpayment of child support in 1951. He died, either from the effects of alcoholism or, as some suspected, from police mistreatment, in an Austin jail.

Another short-lived, tragic hero of Cajun music was Iry Lejeune, an almost blind songwriter who spearheaded the revival of the accordion in the late forties and fifties. Lejeune was a country boy from the Pointe Noir area, northwest of Lafayette, who carried his instrument in a flour sack. His works probed the heart, telling poignant tales of love and loss, of suitors made miserable by fathers of girls they yearned for, of prison and hard labor. Going against the tide of hybridization, he sang in French in the plaintive, crying style of older, non-amplified vocalists. Lejeune died in an auto accident in 1954, at the age of twenty-six. But others, including Nathan Abshire, Lawrence Walker, and Aldus Roger followed his lead in the return to accordion-based Cajun music.

However, by the time the postwar generation came of age, French had begun to die out. Youngsters who attended school in the thirties had been punished for speaking the language of their heritage in school. By the forties and fifties, children might learn French from their grandparents, but few in their parents' generation kept to the old ways of back-porch playing and singing. The children of the war years and later paid more attention to R&B, country and western, and rock and roll than they did to Cajun folk music.

Thus, the next group of Cajun performers such as Belton Richard, a popular singer, and D. L. Menard, a guitarist and singer, Jimmy C. Newman, guitarist, and Doug Kershaw, the first "modern" Cajun country star, exhibited a form of split musical personality. They recorded in both French and English but were in some ways more in the Nashville orbit than in that of Lafayette. Menard, for example, born in 1932, once explained that he had never heard a Cajun band until he was in his teens. Raised in a farming family, he discovered music by listening to a Texas country station on a battery-powered radio. The batteries regularly died each year about a month before the family harvested its cotton. D.L. (whose actual first name was Doris) had to wait until the cotton was picked and sold to get money to buy a new battery.

After World War II, Menard's family moved to town so his father could work in a sugar refinery. At the age of sixteen, Menard saw his first live band and begged the guitarist to teach him how to play. He was such a quick learner than within a few months he joined a band with a regular gig in Abbeville. His first recordings were in French, and he wrote his most famous song, "Back Door," in French; it was an instant hit on record and he and his band often were asked to play it as many as seven times a night. "Back Door" became second only to "Jolie Blonde" as a Cajun classic, yet Menard won a measure of fame singing in English, billed as "the Cajun Hank Williams."

Similarly, Kershaw initially became a regional star as a youngster on the "Grand Old Opry," performing with his brother Rusty as a duo called, naturally enough, Rusty and Doug. In the late sixties, his appearances on Johnny Cash's television show allowed him to make a big comeback, this time with billing as a "Cajun hippie." Something of a clown, Kershaw, who sang and played the fiddle, was nevertheless the real thing—a native of the swamps near the Gulf of Mexico where his father was a trapper and alligator hunter. He was the first to gain a national audience for a blend of country and Cajun sounds. A headline about him after he made yet another splash on an all-Cajun tour in the eighties said it all: "He was Cajun before it was cool."

Despite the headlong march of assimilation, a handful of folklorists recognized the unique qualities of early and traditional Cajun music and made it their business to preserve them. These purists collected old songs, put together collections of lyrics and music, and kept the flame burning. Their interest persuaded the Newport Folk Festival producers to send a scout to South Louisiana in 1964 to round up musicians who could introduce this authentic regional style at the famous Rhode Island extravaganza. Thus, Gladius Thibodeaux, Louis "Vinesse" Lejeune, and the Balfa brothers made the journey to Newport that summer. Without realizing it immediately, they helped kick off a full-blown return to roots that Dewey, one of the Balfas, turned into a crusade.

Dewey Balfa, an exuberant fiddler with a robust, if untutored, singing voice, was an unlikely candidate for Cajun Pied Piper. Like most of his peers, he was a part-time musician; he drove a school bus for a living. He had just high school education, yet he was a natural teacher.

The Balfa musical saga began in the community of Grand Louis, near Mamou. The brothers grew up in a French-speaking household of nine children. Their father, a sharecropper, played the fiddle, and as a child, Will, the oldest son, would try to imitate him by rubbing sticks together. His father finally decided to get the boy his own instrument. The family was so poor that he traded a pig to a neighbor in order to get a used fiddle for his eleven-year-old son.

Dewey, ten years Will's junior, was born in 1927. As a boy, he was punished and beaten for speaking French on school grounds. But his musical education was in English as well as French; he was exposed to country music by such masters as Jimmy Rodgers and Ernest Tubb via the radio. Still, he was much more influenced by the informal dances and performances of his father and brother. The men would perform songs that had been passed down from generation to generation.

When he reached his teens, Dewey left home to work in a World War II shipyard in Texas and then served in the merchant marine. During this time, he played Texas swing music with other amateurs. When he returned home to Louisiana he got married, and, in addition to farming, he sold insurance and drove a school bus to support a family that eventually included five children.

One afternoon shortly after the war, Will, who had given up music to devote his time to farming, was surprised by a visit from his father and a neighbor, the owner of the Wagon Wheel Club in town. The club owner plied Will with drinks, prevailing upon him to show off his fiddling skills. He convinced Will to perform with his brother Dewey at the club that Saturday night. It was just the two brothers plus a guitar; they were paid five dollars. The audience was enthusiastic, and so the Balfa Brothers Band was officially launched. For the next few years, the brothers played different dance halls, usually barnlike buildings with bleachers along the wall where dancers could sit down and rest during breaks. Their repertoire was made up of old-time songs delivered by dual fiddles, with a bass, triangle, guitar, and occasionally drums. Some tunes were unfamiliar to others; they were family numbers like the "Balfa Waltz," which they had learned from their father.

At the time of his Newport appearance, Dewey had never played outside the Gulf Coast and had never seen an audience larger than could be collected in a dance hall. Lafayette newspapers, caught up in the rush to Americanization, belittled the music. Local papers, perplexed by the choice of what they considered unsophisticated bumpkins for a spot at Newport, predicted in print that the Balfas would be booed and laughed off the stage. Who could possibly want to hear a bunch of hicks playing "chanky-chank" music? (The phrase, originally one of derision, referred to the tinkle of the ti fer, or, as Dewey described it, "the sound of two hogs stuck in a fence.")

At Newport that year, his fellow performers included Peter, Paul and Mary, Mississippi John Hurt, Doc Watson, and Johnny Cash. They had never heard of the Balfas and vice versa—except for Cash, whom Dewey had heard in a local bar. The Cajuns were nearly overwhelmed by the sheer size of the crowd. "I didn't know where I was. I couldn't understand what was going on, with so many people together at one time," Balfa recalled. Not only wasn't he booed, he was welcomed with open arms by the folk fans as an authentic artist. "We got a standing ova-

tion, and it blew my mind," he recalled, with a catch in his voice. "Can you imagine a crowd of seventeen thousand people giving a standing ovation to music that is supposed to be nothing?"

Returning to Louisiana, Dewey Balfa made up his mind to fight the forces that he felt wanted to "smother" his language and his culture. "I became very disturbed at not being accepted as an American," he later explained. So he began visiting colleges, universities, festivals around the country, "talking about my culture, my music, and doing workshops." When people asked whether the music could survive, he replied, "Not unless we bring it to the Americans of tomorrow."

It was not an easy sell. In an era where television brought mainstream culture into the Cajun home, "nobody listened to the stories of the ancestors, the grandfathers, grandmothers." But Balfa, who eventually got grants from the National Endowment for the Arts and other organizations, was determined to acquaint them with the music of their forebears. How else, he asked, could they "preserve this culture that they don't hear?" He soon found an ally, a member of the next generation— Michael Doucet, the leader of the modern Cajun band Beausoleil. Doucet, who himself was in the process of exploring his roots, joined Balfa in lectures and demonstrations in the schools.

Their mission did not always succeed. "On one occasion, we were turned down by a principal in Southwest Louisiana who didn't want this music in his school," Doucet noted. But Balfa urged him not to lose heart, advising him, "You've just got to do what you believe in, even though people don't respect it. The reward will find you."

Ultimately, it did. Schoolchildren and even some parents responded. People began dusting off scratchy records they hadn't listened to in years. They started asking their grandparents to tell them old stories, and to revive the tradition of back-porch family musicales. Traditional culture—from the unique Mardi Gras parades on horseback, to informal "fais do dos," to meals featuring spicy gumbos and sausages and roast pig—

made a major comeback in the Cajun communities. A non-profit organization whose acronym was CODOFIL, the Council for the Development of French in Louisiana, focused new attention on teaching French in the schools. "I think it awakened a lot of people," said record producer Floyd Soileau, a longtime booster of Cajun music. "We had to raise a hoorah about it. It got a lot of closet Cajuns out in the street." People whose parents had tried so hard to become homogenized "Americans" developed a new pride in their stories, their language, and their cuisine, as well as their music.

The regeneration of French Cajun culture did not happen overnight. Ancelet noted that in 1974, when the first Tribute to Cajun Music Festival was staged, "we could have looked all year long for a young Cajun musician and never found one." Still, with the encouragement of Balfa, Doucet, and others, such as accordion maker and player Marc Savoy, the musicians multiplied. Soileau, for example, continued to issue "Saturday night honky-tonk" records, but Balfa "was insistent. He said, 'You've got to start recording some of the roots sound.' " And Soileau did. By the late seventies, the Festivals Acadiens, a weekend-long celebration of folk crafts, food, and music in a lovely public space in Lafayette, Girard Park, blossomed into an annual showcase for Cajun music.

The Balfas were rewarded for their efforts with gigs all over the country, culminating in invitations to Washington to play at Richard Nixon's and later Jimmy Carter's inauguration. They went on to triumph in Europe as well. Soileau remembered watching in amazement when an audience in Toulon, France, kicked aside the folding chairs halfway through a Balfa brothers concert and started to dance. "We said to ourselves, here it is, *France!* and they can relate to this music. It gave me one hell of a boost," he recalled.

In 1979, tragedy struck when Will Balfa and another brother, Rodney, who played guitar in their group, were killed in an auto accident. Dewey soldiered on, even after his wife died in 1980. At the start of the nineties, he was still performing

numerous concerts and festivals a year, in a group that included his youngest child, Christine, on the stage as triangle player and singer. "I think of the Balfa Brothers Band as a brotherhood of musicians, not just as the three or four blood brothers," he said. A much-loved figure, Dewey Balfa died of cancer in 1992.

The seeds sown by Dewey Balfa bore fruit musically even as the everyday, conversational use of French declined in Cajun country. Balfa was skeptical about some of the music. He and other guardians of the past regarded the unadorned, old-time music as an integral part of their Cajun identity. To them, innovation was less valued than the preservation of stories and folklife, which could then be transmitted to younger generations through song. Some preservationists resented music lumped under the umbrella term Cajun, when it was actually blues or rock with a French accent. Marc Savoy, for instance, blasted any aspect of "American" encroachment, in music or any other aspect of life, charging that some Cajuns were "turning their backs on a hot bowl of gumbo for a cold, tasteless American hot dog." Balfa compared modernizing the music to spicing up a snack food and calling it Cajun potato chips. But he knew he had allies, and Balfa was deeply moved by youngsters who insisted on playing acoustic French music in the old style.

One such player was Cory McCauley, a student at the University of Southwest Louisiana in Lafayette. An accordion player, McCauley and two other young men who played fiddle and bass formed a group called McCauley, Reed and Vidrine. They featured traditional numbers sung in French, which he had learned at family get-togethers. By the time McCauley reached his twenties, personalities such as Balfa and chef Paul Prudhomme had transformed Cajun culture into a national trend. His generation, said McCauley, was now saying, "Hey, what my daddy and my mommy do is not so bad. I don't have to go to McDonald's and eat cheeseburgers. I can stay home and cook food I raised and play the music of my grandparents."

McCauley, Balfa, and numerous of their Cajun brethren also shared traits as important as their music: they were emotionally outgoing, good-natured people whose response to hardship was a dose of dancing and general *joie de vivre*. Their zesty attitude was embodied in four-time Louisiana governor Edwin Edwards, whose rogue image did not prevent him from decisively defeating Klansman David Duke in the 1991 gubernatorial election. But Trent Anger, a Cajun writer, emphasized that his people's love of a good time was "not a state of euphoria that can be induced by the consumption of alcohol." It was instead "a condition of the mind and of the heart." Moreover, after seven generations in the United States, the Cajuns had resuscitated their traditions, an accomplishment few other ethnic groups have achieved.

TRADITIONALISTS AND PROGRESSIVES

At the very nadir of Cajun music in the sixties, when assimilation seemed like it would wipe out French song in South Louisiana, two boyhood pals from Lafayette were envisioning themselves as the Cajun answer to Keith Richards and Mick Jagger. Although they took separate paths, the two were destined to become leaders in South Louisiana contemporary music, a sound that had one foot in the older world of fiddles, accordions, and folk, and the other in the rock and roll that permeated their youth. Their names were Michael Doucet and Zachary Richard.

Neither was the first musician of Cajun background to spread the news about their locality beyond the bayous. In the fifties there was Bobby Charles, who recorded his own composition, "See You Later Alligator," only to see it eclipsed by a cover version done by Bill Haley and the Comets. In the sixties, Doug Kershaw and Jimmy C. Newman rode the Nashville express, expanding the reach of Cajun styles to country fans. Another promoter of early Cajun country/rock was a Houston barber turned disc jockey, Huey P. Meaux. He produced acts such as Jivin' Gene (he did not use his last name, Borgeois), who had a regional hit in "Breaking Up Is Hard to Do." In Ville Platte, Floyd Soileau developed the Jim and Swallow labels, which released various Cajun hits. There were black regional hits produced by independent labels in the area as well.

Nevertheless, no white artists before them produced as sustained a body of work as Beausoleil, the band led by Doucet, or as exciting a brand of Cajun rock as Richard. Their synthesis of Louisiana themes and instrumentation powered by a rock back-beat at once harked back to the Cajun past while laying a foundation for a viable future.

Doucet was the more intellectual of the two, and the first to deliberately return to his roots. He was born in Lafayette in 1951 and began learning the guitar in grade school. His father, an Air Force colonel, "plays the radio," as he put it, and his mother played clarinet. Both parents preferred jazz to other forms, but an uncle was a Cajun music man. Throughout his school years, though, Michael Doucet was very much a child of the times. He once listed among his influences Tennessee Ernie Ford and Elvis Presley. And when he began playing at the age of twelve with his friend Ralph Zachary Richard, the form was folk rock, in the manner of Bob Dylan. His instrument remained the guitar, not the violin.

Coming from a middle-class, assimilated family, Doucet spoke English primarily, but he did learn French at home. His awareness of things Cajun got a nudge when he was a student at Louisiana State University and took a course in American folk music, but Doucet remained in the folk-rock orbit. He and Richard put together the Bayou Drifter band, seeking with only minor success to get bookings in local clubs. Then, in the mid-seventies, both Doucet and Richard had an opportunity to play in France.

In the land of their ancestors, both men made a startling discovery; the younger French pop fans "accepted Cajun music as the new folk music," said Doucet. Indeed, at a French folk festival, he listened with fascination to "eight fiddlers playing 'Jolie Blonde' the old way," as he recalled later, "accompanied by a hurdy gurdy and all sorts of different sounds." The acceptance of Cajun sounds by Europeans had a profound effect on the young performer. "I began to understand what we had and what we stood for," Doucet said. At that juncture, Doucet and Richard set off on different routes in search of their ethnic identity, with both straying from the Anglo mainstream.

Upon his return to Louisiana, filled with an "incredible amount of energy," Doucet embarked on a fiddle pilgrimage. He was supposed to go to graduate school in New Mexico to study English literature. But, in his own words, he "traded Blake for Balfa and came home instead." Picking up a violin after a long hiatus, he apprenticed himself to older musicians such as Dennis McGee and Balfa and steeped himself in the legacy of his fiddling forerunners.

His decision to dig deep into the Cajun musical past came at an opportune time. Balfa and others were zealously building a new awareness of the Cajun heritage. Thus Doucet not only visited schools with Balfa, he got his own NEA Folk Arts grant in order to learn various fiddle styles. But that was only the initial step. In 1975, he formed a group to play traditional music in a contemporary setting with young instrumentalists. The name he chose for the band, Beausoleil (literally "beautiful sunshine"), resonated with history. It was the *nom de guerre* of Joseph Broussard, a captain of the Acadian resistance, who settled in Louisiana after the Acadians were chased from Canada.

The idea of a contemporary Cajun folk-music band was, at that time, risky business, a concept as far from commercial as one could get. Almost no one, especially those in his own age group, gave a hoot about ancient folk songs sung in nasal hillbilly-like voices accompanied by a whining fiddle. Still, Doucet recruited colleagues for Beausoleil such as Bessyl Duhon, an accordion, fiddle, and guitar player who came from a long line of Cajun fiddlers. The band was determined to carve out a territory it could call its own. Its goal was to seduce younger listeners—those who had never spoken French, who had never heard of Dennis McGee—back into the ethnic fold. In Doucet's words, "We thought, well, this is a really good thing. We can't lose it, so let's share it."

Beausoleil, in its earliest incarnations, did not win over everyone who heard one of its concerts. The band occasionally did such overlong improvisational takes on songs in live performance that they were called "the Grateful Dead of Cajun music"—and that was not meant as a compliment. Chris Strachwitz, who was building the important independent record label called Arhoolie, in California, said at the time, "Here's this incredible fiddler stuck in this mushy band."

Neither Doucet nor Duhon turned his back on rock and roll, however. In the same period, Doucet started a second band, Coteau, with Duhon on the accordion. While Beausoleil was acoustic, Coteau was electric—a rock band first and foremost. Indeed, with its French name and rock licks, it pointed the way for acts like Richard, Wayne Toups, Filé, and others who strove to carry Cajun rock to the millions of potential fans beyond South Louisiana.

Coteau broke up in 1977 without even making an album. Beausoleil, however, began to hit its stride as what Doucet called "the Cajun renaissance" took hold. He and Dewey Balfa had introduced plenty of schoolchildren to the old music. Dance halls had never gone out of fashion among older people. Cajun political and community officials contributed to the cause by importing teachers from Canada and Europe to teach French in local schools. Doucet and others also helped CODOFIL establish the Festivals Acadiens to spotlight the previously neglected treasure trove of Cajun musicians.

Perhaps most significantly, American "foodies" fell in love with a mountainous Cajun chef and his sizzling cuisine. "All of a sudden Paul Prudhomme burnt a fish and boom!" said Doucet. Because Prudhomme "used the word Cajun," in Doucet's opinion, the word finally won acceptance instead of derision. "The rest is history," concluded Doucet. "It really helped the musicians a whole lot."

Suddenly people wanted to hear accordions and fiddles, and songs sung in French, whether or not they were backed by drums and a modern beat or not. While Balfa, Savoy, and others stuck to standard older arrangements, Beausoleil provided a fresh take on those sounds with skill and spirit for the younger crowds. Onstage, Doucet was tireless, a rollicking performer who resembled a slimmer David Crosby with his walrus mustache and unruly tufts of hair above his ears. When he wasn't leading Beausoleil, he was sitting in with old-timers like Balfa and the great Creole team of "Bois Sec" Ardoin and Canray Fontenot, or joining Savoy and his wife, Ann, in yet another acoustic band, or encouraging newcomers like Wayne Toups.

Beausoleil took its crusade abroad, playing at a bicentennial exhibition in Paris in 1976 and touring Canada as well. It made its recording debut on the local Swallow label soon thereafter. Doucet put Floyd Soileau, the label owner, on notice ahead of time, guaranteeing him that the record, albeit in French, would be "like none you ever heard before." Soileau was game. "I'll turn you loose with the engineer. Just give me something we can both be proud of," he told Doucet. The album, "The Spirit of Cajun Music," lived up to that billing, consciously bringing together a mélange of medieval songs, jazz, Cajun ballads, blues, and waltzes. At the start of 1977, Beausoleil was invited to be among the popular bands that played at President Jimmy Carter's inauguration.

A while later, Doucet produced an even more eclectic Beausoleil album himself and licensed it to a Canadian company. But he wanted a U.S. version so badly that he bought back rights to the master tapes and beseeched Soileau to release it in Louisiana. Soileau's business was not doing that well; he demurred. Finally, Doucet plunked the record right down on Soileau's desk in his Ville Platte office. "I promise you won't regret it—put it out," Doucet begged. Reluctantly, in 1984,

Soileau agreed. The album, "Zydeco Gris-Gris," was destined to become one of Swallow's top-selling releases ever, and a Grammy nominee to boot. Beausoleil had by then stirred its eclectic blend of Cajun songs and saucy arrangements into a bubbling, danceable gumbo that appealed not just to Cajuns but to the much wider U.S. collegiate record-buying public.

On this and subsequent albums, Beausoleil was anchored by Doucet on fiddle and a stalwart group of sidemen including his brother David on guitar; Errol Verret, Joel Sonnier, or Jimmy Breaux on accordion; and Tommy Alesi on drums. On occasion a female vocalist, a steel guitar, and/or a second fiddle were added. Together they explored a universe of popular music all centered on an immediately identifiable Cajun core. By the late eighties their repertoire had grown to encyclopedic proportions, in line with Doucet's credo that "you can take any song and cajunize it." Whether reviving the old folk song "Paquet d'Epingles" ("Packet of Pins"), which Doucet dug out of the Library of Congress field recordings from 1934, or interpreting a Hackberry standard such as "Fais Pas Ça," or cajunizing Buddy Holly's "Not Fade Away," Beausoleil reached out into every corner of popular music and carried its fans merrily along.

Not every Cajun listener approved of this audacious journey. "You can't call it country any more," protested D.L. Menard. But Doucet argued that "if you play exactly like somebody did years ago, you're not playing yourself. That's not an evolution. That's a decadence." He was careful not to discard the old-time material entirely, playing often with the Savoys. In Doucet's vision, Cajun music could be "not just the two-step and the waltz, but the blues, the zydeco, the ballads, the Tin Pan Alley songs, accordion music," just so long as it maintained its link with its ethnic past. While resurrecting songs from old folk archives, he also wrote new songs. "We don't want to leave any of it out," declared the indefatigable troubadour.

If these moves were gambles, they paid off handsomely. By the nineties, Beausoleil had ascended to the status of young old masters throughout Louisiana, at folk festivals around the country, and at major industry events like the Grammys.

In the meantime, Doucet has pursued his own musical education, which encompassed everything from Bach to Lyle Lovett's droll Texas fables. "I'm kind of enamored with the fiddle," he said with a chuckle, "so my favorite thing is to listen to the unaccompanied violin partitas. I look at music as art, and sort of resent classification," he added. Whatever he might hear, however, is certain to be siphoned through a Cajun filter. Clearly, Michael Doucet spoke for himself when he sang, on one of Beausoleil's albums, "On a trouvé nôtre paradis dedans le sud de la Louisiane." (Our paradise is to be found within South Louisiana.)

No matter what Beausoleil performed, the band's style remained stubbornly, recognizably Cajun—in its instrumentation, its sense of rhythm, its hollering vocalizing. Doucet's childhood friend Zachary Richard, on the other hand, represented a whole different kettle of blackened fish. Even when he sang in French, played the accordion, or interpreted traditional tunes, Richard could not hide his rock-and-roll roots. As wiry as a water moccasin, radiating Jagger-like heat on stage, he presented a classic rocker's disarmingly dangerous sexual machismo, far different from Doucet's almost furry warmth. At one time an altar boy, later a brilliant student, he had swapped his intellectual leanings long ago in favor of show biz. The effect was dazzling to fans in three countries, but controversial in his own South Louisiana backyard.

A year older than Doucet, Richard was born in Lafayette in 1950, the only child of the mayor of Scott, Louisiana, and his homemaker wife. Like Doucet, he came from an assimilated family that was comfortably middle class. Like Doucet, he belonged to the last generation to learn French in the home, in his case from his grandparents. "The whole Cajun experience was a compartment of my life which was associated with my grandparents and with Sundays or holidays," he remarked.

Otherwise, his upbringing was "Anglicized." His parents' favorite music was that of the big bands.

Throughout his youth Richard reaped the benefits of belonging to South Louisiana's *haute bourgeoisie.* He was given art and music lessons at a very young age and by the fourth grade was first soprano in the Lafayette Catholic bishop's choir. Pop music, however, was as important as the church to this altar boy. First came New Orleans early rock and roll; then, when he was fourteen, "the Beatles hit Ed Sullivan and that was it," he said.

Richard's musical tastes followed the pattern of his peers: the Rolling Stones, Simon and Garfunkel, Eric Burdon and the Animals, and the Byrds were his initial loves. When he got to Tulane in the late sixties, a fellow student introduced him to Chicago blues. For Richard, like other young Cajuns, French music as "a parenthesis." They knew about Clifton Chenier, but when Michael Doucet and Zachary Richard practiced, they imitated the Stones, not zydeco.

Nor did the young Richard exhibit any special leaning toward things Cajun. A nearly straight-A student in college, he was expected to become a doctor or lawyer. For his junior year abroad in 1970 he went to Scotland, where he studied the history of white colonization of Africa. Then he began to veer from the mainstream. He joined the hippie rebellion by growing his hair long, and began playing rock guitar.

Upon graduation from Tulane, safe from Vietnam thanks to a high draft number, he traveled to New York to begin a career in music. His timing was excellent; in the early seventies, country rock, pioneered by the Byrds and carried forward by groups like Asleep at the Wheel, was growing in popularity. Fancying himself as legitimate southern rock singer-songwriter, Richard set out to become a star. He began by making a demo tape featuring Doucet on guitar. "I shlepped it to all the record companies in New York," he recalled, and struck pay dirt—or so it seemed—when Elektra, an important folk label, gave him a contract and a $2,500 advance.

Richard used some of the money to buy himself an accordion from Marc Savoy's shop. He was becoming curious about Cajun music. When the record deal turned sour, Richard, along with Doucet, accepted an invitation to play at a folk festival in France. Richard, too, was transformed by the experience. "We played in a duet situation for twenty thousand French people and they loved it," he recalled. Back home in Louisiana, the two formed the Bayou Drifter band, a rock ensemble with a French accent, but their expectations of becoming local heroes simply did not happen. The only fans who came to hear them, he said, were Quebecois and French schoolteachers vacationing in Louisiana.

In 1975, the boyhood pals parted ways for good. Richard was asked to play in Canada and at a Mardi Gras celebration in Mamou at the same time. He chose Canada, believing that there were greater opportunities in Montreal than in French Louisiana, where the music scene was still stagnant. His judgment was correct. Within a short time, he was a major attraction in Canadian clubs and on television. At an Acadian festival in New Brunswick, his heritage, as he put it, "grabbed me by the scruff of the neck and shook me up real hard." Soon, he blossomed into a full-fledged Cajun militant. In Lafayette bars, he insisted on speaking nothing but French, and insulted people who tried to talk in English. Once, upon arriving at the Canadian border, he tried to change his status from visitor to "diplomat of the Acadian people, coming to see my lost brothers." While driving one day on a freeway outside Lafayette, he began to think about a song telling how the Acadians were thrown out of Canada. The idea was so powerful, he said, that tears came to his eyes as he composed it in his head. "Awaken!" the song began. In stark descriptive images, the lyrics told of Acadians being warned about the English forces, who were coming to burn the French farms. The soldiers were about to run these hard-working people off their land "like cattle," and cast them "to the winds." Now, the lyrics declared, "I am left an orphan of

Acadia." Not long afterward, at a festival, he brought eight thousand listeners to their feet with an a capella version of this stirring anthem, "Reveille!" ("Wake Up!") The albums he made in Canada were all in French, even though the music remained undeniably rock.

Richard bounced back and forth between the two countries until the late seventies. "I was being a musical pinball," he said afterward, noting that while he performed traditional Cajun music on some albums, he did an about-face on "Allons Danser," a late seventies release that featured the Meters and paid homage to the Professor Longhair / New Orleans style of rhythm and blues.

Richard's credited his lengthy stays in Canada with allowing him to experiment and broaden his musical appeal. "There were no stylistic limitations placed on me," he explained. "I was known for being rhythmic and colorful—anything with a backbeat is pretty exotic to French Canadians." So he performed in French, playing traditional tunes along with his own compositions, seeking new ways to interpret old and new themes. He was very caught up in Canadian politics, especially the French separatist movement. He danced in the street in the seventies alongside French Canadians when key electoral votes were won by the separatists. By 1980, however, the movement was losing steam and so was the once-lively French Canadian music scene. Richard took note of Coteau, Doucet's band, which was developing a following for rock in Louisiana. Besides, Richard was having fits of homesickness. He longed to build his own house in Scott. So he returned to Cajun country, borrowed money from his father, started the house, and put together a new band featuring Sonny Landreth, a wonderful slide guitarist. For the next several years, he established himself on the "crawfish circuit."

His pinball days were not yet over. During the eighties, Richard was a hit at the Jazz and Heritage Festival almost every year, but he lived in Paris for long stretches, recorded for a French label, and made a name for himself in the pop-music ranks in France. He recorded an album, "Zach Attack," in 1984 in the first digital studio in Paris that was so full of both French and Cajun influences he viewed it as "schizophrenic." When he played Louisiana, he brought a French band to back him.

Admittedly, though, he did not set the world on fire as a "French" pop star. When Rockin' Sidney's "My Toot Toot" became an international hit, Richard sensed that his future lay on American soil. He moved back to Scott permanently in 1986. "I was at a point where I needed to make a decision in terms of my own identity," he said. On his first American album, "Zach's Bon Ton," released by Rounder in 1988, he even sang most of the songs in English.

Richard had always put on an incendiary live show, especially at the cavernous Grand Street Dancehall in Lafayette. In 1990, he finally got his chance to show off on a major record label, A & M. The result was "Women in the Room," a collection of original ballads and rhythm numbers, which won hallelujahs from critics. To promote the single from the album, a lively dance tune called "Who Stole My Monkey," A & M sent Richard on tour with Jimmy Buffett and gave out free cassette singles—with a rubber monkey dangling from each cassette.

Richard was aware that he might never be able to reconcile the two conflicting influences that inform his music. On the Cajun side, he acknowledged that he was "seduced" by his musical heritage and wanted very much to play in the manner of Iry Lejeune and others, but he simply was "not a traditional player." Instead, he analyzed his work as something he "stumbled on" in the process of "integrating certain elements of South Louisiana dance traditions, not only Cajun and zydeco but also New Orleans rhythm and blues, into a basic rock-and-roll format." A perfect example, he suggested, was his ballad "No French No More," which he called "a quintessential Cajun song" about the experience of a generation of Louisianians who were denied their language, but which nevertheless "in a musical sense is American folk rock," having more to do "with the Byrds than with Aldus Roger."

Zachary Richard might never satisfy Cajun purists or Anglo disk jockeys. Nevertheless, he looked toward artists with hybrid sounds such as Los Lobos, Robert Cray, the Neville Brothers, and Bonnie Raitt, and told himself that "one can have a significant career without radio airplay." Ultimately, he declared, "I'd like to be able to touch people with my songs, whether they know anything about Cajuns or not."

LE ROI, CLIFTON CHENIER

Clifton Chenier was to zydeco what Fats Domino was to New Orleans rock and roll—not simply a pioneer, but its biggest star. He just about invented zydeco, although he called it French music. Well, Debussy might not have understood this driving, soulful, percussive creation, but Ravel, that keen student of American jazz, would surely have enjoyed it.

What is zydeco? Imagine a Cajun band—fiddle, accordion, guitar, and triangle. Now subtract the fiddle and substitute a rubboard, which looks like a corrugated metal chest protector. Add a drum kit and perhaps a tenor sax, even a piano. With the accordion pounding out a melody and the other instruments providing an incessant two-step or waltz rhythm, imagine the leader singing an R&B-type fast tune or an old blues number using country, rather than urban, imagery ("I'm a hog for you, baby") in French. That's zydeco.

Clifton Chenier, as dynamic a performer as ever bestrode a honky-tonk stage, represented the eruption of a volcano of music that had bubbled among French-speaking black musicians in Southwest Louisiana for a century. The earliest blacks in Cajun country were slaves brought to the region from Africa and the Caribbean, who either spoke French themselves or learned it from the dominant whites. After the Civil War, large numbers became sharecroppers, just like the poor whites did. The earliest blacks, who called themselves Creoles, brought with them songs and chants that they first sang without instrumental accompaniment. But they soon became adept at both the fiddle and the accordion.

The first French black musician to make a record was Douglas Bellard, a fiddle player who added elements of blues to his songs. In the twenties and thirties, the best-known player was Amédé Ardoin, the accordionist who appeared at local dances and on record with Dennis McGee. This early music, referred to by French-speaking blacks as "Creole music," sounded more like early white Cajun music than anything else. (In recent years, the best-known players in this older style were Ardoin's nephew, Alphonse "Bois Sec" Ardoin, and fiddler Canray Fontenot.) But the blacks quickly absorbed blues sounds from the Mississippi Delta and inserted more lively rhythmic elements that gave the music a whole new vocabulary. At first, performers would clap their hands, stamp their feet, or slap spoons together. Then, someone began rattling a spoon (or a bottle opener) against a washboard, and the frottoir, or rubboard—the instrument that became the corrugated steel vest—was born.

By the end of World War II, blacks were calling this French-derived style, which assimilated influences from R&B as well as the blues, "la la music." Eventually, however, it got a new designation, either from an African word, as some believe, or from a phrase that refers to the lowly snap bean: zydeco.

Zydeco relates back to "juré" singing (pronounced joo-RAY), a style taken from the word "jurer," to testify. Juré singing was a form of music that was most common during Lent, when instruments and dancing were taboo. It consisted of both religious and secular shouts and call-and-response songs. One song used the sentence "Les haricots sont pas salé"—the snap beans aren't salty—alluding to hard times when there was not enough salt meat with which to cook the beans. Say the words "les haricots" aloud in Cajun-inflected French with its hard "r" and you can understand how, in print, it became "zydeco." A song about "les haricots" was recorded in the thirties by folklorist Alan Lomax for the Library of Congress. Even in its most primitive form, accompanied by nothing more than hand-clapping, it had a sound distinct from Cajun folk music. Nonetheless, it took Chenier, a farmer's son from Opelousas, to turn it into a regional phenomenon.

Clifton Chenier, born in 1925, grew up hearing his father play the single-row button accordion. From a friend, he learned to master the larger, more complex piano-key accordion. At the age of eight or nine, Clifton began to trail after a local accordionist and songwriter named Claude Faulk. As he later explained, Faulk and his fellow musicians "had an old Model A Ford with a rumble seat. When they'd pass my daddy's house to go play a dance, I'd jump in the back seat." The youngster would listen while people carrying cakes gathered at a private house, pushed the furniture aside, and began to dance.

At the end of World War II, Clifton followed his brother, Cleveland, to work in Lake Charles, a bustling oil patch town. There were plenty of jobs at the refinery there, and there were also opportunities for the two men to play local dances. Clifton sang and played the accordion, while Cleveland provided the rhythm on a rubboard. He already knew old French songs, and he had soaked up the blues from southern performers such as Muddy Waters and Lightnin' Hopkins. He was not an instant success. "It took a long time for me to get people to listen to my music," he later said. From 1947 through 1951, the brothers drove refinery trucks and spent their spare time playing in towns from Lake Charles to Beaumont. By 1952, he continued, "they started listening a little more," and by 1955, "they were really listening!" Chenier himself was listening as well—to the music of stars like Ray Charles and especially Fats Domino, both of whom clearly influenced his hoarse, urgent singing style.

As it happened, a talent scout was also listening. J. R. Fulbright of Elko Records was driving along a highway outside Lafayette one day in 1954 when he saw a crowd by the side of the road. In the middle of it, playing their music, were the Chenier brothers. Fulbright offered to help them cut a record. He brought them to a radio station in Lake Charles. The Cheniers recorded a single they called "Clifton's Blues" backed by "Louisiana Stomp," with Fulbright doing all the work; the station's racist white engineer refused to lift a finger to help.

The record sold well in the area, and masters were leased to Imperial. Soon Chenier was en route to California to record for Specialty, the label that made Little Richard famous. His first two Specialty releases, "Eh 'Tite Fille" and "Boppin' the Rock," did well along the Gulf Coast, and Chenier soon was touring full time with such blues and R&B stars as Lowell Fulsom, Jimmy Reed, and Etta James.

Chenier was not modest about the fact that zydeco was both great dance music and an important storytelling genre. "If you can't dance to zydeco," he told crowds, "you can't dance, period!" Still, the lyrics had meaning. "I like to hear something with ideas," he said. "Maybe your wife done walked off and left you. Why she left you? That's the point. . . . You did something you ain't had business doing." A lot of musicians, he went on, could make a decent record, but "they don't tell a story. You got to go through the mill for that." Performers like himself and B.B. King, Big Joe Turner, and Fats Domino, on the other hand, "them fellas can tell you something, 'cause they've been out there."

During the sixties, when assimilation ruled among Creoles and Cajuns alike, times grew hard for Chenier. He was forced to let his band go and he moved to Houston. He was barely getting by, playing small clubs and beer joints in the section of Houston called Frenchtown, when a producer, Chris Strachwitz of Arhoolie Records in California, heard him.

Strachwitz was taken to a little tavern by Chenier's friend Lightnin' Hopkins. "I couldn't believe it," Strachwitz recalled. "Here was this light-skinned black man with this huge accordion on his chest, and just a drummer, playing the damnedest blues I ever heard and singing it all in French."

Hopkins introduced Strachwitz to Chenier as a "record man." Immediately, Chenier beseeched the visitor to help him make a record. He had not recorded anything in nearly five years and he needed a single on jukeboxes so he could generate more work. Strachwitz could not turn Chenier down. He booked studio time. To his astonishment, Chenier showed up with an entire band. Unfortunately, the bass player's speaker was broken, the guitarist had an amplifier that started smoking, and Strachwitz wound up capturing a few songs with just the drums, accordion, and piano.

It was enough. The singles made that day sold well in Houston. It was the beginning of Clifton Chenier's golden years.

For the next twenty years, Chenier reigned along the Gulf and in Creole pockets of California. Depending on the audience, he might play southern blues, the latest soul hits, or his own "French" music, although he had to be coaxed into a zydeco mode. According to Strachwitz, "he was ambitious, and he knew his audiences." Chenier realized that zydeco might be his bread and butter in Louisiana and Texas, but he did not have much faith that it would catch on outside those areas. He was often reluctant to put more than a nominal French tune on an album.

Black churches, Strachwitz believed, were responsible for elevating Chenier to star status in the late sixties and for burnishing the Chenier legend. In California, where there were Roman Catholic congregations with a large number of Creoles, "priests found that in order to keep their Louisiana people happy they needed to get that music they loved," Strachwitz said. So they booked Chenier to play the church halls, a venue that made zydeco and its leading interpreter more respectable than they had been when Chenier was playing only in beer joints and dives. Whole families—parents, children, grandchildren—would turn out to hear him. The church halls in Houston and Louisiana followed suit.

It was not long before Chenier, a proud and tough-minded man, realized the churches were booking him on the cheap. He would agree to a $500 fee, then discover a hall filled with hundreds of people. At that point the artist demanded an extra $500 from the priest in charge before taking the stage. Later, according to Strachwitz, Chenier got even more savvy about fees and insisted on a percentage of the door receipts.

Whatever those churches or clubs paid him, Chenier put on a 150-proof show, sometimes a marathon of four hours and more, that covered the history of black popular music from country blues to R&B to soul to zydeco. His repertoire included local favorites such as Louis Jordan's "Caldonia," Joe Turner's "Shake Rattle and Roll," and Huey Smith's "Rockin' Pneumonia," covers from the Otis Redding and Ray Charles songbooks, plus his own compositions such as "Ça M'Appelle Fou" and "Hot Tamale Baby." "Old people come to my shows with canes, and at the end of the night they can't find 'em," he would boast in French to his fans.

Most critics agree that his records never fully captured the sweaty brilliance of his live appearances. A music writer named Ben Sandmel, who is also a drummer, found the live performances thrilling, even when the equipment was not up to par. One night in some joint in Southwest Louisiana, Chenier invited Sandmel to sit in; once he got behind the drum kit, he discovered the high hat was missing and the sticks were broken. Still, Sandmel discovered after a few hot, driving numbers that whether or not the hardware was good or poor, Chenier's sidemen were superb.

As Chenier hit his stride in the seventies, he and Cleveland traveled with a band that could match the star's energy. It began to feature a tenor sax, rarely heard before in zydeco, to further emphasize the link between zydeco and R&B. He also set up his own club out in the country near New Iberia, where his wife, Margaret, collected the cover charge nightly at the door.

Because the heart of his art was the live show, Chenier did not waste a lot of time in the recording studio. Strachwitz always had to nag him to include more French numbers. "That isn't what the kids like!" Chenier would argue. Most of the time, the band came to the studio with no clue about what they would be playing. "That's why all the numbers start with the accordion," Strachwitz noted. Chenier would say, "All right, boys, come on in, this is the way it goes," and begin an introduction. The others would then find their places behind him. In addition, he often refused to do a tune over again, having learned from fellow musicians like Lightnin' Hopkins that unscrupulous companies would issue alternate takes under different names while paying a band for just a single recording. Both at live shows and in the studio, Chenier could get ornery and physical, especially when he was drinking. At one date, he fired his entire band because he didn't like the way they were playing. At another, he threw a whiskey bottle at Cleveland. As Strachwitz remarked, "This was no string quartet."

By the eighties, Chenier was a hero to his own people in Southwest Louisiana. Furthermore, he began to reach a much wider audience. His appearances at the New Orleans Jazz and Heritage Festival gave him exposure to foreign producers, who booked him for such prestigious gigs as the Montreux Festival in Switzerland. Chenier was finally being paid off for the faith he had in himself. "I know one thing: the way I was playin' that accordion it was going to go somewhere, and that's what it did," he said later. "It took me all the way from here to Israel."

He enjoyed his trips to France, not just because fans there were so receptive but because he could communicate with them. He loved telling about one European tour with a bunch of blues artists including Earl Hooker and Magic Sam, who kidded him about French. Then, in France, they went to a café and a waitress asked, in French, "Can I help you?" He replied, "Oui, Madame," and proceeded to order a big meal of "les oeufs . . . et du pain." But the others were struck mute. Chenier then ordered for his non-speaking friends; they were presented with a platter of raw fish. "And from that day on, all our tour in Europe, they never would tease me no more," he chortled.

In the final years of his career, Chenier was a royal personage. He won his title on a trip to Europe. There was a contest featuring five hundred accordion players. Chenier could imitate their styles, but they couldn't copy his, and he was awarded a crown. From that moment on, he unabashedly billed himself as the King of Zydeco, and often wore a crown during appearances. As his status grew, he inspired others, including Rockin' Dopsie and Boozoo Chavis, to play their own accordions with renewed dedication. Both those men began getting gigs around the South and nationally. Chenier's success also affected established players in other styles. Canray Fontenot, the handsome old-style fiddler with the beautiful smile, was a few years older than Chenier. He recalled running into the "king" in a bar, and telling him he was thinking of giving up music. Chenier was so distressed at the news that he turned to the other patrons and declared, "Among us Creoles, find me another black man who can do what he does with the fiddle." He urged Fontenot to keep going; fans were just beginning to appreciate French music, he said. Fontenot heeded his words, and was still making appearances at folk concerts and festivals in the early nineties.

Some of the finest band leaders of the next generation served their apprenticeship with Chenier, including Stanley "Buckwheat" Dural and, in his last years, his son, C.J. Chenier. Sadly, a life of hard drinking and touring began to catch up with Chenier in the mid-eighties. Physically, he suffered from diabetes, and needed kidney dialysis several times a week. Emotionally, he grew more and more remote from many people. Yet he was still capable of great music. According to Sandmel, winning a Grammy in 1984 for best ethnic recording was like a shot of adrenalin for him. Chenier might look like a shriveled old shell one night, but the next night he might go on a tear at Tipitina's.

By 1987, he was fading quickly and had to play sitting down. Although he was hospitalized in November after a short tour of New England, he played right up until the day he died in December 1987.

The wake was in the black section of Opelousas. Chenier lay in an open coffin with his trademark headband on. Dozens of fellow musicians, including Cleveland, were there. His son C.J. played at his funeral. Then, the very next night, C.J. and the rest of the Red Hot Louisiana Band climbed onstage at a previously booked private party in a Houston steak house and carried on the legacy of the king of zydeco.

EVERYONE'S TOOT TOOT—ZYDECO ROCK

Ironically, zydeco went into orbit in the last years of Clifton Chenier's life, not because of anything he did, but because of a worldwide craze for a novelty song by veteran accordion player Rockin' Sidney. "My Toot Toot" was in the great tradition of Louisiana "Ooh Poo Pah Doo" tunes—it was nonsense but you couldn't keep your toes from tapping.

The song had its origins outside of Ville Platte, the county seat of Evangeline Parish. Producer Floyd Soileau had worked for years with Sidney Simien, although two albums by Simien had gotten only lukewarm response and little airplay. Then, in 1985, Sidney walked into Soileau's office with a tape he had made at home, playing all the instruments. Soileau thought the recording quality was not great, but he told Simien, "I'll gamble on it." He put together an album from the homemade tapes, calling it "Zydeco Shoes," after what Soileau judged to be the strongest song of the lot. To the surprise of both artist and producer, "My Toot Toot" was the song that kept getting requested on the radio. The phrase came from the French expression "Ma Cher Tout Tout," which could be translated as "My dearest dear," but once Simien dropped the "cher," people took it to mean any number of things, from the male sex organ to the slang word for cocaine.

"It was the weakest song in terms of recording quality," Soileau recalled. If the tune were going to get anywhere, it had to be beefed up. He asked Simien to return to the studio, where the artist "added a little more meat around the bone." When "Toot Toot" was issued as a single, it was an immediate hit, first in local circles and then on country radio. Soon it made its way abroad, where it was as big as or bigger in Portuguese,

French, and Spanish than it was in the U.S. version. The original Rockin' Sidney version sold 100,000 copies on the Maison de Soul label. Soileau then leased it to Columbia and Sidney sold another 750,000. Back in Ville Platte, an agricultural center of nine thousand people on the northern border of French-speaking Louisiana, a delighted Soileau chalked it up to the Cajunization of America, which had begun with Paul Prudhomme's cooking. "Toot Toot," he believed, "shed a favorable light on Louisiana music as a whole. First there was Fats and Little Richard. Now comes a new hit out, and people were saying, hey, those guys in Louisiana are still at it!"

For a while, it seemed like 1955 all over again. There were a host of talented performers, black and white, throughout Cajun country who had labored for years in the region's dance halls for small change. Suddenly, booking agents and scouts for major labels were driving their rental cars through the cane fields to check them out. Seasoned zydeco performers such as Rockin' Dopsie, Boozoo Chavis, Stanley "Buckwheat" Dural, John Delafose, Fernest Arceneaux, and, on the West Coast, Queen Ida, found themselves with weekend gigs from New York to San Francisco. Younger acts, including Terrance Simien and the Mallet Playboys, Joel Sonnier, Wayne Toups and Zydecajun, Steve Riley and the Mamou Playboys, Filé, Bruce Daigrepont, and Nathan and the Zydeco Cha Chas were entertaining young, predominantly white audiences who wanted desperately to learn the Cajun two-step.

The bonfire of interest in things Cajun and zydeco was fanned by two other cultural events in 1987: the release of the movie *The Big Easy*, whose soundtrack was loaded with zydeco music, and the popularity of Paul Simon's album "Graceland," which featured contributions from Rockin' Dopsie and a bow to Clifton Chenier. Within the Southwest Louisiana musical community, some welcomed "Toot Toot" and subsequent developments; others were wary.

For Zachary Richard, "Toot Toot" was a signal that it was all right to return to his roots and reintroduce himself to American audiences. Michael Doucet, on the other hand, watched the action with considerable skepticism. "People could see that Clifton was getting very ill," he observed, and many performers—"born-again musicians," he called them—jumped on the Cajun/zydeco bandwagon without the proper credentials. "Basically they only had to learn a couple of songs and everything else they did was rhythm and blues," he concluded.

It could be argued that this definition applied to Chenier as much as it did to anyone else. Asked to define zydeco, the king would reply, "Zydeco is rock and French mixed together, with a beat to it." In any case, good musicians with French names and accordions strapped to their chests got plenty of work and bigger paydays thanks to the path Chenier and "Toot Toot" had pioneered. Perhaps the most accomplished among them was Stanley Dural.

Born in 1947 in Lafayette, Dural had actually spent many years "running away from the accordion" and from his nickname. He was dubbed Buckwheat as a boy, by way of the character in the television show "The Little Rascals," because his mother let his hair grow long and then braided it. He hated the name, but it stuck. Meanwhile, the boy showed an interest in the piano when he was barely out of kindergarten. By the age of nine, he was performing in nightclubs with the drummer Lynn August.

The accordion was an anachronism to him. "It was my father's and great-grandfather's instrument," he explained. "The music my father played wasn't hip enough for me." Instead, as a teenager, he developed into a standout keyboard player, appearing regularly on the crawfish circuit playing funk, soul, blues, and R&B as a sideman for such stars as Joe Tex and Gatemouth Brown. He even led his own funk band, Buckwheat and the Hitchhikers.

The turning point in Dural's career came in 1976 when Clifton Chenier, a friend of his father's, invited him to join his band as an organist. The power and charisma of Chenier's accordion playing finally won him over, and in the next few years he learned to play the piano-key accordion from the master. In 1979, he left Chenier to start his own zydeco band, which he named Ils Sont Partis. It translates as "They're off!"— the cry of the racetrack, a favorite pastime in South Louisiana.

There was not a huge demand for zydeco bands right off the bat, despite Chenier's groundwork. Dural claimed he became his band's vocalist because he could not get anyone to take that job. One of his early club dates, he continued, drew exactly twenty-five paying customers. "They wanted guitar and drums," he said. Nevertheless, he made up his mind to stick it out with zydeco for a while. After more than a year, he began to get occasional dates outside the Gulf Coast, and even traveled to Europe. He worked hard throughout the early eighties, honing his band's tight, danceable sound. Dural updated zydeco and other classic Louisiana music with the addition of a trumpet and a synthesizer, put a new twist on chestnuts like Hank Williams' "Hey Good Lookin'," and dared to cover a minor Rolling Stones hit, "Beast of Burden." If any single recording summed up zydeco's integration into the Louisiana heritage, it was Buckwheat Zydeco's rendition of "Tutti Frutti," a rousing, accordion-driven illustration of the swamp absorbing R&B and making that city music its own.

Dural's practice of punctuating his zydeco with rock, blues, and country licks was really not far from Chenier. After he became one of the first zydeco musicians to sign a major record label deal (he made several albums for Island) he boasted that he had helped the younger generation—his own—cross over to hear an older style of music. "Now you, Mom, and Dad can go to hear Buckwheat Zydeco and all have fun at the same time," Dural, a hearty, bespectacled man who traveled everywhere with his pet raccoon, told one crowd. He was keenly aware of how to please them all—by mixing "the traditional and the more modern beat. That's one reason why the younger generation is still coming out for this," he insisted. "You give them fifty percent, and they give you fifty percent, and you can't go wrong."

Furthermore, he saw zydeco as a cultural bridge to the French language. "Our parents wouldn't speak French to us," he said. "I never spoke French in my life until '79." The one aspect of the French Louisiana renaissance he bristled at, however, was the use of the word Cajun when applied to black sounds. Cajun was music "played straight," he declared; zydeco was "played wavy."

At times, Buckwheat laid claim to Chenier's crown, to the distress of die-hard Chenier worshipers. But he meant no disrespect, he said. "There is more attention and thought given to zydeco now than there was when Chenier was around. It should have been done when he was alive," Dural said.

The truth is that no one has ascended to Chenier's throne, although Buckwheat Zydeco, Rockin' Dopsie, and Boozoo Chavis—the latter an artist with a simpler, more rural sound grounded in Afro-Caribbean drumming—each had their moments. There was, however, no dispute about the queen of zydeco, Ida Guillory. Originally from Hammond, Louisiana, she grew up in Texas, lived in California most of her adult life, and was one of a handful of women who ventured into Creole music. "We were brought up to leave those instruments to the male," she said. "The accordion is not very ladylike."

Queen Ida picked up the accordion while she was raising a family in the San Francisco area. She drove a school bus, and to fill up the hours during the day that she spent waiting for the children, she began practicing the instrument. Her brother had a zydeco band, and one day in the mid-seventies she asked if she could sit in. Her brother, she recalled with a grin, was "in shock," but the appearance launched her career. For the next fifteen years, Queen Ida, a petite, friendly woman with pecan-colored skin who radiated energetic charm from the stage, toured the U.S. constantly, delivering pleasant, simple zydeco dance music to her fans. She won a Grammy in 1982.

By the beginning of the nineties, both black and white performers were mining the rich zydeco vein but rocking harder and harder. Zydeco might be "roots" music, but its melodies were propelled by a solid rock backbeat. Two of the best examples of this crossbred sound were accordionist/singers born in the late fifties in Cajun country, who came of age in the soul era—Wayne Toups and C.J. Chenier.

Toups was a product of the white generation that grew up understanding scraps of French without speaking it much. (His parents, he said, spoke it when they didn't want the kids to understand what they were saying.) Raised in Cowley, Louisiana, he knew about Cajun music from the time he was a child, and learned the accordion from his brother at the age of thirteen. But his own listening habits were molded by artists such as James Brown, Otis Redding, Aretha Franklin, and the Motown hit makers, along with a dollop of modern country music. He said he didn't even know who Clifton Chenier was until he was in his twenties.

At first, Toups worked in the oil fields and played with a band on the side. Then, in the late seventies, he formed a band called Cajun Creole with a drummer and bassist who had a rock background, plus a steel guitarist. When that group broke up, he came up with a new band, which he called Zydecajun to reflect the dual cultural impact on his sound. Toups began playing with Michael Doucet two nights a week at Mulate's, the well-known dance hall in Breaux Bridge, and he added much traditional Cajun music to his repertoire. Still, he noted, "when I finally found out who Clifton Chenier was, I fell in love with him."

A pint-sized dynamo with a mass of black curls poking out of his ever-present headband, Toups sang in a husky baritone and danced like a dervish on stage. As Zydecajun began to get bookings in the "Toot Toot" era, he was signed by Mercury/Polygram and made four fine albums for them, one of which, "Blast from the Bayou," became the first Cajun or zydeco release to make the *Billboard* pop charts. His record sales were undoubtedly helped by his high-octane live show. Carole King chose Toups as the opening act for her 1989 tour, and he co-hosted a Mardi Gras special on MTV.

Zydecajun might offend a few purists, but the band was definitely the wave of the future, with tours of Southeast Asia and Latin America as well as numerous appearances at American clubs and festivals. His aim, Toups said, was to introduce zydeco rock "to a whole different new audience but still keep true to our people back home." Cajun music is special, he argued, because "it's not a fad." In mainstream pop rock, acts might "come and go, whereas this kind of music, once you make a fan, you have a fan for life." Like Zachary Richard, he was interested in advancing the music, but unlike Richard, he emphasized that he almost always included in a show "twenty or thirty minutes of old-time Cajun music to show that I haven't forgotten where I came from."

C.J. (Clayton Joseph) Chenier had the opposite problem; he and everyone else knew quite well where he came from. He needed to emerge from beneath the dauntingly large shadow cast by his father. And emerge he did, though it was anything but easy.

He was born in Port Arthur in 1957 to Mildred Bell, a house cleaner. (Clifton Chenier did not have any children with his wife, Margaret.) During his childhood, C.J. saw his father only every four or five months, and had no idea Clifton was a musical star. "I knew he was a songwriter; I didn't know what magnitude," C.J. explained. "The first time I saw him perform I was about sixteen." He was interested in music at an early age, though. His first choice of an instrument was the trombone, but his mother, well versed in the blues, persuaded him to take up the tenor saxophone instead. By the time he was in high school, the burly youngster chose the school band over football, and also played in a garage band. He and his friends shunned zydeco music; that was for old folks. Unfortunately, there was very little live music in Port Arthur to inspire him, so he got an education from records after a friend turned him on to fusion jazz—Grover Washington and Spyro Gyra were among his favorites. Most of all, C.J. longed to get out of Port

Arthur, a town which was as dull to him as it had been to Janis Joplin a generation earlier.

He got his chance when he was barely twenty years old. C.J. had been working at a refinery, doing everything from digging holes to chipping sulphur off walls, and hating every minute of it. Then, his father called his mother out of the blue one day in 1978. His regular saxophone player was indisposed. Could she send C.J. to Bridge City, Texas, to fill in? C.J. went, more frightened than excited. He figured the regular sax player was there at the Sparkle Paradise Club and could show him the ropes. "Instead," he recalled with a laugh, "it was just me, and it was like, 'what am I supposed to play?' I didn't know anything about the music." Nor did he speak a word of French; his father's drummer taught him song lyrics phonetically.

C.J.'s trial by fire continued as he stayed with the band on a coast-to-coast tour. Gradually, he grew more comfortable. "All the guys were so friendly, they made me feel at ease," he said. He was impressed by the fans: "I started seeing these people who were so crazy about my dad." His father remained somewhat distant—"he wasn't an emotional person," C.J. said—but a life of one-night stands and miles of highway roads in a van were still preferable to Port Arthur. For a young man who had barely been out of Louisiana before, places like Canada and especially California were exotic and wonderful.

By 1983, the elder Chenier judged that his son had won a unique role for himself. Clifton had been sick, and even after he recovered he was too weak to play an entire set. So he began to teach C.J. the accordion. At first, C.J. found it complicated. Somehow, though, this genial youngster, whose eyeglasses made him look more like a student than a stage/pop performer, persevered. It became his job to warm up the crowd, out front, on the accordion, until his father joined the band onstage. "He didn't say a whole lot," admitted C.J. "When I did good, he'd tell me. He let me do it my own way."

In the last years of Clifton Chenier's life, C.J. became the official leader of the band. He had undergone a remarkable apprenticeship, and it paid off. When the king died, C.J. and the Red Hot Louisiana Band endured. After the funeral, the entire group drove from Opelousas to Houston and played their scheduled party gig. What did they sound like? C.J.'s memories were vivid: "Whoa! Full of energy. Like we had something to prove."

The younger Chenier showed musical growth both within the zydeco tradition and beyond it as the years passed. In somewhat the same fashion as Ziggy Marley, he built on his father's legend without attempting the impossible task of surpassing it. "I guess everybody tries to contribute a new sound," he remarked. "My style might differ from my father's. Because I'm a Texas boy, I didn't grow up around sheep and pigs out in the fields. So I write about different things." By the time the second album featuring C.J. came out on Slash Records, produced by his father's loyal friend Chris Strachwitz, the younger Chenier was contributing songs of his own, mostly in English, with a dash of French. For someone whose only exposure to live music as a kid was Tower of Power, C.J. Chenier proved that he had grown into a zydeco man to be reckoned with. His nimble work on the accordion, especially on his father's tunes, like "Hot Rod," was matched by an excellent baritone voice, less rousing, perhaps, than Clifton's but full of warmth.

More than anyone, C.J. recognized that he had inherited a gift that he must strive to live up to. In a touching homage, "He's Still a King to Me," he sang:

> There was a lot of folks
> Always hanging round
> Telling a bunch of jokes
> like hey I got the crown
> But like he used to say
> you can have this crown you see
> but if you want to wear this crown
> You gotta take it away from me.

⑥ Back to the Future: Contemporary Jazz

BRASS BANDS REDUX

As New Orleans approached the end of the twentieth century, some of its brightest—and youngest—stars were those devoted to contemporary jazz. Indeed, the resurgence of interest in jazz nationally was due in large measure to such Crescent City natives as Wynton Marsalis, Branford Marsalis, and Harry Connick, Jr. Moreover, the performing arts high school all three attended, the New Orleans Center for the Creative Arts, was regularly turning out even younger aspiring jazz artists, some of whom, such as Nicholas Payton, were in the spotlight long before they were out of their teens.

Just about every product of this renaissance was labeled a "new conservative," "new traditionalist," or "neo-bopper." Rather than reach toward the avant-garde edge of jazz, these players studied, adapted, and modernized earlier styles. Nor was it coincidence that the most heralded of the new breed in the city of Jelly Roll Morton and Louis Armstrong were pianists and horn men.

It seemed appropriate, too, that the introductory notes of this jazz explosion were sounded by a group dedicated to one of New Orleans' most senior traditions, the brass band. Brass bands had never really left the streets of the Crescent City. They were there in Buddy Bolden's day, present throughout the blossoming of jazz in the years before and after World War I, and available in various configurations thereafter. Brass bands were not allowed to die out because they served indispensable functions, such as playing at social club parades and funerals.

Still, all these bands played traditional music, whether they were new incarnations of famous old-time bands, such as the Eureka and Onward, or newly formed coalitions, such as the Olympia (founded in 1960) and the Young Tuxedo (founded 1935). The second generation of brass-band players did introduce a few fresh tunes—"Iko, Iko" and "Blueberry Hill," for example—to the repertoire. But by the sixties they were so close to being an endangered species that in 1965 Danny Barker created a new band, the Fairview Baptist Church Band, to make sure younger people learned about the tradition. Then, in 1977, the Dirty Dozen Brass Band appeared and made up new rules for the oldest game in town.

However unusual this eight-piece ensemble might seem to listeners unfamiliar with New Orleans traditions, they must have sounded weirder when they were first organized—as a band of kazoos. Soon, though, bass-drummer Benny Jones added snare-drummer Jenell "Chi-lite" Marshall, trumpeter Gregory Davis, baritone-saxophonist George Lewis, and two sons of a famous trombonist, Walden "Frog" Joseph: trombonist Charles Joseph and sousaphone (tuba) player Kirk Joseph. Lewis and Davis, both schooled musicians, led the group away from the kazoo. Several of the musicians had been in Barker's Fairview band. Others had grown up in the same neighborhood.

Their idea, according to Davis, was to re-create "what we remembered from our childhoods—the brass bands playing the funerals and the second lines." They rehearsed diligently in the backyard of the Joseph family's home in hopes that they might get an occasional gig. Their name came not from the number of players but from the Social and Pleasure Club that used them for their annual parade. The group's lineup was similar to traditional parade bands, except that it lacked a clarinet and included a baritone sax, which had been eliminated from most bands after World War I.

As Lewis, a student of modern music under Kidd Jordan at Southern University and a veteran of Fats Domino's band, recalled, they were playing a street parade one day when he suggested that they play the jump band classic "Night Train." A few onlookers thought they were crazy. You can't play that kind of music out here, they said, to which Lewis replied, "We did and it worked."

The band got a Monday night gig at the Glass House, a late-hours Uptown bar. For six years, they jammed and practiced, adding all kinds of music—Stevie Wonder songs, Charlie Parker tunes, plus their own compositions—to the basics like "The Saints Go Marching In." By spicing up the repertoire with bebop and R&B and by devising novel arrangements, they invented a new form: a contemporary jazz octet that played funky rhythms in a turn-of-the-century instrumental configuration.

One gig led to another, until the group was invited to play at the Umbria Jazz Festival in Perugia in 1984, where they got such a rousing reception from young listeners that the police almost thought they had a riot on their hands. The next year, they played New York's Kool Jazz Festival on a "Young New Orleans" bill with Wynton Marsalis and others. Their first album, "My Feet Can't Fail Me Now," was released that year. Critiquing it in *Stereo Review*, Chris Albertson hailed it as "curiously refreshing. These eight musicians are no relics from Preservation Hall," he wrote. "They are young, and their ears are close enough to the ground that their music also reflects the present time."

The Dozen's "Voodoo" and "New Orleans Album" releases, which featured Buckwheat Zydeco, Elvis Costello, Dizzy Gillespie, and Dr. John as guests, solidified their reputation. Not only were they sassy second-liners who transformed music borrowed from every era into a sophisticated, syncopated mosaic, they were excellent instrumentalists. Kirk Joseph, above all, came to be recognized as a master of the sousaphone. (Joseph left the Dirty Dozen in late 1991 to form a new group, the Frappe Brass Band, with his brothers Charles and Gerald, as well as the youngest Marsalis, Jason, and others.) The whole concept of the Dirty Dozen was admired by fellow musicians and cheered by the public. As Davis pointed out, "We do what people pay thousands of dollars for a synthesizer to do."

The Dirty Dozen inspired many young New Orleanians. Especially impressed were a handful of kids from Treme, a poor black neighborhood near Armstrong Park, who were playing and parading for tips in the French Quarter. The group called themselves the ReBirth Brass Band.

The ReBirth came into being in the early eighties when teen-aged tuba player Philip Frazier asked his Clark High School friend, trumpeter Kermit Ruffins, to join a "second line" band he was organizing. Frazier's mother, Barbara, a church organist, allowed the boys to practice at her home; his brother Keith became the band's bass drummer. Soon the student group started playing on street corners, just as brass bands had done seventy years before. "When we found out we could make a little money," explained Ruffins, "we started doing it every day of the week, playing on the street and learning on the street at the same time." The players named themselves the ReBirth in honor of a youth center whose leader got them a lot of bookings.

Some band members were still in high school when the ReBirth took up residence at the Dirty Dozen's old stomping ground, the Glass House. One night there, a booking agent heard them and was so bowled over he signed the group for an appearance at New York's Lone Star Café. On the first night in the big city, the youngsters did what they were used to doing back home; they marched outside and began playing on the street. "Before you knew it, we had police all around," laughed Ruffins.

The ReBirth couldn't play in New York streets without a permit, but the group was well received indoors, not just in New York but in Europe and Japan. Following the work pioneered by the Dirty Dozen, the ReBirth expanded its repertoire to jazz and R&B, the latter, according to Ruffins, so it could appeal to a wider audience, "especially our parents." To widen his horizons further, Ruffins trained himself to get up at six every morning in order to listen to and tape a traditional jazz program broadcast on a local radio station, WWOZ.

By the early nineties, the ReBirth was as eclectic and nearly as successful as the Dozen, though perhaps not as smooth in arrangements or execution. The ReBirth's first two Rounder albums, "Feel Like Funkin' It Up" and "ReBirth Kickin' It Live," featured numbers made famous by musicians as different as Louis Armstrong, Fats Domino, and Michael Jackson. Meanwhile, taking a cue from another hometown idol, Wynton Marsalis, ReBirth's members, still barely old enough to order a beer in the clubs that hired them, were busy encouraging the next generation of New Orleans musicians. They helped a second band, called the New Birth, get started, and they were planning a third, centered on Ruffins' and Fraziers' baby sons. They already had a name for this offspring: the Afterbirth.

KEEPERS OF THE FLAME—
THE MARSALIS FAMILY

No less an authority than the dean of jazz critics, Leonard Feather, declared that the eighties would "go down in jazz history as the Marsalis decade." He was referring primarily to Wynton, but also to the trumpeter's father and brothers, who were crucial partners in making the family the rulers of the contemporary jazz world. As an educator, Ellis Marsalis, the father, taught some of the finest New Orleans talents to make an impact on the national scene, including Harry Connick, Jr., and Terence Blanchard. As performers, Wynton, his older brother, Branford, and Connick dominated the spotlight to the point where, in the fall of 1990, their albums claimed all five top spots on the *Billboard* jazz chart. What these musicians had in common with the new brass bands was a devotion to acoustic sound, a knowledge of and respect for past masters, especially those from their hometown, and an attitude so self-assured that occasionally it was taken for arrogance.

The literal and spiritual father of New Orleans modern jazz was a great teacher who went into education because he could not support his family on his music bookings alone. Ellis Lee Marsalis, the son of a motel owner, was born in New Orleans in 1934. His first instrument was the clarinet, although he switched to saxophone early because it was the jazz instrument of choice during his formative years. As a teenager, he played R&B and pop music with friends in a band that accompanied school dances. But in 1949 he heard Dizzy Gillespie at a local concert; soon he was a "confirmed bebopper."

Ellis took up piano while attending Dillard University in New Orleans. He was still primarily a saxophonist when he met Harold Battiste, a senior at Dillard, who invited him to join his new bebop group. Since Harold himself played the tenor and Alvin Batiste (no relation) was on clarinet, Ellis found himself on piano. "I didn't really object," he said, "because I just wanted to belong."

There were not many other beboppers around New Orleans in the mid-fifties. It was, after all, "a music that was relatively new to the universe." But Marsalis glimpsed the shape of jazz to come on a trip to Los Angeles in 1956 just after graduating from college. Drummer Ed Blackwell, a band mate, had been invited to play with Ornette Coleman. Marsalis and Battiste went along for the ride, and Ellis got a chance to play a few gigs with Coleman, soon to be a key figure in the post-bop era. At that point, recalled Marsalis, Ornette was still trying to "figure out what the piano was supposed to do" in his experimental new music. After a few months, a family illness required Marsalis to return to New Orleans. He served a stint in the

Marines, worked for his father, got married in 1958 to Dolores, and began teaching.

During this period, he convinced his father to turn the family home across from the motel into a club, the Music Haven. It lasted only about six months. However, he used the site to make his first record, "Monkey Puzzle," with his quartet, which included Nat Perrilliat on sax and James Black on drums, for Battiste's AFO label. (It was reissued as "Classic Ellis Marsalis.") Meanwhile, Branford was born in 1960, followed by Wynton in 1961 and Ellis III in 1963. With gigs harder to come by, Marsalis began his career as a teacher, and the family moved in 1964 for two years to the Cajun town of Breaux Bridge, where he also directed the chorus.

By 1967, the Marsalises were settled back in Kenner, a New Orleans suburb. Not much was happening in modern jazz in the city then, so Marsalis played with Al Hirt's Dixieland group, one of the first integrated bands on Bourbon Street, for three years. Like every other New Orleans musician, he had to be versatile to survive. He hit his stride as a teacher when a position opened at the New Orleans Center for the Creative Arts (NOCCA). During school breaks, he would travel to New York to play piano at the Carnegie Tavern, around the corner from Carnegie Hall. New York musicians, he felt, had a much more professional attitude toward their work than those at home. "Most of the musicians in New Orleans live on what we call Mom Street. They can go to Mom and get a little breakfast— or to Auntie, or to Sister," he commented.

While Branford and Wynton were youngsters, Ellis had a fairly steady gig at Lu and Charlie's, a restaurant and bar on Rampart Street that was the Crescent City's major modern jazz venue. "I was fortunate in that Lu and Charlie's served food," he said, because thus his kids could visit him on the job, and hear music "in a favorable environment and atmosphere. They learned that jazz didn't have to come out of a cathouse."

He never pushed Branford or Wynton into music, but clearly they absorbed his message. "Just having the opportunity to listen to his sound when I was growing up was a tremendous inspiration for me and for my brothers," said Wynton. "The greatest influence on me was seeing his dedication to music during the many times when he wasn't playing gigs that much."

Ellis instilled that dedication in other youngsters at NOCCA, as well as in his spare time. "My father would stay up with anybody" who came to the house late at night to ask him about how to play changes, or to learn tunes, Wynton remarked. Among Ellis's NOCCA students was a precocious pianist who was the son of the city's district attorney. "I learned everything from Ellis," Harry Connick, Jr., said later. "In four years he brought me from an undirected goof-off to a very directed, potential jazz musician. And he impressed upon me the seriousness of the music."

Lu and Charlie's closed in 1977. The city was a typical southern town, Ellis felt, not inclined to be "open to that much that was new." He found fewer and fewer playing opportunities for the next several years in New Orleans, even as his sons were beginning to make both the jazz and classical world take notice of them. When it seemed as though no one else was ever going to record him, Ellis went into a studio and put a record out on his own Elm label. He did appear with Wynton and Branford on one of their earliest albums, "Fathers and Sons," in 1982. The next year, Ellis's quartet made another Elm album, with Delfeayo, then a high school senior, making his debut as producer.

Gradually, the modern jazz scene improved in New Orleans. By 1984, Ellis was a headliner at local clubs, such as Tyler's and Snug Harbor, as well as an occasional guest in Wynton's band at rooms such as Blues Alley in Washington. But the number of jazz students at NOCCA was dwindling, so in 1986, Marsalis accepted a position at Virginia Commonwealth University. "It's the same old story," wrote a New Orleans critic. "In the Big Easy, nobody loves you until you're gone. When you're here, you're taken for granted."

After three years, though, Marsalis was wooed back to the

Crescent City by New Orleans University and a local Coca Cola distributor, who endowed a chair for him in the Jazz Studies program. The first name on his hiring list? Harold Battiste, his old college buddy, who had been busy in Los Angeles producing such groups as Sonny and Cher.

Marsalis's students told countless tales of his inventiveness as a teacher. Victor Goines, a tenor-sax man, studied with him and became a member of his band. "Every time we played on the bandstand was like a lesson. For practical exercises, we'd go to a gig and play a song like 'Cherokee' in all the keys, a chorus apiece. One night it took about thirty minutes to get through the song. It was definitely an ear-training course," Goines said. Marsalis also imparted his fondness for the standards to sons and students alike. When Wynton went into the studio to do his "Resolution of Romance" album, released in 1990, his father was at the piano. "I heard my father playing these songs in clubs so beautifully," said the trumpeter of numbers like "Where or When" and "How Are Things in Glocca Morra," adding that he had always wanted to do an album with his dad but "I never felt prepared because I didn't play well enough on changes." The album was acclaimed as a masterpiece.

A low-keyed, soft-spoken man, Marsalis eventually signed with Columbia, made new records, and started playing many more club dates throughout the country, as well as in New Orleans. The recognition was sweet, but it came late; he was sorry that he hadn't been able to record more in the sixties when his "Monkey Puzzle" group was at its "zenith." Nor did he see any reason to give up teaching for a full-time performing career. "I see them as the same thing," Ellis Marsalis remarked. "Its just a different audience."

For his second son, Wynton, it was a different story. Recognition came early and never let up. He made his first splash at fourteen, when he played the Haydn trumpet concerto with the New Orleans Philharmonic. At twenty-three he became the first musician to win simultaneous Grammies for a classical album and a jazz album. By his mid-twenties he was an international star. Before he reached thirty, his renown was so immense that at a Chicago jazz festival the announcer introduced him by saying, "Wynton Marsalis is to jazz what Michael Jordan is to basketball." Especially in the Windy City, there was no higher compliment.

More important, he was credited by fellow musicians, not to mention *Time* magazine, with ushering in "a new jazz age" on "what was once barren soil" and opening doors for a host of equally committed younger players. At the time Wynton burst on the scene, jazz was somewhat becalmed. The free jazz movement of the sixties was just about played out; an electrified music usually referred to as fusion was popular but unacceptable to purists. Other artists such as Anthony Braxton appealed to a very narrow audience. Into these waters cruised Wynton Marsalis. It didn't hurt that he was articulate and unafraid of musical controversy, an appealing straight-arrow role model for black youths and a willing crusader for his brand of acoustic jazz. He seemed prepared for fame and carried its burden gracefully.

But the Marsalis saga was even more remarkable. Besides Wynton, there was his brother Branford, older by thirteen months. Branford's relaxed, good-natured personality was an interesting contrast to Wynton's intensity. He played tenor and soprano sax with what some critics thought was a more instinctively lyrical improvisational style. Branford, for all his talk of being laid back, built an impressive résumé well before his thirty-fifth birthday. He made jazz recordings, first as a member of Wynton's band and then on his own; he played rock behind the British pop idol Sting; he turned in respectable acting performances in Hollywood films, wrote the score for two Spike Lee movies, and took over the leadership of the "Tonight" show orchestra from Doc Severinsen on television.

Ellis and Dolores Marsalis had four more sons, of whom two gave every indication of following in their brothers' musical footsteps. Delfeayo, four years younger than Wynton, was a skilled record producer and trombonist. Jason, twelve years younger than Delfeayo, was a teenaged drum prodigy. Ellis, Jr., a computer consultant a year older than Delfeayo, and Mboya, the next to youngest, who was autistic, rounded out the roster.

Wynton was born on October 18, 1961, and spent his early years in school in Kenner, a white New Orleans suburb. He and Branford were among eleven black children in a predominantly white local elementary school. He got his first trumpet when he was six years old. Ironically, Miles Davis, who cast such a long shadow over modern jazz, and who was to become an antagonist of Wynton's, happened to witness the event. It took place in Al Hirt's club, where Ellis was a member of Hirt's band. A group of players including trumpeters Hirt, Davis, and Clark Terry were gathered at a table. Ellis, noting all the horn men, said, "I better buy Wynton a trumpet." Hirt insisted on giving the boy one of his. Davis protested. "Don't give it to him," said Davis, "Trumpet's too difficult an instrument for him to learn."

The boy accepted the gift anyway, and within two years was progressing well enough to be part of Danny Barker's Fairview marching band. But at first, music took a back seat to academics—Wynton was a straight-A student—and sports. Then, when he was twelve, he was transported by an album featuring Clifford Brown, the great bop trumpeter. "Nobody could go like that," he thought. "I've just got to learn how." Whereupon he began practicing in earnest—four hours a day, when he woke up in the morning and after school. He entered NOCCA after the ninth grade, and was eager to play just about anytime, anywhere. Happily, New Orleans afforded him numerous opportunities—classical orchestra, concert band, funk band, weddings, parades. "The best thing about New Orleans for me and other young musicians," he noted later, was that it had a corps of older musicians "who loved music so much they would do anything for us." Among them was John Longo, whom Wynton called his first teacher. "I hardly ever paid him, and he used to give me two- and three-hour lessons," he recalled. Another was Alvin Batiste. Wynton dreaded seeing him arrive at the door because Batiste gave him so much homework, but the older man also hammered home invaluable habits. "He taught me about the importance of having good embouchure, good breathing, practicing every day, studying, the importance of seriousness and professional deportment," Marsalis said.

At NOCCA, Marsalis was considered a brilliant student. (Since NOCCA is a part-time school, he was attending a tough academic high school, Benjamin Franklin, at the same time.) Not only did he perform the Haydn at fourteen; he also played in a funk band, doing covers of Earth, Wind and Fire and the like. Jazz pianist Marian McPartland, who heard Wynton at the age of fifteen playing with Branford, was "flabbergasted. They were so together it was unbelievable," she said. "I give clinics for kids all over the country, and I hear a lot of people with great potential. But Wynton seemed fully grown from the first," she continued. "His mother says he has always been a little man, that he was never a little boy."

Even more impressive to some than his Philharmonic debut was a concert Marsalis gave in 1979 at the Contemporary Arts Center; he devoted the first half to the Hummel trumpet concerto, the second half to jazz. That same year he auditioned for a spot in the illustrious Tanglewood summer music school. Conductor Gunther Schuller remembered that Wynton moved behind a pillar to prepare himself—and to talk to his horn. "Now don't let me down," he said. According to Schuller, he "didn't miss a note" in Bach's Second Brandenburg Concerto. "We were overwhelmed by his talent," Schuller said. Marsalis, though officially too young to attend the Tanglewood program at seventeen, nevertheless was voted Outstanding Brass Player that summer. "I could always tell how shocked they were," he recalled, "that a black kid my age could play *their* music." Later, he explained that he was diligent in his classical studies because "so many black musicians were scared of this big monster on the other side of the mountain called classical music," adding, "I think—I *know*—it's harder to be a good jazz musician at an early age than a classical one. In jazz, to be good means to be an individual, which you don't necessarily have to be in classical music performance."

During the next decade, he made both disciplines look deceptively easy. He went to Juilliard in New York, on a scholarship, where he was frequently the last to leave the practice rooms. He left Juilliard early, however, to go on the road with Art Blakey's Jazz Messengers. His jazz graduate studies had begun.

Juilliard is considered the Harvard of music conservatories; the Messengers might be called the Juilliard of modern jazz small bands. (Wayne Shorter, Freddie Hubbard, Lee Morgan, Donald Byrd, Keith Jarrett, Chick Corea, and Horace Silver are among its alumni.) Wynton later admitted, with embarrassment, that not only had he never listened to Blakey's albums before joining the band, his jazz chops left something to be desired. The first night he sat in with the band, he said, "I got lost in 'Along Comes Betty.' " A year with Blakey proved to be great on-the-job training.

Inevitably, Wynton came to the attention of George Butler, who headed Columbia Records' progressive jazz department. He signed the young man to a contract for both classical and jazz recordings, tapping Herbie Hancock to be the jazz producer. It is Wynton's firmly held viewpoint, however, that Columbia really wanted him to play pop, not jazz, in the style of Tom Browne, a young trumpeter who made a splash about the same time. He had to fight "every step of the way" to play his own brand of jazz.

Barely twenty-one years old, Marsalis made his self-titled first album with bassist Ron Carter and drummer Tony Williams—both former members of Miles Davis's classic sixties quintet—plus his brother Branford as sidemen. A glittering display of hard-bop instrumental gymnastics, the album was a sensation in 1982. He capped a remarkable year by winning *Down Beat's* listener poll as both Jazz Musician of the year and by beating out Davis as Number 1 trumpeter. He toured with Hancock again in 1983. According to Hancock, Wynton was his own worst critic: "After playing some incredible stuff, he'd walk off the stage and say, 'That was sad.' I'd be thinking, 'Is he crazy?' He got better and better."

Columbia Records launched Marsalis with the kind of full-scale publicity campaign it usually reserved for rock stars. Whether it was that hype, his music, or a combination of both, the investment paid off handsomely. The following year came his double shot at the Grammies, one for the jazz album "Think of One," the other for his album of the Haydn, Hummel, and Mozart concertos.

At the Grammy awards, Marsalis caused a flap by appearing to knock Hancock (who had also performed on the telecast, in a glitzy outfit) and people like Miles Davis, who, he felt, had strayed from jazz into rock-accented fusion. In his acceptance speech he dedicated the jazz award to Charlie Parker, Thelonious Monk, Louis Armstrong, and others "who gave an art form to the American people that cannot be limited by enforced trends or bad taste." Hancock was obviously hurt. Wynton was "a little harsh and opinionated," he said.

The "young lion" (as fresh faces in jazz are dubbed) was outspoken and humble by turns. He insisted he had much to learn. (Most critics and older jazzmen agreed; they were dazzled by his skill but thought he had not yet found his own "voice.") Nevertheless, he willingly accepted the mantle of a jazz savior. Jazz, he declared, had lost its way in the seventies. "The established cats were bullshittin' and trying to act like rock stars," he said. "So when people heard me, they knew it was time to start takin' care of business again. At least I was playing some real music." He was equally harsh on the avant-garde. "There's a whole school of musicians who are called the avant-garde, and you don't really [need] any craft requirements to join. All you have to do is be black and have an African name," he said.

What knocked out listeners about his playing was a superb technique and round tone married to a style that had been handed down from Fats Navarro, Brown, Davis, and other boppers. Whitney Balliett of *The New Yorker* marveled that Marsalis could "play with or without a vibrato. He can growl, trill, half-valve, and use any sort of mute. He has complete possession of all his registers. And how he moves through them! His descending arpeggios are sometimes so crowded they almost flatten into glissandos." Years of radical change in jazz had prepared many to welcome Marsalis's beautifully honed orthodoxy.

At that time, Branford, though older, was clearly the junior partner. The brothers shared a brownstone in Brooklyn, and Branford played on Marsalis's next two albums, "Hot House Flowers" and "Black Codes from the Underground." But that harmony was shattered in 1985 when Branford, along with Kenny Kirkland, Wynton's pianist, took off to join Sting on tour. Wynton fired them both. The trumpeter was so upset over the defections that he contemplated quitting jazz altogether. "It wasn't so much that they left," he later explained. It was their use of jazz as a "high-class calling card" to get popular gigs.

He felt that, as was the case with his Columbia Records disputes, he was facing issues that went beyond who would play in what band. "With my brother, the whole battle has been over the question of what is jazz's place in American culture," he said. "Is it some lightweight music that has no substance, or is it an art form that informs us about American democracy, about what it means to live in the twentieth century?" On the phone, he told his father that he felt like he was "out there all by myself," that he was disillusioned at being the lone member of his generation who was trying to extend the great traditions of jazz. Words of encouragement from Ellis, plus a sensational new pianist, Marcus Roberts, who was as serious as he was, went a long way toward boosting his morale.

Marsalis's most famous feud, however, was with the jazz legend who embodied cool, Miles Davis. On the one hand, Davis was among the greatest jazz trumpeters of the modern era. In Marsalis's eyes, though, he was a former hero who had defected, who had forfeited his leadership post in quest of mass popularity. Davis, of course, was never a man to let an apparent insult go unanswered, and he was clearly piqued by the youngster's comments. ("I've got every record Miles Davis ever made," Marsalis said, "I know how great he was. But then, man, he wanted the kids, and he came down to all that electric shit.") The two were on the same bill at jazz festivals around the world, Wynton added, "and I had to listen to him play pop. Although he was one of my biggest influences, I didn't have that much respect for him." At one confrontation in 1986 at a Vancouver jazz festival, Wynton came onstage while Davis and his band were in mid-set. Davis signaled to his band stop playing; Marsalis withdrew. He didn't want to fight, he said scornfully, with a man old enough to be his grandfather. (Davis was sixty, Wynton twenty-five.) The bitterness lingered until Davis's death in 1991.

One of the fascinating aspects of Marsalis's career was that as his playing matured, he undertook longer and deeper explorations of the music that had come before him—especially that of New Orleans. "I heard that music from birth," he noted. When he was younger, he had wrongfully dismissed the likes of Louis Armstrong and parade music as "Uncle Tom" music. Still, "at the end of every gig, we played the second line," he noted. By the age of nineteen, he had begun listening more thoughtfully to the earlier music. On his own first albums, the call-and-response patterns between his trumpet and his brother's sax were taken from the oldest New Orleans music, he said. Then, in "Black Codes," he borrowed a bass line from the old Mardi Gras Indian tune "Pocky Way."

Marsalis also examined the music of his father's generation, the vintage songs of composers like Gershwin and Porter. He made his first album, called "Marsalis Standard Time," in 1987. Another, in 1990, featured Ellis on piano, while the third, in 1991, included Roberts at the keyboard.

Next came the blues and traditional jazz. In the view of many, his "Majesty of the Blues" album of 1988 was an artistic break- through. For it, he brought in eighty-year-old legend Danny Barker, Freddie Lonzo, Teddy Riley, and the young traditional clarinetist Michael White, all New Orleanians. "Majesty," Mar- salis proclaimed, was an attempt to express the feelings that grew out of "all the things I experienced growing up in New Orleans, those kinds of feeling of fraternity, of humor, of style, food, dances, parades, churches, ribbing, family, sports, girls— all of it." The album contained a long piece interpreting an entire jazz funeral, with a dirge at the outset, a sermon in the middle (written by his friend the critic Stanley Crouch), and a celebratory march at the end. On this album, as well as on "Thick in the South" and "Uptown Ruler" (both made around the same time but not released until 1991) and in concerts he organized over the next few years as overseer of Lincoln Cen- ter's classical jazz program, Marsalis spearheaded a major revival and reworking of the Crescent City's original gift to music.

These investigations of older idioms were not universally applauded. They caused furrowed brows among some critics and jazz buffs who saw him becoming reactionary, elitist. On the other hand, as a *Down Beat* reviewer said in 1991, "If Wyn- ton has sacrificed exuberance for dignified reflection, give him time. He's only thirty."

No one questioned his virtuosity. Marsalis was the first major jazz figure since Benny Goodman who was as at home with classical playing as he was with jazz, and the only trumpet player ever to excel in both fields. He withdrew from almost all classical recording in the mid-eighties, though, because he did not feel he could do both genres justice. "Every time I would mess up Haydn's concerto, I would have nightmares about him attacking me with a long dagger," he said. "Conversely, I would cringe when imagining the outrage Pops must have felt in heaven when a trumpet lesson he was giving Gabriel was interrupted by the sound of people like myself."

Looking at Marsalis at thirty, it would be hard to overstate his contributions to modern jazz. Clearly, he had breathed new life into acoustic playing and stimulated a new appreciation of older forms. But his influence went further; New Orleanians like Victor Goines and Kermit Ruffins sought his advice on their careers, and Marsalis, in turn, sought out them and others like them across the country. Almost from the beginning of his career, he made it a habit to visit schools and seek out promising youngsters in the course of his travels. In New Orleans, he would pick up Marlon Jordan at school. "We'd play basketball, then have a trumpet lesson," Jordan recalled. His stature among young players was such that many adopted his sober demeanor, his dress code, and his interest in jazz history.

Happily, Marsalis also had a sense of humor and seemed capable of keeping things in perspective. He wouldn't clown around when talking about jazz in American culture, but to someone like Kermit Ruffins, who spent time with him at a jazz festival in France, he was "just a down-home guy." He realized that however lionized he might be in jazz, in terms of popularity he wasn't in the same league as Hammer or Guns N Roses. Pointing to a junior high school across the street from Lincoln Center, Marsalis bet a *Newsday* reporter "any amount of money I can walk through that whole place and not get recognized." True enough, although if he had walked through the school next door, La Guardia, the New York performing arts high school, he would have drawn worshipful stares.

In any event, popularity, to Marsalis, was not the issue. Creating something "significant" was. And no one who heard him play doubted that as he matured, he was in the process of achieving that goal.

Meanwhile, Branford, the self-styled "lazy" Marsalis, was, in his own affable way, building an equally formidable career. From the start, the brothers, though quite close to one another, were very different individuals. Their father associated the difference with learning styles. Wynton, he said, was "concrete and sequential," someone who moved from "step one, step two, right on down the line." Branford, on the other hand, was "random and abstract," the type who went "from a lot of general information" to the specific. Imagine how amused Ellis was when, just a few days after using these phrases in an interview, he passed a record store window with a poster for Branford's upcoming album. The title? "Random Abstract."

Branford was born in Breaux Bridge, a Cajun town, in 1960, and went, as Wynton did, to a newly integrated grade school in Kenner. His first choice of an instrument was the drums, but his parents, fearing a racket, persuaded him to learn the clarinet instead. Ellis felt a clarinetist would always be able to get a job. He also tried to get the boy to learn oboe and bassoon, but Branford stubbornly resisted. He absolutely hated the clarinet, he said, and finally got an alto sax for Christmas a few years later, whereupon he joined his high school jazz band.

From the start, he was energetic at listening and lazy at practice. He liked a wider variety of music than Wynton—everything from Led Zeppelin to Funkadelic—and drove his mother a bit crazy playing Donna Summer's "Love to Love You Baby." (Dolores thought it obscene.) As the boys grew older, Wynton was the hard-working pupil, Branford the cut-up. "Wynton used to keep after me to take jazz more seriously and to practice more, but I didn't care. I just wanted to be a pop arranger and record producer—the next Quincy Jones," Branford maintained. "I figured I'd learn just enough about jazz harmony to drop the big chord at the right moment, go to L.A., and make the big money."

First, he enrolled in what he looked upon as an "easy" college, Southern University in Baton Rouge. It also happened to be the school where his father's old friend Alvin Batiste was teaching reed instruments. Branford roomed there with Donald Harrison and played in Southern's nationally famous football marching band, although he claimed he was awful. After a year, however, Batiste saw that both Marsalis and Harrison were too advanced for the school, and threatened to fail them if they didn't move on to someplace more challenging.

As a result, Branford wound up at Berklee, the music conservatory in Boston known for jazz. What changed his lackadaisical attitude was a classmate who introduced him to a record collection that included the great Miles Davis quintet albums of the sixties with Wayne Shorter on tenor. Suddenly, Branford was hooked. "I became immersed in music, almost to the exclusion of having a social life or remembering to eat three times a day," he recalled.

After Berklee, he played alto in Clark Terry's big band for several months. Wynton helped him land a job with Blakey in 1982, replacing Bobby Watson on alto. Then he switched to tenor when he joined Ellis and Wynton for "Fathers and Sons." Here again, Branford thought he "sounded awful," but he loved the instrument's sound. "I found out that I had been playing the alto like a tenor," he noted, "concentrating on the lower registers."

The next year, he and Wynton found themselves playing alongside Davis's former rhythm section—Herbie Hancock, Ron Carter, and Tony Williams on the VSOP II tour. Branford was awed by being on the bandstand with men whose albums had dominated his college days. Finally, Carter took him aside one day. "Look," he said, "we ain't paying you to stand there admiring us. PLAY!" After that, said Branford, "I was all right."

He next played tenor in Wynton's quintet, and for a good period of time he was quite content to be a sideman. No, he did not mind his younger brother getting so much attention, he would reply in response to the inevitable questions. Wynton was the one in the hot seat, he pointed out. He, on the other hand, was "sitting back, observing." Wynton, meanwhile, made it clear Branford was there not because he was his brother, but because he was a terrific player. Besides, it was Branford who had recommended Jeff Watts, a Berklee classmate, to become the drummer in Wynton's first group.

In fact, George Butler soon had Branford in the Columbia

studios as a leader himself. Borrowing pianist Kenny Kirkland, bassist Charnett Moffett, and Watts from Wynton, he made his first album, "Scenes from the City," in late 1983. It got excellent notices, although he was tired of the critics' "he sounds like Wayne Shorter" refrain. He insisted that he sounded at times like Coltrane, Sonny Rollins, or Lester Young as well, preferring to call it "reference, not imitation."

Branford strayed from the jazz fold in 1985, leaving Wynton's band for what he thought was a temporary gig on Sting's "Dream of the Blue Turtles" tour. The English star saw in Branford a spiritual brother who "didn't have any prejudice about music." For his part, Branford enjoyed playing rock; it was a breeze compared with jazz and it allowed him to see a wider musical world. Kirkland, too, jumped at the chance to play with Sting. Branford, in Kirkland's opinion, "needed to define himself outside of Wynton," and the move worked. He came off the tour a more confident and assured musician.

Unfortunately, his stint with Sting caused a rupture with Wynton that took several years to heal. By the time Branford returned to the Brooklyn brownstone with his bride, Teresa Reese, the two brothers were not talking. Though upset, Branford was philosophical. "I am a jazz musician, but sometimes I play rock. For some reason, that makes people mad," he remarked. (No one got mad when he followed in Wynton's footsteps by making a classical album around the same time.)

His jazz chops were rusty after a year and a half on the Sting tour, but Branford went right back to the studio to record his next album, "Royal Garden Blues." (Later, he acknowledged that he might have sounded "100 percent better" if he had given himself more time to practice.) His producer for this record was his brother Delfeayo. The fact that Columbia allowed him to hire Delfeayo, who had majored in producing at Berklee, was seen by some as evidence of Branford's "post-Sting clout."

The title of his next album, "Renaissance," said it all. Here was a young man who refused to be boxed in. During the next few years, Branford played club dates, toured again with Sting, made albums as leader of both a quartet and a trio, wrote music for Spike Lee's film *Mo' Better Blues,* acted in Danny de Vito's *Throw Momma from the Train,* and even made a guest appearance on one of Miles Davis's last recordings. He sat in with everyone—his good friend Harry Connick, Jr., the Grateful Dead, the rap group Public Enemy, the avant-garde World Saxophone Quartet. This was supposed to be the lazy brother?

All the while, Branford projected the image of an easygoing guy. His first trio album, "Trio Jeepy" (Jeepy was one of his nicknames), came about because he had no band at the time. So he called Watts and elder bass statesman Milt Hinton and they did what he called "a jam session, essentially." In the liner notes, Branford twitted his critics by including "a different kind of thanks" to Coleman Hawkins, Don Byas, and Paul Gonsalves "because I don't play like any of them!"

In fact, the consensus among critics was that Branford was finding his own voice, one that was lyrical and adventurous. By the time his highly praised album "The Beautyful Ones Not Yet Born" topped the *Billboard* jazz charts in 1991, Branford was climbing into first place in revised standings of the Marsalis League. "Of the two brothers, Branford is the one who seems the more natural jazzman," *GQ* declared. If there was a competition going on, however, neither brother acknowledged it. Instead, they quietly ended their estrangement, appearing together in television shows and on record. Anyway, it was their opinion that neither one of them nor Delfeayo was the ultimate star in the family.

Watch out for Jason, father and brothers told everyone with a smile; he could surpass them all. Why? "It's too early to tell," said Wynton, "but he has more talent than anybody I've ever seen." Ellis seconded the motion. "He's just musically gifted," Marsalis père said knowingly of Jason. "More so than my other kids."

IS THE D.A.'S SON THE NEXT SINATRA?— HARRY CONNICK, JR.

Of all the wunderkinder to toddle into the modern jazz world from New Orleans, none reached stardom as fast or at such a tender age as Harry Connick, Jr., the son of the city's district attorney. An ambitious unknown when he left high school, he was a recording sensation on the piano within three years and a Broadway headliner shortly thereafter.

Was he the good turtle soup, or merely the mock, to borrow a phrase from a Sinatra standard? Was he the current yuppie hype or Young Blue Eyes? Was he a jazzman at all, or simply a pop dreamboat? As Connick reached the quarter-century mark, one thing was certain: female fans from teens to grand-mothers—and plenty of men as well—were wild about Harry, whose swanky suits and pomaded hair bespoke a retro style in much the same way his music did.

His background was not as distant from show business as it might seem. Harry Connick, Sr., and his wife, Anita, were music lovers who owned a record store before their son was born. It paid for the tuition of both at law school. Afterward, Dad (Harry described him as "a great shower singer") became a prosecu-tor, Mom a judge in small claims court, but there were always records and radio music around the house. One day music was playing and baby Harry started banging on his high chair. His astonished parents realized the one-year-old was keeping time with the downbeat. When he was three, friends gave the Connicks a piano as a Christmas present. The moment he touched it, he knew what he wanted to do.

At the age of six, Junior got his first opportunity to strut his stuff before an audience. Harry Senior was being inaugurated as the city's district attorney; Mrs. Connick demanded that a piano be trundled to the ceremony on the back of a flatbed truck so their son could perform "The Star-Spangled Banner." The little boy reveled in the applause that followed. "That sound generated my interest to continue to play," he said. "I've always wanted to hear that applause."

Part of the family routine was to wander through the French Quarter on weekends, so Junior heard plenty of Dixieland. He sat in with so many bands that, at nine, he joined the musicians' union. His doting father then recruited some Dixieland players to help the boy record an album for a local label. The next year, he appeared in a film with Eubie Blake, the elder statesman of jazz pianists. A year after that, the boy made a second album, accompanied by major traditional jazz players including saxophonist Walter Payton and trumpeter Teddy Riley. But his privileged world was shattered at thirteen, when his mother died of cancer.

The tragedy did not take Harry off the piano bench for long. To his own surprise, his father let him sit in late at night at the Famous Door on Bourbon Street when the band there needed him. "I learned a lot from the musicians on Bourbon Street," he said. He also realized what a delicate position he was in, since the French Quarter was full of activity that was less than law-abiding. "My father came down there to clean up the prostitution and to bust a big heroin ring," he recalled. "I'd be playing down there and he'd be down there at the same time." Young Harry did not find it hard to stay clean and sober.

He did begin taking private lessons from a man who had plenty of experience on the wrong end of the law, James Booker. (Little Harry made it a practice to introduce himself to pianists; a fan letter in his childish scrawl to Armond Hug, an older man who had given him some records, is now framed in the Louisiana State Museum's jazz collection.) The youngster worshiped Booker, despite his eccentricities. He said later he didn't realize the Ivory Emperor had a drug problem, even though Booker occasionally would throw up in the middle of a session. "I didn't know what was wrong. I wasn't thinking about dope when I was eight," he said.

By the time he entered Jesuit high school, Connick was a seasoned performer. And perform he did—even during lunch in the school cafeteria. A fellow student recalled that he could play "almost anything" the students asked for, "even if he had only heard it once." Connick not only was a ham, he was a teenager who, by his own admission, wanted to be popular. "So I'd do Stevie Wonder imitations, Bee Gees, Donna Summer, Michael Jackson." Connick might have chosen Sinatra later on as his vocal role model, but neither students nor teachers remembered hearing him sing like Sinatra in high school. What they did remember was his uncanny impersonation of Stevie Wonder.

He wasn't concentrating on vocals; he was first and foremost a keyboard player. In the afternoons, he went to NOCCA for lessons from Ellis Marsalis, who introduced him to a vast universe of modern jazz. Marsalis showed him bebop and new harmonies. He taught him about Herbie Hancock, Thelonious Monk, Bud Powell, and "just about everybody," said Connick. One problem was that his classical piano teacher fretted about how little he practiced his Bach. There were regular competitions for such students; Ellis figured the kid soon would get his comeuppance. "As soon as he gets into competition and loses, he'll practice," Marsalis assured Betty Blanq, the classical teacher. Marsalis was wrong; Harry never lost. One year, Ellis brought him to perform at a jazz educators' conference in Kansas City. George Butler, the Columbia jazz A & R man, was there and he was impressed. "Call me when you get to New York," he told Harry. Little did he know that the young man could barely wait to make that call.

Connick was impatient about fast-forwarding his career. He paid little attention to his academic studies. In 1983, he made yet another record. Steve Masakowski, a New Orleans jazz guitarist and teacher, was part-owner of the studio where Harry booked time. "He came in with a rhythm section," said Masakowski. "He said he wanted to make a record before his seventeenth birthday. He was an amazing piano player. Later, we did a duet gig at Snug Harbor. I would play a complex line and he could play it right back."

Without graduating from high school, Harry fled New Orleans at eighteen to seek his fortune in New York. He took a room at the Y, got in touch with Branford and Wynton Marsalis, whom he had known for years, haunted bars and restaurants for gigs, and dogged George Butler with almost daily phone calls. Butler did not return them.

His early dates were not at Carnegie Hall. One night a week he played at the Empire Diner, a hip twenty-four-hour grill in Chelsea on the West Side frequented in the wee hours by a typically motley crew of New York bon vivants. On Sunday mornings, he was organist and choir director for a church in the Bronx. Eventually he picked up a steady gig at the Knickerbocker, a Greenwich Village saloon.

In person, Connick even then was a scintillating one-man act who could segue from Billie Joel to Thelonious Monk to Stevie Wonder on the ivories and engage his listeners in banter at the same time. One patron, whom he later described as "an oil guy from Zimbabwe," handed him a thousand-dollar tip. Still, as Branford Marsalis recalled, plenty of people at the Knickerbocker would pay no attention, talking throughout his show.

Connick was getting nowhere in his quest for a record contract. Then one night he went to hear Wynton Marsalis play at Mikell's, an Upper West Side club popular among the city's jazz musicians. Noticing Connick, Marsalis made piano-playing motions with his fingers, a signal that his friend might sit in. Connick didn't need a whole lot of encouragement and played a few tunes. As luck would have it, Butler was also at Mikell's that night. Afterward, he reminded Connick how interested he had been in him: "You were supposed to call," he said. The next day, Connick phoned Butler at 9 A.M. At last, Butler accepted the call and arranged for Harry to make a demo.

Connick, of course, was thrilled. But there were a few more twists of fate in store. A bassist and drummer backed out of the demo right before his audition, so he entered the studio all by himself, gripped by tension. Inside was a big white piano and a sound technician. The technician convinced him that he sounded just fine. It was the moment Harry Connick had been awaiting for most of his eighteen years and he did not let himself down. He played a few numbers but did not sing a note. Once Butler heard the tape, he offered him a contract.

Connick put together most of his first album accompanied only by Ron Carter, who had also worked on Wynton's debut album. "We had no rehearsal. We just did it," said Connick. The songs—"Love Is Here to Stay," "On Green Dolphin Street," "I Mean You"—showed him to be a derivative virtuoso with chunks of Oscar Peterson, Errol Garner, Monk, Booker, and everyone else in his style.

The album was very much a New Orleans musical family affair. He dedicated "On the Sunny Side of the Street" to Booker's memory. (Indeed, a half century of New Orleans piano can be traced by listening to versions of that number as recorded by Tuts Washington, James Booker, and Harry Connick.) One number, "E," written for Ellis, was performed with Wynton's sidemen Reginald Veal and Herlin Riley, themselves both New Orleanians. The producer: twenty-two-year-old Delfeayo. Wynton and Branford both pronounced his debut "a killer," Harry said later. He was nineteen years old.

Connick went on to audition for any piano gig available. Over the course of two years, he appeared on both the "Tonight" and "David Letterman" shows, but they were not happy experiences. At the "Tonight" show, he said he was forced to play with one of Doc Severinsen's bassists because a solo piano wouldn't be loud enough coming on after the studio band. "I'm from New Orleans. I play loud!" he replied. On the Letterman set, he was hurt by Paul Shaffer's suggestion that he sounded like a lounge act.

Connick was gaining recognition. Clubgoers clamored for more singing from him, although he felt vocals were still secondary to his piano work. But on his next album, entitled "20" (his age), he sang quite a bit more. Before making the record, he wisely went for his first visit ever to a vocal coach. What happened? "I opened up my throat, and my range and style totally changed," he said.

The record quickly sprinted to Number 6 on the *Billboard* jazz charts, setting the stage for his next major break—a month's booking in January 1989 at the swank Oak Room in the Algonquin Hotel. The environment and audience were as tailor-made for Connick's style as his extravagantly cut suits. Here was a handsome, charming, clean-cut young man who played and sang Arlen, Gershwin, and Porter with freshness and panache, who could swing into a jazz tune at will, who would swap places with his bassist, Ben Wolfe, just for fun. He wasn't just a performer, he was an entertainer. Patrons swooned and reviewers raved.

The Connick buzz was all over New York—including Black Rock, the building where Columbia Records was housed. He was not naive about why, all of a sudden, he was getting the attention he had courted so ardently. "I sing, and I'm young, and I wear baggy suits, and I play jazz, and I'm white," he told *Rolling Stone*. "I'm a novelty. The sounds that come out of me shouldn't be coming out of someone so young."

Nonetheless, he denied that he was crafting an image based on stars like the early Sinatra. The gel in his hair was to keep it out of his eyes. His suits were loose because it was hot onstage. "I don't want to be a revivalist. I was born in 1967; I could care less about the forties," he declared. He paid obeisance to the Crescent City jazz tradition, asserting that he was continuing a line begun by Wynton and Branford. "I roll my socks down because Louis Armstrong did," he said. His music was "not that Lite jazz, it's the real thing." Then again, when Tony Bennett said Harry could become the next Sinatra, Connick had the good sense to say he was honored.

Connick's biggest break of all was just around the corner. A Columbia executive introduced him to director Rob Reiner, who was completing *When Harry Met Sally*. The film itself was filled with famous versions of standards by Sinatra, Armstrong, and Ella Fitzgerald. But Reiner was looking for someone to cover

them for a soundtrack album. Because either the stars themselves or their estates "didn't want to be part of the album,"
according to Connick, "I ended up doing all the songs." He was
modest, at least out loud, about his vocal talent. "I don't think
I'm anything that special," he protested. "I'm not really a jazz
singer like Betty Carter. I'm not on a level with Sinatra." It
hardly mattered by then. The soundtrack album sold 200,000
copies in the first month, rocketing Harry Connick, Jr., into
show-biz orbit.

Hometown fans had jammed the jazz tent when he played
the 1989 Jazz Festival. A few months later, a four-night stand
at Snug Harbor was sold out almost the minute tickets went
on sale. Before you could say *Memphis Belle*, Connick was
playing a featured role in a movie by that name, set, naturally,
in the forties. Within a few months, he, conductor Mark Shai-
man, and a thirty-piece orchestra, billed as the "When Harry
Met Sally Tour," were being booked into 3,000-seat halls rather
than 300-seat clubs. The record won him his first Grammy.

Connick now had an opportunity to stretch as many new
directions as he wanted. And he did, but not in the way fans of
his piano jazz days might have expected. He released two
albums at once in 1991, an acoustic jazz excursion called "Lofty's
Roach Soufflé" with Wolfe on bass and Shannon Powell on
drums, and a collection of romantic ballads called "We Are in
Love." At the same time, he went on tour leading his own six-
teen-piece orchestra. He presented a show so reminiscent of
fifties Las Vegas pop that it could have been a copy of a Sinatra
program under the baton of Nelson Riddle. Connick even joked
that during a stop in Palm Springs; he fantasized about breaking into Sinatra's house. "He's like a god to me," Harry
acknowledged.

In fact, Harry worshiped more than one Hollywood deity. A
wintertime gig took him to celebrity-filled Aspen. Having a drink
one night at the Little Nell Hotel, Connick spotted Arnold
Schwarzenegger at a nearby table. He was thrilled, and not
embarrassed to admit it. "He's an idol of mine. I started lifting

weights years ago because of him," the musician said to his companions. "Do you think he would mind if I introduced myself?" Assured that the Terminator would probably be delighted, he paid a call on Schwarzenegger. At his concert the next night, Connick proceeded to tell his audience all about the incident with Arnold.

The exponential growth of his celebrity did bring him a few negative reviews, to which he retorted, "There's nothing wrong with being popular." Testily he declared that critics and musicians hated him but he didn't care. "I say, 'bye, I see you later.' I put all my money in the bank."

Not all musicians knocked him. "The main difference between Harry and me is that Harry can sing," Branford Marsalis said amiably. "Harry sold a million records. I will *never* sell a million records." Concluded Branford, "There is the advantage of being white that you can't ignore."

It remained to be seen where Connick would take his prodigious gifts next. A *Down Beat* reviewer disparaged his 1992 chart-topping album "Blue Light Red Light," saying Harry had become "the light beer of crooners. To the whitebread masses, he tastes great. To surly jazz critics, he's less filling." There was, happily, loads of time for Harry Connick, Jr., to develop into a full-bodied brew.

WYNTON'S FLOCK
....

Wynton Marsalis became the "shepherd," as one of his followers put it, for a flock of accomplished acoustic jazz soloists in the late eighties and early nineties. "It is as if someone recently woke up a sleeping giant in New Orleans and unleashed a new school of players bent on rerouting modern jazz from its disastrous electronic course," marveled critic Chris Albertson. Besides Branford Marsalis and Harry Connick, Jr., the New Orleanians among Wynton's flock included his sidemen, bassist Reginald Veal and drummer Herlin Riley, his brother, trombonist Delfeayo, as well as trumpeters Terence Blanchard, Marlon Jordan, and Nicholas Payton, flutist Kent Jordan (Marlon's brother), alto saxophonist Donald Harrison, and tenor saxophonist Victor Goines.

Among these younger players, the baby-faced Blanchard was the most immediate heir. Born in 1964, he knew Wynton and Branford in elementary school. He started high school at St. Augustine, but once he heard how far the Marsalises had progressed, he enrolled at NOCCA. Trained on the piano, he had never had a formal trumpet lesson before. "From what I knew about the trumpet, probably the most involved thing you could play was the call at the racetrack," he said. Upon graduation, he continued his studies at Rutgers University in New Jersey and put in some time with Lionel Hampton's big band.

When the Marsalises decided to leave Art Blakey's Jazz Messengers, Wynton recommended Blanchard and Harrison, who had been Branford's roommate at Southern University, for auditions. They got the jobs and spent three fruitful years on tour with Blakey. They then formed their own group, and put out several records for George Butler at Columbia. Meanwhile, Blanchard got a chance to work with filmmaker Spike Lee, first appearing on the soundtrack of *School Daze,* then playing the trumpet parts for Denzel Washington's character in *Mo' Better Blues.* Lee next took advantage of Blanchard's composing skills, hiring him to write the soundtracks for *Jungle Fever* and *Malcolm X.*

The comeback of acoustic jazz additionally helped New Orleans musicians not directly associated with either the Marsalis family or brass bands. They included vocalist Germaine Bazzle, a music teacher whose style incorporated singing both scat and the horn parts of songs, and Rick Margitza, a tenor saxophonist who spent time with Maynard Ferguson's big band as well as with small combos.

Another was Tony Dagradi, a fluid post-bop tenor and soprano saxophonist, born in New Jersey and educated at Berklee. After settling in New Orleans in 1977, he began playing with local musicians, many of whom he met at Lu and Charlie's. He made six albums with various combinations of players. His group, Astral Project, was a quintet comprised of Steve Masakowski on guitar, David Torkanowsky on piano, James Singleton on bass, and John Vidacovich on drums—all of them among the busiest artists in other jazz and R&B bands, solo dates, and recordings in New Orleans. The band's featured singer in the mid-eighties was Bobby McFerrin, before he went on to "Don't Worry, Be Happy" fame. Masakowski was spotlighted on record and in concert with his own group, Mars. Pianist David Torkanowsky, too, had a solo career and played an important part alongside such noted singers as Dianne Reeves. Bassist James Singleton and drummer John Vidacovich provided rhythms for countless recording sessions and live performances by everyone from Professor Longhair to Chet Baker.

Dagradi was on the road with an R&B group, Archie Bell and the Drells, when he and his wife decided not to return to the northeast but to settle in New Orleans. What he found, he said, was a city different musically from any other in that "here like no other place anywhere, all the styles of music such as brass bands, traditional jazz, and R&B are being practiced in their original forms." The result was, first, a corps of musicians who were *required* to be versatile, in order to play all those styles, and second, an indigenous sound rooted in drumming that came from the second-line beat, which pulsates through bands as diverse as Astral Project, the Neville Brothers, and the Wynton Marsalis quintet.

To Masakowski, a New Orleans native, the music reflected the complex mix of cultures in this most sophisticated of port cities. "It brings on its own kind of flavor," he said. "In a melting pot, it's a gumbo." Ellis Marsalis viewed it in a slightly different light: a town with a relaxed atmosphere and "laws that permitted the flow of music. There always was an opportunity to play." Today, he continued, the strong tourism industry "has managed to sustain" many musicians. Nonetheless, he worried about students not being "inculcated with values of practice and discipline." The music was still "spirited," but how long would the latest flow of talent last?

Stay tuned.

7 Where to Hear It— Where to Find It

JAZZFEST
....

From the era of Jelly Roll Morton to that of Harry Connick, Jr., New Orleans, with its love of public spectacle, nurtured live music with a devotion no other city in the United States could match. In earlier times, the city boasted opera companies and symphony orchestras as well as marching bands, dance galas, musical picnics, and nightclubs. Although its classical music outlets atrophied, New Orleans and nearby areas still supported a galaxy of venues, outdoor as well as indoor, for popular music. The oldest, Carnival, continued to be the city's biggest tourist attraction. However, in terms of music, the most important was a relatively recent creation: the New Orleans Jazz and Heritage Festival, known to music lovers everywhere as "Jazzfest."

Just as Nashville had the "Grand Old Opry," and Texas "Austin City Limits," New Orleans had the Jazzfest to showcase its musical treasures before a national and increasingly international audience. Since the first event was staged in 1970, this annual spring bash grew into a two-week ten-ring circus of sound, considered by many to be the happiest, freshest, most engaging celebration of popular culture held anywhere. "*The* festival," *Esquire* calls it. "The richest, liveliest" presentation of "American music and its roots," says *Rolling Stone*. Jazzfest producer Quint Davis liked to refer to it as "the world's biggest backyard barbecue."

Jazzfest undoubtedly played a big part in the renaissance of the region's remarkable diversity of music. It is probably also true that given the Crescent City's penchant for partying, Jazzfest had a leg up on other cities even before the first festival was produced. Nevertheless, it took years of roller-coaster revenues for the Jazzfest to reach its potential as the second mightiest party of the year.

In the sixties, various concerts were staged under the name Jazz Festival in New Orleans. But entrepreneur George Wein was the force behind the multi-dimensional festival at Congo Square in April, 1970. The concept was based on the idea Wein and Pete Seeger had in 1959 that gave birth to the Newport Folk Festival, when traditional music held sway in the Rhode Island town on several stages. New Orleans officials urged Wein to develop a Newport-style festival as early as 1962, but he told them it was impossible as long as the city's Jim Crow laws were in effect. (They forbade integrated bands and public assemblies and would have put musicians in segregated hotels.) By 1968, the city had a civil rights law, but the mayor felt the fact that Wein's wife was black might be embarrassing.

Two years later, when the city had a new mayor and apparently a new attitude, Wein was able to proceed. Interested in a program that would celebrate southern Louisiana's unique music, food, and crafts, he approached Quint Davis and Allison Miner, two young music buffs then working at the Tulane Jazz Archives, to help him line up local musicians.

Congo Square, the historic slaves' gathering place, had long been called Beauregard Square. It was a grassy area outside the Municipal Auditorium on the edge of the French Quarter. For the first festival, the organizers set up a 20 × 30-foot tent for gospel acts and three other stages to feature Cajun, blues, and "street" music. Buster Holmes, a long-established restaurant, signed on to sell red beans and rice. Admission for the day-long programs was three dollars. Meanwhile, evening programs at higher prices were scheduled aboard the riverboat *President* and at the Municipal Auditorium. Opening night on the *President* was a festive occasion starring hometown hero Pete Fountain, and the subsequent evenings were gala indeed: they were highlighted by Duke Ellington, who wrote a special suite for the occasion, and Mahalia Jackson, at last starring in her native city. For the Heritage Fair, as the daytime shows and exhibits were called, a brass band paraded through the streets of the city, leading people to Beauregard Square. It was not exactly a throng; over the weekend three hundred musicians played for about two hundred paying customers. Among them was a part-time clarinetist named Woody Allen, who interrupted filming of his movie *Bananas* in Puerto Rico to catch the action. "It's like watching Willie Mays all your life and then finding yourself in the outfield with him," Allen said.

All the elements that would make the festival unique were in place, in embryonic form—the multiple stages, the food booths, the crafts, the emphasis on homegrown musical styles. The most remarkable moment of the weekend happened spontaneously. Joyce Wein, the wife of the producer, brought Mahalia Jackson to the Heritage Fair to see what was going on. On the spot, the first lady of gospel took a mike from the stage and began singing "Just a Closer Walk with Thee," backed by a band of Mardi Gras Indians and the Olympia Brass Band, while Ellington held an umbrella to shade her.

Mahalia Jackson's return set the stage for subsequent welcomes. The next year, the festival scored a coup by bringing home eighty-four-year-old trumpeter Kid Ory (who was greeted by a band at the airport) for his first local gig since 1919. The 1981 festival saw the great Roy Brown, a nearly forgotten yet important figure in the history of rhythm and blues, take the stage. In 1990, it was Champion Jack Dupree's turn to become reacquainted with his hometown.

Jazzfest might have been a spiritual success from the start, but economically it foundered. Although the Miller Brewing Company sponsored the shows, the early productions lost so much money that Wein was asked to cancel the daytime music and concentrate on the money-making evening shows. He refused, arguing that the show would be robbed of its unique regional spirit. Instead, around 1972 the presentation was restructured. George Wein and Davis's father, Arthur Q. Davis, a prominent architect, signed notes at the bank to keep it solvent. A nonprofit organization was set up as overseer. For the next ten years, the shows did not make money, but Wein and young Davis, an acting major who dropped out of Tulane to work full time for Wein, enlisted additional sponsors to keep the festival afloat.

By 1972, the festival's daytime activities had outgrown Beauregard Square. They were relocated on five stages, including an enlarged tent for gospel, in the infield of the Fairgrounds, the New Orleans racetrack. Homegrown favorites Professor Longhair, Deacon John, Snooks Eaglin, and Allen Fontenot were among the performers. Local chefs stirred up jambalaya and gumbo in twenty-five food stalls. And where else but Louisiana would such a festival open with a former governor, Jimmy Davis, singing "You Are My Sunshine"? It was hailed by the *Times-Picayune* as "some of the best sounds and foods ever to represent the real South Louisiana traditions."

Benny Goodman headlined the opening night in 1973, but local musicians once again held sway at the Fairgrounds. There were so many acts by this time that *Figaro,* a New Orleans alternative weekly paper, put out the first tout sheet with capsule descriptions of every act, a practice that was to be continued by the weekly newspaper *Gambit* in subsequent years. Stevie Wonder, in town for an evening show, got up onstage with the Meters for one memorable moment, and the set that closed the Jazzfest that Sunday was magical: Professor Longhair on a big stage, with Eaglin, George Porter, and Ziggy Modeliste as his sidemen.

Year by year, Jazzfest grew in numbers of both performers and visitors. By 1974, there were six stages. By 1978, they numbered ten, including two gazebos and a jazz tent. The gospel tent got larger and larger each year. In the crowds were visitors from Europe and Japan, who had read about this cultural phenomenon in their own jazz publications. By 1978 the program stretched into two weekends at the Fairgrounds, accommodating several hundred acts and thousands of listeners. For the tenth anniversary, Ella Fitzgerald headlined an evening concert, while Earl "Fatha" Hines and nonagenarian Eubie Blake were at the keyboards another night. In the years that followed, the Jazzfest finally grew profitable. It became the scene of thrilling reunions and remarkable guest shots. The Neville Brothers appeared onstage with Wild Tchoupitoulas, Aaron Neville began making regular trips to the gospel tent to sing with the Zion Harmonizers, an adolescent Harry Connick, Jr. shared James Booker's piano bench, Irma Thomas made her triumphant Crescent City return, Stevie Ray and Jimmy Vaughan jammed together, and the Marsalis family took over the jazz tent.

As Jazzfest entered its third decade, it boasted three hundred thousand fans who packed the tents and stage areas over the course of two long weekends to hear more than five thousand musicians. "We pay everyone market value," Davis, now the year-round director, said. "In some cases, we set their market value." And what value listeners got for their money! Even when the daily Fairgrounds ticket reached seven dollars (ten dollars if you did not buy it in advance), it was the biggest bargain in the entertainment field. On a Sunday in 1990, for instance, you could hear the Southern Bells, Snooks Eaglin, Dewey Balfa, Mahlathini and the Mahatolla Queens, Danny Barker and His Jazz Hounds with Blue Lu, the Mighty Clouds of Joy, Alvin Batiste, Germaine Bazzle, Ramsey Lewis, the Dirty Dozen Brass Band, Zachary Richard, the Radiators, Johnny Adams, Allen Toussaint, Linda Ronstadt, and Aaron Neville, to name just some of the more than fifty acts scheduled for the day. That is, you could hear them if you could somehow manage to dash from stage to stage, tent to tent, from one end of the racetrack infield to the other during the eight hours the festival was in progress, without collapsing from the humidity or turning crawfish red from the relentless sun. Sooner or later, you would be side-tracked by the scents wafting across the infield from the food booths, which offered the most luscious fast food available in the United States—jambalaya, cochon du lait, soft-shell crab po'boys, oysters Rockefeller, alligator pie, sweet potato pone—all priced at no more than five dollars per portion. You could wash them down with beer, soft drinks, or free bottled water, but en route your eye might be caught by one of the dozens of unusual crafts offered by jewelers, painters, furniture makers, quilters, and even a canoe maker.

By the end of that Sunday, however, you would have experienced only the *first* weekend; then you would need to rest up for three days more the following weekend. (In 1991, the festival added a full program on Thursday of the second week, making a total of seven days at the Fairgrounds in the course of two weeks.) As Mason Ruffner remarked after playing the Jazzfest, "Part of the charisma is that you have to go back next year to catch all of the stuff you missed."

For New Orleans, a city nearly crushed by the slump in the oil industry, the festival became more than just a party. It was a financial bonanza as well. A 1988 economic survey reported that Jazzfest brought in $31.9 million in revenue to New Orleans, making it the equal of the Sugar Bowl and the NCAA Final Four. More than a third of the listeners were from out of town, putting an additional $15.1 million into the coffers of local merchants. The Jazz and Heritage Foundation also squirreled away enough surplus to buy WWOZ, a local radio station that is now devoted to New Orleans music almost exclusively, and to support individual grants and special programs in schools.

Naturally, there were bumps and potholes on the road to success. Although the Jazzfest was acclaimed by many as the nation's premier music showcase and spawned imitations, musicians periodically complained that nationally known acts, such as the Temptations, Los Lobos, Linda Ronstadt, and Al

Green, were squeezing local players out of choice spots on the big stages. There was grumbling every time a "tradition" in the short life of the festival was changed. For instance, where once the stages had numbers and/or names, they later were identified by sponsors, so that, for example, the Fess Stage became the Ray Ban Stage and Economy Hall found itself with the moniker Cox Cable Economy Hall. In this, the producers took a page out of the college football playbook, in which the Sugar Bowl became the USF &G Sugar Bowl, but some observers dislike the commercialism. Critics such as Jon Pareles of the *New York Times* expressed disappointment at local performers who transformed themselves into "generic oldies acts." Many fans were upset when, in the eighties, the festival instituted a ban on outside bottles and cans; dragging a red wagon heaped with twelve-packs of beer had been the mark of the experienced festival goer. Periodically, Jazzfest was accused of importing too many "outsiders" as headliners of the evening shows, even though that had been done from the beginning. As it turned out, natives Wynton Marsalis and Harry Connick, Jr., became such national figures that they were the stars of the first three evenings in 1991.

If anything, the national and international acclaim the festival received could be its most serious problem. Longtime fans fondly remembered how, in the first fifteen years and more, there was plenty of room at the Fairgrounds for everyone to get close to a stage, to have a picnic, even to pitch tents on the outskirts of the infield. The first day of the Heritage Fair, a Friday, was especially popular with schoolchildren and thousands of adults who played hooky from work to attend. Lately, however, the crowds became so enormous (there were 75,000 people at the final Sunday show in 1991 alone) that Jazzfest lost a bit of its relaxed atmosphere. According to *Wavelength*, the city's now-defunct music magazine, it had become "a Dionysian rite," for which "respectable citizens begin preparations immediately after the [Mardi Gras] courts of Rex and Comus meet." Where once the event was simply a stroll through the Fairgrounds, *Wavelength* declared solemnly, now "Jazz Festival is serious business."

MARDI GRAS AND OTHER PARTIES
....

Even more serious, in the minds of many old New Orleans families, was Carnival. The word refers to the season of merriment that begins January 6, Twelfth Night, and ends at midnight on Mardi Gras, after which the season of Lent begins. Mardi Gras means Fat Tuesday, when the party season culminates in a whirlwind of parades and balls.

Carnival is a French celebration that dates back to the Middle Ages. Imported by Louisiana's first European settlers, it took hold quickly in the New World. By 1750, less than thirty years after their arrival, the French colonists were already staging rather elaborate balls in their frontier village. The first formal parade was mounted in 1837. Festivities degenerated into brawls by the 1850s. Roving bands of masked thugs became violent enough for some to demand a moratorium on Carnival. However, a group of civilians calling themselves the "krewe" of Comus (Greek for "revelers") staged an orderly, torchlit parade of floats in 1857, restoring some legitimacy to the proceedings. Comus also employed a black band to set the tempo for the flambeau carriers, although Carnival was an entirely Caucasian phenomenon until the end of the century.

After the Civil War, Carnival grew and grew, to the point where there were scores of krewes, each of which poured endless money and time into their costumes, floats, and masked balls. By the 1990s, the public side of Carnival—the elaborate parades through streets packed with celebrants shouting "Throw me something, Mistah!"—had become basically a tourist attraction. Marching bands—both New Orleanian ones such as The Onward Brass Band and the St. Augustine High School band, plus famous collegiate ones such as the Southern University band from Baton Rouge—wound through the streets along with the floats loaded with masked krewe members. The krewes flung plastic beads, drinking cups, and specially embossed coins at the shouting legions of onlookers, some of whom stood for hours to witness each event.

The city's African American population won first-class status in Carnival in 1969 when the Zulus, a well-known "social aid and pleasure club," staged its Zulu parade along a standard parade route. But the Zulu celebration, like that of other black clubs, had been a fixture in the black community on Mardi Gras day for years before the city fathers chose to "recognize" it. Zulu started out as a parody of white festivities; the king of the Zulus tossed coconuts to eager throngs in a sendup of the likes of King Rex, who showered crowds with beads and coins. By the late twentieth century, Zulu was very much a part of the mainstream.

Meanwhile, there was a second Carnival tradition among blacks, one that went back perhaps as far as the eighteenth century. These were the Mardi Gras Indians. Since at least the turn of this century, tribes, or gangs of Indians, from all over the city gathered in African American neighborhoods on Mardi Gras day (and selected other days as well), dressed in colorful beaded and feather-laden outfits they spent months sewing by hand. Led by a chief (the equivalent of a king of a krewe), each tribe snaked through the streets, dancing to the thunderous Afro-Caribbean pounding of drums and other marching instruments. They were trailed by a long procession of second-liners. Although the private balls and police-protected parades of whites attracted most of the media and tourist attention, Indians were considered by many the heart of black Carnival.

The holiday had its own traditions in Cajun country as well. Celebrants in the *Courir du Mardi Gras* rode on horseback from town to town collecting contributions for a communal Mardi Gras gumbo pot. Led by a "capitaine," the riders (along with a "second line" consisting of a beverage truck, a bandwagon, and numerous cars) were not permitted to throw anything. At each home owner's yard, they dismounted, performed songs, danced, and had a good time until everyone was ready to go on to the next stop. There would be a public dance and gumbo when the riders returned late in the afternoon to an appointed spot.

In recent years, all of South Louisiana caught Mardi Gras fever for the first two months of each year. Drinking, more than eating or dancing, appeared to be the major activity in New Orleans, especially toward Fat Tuesday itself. If there were any sober celebrants in New Orleans by noon, after the Zulu and Rex processions wound through the streets, they were probably indoors, trying to avoid the carousing hordes. Not everyone thought that was a good thing; a local economics professor provoked considerable discussion in the sixties when he theorized that the "Mardi Gras Syndrome" drained New Orleans of valuable investment dollars and energy, which might otherwise be spent on civic improvements.

Nevertheless, for the city's music industry, Mardi Gras was a boon. Bands were kept busy playing public and private parties (some of the balls are so exclusive they make the ritziest country clubs seem democratic), while the yearly influx of tourists guaranteed musicians plenty of bookings at clubs and hotels. Paradoxically, numerous residents of New Orleans deserted the city during the hectic final two weeks of Carnival season, preferring to enjoy a respite from partying and at the same time collecting a small fortune from visitors who rent their houses and apartments.

In that it sparked a similarly jovial spirit, the Jazz Festival, which begins in late April, continued the Mardi Gras theme. Also, like Mardi Gras, it motivated organizers in other towns to stage their own festivals. As of 1991, there were more than one hundred celebrations throughout the year in South Louisiana, many of which featured live bands. The most important, in terms of music, were the Festivals Acadiens (September, Lafayette); the Festival International de Louisiane (April, Lafayette); the Southwest Louisiana Zydeco Music Festival

(August, Opelousas); the River City Blues Festival (Labor Day weekend, Baton Rouge); the Jam-Bal-aya du Musique (September, Lafayette); and the Festforall (May, Baton Rouge).

All the festivals mentioned here are subject to change. Readers are urged to consult the local chambers of commerce about dates and acts. Also, the authors would be derelict in their duty if they did not mention some of the food-related festivals. These include The Louisiana Crawfish, Ponchatoula Strawberry, Cochon de Lait, Tomato, Dairy, Jambalaya, Bayou Lacombe Crab, Louisiana Catfish, Louisiana Oyster, Delcambre Shrimp, Rayne Frog, Bridge City Gumbo, Louisiana Gumbo, Greater Mandeville Seafood, Andouille, Gueydan Duck, and Cracklin' Festivals, as well as our personal favorite, Basile's Louisiana Swine Festival. (The latter is described by the New Orleans *Times-Picayune* as "a tribute to the pig and its many products. . . . Hog calling, greasy pig and boudin eating contests.") Bon Appetit!

The most ambitious of the Louisiana musical events beyond the Jazzfest was the Festival International de Louisiane, which presented both classical and pop music performers from fourteen "Francophone" countries. In a given year, they might include drumming groups from Africa, a Congolese ballet troupe, a Belgian rock group called Les Gangsters d'Amour, and a Nova Scotia folk music band, along with local performers such as Beausoleil and Boozoo Chavis. The attendance at the 1991 Festival exceeded 250,000, making it the biggest event in Southwest Louisiana.

The Festival International was deliberately multicultural, stressing the connections between Louisiana's French heritage and that of other French-speaking people from Quebec to Brussels to Burundi. It was also consciously highbrow; visitors saw and heard not just popular music but art exhibits, dance troupes, and string quartets. As another manifestation of Cajun pride, the festival was especially successful. Said Canadian folk singer Edith Butler, a native of New Brunswick, "I feel like I am coming back home. Two hundred years have separated us, but you have not lost the Acadian accent that we have up north. You have not lost your *joie de vivre*," she told the Lafayette newspaper.

The flip side of this deliberately international roster was the Festivals Acadiens. This gathering was an extraordinary, weekend-long summit meeting on things Cajun, presented almost entirely free of charge. Begun in 1974 under the sponsorship of CODOFIL, it was later overseen by the Lafayette Jaycees and other local groups. In contrast to its New Orleans cousin, this fete had but one stage, set in the middle of a public park, but some of the most charismatic musicians of the region appeared on it, from legends such as the Balfa brothers and Clifton Chenier to younger artists such as Bruce Daigrepont and Zydeco Force.

Each year, from early on Saturday morning, Girard Park, the festival site, was covered with the blankets and folding chairs of picnicking families. But a large patch directly in front of the stage was always left empty to accommodate dancers. A roadway from the music area led to the booths set up in front of the Natural History Museum, where Cajun crafts people demonstrated everything from cooking jambalaya to skinning alligators.

The New Orleans spirit reached beyond the state's borders in recent years as distant cities identified a market for Louisiana-style food and music celebrations hundreds of miles from the source. There were numerous out-of-state festivals staged along Jazzfest lines each year. Among the best known: the Big Easy Bash and Cajun Festival, both in Rhode Island; the Bay Area Cajun/Zydeco Festival in California; and Jambalaya Jam in Philadelphia.

THE CLUB SCENE

One reason New Orleans has been so rich in music is the large number and great variety of venues—indoor as well as outdoor—where performers can polish their techniques and their entertainment skills.

In the earliest days of jazz, honky-tonks, dance halls, restaurants, and brothels all contributed to the spread of the new music because they employed the hottest musicians. Funky Butt Hall on Perdido Street, owned from the end of the Civil War by the Unions Sons Relief Association, was perhaps the most famous. That was where a very young Louis Armstrong, who grew up on the same block, heard Buddy Bolden play. Also important were clubs such as Big 25, a gambling house and bar run by Johnny Lala near North Franklin and Customhouse Street in Storyville. Even accomplished Creole musicians, violinist Paul Dominguez, for one, found the money there seductive. As he told Alan Lomax, he could work seven nights a week, making $1.25 plus tips a night. "That's how they make a fiddler out of a violinist," he said. Freddie Keppard played his last New Orleans gigs at Pete Lala's Café at 1300 Customhouse Street (now Iberville) before heading north; his replacement there, in 1911, was Joe Oliver. Economy Hall, a dance hall at 1422 Ursuline Street; Tom Anderson's, a cabaret owned by the boss of the red-light district; the Tin Roof Café; and Mahogany Hall, Lulu White's famous brothel at 235 Basin Street, which employed such pianists as Tony Jackson and Jelly Roll Morton, were also key sites. Unfortunately, all have been demolished.

In the decades following the abolition of Storyville, there developed dozens of nightclubs on Rampart Street and later on Bourbon Street, ranging from the most tawdry to the most elegant. The Pelican Roof Ballroom at 407 South Rampart and the Old Absinthe House at Bourbon and Iberville, which still exists, were two of them. Older traditional jazzmen found a new home in 1961, however, when Preservation Hall opened at 726 St. Peter Street in the French Quarter. It became an internationally known spot for hearing the finest of these venerable musicians.

The headquarters of New Orleans R&B in its heyday following World War II was the Dew Drop Inn at 2836 La Salle Street, owned by African American businessman Frank Painia. An extension of a hotel where entertainers stayed, it was considered the first "decent" nightclub for blacks, with a floor show, an emcee, and a house band. In the early fifties, musicians playing or recording in town habitually hung out in front of the Dew Drop after their shows, or went inside and jammed. Allen Toussaint, for one, had fond memories of shake dancers and an emcee, Patsy Valderer, who dressed as a female impersonator in a fancy gown and gestured with a long cigarette holder. Just a boy at the time, Toussaint reminisced about "the drop-outs and the drop-ins" who made the place a "music haven."

Beginning in the fifties, the Dew Drop served as both hangout and hiring hall, a round-the-clock site where the key movers and shakers could collect people for a band or record date, listen to one another, and play together. Headliners like Dinah Washington and Little Willie John, up-and-coming stars like Ray Charles, Little Richard, and James Brown, visiting celebrities like Duke Ellington and Ella Fitzgerald, local performers like Smiley Lewis and Huey Smith, major band leaders like Dave Bartholomew and Paul Gayten, and the best instrumentalists like Lee Allen, Red Tyler, and Earl Palmer, all congregated night after night at the Dew Drop. White R&B buffs made forays to the Dew Drop, although the segregation laws of the time forbade real contact. The most notorious event to take place there occurred when white movie star Zachary Scott and his party came one Saturday night in 1952 to catch the show. They were socializing at a table with blacks when the police, acting on a tip, raided the place and arrested Scott, Painia, and others on charges of race "mixing." (By Monday, the charges were dropped.) The Dew Drop's chief rival was the Club Tiajuana on Saratoga Street, which included stripteasers in its floor show and drew a less affluent, younger crowd.

In the sixties, such great acts as Sam Cooke and Otis Redding played the Dew Drop, and Little Richard even immortalized it in a song. But the Groove Room, as the nightclub portion was officially called, closed after Frank Painia got sick in the late sixties and the scene faded. In the seventies, *Shangri La*, a musical developed by Charles Neville and written by white playwright Dalt Wonk, along with special Jazzfest "Dew Drop Inn Revisited" shows, paid tribute to this special breeding ground for the New Orleans sound.

Modern jazz in New Orleans had a mecca, too, but only for a few years beginning in 1972. Jazz lovers and musicians made Lu and Charlie's, the Rampart Street restaurant and club, their haunt. According to co-owner Charlie Bering, it was a monopoly. "We were the only modern jazz club in town," he said. "We walked right into it and found a ready and waiting crowd for the music." Before it closed on New Year's Eve, 1977, Lu and Charlie's hosted such musicians as the Ellis Marsalis Quartet, Milt Jackson, James Moody, Art Pepper, and Nat Adderly.

Lu and Charlie's music room seated only ninety people, the bar no more than sixty, so that it never really was cost-effective and could never afford large ensembles. Still, musicians looked back at the place with great affection. Hearing his father play there, said Wynton Marsalis, "made me want to be a jazz musician. I liked the environment, the stories people would tell." The club, he added, "took musicians and put them with listeners and the two made a special feeling together. It was very different from hearing my father and other musicians rehearse. There was something ceremonial about it," he concluded, "the intensity of a New Orleans parade compressed into one room."

Beginning in the seventies, the phrase "going to school" took on a literal meaning as the New Orleans Center for the Creative Arts (NOCCA) and the music departments of local universities became places where the brightest students benefited from the tutelage of master teachers such as Ellis Marsalis (NOCCA and the University of New Orleans), Clyde Kerr

(NOCCA), Tony Dagradi (Loyola), Harold Battiste (UNO), and Alvin Batiste (Southern University in Baton Rouge).

NOCCA, founded in 1974, was established as a part-time institution that admitted high school students by audition only. Students would take academic courses at a regular school, then go to NOCCA for music instruction. Stellar graduates such as Wynton Marsalis, plus those who attended but did not complete formal course work, such as Harry Connick, Jr., returned to the school regularly to give pep talks or put on fund-raising concerts. Performances were a key element in New Orleans musical education. NOCCA students were required to participate once a week in ensemble groups. The UNO campus even had a nightclub called the Sandbar, where jazz students could get together and jam.

Still, however many Marsalises graduated from NOCCA, however huge the Jazz and Heritage Festival grew, however many chances Aaron Neville or another local star might get to sing the national anthem in the Superdome, the raffish nightclubs of New Orleans and the roadhouses throughout Cajun country were the places where new sounds and new acts could be birthed and nurtured before being released into the wider music world.

In Cajun country, the most famous sites for live music were two huge dance halls. Mulate's, near Breaux Bridge, and Randol's, near Lafayette, were both located out in the countryside and featured the best-known Cajun bands of the day. (Mulate's recently opened a New Orleans branch in the Warehouse District.) At both, heaping plates of food were as much a part of the ambience as the musicians, who played tirelessly for hours each evening. Unlike New Orleans, where music at some places did not begin until 10 P.M., the Cajun halls kept earlier hours; many bands packed up well before midnight. Zydeco was more apt to be heard at clubs like Slim's Y Ki Ki, north of Opelousas, which catered more to a black crowd; Richard's, between Lawell and Opelousas; and El Sido's in Lafayette.

In recent years, the most famous club in New Orleans was Tipitina's at 500 Napoleon Avenue in the Uptown area. First opened in 1977 under a cooperative ownership by admirers of Professor Longhair, it quickly became an institution. *Esquire* touted it as a "classic" bar, a "fabulous funky place." It fell victim to the economic decline of New Orleans and was forced to shut its doors in 1984. Soon, however, a new group of business people renovated and reopened it. A good-sized, plain-jane hall with a handful of chairs and tables, two long bars on either side of the room, a balcony overhanging the dance floor, and a bust of Professor Longhair at the entrance, Tipitina's remained a shrine to the late piano master and a magnet for every kind of visiting and local act from the Indigo Girls to the Neville Brothers. A scene from the 1987 movie *The Big Easy* was filmed at Tipitina's, which was gussied up by a set designer for that occasion. Unsuspecting outsiders who subsequently sought it out were shocked to find that it was not an upscale yuppie fern bar. As a concession to its tourist trade, however, Tipitina's did eventually start selling souvenirs and accepting credit cards.

For up-to-date information on clubs in New Orleans, readers are urged to consult the monthly magazine *Offbeat* or the weekly *Gambit*. Both are available free at many hotels, clubs, coffee houses, and record shops. The Friday "Lagniappe" section of the New Orleans *Times-Picayune* also carries extensive listings. For Cajun music sites, consult *The Cajun Country Guide* by Macon Fry, published in 1992 by Pelican.

All in all, New Orleans continues to have a vibrant club scene, although individual nightclubs have had their financial ups and downs. No other city in the hemisphere makes available so much live music at such low prices. Musicians complain that such clubs do not pay enough for them to make a living in their hometown. Nevertheless, the Crescent City (and its nearby Cajun country cousins) remains as drenched in music as it was in the heyday of Funky Butt Hall.

ROUNDER, RECORD STORES, AND RADIO

Rounder and Other Labels

South Louisiana musicians have been blessed with several fine independent record labels, retail stores, and radio stations devoted to their music, be it jazz, R&B, pop, Cajun, or zydeco. In addition, the tremendous interest in this music shown by European and Japanese fans has led to a huge volume of releases by overseas companies, especially in the field of New Orleans traditional jazz and early R&B.

A carefully selected discography is included in this chapter. However, it is intended as a guide by the authors to the most widely available major and/or historic recordings by artists covered in this book. We have limited it to compact discs, except in certain cases where very important recordings have not yet been issued in the CD format. The discography is by no means complete; an all-inclusive one would run to hundreds of pages. It includes recordings released through spring 1992.

The most important of the American record companies that issues a great deal of South Louisiana music is Rounder, based in Cambridge, Massachusetts. In its more than twenty years of existence, Rounder has made it a policy to produce albums by both well-known and neglected local artists, from Irma Thomas and Johnny Adams to Beausoleil and Bruce Daigrepont to Buckwheat Zydeco and John Delafose. In addition, Rounder is the distributor for a variety of other independent labels, including the New Orleans–based Black Top (which specializes in blues), Ace, Arhoolie, Alligator, Charly, Antone's, Mardi Gras, and Rhino.

The easiest way to buy records not available in a neighborhood store is through the specialized record stores listed below. Also, some labels will fill orders directly from individuals at retail prices, send a catalog on request, and/or answer questions about their titles. The following is a selected list of labels and their addresses, phones, and Fax numbers:

Alligator Records, P.O. Box 60234, Chicago, IL 60660. Phones: (800) 344-5609, (312) 973-7736. Fax: (312) 973-2088.

Antone's Records, 2928 Guadalupe, Austin, TX 78705. Phone: (512) 322-0617. Fax: (512) 477-2930.

Arhoolie Records, see Down Home Music Co. under Retail Stores.

Black Top Records, P.O. Box 56691, New Orleans, LA 70156. Phone: (504) 895-7239.

Qualiton Imports, Ltd. (Distributor for Classics, Hot'n Sweet, Vogue, and other labels), 23-02 40th Avenue, Long Island City, NY 11101. Phone: (718) 937-8515. Fax: (718) 729-3239.

Rhino Records, 2225 Colorado Avenue, Santa Monica, CA 90404. Phone: (310) 828-1980.

Rounder Records, Main office, One Camp Street, Cambridge, MA 02140. Phone: (617) 354-0700. Fax (617) 491-1970.

Specialized Record Stores

New Orleans and surrounding areas are chock-full of record stores that cater to fans of local music, both old and new. Most of the stores listed below have friendly owners and/or clerks with a great deal of experience fielding questions from all over the world. They are delighted to fill requests or simply chat about music and collecting. During peak seasons such as Mardi Gras and Jazzfest, the shops try to stock up on local and/or featured acts in anticipation of heightened demand.

The largest stores, like Tower, tend to have discounted prices and a large stock of new or newly reissued CDs by leading artists in every category. Readers who seek titles that may be out of print (including those from this book's discography) are urged to contact the smaller stores. Some, such as Record Ron's, Ace, and Jim Russell, specialize in rare and out-of-print titles, as well as LPs otherwise difficult to find. The stores listed in Church Point, Crowley, Lake Charles, and Ville Platte specialize in Cajun, zydeco, and "swamp pop," as they like to refer to local R&B and rock 'n' roll. Many stores will accept phone orders with a major credit card and will ship items anywhere in the world. Hours shown are Central Time. All area codes 504 except where noted.

ACE VIDEO & MUSIC

Mail-order outlet specializes in thousands of New Orleans and South Louisiana R&B, Cajun, and zydeco CDs, LPs, 45s, cassettes, videos, books. Catalog available for $3 (U.S.); $5 (foreign).

P.O. Box 1934, Biloxi, MS 39533-1934.
(601) 374-0777
10 A.M.–4 P.M. Mon.–Fri.
Phone orders? Yes, with major credit card.

ACORN RECORDS & TAPES & MEMORY LANE

A varied stock of CDs, cassettes, and "LPs while they last." All unplayed; does not carry used titles. Especially strong in R&B. Inventory is shallow in jazz, although does carry "hot stuff" like Harry Connick, Wynton Marsalis, etc.

Chalmette—9073 W. Judge Perez Drive. 277-2120.
Metairie—Metairie—6417 Airline Highway. 733-2120
10 A.M.–6 P.M. Mon.–Sat., both stores.
Phone orders? Yes, C.O.D. or major credit cards.

BROWN SUGAR RECORDS

Specializes in R&B, gospel, plus good selection of blues. Mostly used records, some new. All three formats.

New Orleans—2334 Louisiana Avenue. 895-8087
10 A.M.–8 P.M. Mon.–Thurs.; 10 A.M.–9 P.M. Fri. & Sat.; noon–
6 P.M. Sun.
Phone orders? No. Visa & MasterCard accepted in store.

DOWN HOME MUSIC

Retail and mail-order outlet for Arhoolie Records and its subsidiaries, including Old Timey and Blues Classics labels. All three formats. Sample newsletter is $2.

10341 San Pablo Avenue, El Cerrito, CA 94530
Store: (510) 525-2129 Mail orders: (510) 525-1494
Fax: (510) 525-2904
Phone orders? Yes, with check or major credit card.

FLOYD'S RECORD SHOP

The retail outlet of record producer Floyd Soileau's Cajun and zydeco empire. All three formats, plus 45s. Carries latest releases and full collection of Floyd's own labels such as Swallow, Maison de Soul, plus lots more.

434 East Main Street
P.O. Drawer 10, Ville Platte, LA 70586
(318) 363-2184 Fax: (318) 363-5622
8 A.M.–5 P.M. Mon.–Sat.
Phone orders? Yes, with Visa or MasterCard.

GOLD MINE RARE RECORDS COMICS CARDS

Since there are no special clerks who sort records, this store requires in-person searches. CDs, LPs, cassettes. Several stores, but Harahan location is best organized for music.

Harahan—6469 Jefferson Highway. 737-2333
11 A.M.–7 P.M. Mon.–Sat. Closed Sun.
Phone orders? Not applicable. All credit cards accepted.

GOLDBAND RECORDING

Large selection of South Louisiana music at label owner Eddie Shuler's store. All three formats. No used copies. Catalog available on request.

P.O. Box 1485, Lake Charles, LA 70602
(318) 439-8839
9:15 A.M.–5 P.M. Mon.–Fri.
Phone orders? Yes, prepaid by check only.

JIM RUSSELL RARE RECORDS

Thousands of items in stock. Mostly older titles, including lots of traditional jazz, R&B, and older gospel. Not much in

contemporary jazz. CDs, 45s, cassettes, LPs, 8-tracks, 78s.
Includes new and used copies except 78s, which are all used.
New Orleans—1837 Magazine Street. 522 2602
10 A.M.–7 P.M. Mon.–Sat.; 1–6 P.M. Sun.
Phone orders? Yes, with major credit card.

MODERN MUSIC CENTER

Large collection of current Cajun and zydeco music, plus
some out-of-print and/or rare titles available at this longtime
recording and retail base for producer Jay Miller. All three formats plus some 45s. No used copies.
413 North Parkerson, Crowley, LA 70526
(318) 783-1601—business phone Fax: (318) 788-0776
9 A.M.–5 P.M. Mon.–Fri. 9 A.M.–noon Sat.
Mail orders? Yes, with major credit card.

MUSHROOM

All New Orleans and South Louisiana music. "Our specialty
is Professor Longhair, Dr. John, Radiators & local rock bands,
plus Mardi Gras music." Also carry good collection of local
contemporary artists. Mainly CDs and cassettes and some old
45s. Mainly new, some used.
1037 Broadway near Tulane University. 866-6065
11 A.M.–10 P.M. 7 days
Phone orders? Yes, with major credit card.

ODYSSEY RECORDS & TAPES

Canal Street store has large selection of traditional jazz and
other South Louisiana music. All three formats.
1012 Canal Street, near French Quarter. 523-3506
10 A.M.–6 P.M. Mon.–Sat. Closed Sun.
Phone orders? Yes, with major credit card.

RECORD RON'S

Mostly rare and out-of-print records in every category. Very
strong New Orleans section and blues. Mainly LPs plus CDs

and cassettes. New Orleans material is mostly new CDs. Other CDs are used for outside Louisiana. "We have a really amazing amount of Louisiana music from Professor Longhair, Smiley Lewis, etc. When the labels were dumping vinyls, I stocked up," says owner Ron Edelstein. Average price $12–$15 for an old R&B LP. Over 800 different titles.

New Orleans—1129 Decatur Street in French Quarter. 524-9444

Also in the French Quarter at 407 Decatur. 525-2852

11 A.M.–7 P.M., 7 days, both stores.

Phone orders? Yes, with Visa, MasterCard, and American Express.

ROCK N ROLL RECORDS & COLLECTIBLES

Large selection of well-maintained used LPs, including some original pressings. Strong in traditional jazz, blues, rock. Also large stock of traditional jazz on 78s. Some CDs and cassettes.

New Orleans—1214 Decatur Street in French Quarter. 561-5683

10 A.M.–10 P.M. 7 days a week.

Phone orders? Yes, with check, money order, or major credit card.

SOUND CENTER

Specializes in Cajun, zydeco, and Swamp pop CDs, cassettes, LPs. No used records.

329 N. Main Street (P.O. Box 233), Church Point, LA

(318) 684-2176

9 A.M.–5 P.M. Mon.–Fri. 9 A.M.–3 P.M. Sat.

Phone orders? Yes, with major credit card.

SOUND WAREHOUSE

Good varied collection of CDs and cassettes in every category of South Louisiana music at good prices. See phone book for locations throughout metropolitan New Orleans.

SOUNDS FAMILIAR

Full range of local music as well as jazz in general. Not strong in Cajun or gospel titles. "Lots" of out-of-print titles. Specializes in LPs and/or hard-to-find titles. No cassettes. Mostly used recordings.

829 Chartres Street in French Quarter. 523-4839

Phone orders? Yes. with check or major credit card.

11 A.M.—6 P.M. 7 days a week. Closed Mardi Gras day. Open late during Mardi Gras and Jazz Festival seasons.

TOWER RECORDS

Large, well-priced CD and cassette collection of all types of New Orleans and South Louisiana music, old and new. Also good selection of blues, rare imports on CD, plus many locally produced cassettes by local artists. Numerous reissues of early and traditional jazz.

New Orleans—marketplace at Jackson Brewery, 408 N. Peters Street at Decatur Street. 529-4411

9 A.M.—midnight every day of year except Mardi Gras.

Phone orders? Yes, with major credit card.

Special mention should be made of Marc Savoy's music store in Eunice, 40 miles northwest of Lafayette. This store is the center for the husband and wife team of Marc and Ann Savoy, who play traditional Cajun music and write about it. Marc is known for his handmade accordions, which are sold here. The store is a noncommercial haven for serious musicians, who come to talk and especially to jam on Saturday mornings.

Radio

If this book had a soundtrack, it would be the daily broadcasts on WWOZ. This listener-supported station is owned by the Jazz and Heritage Foundation, the sponsor of the Jazz Festival. From early morning until late at night, WWOZ (90.7 on the FM dial) features shows on traditional and contemporary jazz, blues,

R&B, pop, and ethnic music—a great deal of it specifically by South Louisiana artists. WWOZ also broadcasts a Cajun music show in French each Sunday afternoon. The WWOZ producers and disc jockeys are for the most part volunteers. They are not slick but they are knowledgeable, and they include several working musicians.

Other New Orleans stations that pay special attention to local music are the college stations. Tulane's student-run station, WTUL (91.5 FM), broadcasts a live show Monday nights from Tipitina's and the University of New Orleans' WWNO (89.9 FM) features jazz as well as classical music. For contemporary gospel, there is WYLD (940 AM) and WBOK (1230 AM).

In Cajun country, there are a number of radio stations that broadcast Cajun and zydeco music shows in French, the vast majority on Saturdays and Sundays. The best-known station is WRVS, the public radio station in Lafayette (88.7 FM). Its best-known show is "Zydeco Pas Salé" on Saturday mornings. Among the others are:

Abbeville: KROF 104.9 FM or 960 AM
Baton Rouge: WKJN 103 FM, WYNK 101.5 FM
Crowley: KSIG 1450 AM
Donaldsonville: KKAY 104.9 FM or 1590 AM
Eunice: KEUN 1490 AM, KJIB 105.5 FM
Golden Meadow: KLEB 1600 AM
Houma: KJIN 1490 AM
Jennings: KJEF 92.9 FM or 1290 AM
Lake Charles: KAOK 1400 AM, KLCL 1470 AM
Marksville: KAPB 1370 AM or 97.7 FM
Opelousas: KSLO 1230 AM
Thibodaux: KTIB 640 AM
Ville Platte: KVPI 93.5 FM or 1050 AM
Washington: KNEK 1190 AM

MUSIC LIBRARIES, ARCHIVES, JAZZ MUSEUMS

Louisiana is fortunate in having excellent resources for scholars and researchers who seek books, scores, record collections, and archival materials on the state's jazz and popular music. Here is a selected list with notes on each. Call for further details, admission policies and entrance fee (if any), names of contact persons, and hours. All area codes are 504 unless noted.

AMISTAD RESEARCH CENTER AT TULANE UNIVERSITY

This large American ethnic archive includes manuscripts, personal papers, and other materials. Among them: Louisiana Music Collection, 1848–1987, which includes material on music of black Americans, mostly Creoles of Color, principally nineteenth century.

Tilton Hall
6823 Street Charles Avenue, New Orleans, LA 70118
865-5535

HISTORIC NEW ORLEANS COLLECTION

Library Manuscripts Division includes records of the New Orleans Jazz Festival in the seventies. Curatorial division has photographs of New Orleans jazz musicians and jazz funerals.

533 Royal Street, New Orleans, LA 70130
523-4662

NEW ORLEANS STATE MUSEUM

Its New Orleans Jazz Museum section, at the old U.S. Mint, across from the French Market, is a fascinating series of exhibits on the history of jazz, including photos, instruments, posters, and historical displays.

Also houses collections of the New Orleans Jazz Club, including tapes of club's radio programs; recordings; piano rolls;

Don Perry film collection of some 400 reels of 16-mm. film depicting jazz funerals, festivals, and performing jazz bands; sheet music; some 10,000 photographs; newsletters from international jazz clubs; vertical files arranged by musician and subject; etc.

400 Esplanade, P.O. Box 2448, New Orleans, LA 70176
568-6968 (Museum) or 568-8215 (Curator)

LOYOLA UNIVERSITY MUSIC LIBRARY

Books, periodicals, videos, and large collection of recordings (LPs and CDs) on Louisiana music other than traditional jazz, including pop, R&B, zydeco, Cajun, and contemporary jazz.

6363 St. Charles Avenue, New Orleans, LA 70118
865-2774

NEW ORLEANS PUBLIC LIBRARY

Book, recordings, and picture file collections include musical subjects. Graumann-Marks Collection has photographs of jazz musicians taken during performances. Jambalaya Program includes reel-to-reel tapes of lectures and performances (cassette copies available).

Main Branch
219 Loyola Avenue, New Orleans, LA 70140
529-7323

PRESERVATION HALL

Famous home of traditional jazz contains files of annotated clippings, programs, personal correspondence of musicians, and small collection of photos. Not open to public but staff will respond to phone or mail requests.

726 St. Peter Street, New Orleans, LA 70130
522-2481

WILLIAM RANSOM HOGAN JAZZ ARCHIVE AT TULANE UNIVERSITY

Among the best-known jazz research facilities in the United States, this library focuses on traditional jazz. Holdings include an Oral History collection of some 1,500 reels of interviews with musicians and related persons, plus transcripts or summaries of over 1,200 of them. Also thousands of recordings; vertical subject files containing newspaper clippings, correspondence, etc.; photographs; printed and manuscript music; and individual collections donated by scholars, photographers, musicians, and the musicians' union.

Howard Tilton Memorial Library, 4th floor
7001 Freret Street, New Orleans, LA 70118
865-5688

WWOZ-FM LIBRARY
Radio station owned by Jazz and Heritage Foundation includes thousands of commercial recordings and archival tapes of New Orleans and South Louisiana music, performances, interviews. By appointment only.

901 Rampart Street, New Orleans, LA 70116
468-1238

GOING NATIVE

CAJUN DANCE LESSONS AND TOURS
Rand Speyrer is a Cajun music and dance enthusiast whose lessons have helped hundreds of Louisianians and out-of-towners alike learn the two-step, Cajun jitterbug, waltz, and other routines. Beginning and advanced classes are held weekly at seven locations in greater New Orleans area: $50–$60 for six-week course of lessons an hour to an hour and a half long. Call or write for free schedule.

Speyrer also conducts field trips to such Cajun country meccas as Mulate's and such events as the Festivals Acadiens in Lafayette. Information can be found in his free newsletter, *Allons Danser*.

Rand Speyrer
P.O. Box 15908, New Orleans, LA 70175-5908
899-0615

CONTEMPORARY ARTS CENTER

New Orleans' thriving nonprofit Warehouse District home of unusual music programs, theater, lectures, art exhibits, and, of course, parties. Write or call for current schedule and tickets.

900 Camp Street, New Orleans, LA 70130
528-3800

GREATER NEW ORLEANS TOURIST AND CONVENTION COMMISSION, INC.

A great source of guide booklets, event, hotel and restaurant listings, and related tourism information. Office is located in Superdome.

1520 Sugar Bowl Drive, New Orleans, LA 70112
Phone: 566-5011
Fax: 566-5046

LOUISIANA MUSIC DIRECTORY

Annual compilation of musicians, bands, booking agents, managers, clubs, and other people and businesses connected with music in the region. An invaluable source book for professionals. Published each July. Available by mail for $10 including postage and handling.

Offbeat Publications
921 Canal Street, Suite 900, New Orleans, LA 70112
Phone: 522-5533
Fax: 525-2594

NEW ORLEANS JAZZ AND HERITAGE FESTIVAL

Each year, festival lineups are announced in February. A full schedule is usually published upon announcement in the *Times-Picayune* and *Gambit*. Tickets to daytime and evening programs are available in advance from Ticketmaster outlets and other sources. For brochure, tickets, information contact festival office. For material on special accommodation and ticket packages, call Travel New Orleans, Official Tour Operator of the Jazz Festival.

1205 N. Rampart Street, P.O. Box 53407, New Orleans, LA 70116

Phone: 522-4786

Fax: 522-5426

Travel New Orleans: (800) 535-8747 (outside Louisiana) 561-8747 or (800) 654-0577 (within Louisiana)

DISCOGRAPHY

Note to Readers: Listed below are some of the best available recordings, on compact disc, of the many varieties of Louisiana music. We have also listed some important out-of-print recordings on CD, LP, or cassette, which you can still find, with a little luck, in specialized record stores and mail-order catalogs.

Each recording is followed by the manufacturer's name and number. All recordings are single CDs unless otherwise noted.

CHAPTER 2:
THE CRADLE OF JAZZ STILL ROCKS

ANTHOLOGIES

Atlantic Jazz: New Orleans. 1955–71 performances by Paul Barbarin, Eureka Brass Band, George Lewis, Danny Barker; others. Atlantic 81700-2

New Orleans. 1918–34 performances by Jelly Roll Morton, King Oliver, Johnny Dodds, Louis Armstrong with Hot Seven, Freddie Keppard, Kid Celestin's Original Tuxedo Jazz Orchestra, New Orleans Rhythm Kings, Henry Allen and Paul Barbarin, Original Dixieland Jazz Band; others. BBC CD 588

New Orleans Jazz. 1950s–80s New Orleans revival style performances by Kid Thomas Valentine & His Creole Jazz Band, New Orleans Ragtime Orchestra, George Lewis; others. Arhoolie CD-346

ARTIST LISTINGS

Henry "Red" Allen   See also anthologies
1929–1936. With Paul Barbarin, Danny Barker; others. BBC CD 685
World on a String. Recorded in NYC, 1957. With Coleman Hawkins. Bluebird 24972-RB
Allen also is heard on recordings by Louis Armstrong, Sidney Bechet, Jelly Roll Morton, King Oliver, and Clarence Williams.

Louis Armstrong   See also anthologies
Among dozens of great recordings, these are some of the best:
Louis Armstrong and King Oliver. Recorded in Indiana, Chicago, and NYC, 1923–24. Jelly Roll Morton plays on two numbers. Milestone MCD-47017
Louis Armstrong of New Orleans. With Sidney Bechet; others. If you buy only one by Armstrong, this is a good retrospective, covering the years 1926–50. Decca / MCA MCAD-42328
Louis Armstrong: Vols. 1–6, Recorded in Chicago and NYC, 1925–30. Vol. 1–3 contain the Hot Fives and Hot Sevens recordings. Vol. 4 features Earl Hines on piano. Vol. 6 includes Henry "Red" Allen. Columbia CK-44049, CK-44253, CK-44422, CK-45142, CK-46148, CK-46996
Pops: The 1940's Small-Band Sides. With New Orleans sidemen like Barney Bigard; others. Bluebird 6378-2-RB (2 CDs)
Satch Plays Fats. With the All-Stars. Recorded in 1955. Columbia CK-40378.
Armstrong also is heard on recordings by Sidney Bechet, Johnny Dodds, King Oliver, and Clarence Williams.

Paul Barbarin   See also anthologies
Paul Barbarin & His New Orleans Jazz. Recorded in NYC, 1955. With Danny Barker; others. Atlantic 90977-2
Barbarin also is heard on a recording by Henry "Red" Allen.

Danny Barker   See also anthologies
Save the Bones. Solo guitar album originally released in 1988. Orleans 1018
Barker also is heard on recordings by Henry "Red" Allen, Paul Bar-

barin (chapter 2); The Dirty Dozen Brass Band, Wynton Marsalis (chapter 6).

Sidney Bechet   These are some of Bechet's best recordings:
Complete Blue Note Recordings. With Bunk Johnson; others. Recorded in NYC, 1939–53. Mosaic MD 4-110 (4 CDs)
Master Takes. With Jelly Roll Morton, Henry Red Allen; others. Recorded in NYC and Chicago, 1932–43. RCA 2402-2 (3 CDs)
Sidney Bechet: 1924 to 1938. With Louis Armstrong, Clarence Williams; others. If you buy only one by Bechet, this showcases him with both combos and big bands. ABC (Australia) 838 032-2
Bechet also is heard on recordings by Louis Armstrong, Jelly Roll Morton, and Clarence Williams.

Barney Bigard
Barney Bigard & Claude Luter: Paris December 14 & 15, 1960. Vogue VG-655003
Bigard also is heard on recordings by Louis Armstrong, Jelly Roll Morton, and King Oliver.

Oscar "Papa" Celestin   See also anthologies
Two of Celestin's 1950s Jazzology LPs will be issued on one CD shortly as American Music CD 28.

George "Kid Sheik" Colar
Blues & Standards. GHB 47. (LP only)

Johnny Dodds   See also anthologies
Johnny Dodds: Great Original Performances 1923–29. With Kid Ory's Jazz Band, Jelly Roll Morton's Red Hot Peppers; others. Recorded in Chicago. ABC (Australia) 836 202-2
Blue Clarinet Stomp. Recorded 1928–1929. With Jelly Roll Morton; others. Bluebird 2293-2-RB
South Side Chicago Jazz. Recorded 1927–1929. With Louis Armstrong; others. MCA MCAD-42326
Dodds also is heard on recordings by Louis Armstrong, Jelly Roll Morton, and King Oliver.

Pete Fountain   See also Al Hirt and Pete Fountain
Best of Pete Fountain. MCA MCAD-4032 (2 CDs)

Jacques Gauthé   See also listing under New Orleans Classic Jazz Orchestra

Cassoulet Stomp and Doin' the Hambone. With Creole Rice Yerba Buena Jazz Band. Stomp Off CD-1170

Banu Gibson
Let Yourself Go. With New Orleans Hot Jazz Orchestra. Recorded in New Orleans, 1988. Swing Out Records CD 103

Al Hirt   See also listing under Al Hirt and Pete Fountain
All Time Greatest Hits. RCA 9593-2-R

Al Hirt and Pete Fountain
Super Jazz I. Recorded ca. 1975. Monument AK-44359

Percy Humphrey   See listings under Preservation Hall Jazz Band

Bunk Johnson
Bunk Johnson's Superior Jazz Band. Recorded in New Orleans, 1942. With George Lewis; others. His historic first recordings. Good Time Jazz 12048-2
1944. With George Lewis; others. American Music AMCD-3
Johnson also is heard on a recording by Sidney Bechet.

Freddie Keppard   See anthologies

George Lewis   See also anthologies
Complete Blue Note Recordings of George Lewis. Recorded in New Orleans, 1943; Bakersfield, Ca., 1954; Hackensack, NJ, 1955. Mosaic MD 3-132 (3 CDs)
Lewis also is heard on a recording by Bunk Johnson.

Ferdinand "Jelly Roll" Morton   See also anthologies
Jelly Roll Morton Centennial: His Complete Victor Recordings. With Red Hot Peppers, Red Allen, Barney Bigard, Kid Ory, Johnny Dodds, Sidney Bechet; others. Recorded in Chicago, NYC, and Camden, NJ, 1926–30; 1939. Bluebird 2361-2-RB (5 CDs)
Jelly Roll Morton: Library of Congress Recordings. Includes interview with folklorist Alan Lomax. Affinity CD 1010-3 (3 CDs)
1923–24. Recorded in Richmond, Indiana, and Chicago, 1923–26. Milestone MCD-47018-2
Morton also is heard on recordings by Louis Armstrong, Sidney Bechet, Johnny Dodds, New Orleans Rhythm Kings, and King Oliver.

New Leviathan Oriental Fox-Trot Orchestra
Here Comes the Hot Tamale Man. Leviathan Productions 19329

New Orleans Classic Jazz Orchestra
Blowin' Off Steam. With Eddie Bayard, Jacques Gauthé; others. Recorded in 1990. Stomp Off CD-SOS-1223

New Orleans Ragtime Orchestra   See anthologies

New Orleans Rhythm Kings   See also anthologies
New Orleans Rhythm Kings, Vol. 1. Recorded 1922–23. Village (Germany) VILCD 004-2

Jimmie Noone
Complete Recordings, Vol. 1. Recorded 1926–30. Affinity AFS 1027-3 (3 CDs)

King Oliver   See also anthologies
Complete Vocalion / Brunswick Recordings, 1926–1930. Affinity AFS 1025-2 (2 CDs)
King Oliver: Vol. 1 (1923–29) Vol. 2 (1927–30). With Louis Armstrong, Johnny Dodds, Jelly Roll Morton, Kid Ory, Barney Bigard, Clarence Williams, Red Allen; others. BBC 787 and 788
The New York Sessions. Recorded 1929–30. Bluebird 9903-2-RB
Oliver also is heard on recordings by Louis Armstrong.

Olympia Brass Band   See also anthologies, chapters 6 and 7
Best of New Orleans Jazz. Mardi Gras Records MG 1004

Original Dixieland Jazz Band   See also anthologies
Complete Original Dixieland Jazz Band 1917–21. Recorded in NYC. Bluebird BMG 61098-2
Original Dixieland Jazz Band 1921 / 1936. Recorded in NYC. EPM ZET-728.

Edward "Kid" Ory
Kid Ory's Creole Jazz Band 1944 / 45. Recorded in Hollywood. Good Time Jazz 12022-2
Legendary Kid. Recorded in Los Angeles, 1955. Good Time Jazz GTCD-12016-2
Ory also is heard on recordings by Louis Armstrong, Johnny Dodds, Jelly Roll Morton, and King Oliver.

Preservation Hall Jazz Band
Best of Preservation Hall Jazz Band. With Percy Humphrey; others. Recorded in New Orleans, 1976, 1981, 1983, 1986, and 1988. CBS MK-44996

Kid Thomas (Valentine)   See also anthologies

Kid Thomas Valentine & Algiers Stompers. Recorded in New Orleans, 1965. GHB 80 (LP only)

Isidore (Tuts) Washington   See also anthologies, chapters 4 and 7.

New Orleans Piano Professor. Rounder CD-11501

Washington also is heard on a recording by Smiley Lewis (chapter 3).

Dr. Michael White

Crescent City Serenade. With Wynton Marsalis, Wendell Brunious, Walter Payton; others. Antilles 422-848545-2

White also is heard on a recording by Wynton Marsalis (chapter 6).

Clarence Williams

Complete 1923–1926 Clarence Williams Sessions, Vol. 1, 1923; Vol. 2, 1923–25. With Sidney Bechet, Louis Armstrong; others. Includes Bechet's first recordings. EPM FDC-5107; 5109

1927 to 1934. With Henry "Red" Allen; others. Recorded in NYC. ABC (Australia) 836 929-2

Williams also is heard on recordings by Sidney Bechet and King Oliver.

Note to Readers: there are many more CDs—especially on European labels such as Classics (Allen, Armstrong, Bechet, Dodds, Morton, Oliver) and Vogue (Bechet's expatriate period)—currently available. Space limitations (and the varying quality and sources of these discs) prevent us from listing most of them. Contact Qualiton, the U.S. distributor, for more information. The reissues on BBC and JSP (U.K.) and the Australian ABC label are considered excellent—although purists don't always like the digitalized versions on both the BBC and ABC labels engineered by Robert Parker.

George Buck's New Orleans–based GHB, Jazzology and American Music labels feature Barbarin, Barker, Colar, Humphrey, Johnson, Lewis, Ory, and Thomas. CDs issued by Buck include some of Bill Russell's original American Music sessions from the 1940s and 1950s. The label name has also been resurrected. As his older stock is depleted, CDs will replace LPs in Buck's catalogs.

CHAPTER 3:
REBIRTH: THE FIRST WAVE OF R&B

ANTHOLOGIES

Note to Readers: These selective anthologies primarily emphasize performers discussed in the text; however, a few compilations representing "swamp-pop" and "swamp-blues" styles are also included.

Best of New Orleans Rhythm & Blues, Vols. 1–2. 1953–69 performances by Shirley & Lee, Ernie K-Doe, The Showmen, Smiley Lewis, Earl King, Dave Bartholomew, Benny Spellman, Irma Thomas, Spiders, Roy Brown, Bobby Mitchell, Aaron Neville, Jessie Hill, Frankie Ford, Roy Montrell, Art Neville, Lee Dorsey, Meters, Dixie Cups, Lloyd Price, Chris Kenner, Clarence Henry, Barbara George, Guitar Slim, Lloyd Price, Hawketts. Rhino R21S-75765; R21S-75766.

Carnival Time: Best of Ric Records, Vol. 1. 1958–62 performances by Al Johnson, Eddie Bo, Johnny Adams, Joe Jones, Tommy Ridgely; others. Recorded in New Orleans. Rounder CD-2075

New Orleans Gospel Quartets 1947–1956. One of the few anthologies covering this period, with performances by the Jackson Gospel Singers, Famous Soul Comforters, Southern Harps, Famous Four, New Orleans Humming Four, Delta Southernaires, New Orleans Chosen Five, Zion Harmonizers, Crescent City Gospel Singers. Heritage HT 306 (LP)

New Orleans Party Classics. 1954–90 performances by Professor Longhair, Huey "Piano" Smith & Clowns, Fats Domino, A. Tousan (Allen Toussaint), Hawketts, Al Johnson, Lil' Bob & Lollipops, Frankie Ford, Alvin "Red" Tyler & Gyros, Oliver Morgan, Dr. John, Wild Tchoupitoulas, Neville Brothers, Dirty Dozen Brass Band, ReBirth Brass Band; others. Rhino R2 70587

Paul Gayten / Annie Laurie / Dave Bartholomew / Roy Brown: Regal Records in New Orleans. Recorded 1949–1950. Specialty SPCD 2169-2

Sanctifed! Gospel from New Orleans. Recently recorded live at Tipitina's nightclub. With Johnny Adams, Marva Wright, Sammy Berfect, Dimensions of Faith, Joe "Cool" Davis; others. Tipitina's Records 1404

Sounds of the Swamp: Best of Excello Records, Vol. 1. Slim Harpo,

Lazy Lester, Johnny Jano; others. Rhino R2 70896

Swamp Gold, Vols. 1 and 2. 1960s–1980s performances by Cookie and the Cupcakes, Rockin' Sidney, Irma Thomas, Johnnie Allan; others. Jin CD 106–107

Troubles, Troubles: New Orleans Blues from the Vaults of Ric and Ron. Lesser-known 1950s performances by Eddie Lang, Edgar Blanchard & Gondoliers, Jerry Harris with Clarence "Bon Ton" Garlow's Orchestra, Jimmy Rivers Combo. Rounder CD-2080

We Got a Party: Best of Ron Records, Vol. 1. 1958–62 performances with Professor Longhair, Irma Thomas, Robert Parker, Chris Kenner, Bobby Mitchell; others. Recorded in New Orleans. Rounder CD-2076

ARTIST LISTINGS

Lee Allen

Walkin' with Mr. Lee: Golden Classics. Collectable COLCD-5083

Allen also is heard on recordings by Dave Bartholomew, Cousin Joe, Smiley Lewis, Lloyd Price, Tommy Ridgely, Huey Smith, Larry Williams (chapter 3); Dr. John (chapter 4).

Archibald (Leon T. Gross)

New Orleans Sessions. With Dave Bartholomew, Earl Palmer; others. Recorded in New Orleans, 1950–52. Krazy Kat (U.K.) KK 7409 (LP only)

Dave Bartholomew   See also anthologies

In the Alley. With Earl Palmer, Tommy Ridgely; others. Recorded 1949–52. Charly (U.K.) 273

Jump Children. Recorded in New Orleans, 1950–60. With Earl Palmer, Lee Allen, James Booker; others. Imperial (France) 1546601 (LP)

Bartholomew also is heard on recordings by Archibald, Fats Domino, Earl King, Smiley Lewis (chapter 3); Dirty Dozen Brass Band (chapter 6).

Harold Battiste

Battiste is heard on recordings by Larry Williams (chapter 3); Dr. John (chapter 4); Victor Goines, Ellis Marsalis (chapter 6).

Eddie Bo (Bocage)   See also anthologies

Check Mr. Popeye. Recorded 1959–62. Rounder CD-2077

Bo also is heard on recordings by Johnny Adams (chapter 4); Dirty Dozen Brass Band (chapter 6).

Clarence "Gatemouth" Brown
Among Brown's many recordings, these are some of the best:
Original Peacock Recordings. Recorded in Houston, 1952–59. Rounder CD-2039
Pressure Cooker. Recorded in France, 1973, with re-recorded Peacock numbers plus newer material. Alligator ALCD 4745
Real Life. Recorded in Texas, 1985. Rounder CD-2054
Standing My Ground. Recorded in New Orleans, late 1980s. Terrance Simien plays on one number. Alligator ALCD-4779
Texas Swing. With Alvin Red Tyler; others. Recorded in Bogalusa, LA, early 1980s, with material from Rounder albums *Alright Again* and *One More Mile.* Rounder CD-11527
Brown also is heard on a recording by Professor Longhair.

Roy Brown   See also anthologies
Laughing but Crying. Recorded 1947–59. Includes "Good Rockin' Tonight." Route 66 (Sweden) CD 2

Roy Byrd (see Professor Longhair)

Bobby Charles
Bobby Charles. Recorded 1955–57. Chess CHC-92001 (cassette only)

Jimmy Clanton
Very Best of Jimmy Clanton. Ace (US) 2039

Cousin Joe (Pleasant Joseph)
Cousin Joe from New Orleans. Recorded 1946–47. With Lee Allen, Paul Gayten. Oldie Blues 8008 (LP)
Relaxin' in New Orleans. Solo performances recorded in 1985. Great Southern Records GS-11011 (LP)

James "Sugar Boy" Crawford   See also anthologies, chapter 7
Sugar Boy Crawford. Chess CHC2-9292508 (cassette only)

Delta Southernaires   See anthologies

Dixie Cups   See also anthologies, chapters 3, 4, and 7
Dixie Cups Meet the Shangri-Las. Recorded 1964–66. "Chapel of Love," "Iko, Iko"; others. Charly (U.K.) CD 38

Fats Domino   See also anthologies, chapters 3 and 5
My Blue Heaven: The Best of Fats Domino, Vol. 1. Recorded in New

Orleans and Los Angeles, 1949–61. If you only buy one by Domino, this is a good "greatest hits" collection. EMI E21Y-92808
They Call Me the Fat Man:" the Legendary Imperial Recordings. Recorded 1949–62. EMI E2-00-96784 (4 CDs)
Domino also is heard on recordings by Smiley Lewis and Lloyd Price.

Lee Dorsey   See also anthologies, chapters 3 and 7
Great Googa Mooga. Recorded 1960–78. Charly (U.K.) CD NEV3 (2 CDs)
Dorsey also is heard on a recording by Dr. John (chapter 4).

Champion Jack Dupree
Here's a representative sampling of Dupree's many recordings:
Back Home in New Orleans. With Alvin "Red" Tyler, Walter Payton; others. Recorded in 1990. Bullseye Blues CDBB-9502
Blues for Everybody. Recorded 1951–1955. Charly (U.K.) CD 243
Forever and Ever. With John Mooney, Bo Dollis; others. Recorded in 1991. Bullseye Blues BB 9512
From New Orleans to Chicago. With John Mayall, Eric Clapton; others. Recorded in London, 1966. Polydor 820568-2
Joe Davis Sessions. Recorded 1945–1946. Solo sessions. Flyright (France) CD 22

Snooks Eaglin
Baby, You Can Get Your Gun! Recorded in Metairie, La., 1986. Black Top CDBT-1037
Country Boy Down in New Orleans. Recorded in 1958. Includes material from his *Possum Up a Simmon Tree* LP, plus previously unreleased cuts. Arhoolie CD 348
Out of Nowhere. Recorded in Metairie, La., 1988. Black Top CDBT-1046
Snooks Eaglin: Legacy of the Blues, Vol. 2. Recorded in New Orleans, 1971. GNP Crescendo GNPD-10012
Teasing You. With George Porter; others. Recorded ca. 1990. Blacktop BT 1072
Eaglin also is heard on recordings by Professor Longhair and Earl King (chapter 3); Bo Dollis (chapter 7).

Frankie Ford   See also anthologies
Let's Take a Sea Cruise. Recorded 1958–60. The original Ace LP plus six additional cuts. Ace (U.S.) 2036
Ford also is heard on a recording by Dr. John (chapter 4).

Edward Frank See anthologies, chapters 4 and 6

Paul Gayten See also anthologies
Chess King of New Orleans. Recorded 1954–59. Chess CHD-9294
Creole Gal. With Annie Laurie. Recorded in New Orleans and NYC,
    1947–57. Route 66 (Sweden) KIX 8 (LP)
Gayten also is heard on a recording by Cousin Joe.

Barbara George See also anthologies
I Know: Golden Classics. Title song is her AFO hit from 1961. Collect-
    ables COLCD-5141

Guitar Slim (Eddie Jones) See also anthologies
Atco Sessions. Recorded in New Orleans and NYC, 1956–58. Includes
    previously unreleased material and his final recordings. Atlantic
    81760-2
Sufferin' Mind. Recorded 1953–55. "Things I Used to Do" plus some
    previously unissued cuts. Specialty SPCD-7007-2

Hawketts See anthologies, chapters 3 and 7
The Hawketts also are heard on a recording by the Neville Brothers
    (chapter 4).

Clarence "Frogman" Henry See also anthologies
But I Do. Recorded ca. 1961. Red CD 13

Jessie Hill See also anthologies
Y'All Ready Now? . . . Plus. Recorded 1960–62. Includes "Ooh Poo Pah
    Doo." Charly (U.K.) CD 262
Hill also is heard on a recording by Dr. John (chapter 4).

Mahalia Jackson
Gospels, Spirituals, & Hymns. Recorded 1954–60. Compilation of many
    of her best Columbia recordings, including three live cuts from the
    1958 Newport Jazz Festival.
Columbia / Legacy C2K-47083 (2 CDs)

Al Johnson See anthologies, chapters 3 and 7

Joe Jones See anthologies

Ernie K-Doe (Kador) See anthologies, chapters 3 and 7
Burn! K-Doe, Burn! Recorded 1959–63. Includes "Mother-in-Law."
    Charly (U.K.) CD 213

Chris Kenner   See also anthologies
I Like It like That. Recorded ca. 1961–67. Charly CD 230

Earl King   See also anthologies, chapters 3 and 7
Glazed. With Roomful of Blues. Recorded in Slidell, La., and Dallas, 1986. Black Top CDBT-1035
Sexual Telepathy. With Snooks Eaglin, George Porter; others. Recorded in Metairie, La., 1989. Black Top CD-BT-1052
Trick Bag. With Dave Bartholomew, James Booker; others. Recorded in New Orleans, 1960–62. Considered by many to be his best. Imperial (France) 2 C 068-83299 (LP)
King also is heard on a recording by Dr. John (chapter 4).

Annie Laurie   See anthologies
Laurie also is heard on recordings by Paul Gayten.

Smiley Lewis   See also anthologies
New Orleans Bounce. With Dave Bartholomew, Tuts Washington, Earl Palmer, Fats Domino, Lee Allen; others. Recorded in New Orleans 1950–60. 30 Imperial cuts. Sequel NEX CD 130

Little Richard
Georgia Peach. Recorded 1952–56. If you only buy one by Little Richard, this includes all the classics. Specialty SPCD-7012-2
Specialty Sessions. Recorded 1955–64. Specialty SPCD-8508 (3 CDs)

Bobby Marchan
Bobby Marchan: Golden Classics. Collectables COLCD-5113

Bobby Mitchell   See also anthologies
I'm Gonna Be a Big Wheel Someday. Recorded 1953–63. Mr. R & R Records (Sweden) R&B 101 (LP)

Earl Palmer
Palmer is heard on recordings by Archibald, Dave Bartholomew, Smiley Lewis, and Larry Williams.

Robert Parker   See also anthologies, chapters 3 and 7
Barefootin: Golden Classics. Collectables COLCD-5163

Lloyd Price   See also anthologies
Lawdy! With Lee Allen, Fats Domino; others. Recorded 1952–56. Specialty SPCD-7010-2 (CD)

Professor Longhair (Roy Byrd)   See also anthologies, chapters 3, 4, 7

Complete London Concert. Recorded live in London, 1978. JSP Records (U.K.) CD 202

Crawfish Fiesta. With Dr. John, Tony Dagradi, John Vidacovich; others. Recorded in New Orleans, 1979. His last recording. Alligator ALCD-4718

Houseparty New Orleans Style: The Lost Sessions, 1971–72. With Snooks Eaglin, Joseph "Zigaboo" Modeliste; others. Recorded in Baton Rouge and Memphis, 1971–72. Rounder CD-2057

Last Mardi Gras. Recorded live at Tipitina's in New Orleans, 1978. Atlantic CS2-4001 (2 cassettes only)

Mardi Gras in Baton Rouge. Recorded in Baton Rouge and Memphis, 1971–72. Originally produced by Quint Davis, finally released in the 1990s. Bearsville / Rhino R2 70736

Mardi Gras in New Orleans 1949–1957. With the Shuffling Hungarians, the Blue Jumpers or the Blues Scholars. Original versions of many of his signature songs. Nighthawk 108

New Orleans Piano. Recorded 1949, 1953. Atlantic 7255-2

Rock 'n' Roll Gumbo. With Clarence "Gatemouth" Brown; others. Recorded in Bogalusa, La., 1974. Dancing Cat DD-3006

Tommy Ridgely   See also anthologies

New Orleans King of the Stroll. With Lee Allen, Red Tyler, Dr. John; others. Recorded in New Orleans, 1960–64. Rounder CD-2079

Ridgely also is heard on a recording by Dave Bartholomew.

Shirley and Lee   See also anthologies

Shirley and Lee, Vol. 1. Recorded in the 1950s. Includes all their familiar Aladdin material. EMI CDP 92775

Shirley is also heard on a recording by Dr. John (chapter 4).

Showmen   See also anthologies

Some Folks Don't Understand It. Recorded ca. 1961–62. Charly (U.K.) CD 226

Huey "Piano" Smith   See also anthologies

Good Ole Rock 'N Roll. With Dr. John, Lee Allen, Red Tyler; others. Not just the usual "greatest hits." Ace (U.S.) 2038

Pitta Pattin'. Recorded 1966–72. "Rockin' Pneumonia," etc. Charly CD 225

Rock & Roll Revival. Includes Smith's original version of "Sea Cruise." Ace (U.S.) 2021

Rockin' Pneumonia and the Boogie Woogie Flu. Recorded 1957–65. Includes material not yet available on CD. Ace CH-9 (LP only)

Benny Spellman   See also anthologies
Fortune Teller: Golden Classics. Recorded 1959–66. Collectables COLCD-5165

Joe Tex
I Believe I'm Gonna Make It: The Best of Joe Tex. Recorded 1966–72. Rhino R21S-70191
Tex also is heard on a recording by Dr. John (chapter 4).

Allen Toussaint   See also anthologies, chapters 3 and 7
Allen Toussaint Collection. Selections from the albums *From a Whisper to a Scream; Life, Love and Faith; Southern Nights* and *Motion*. Includes Toussaint's own version of "Southern Nights." Reprise 26549-2
Wild Sounds of New Orleans by Tousan. Recorded in 1958. His first RCA album, with original version of "Java." Edsel CD 275
Toussaint also is heard on a recording by Dr. John (chapter 4).

Walter "Wolfman" Washington   See also anthologies, chapter 4
Sada. Recorded ca. 1991. PointBlank 1743-2
Wolf Tracks. Recorded in Slidell, La., 1986. Best of his three Rounder CDs. Rounder CD-2048
Washington also is heard on a recording by Johnny Adams (chapter 4).

Boogie Bill Webb
Boogie Bill Webb: Drinkin' and Stinkin'. Recorded in New Orleans, 1986. Flying Fish FF 70506

Larry Williams
Bad Boy. Recorded 1957–59. With Lee Allen, Earl Palmer, Harold Battiste; others. Specialty SPCD-7002
Best of Larry Williams. Recorded ca. 1957–1958. Ace CDCH-917
Williams also is heard on a recording by Art Neville (chapter 4).

Zion Harmonizers   See anthologies
The group also is heard on a recording by Robbie Robertson (chapter 4). A new CD is due out shortly on Mardi Gras Records.

CHAPTER 4: THE SECOND WAVE OF R&B

ANTHOLOGIES

Big Easy. Soundtrack from the 1987 film, with performances by the Dixie Cups, Professor Longhair, Buckwheat Zydeco, Zachary Richard, Aaron Neville & the Neville Brothers, Beausoleil, Terrance Simien, Wild Tchoupitoulas, Swan Silvertones. Antilles ANCD-7087.

Modern New Orleans Masters. 1982–87 performances from Rounder albums by Irma Thomas, James Booker, Ed Frank Quintet, Walter Washington, Dirty Dozen Brass Band, Tuts Washington, New Orleans Saxophone Ensemble (Tony Dagradi, Earl Turbinton; others). Johnny Adams and Red Tyler, Golden Eagles, Willie Tee, Germaine Bazzle. Rounder 11514

Tipitina's in Person. Live performances recorded ca. 1989 by Marva Wright, John Cleary, Walter Washington, Rebirth Jazz Band, Dash Rip Rock; others. Tipitina Records 1401

ARTISTS LISTINGS

Johnny Adams See also anthologies, chapters 3 and 4

After Dark. Recorded ca. 1986. Rounder CD-2049

From the Heart. With Walter "Wolfman" Washington, Alvin "Red" Tyler; others. Recorded in New Orleans, 1983. Rounder CD-2044

I Won't Cry. Recorded 1959–63. His early recordings produced by Dr. John and Eddie Bo. Rounder CD 2083

Johnny Adams Sings Doc Pomus. With Dr. John, James Singleton, John Vidacovich, Red Tyler; others. Recorded in New Orleans, ca. 1990. Rounder CD-2109

Room with a View of the Blues. With Dr. John, Walter Washington, Alvin Tyler; others. Recorded in Metairie, La., 1987. Rounder CD-2059

Adams also is heard on recordings by Wynton Marsalis (chapter 6).

Marcia Ball See also anthologies, chapter 7

Dreams Come True. With Angela Strehli and Lou Ann Barton; produced by Dr. John. Antone's Records & Tapes ANT-0014CD

Gatorhythms. Recorded in Texas, ca. 1989. Rounder CD-3101

Hot Tamale Baby. Recorded in Slidell, La., 1985. Rounder CD-3095.

Soulful Dress. Recorded in Austin, Tx. Rounder CD-3078.

James Booker   See also anthologies, chapters 4 and 7
Classified. With Alvin "Red" Tyler, James Singleton, John Vidacovich.
Recorded in New Orleans, 1982. His only studio album. Rounder
CD-2036
King of the New Orleans Keyboard. Recorded live in Europe, late 1970s.
Junco Partner JP1
New Orleans Piano Wizard: Live! Recorded live in Zürich, 1977. Roun-
der CD 2027
Booker also is heard on recordings by Dave Bartholomew and Earl
King (chapter 3).

John Cleary   See anthologies
Cleary also is heard on a recording by John Mooney.

Def Generation
Medicine. With Charles Neville, Cyril Neville; others. Endangered
Species ES1701-2

Dr. John (Mac Rebennack)   See also anthologies, chapters 3 and
7
Desitively Bonnaroo. With Allen Toussaint, The Meters; others.
Recorded in New Orleans and Miami, 1974. Atco (Japan) AMCY 235
Dr. John and His New Orleans Congregation. Recorded 1950s–1960s.
With Lee Dorsey, Earl King, Frankie Ford, Ronnie Barron, Joe Tex;
others. Dr. John plays on some cuts, produced others. Ace (U.S.)
2020
Dr. John Plays Mac Rebennack. Solo piano album recorded in NYC,
1981. Clean Cuts CDCC-705
Gris-Gris. Recorded in Los Angeles. Atco (Japan) AMCY 229
Gumbo. With Lee Allen, Harold Battiste, Alvin Robinson; others. Atco
7006-2
In a Sentimental Mood. With Rickie Lee Jones on one number. War-
ner Bros. 25889-2
In the Right Place. With the Meters; arranged and conducted by Allen
Toussaint. Recorded in Miami, 1973. Atco 7018-2
Ultimate Dr. John. With Allen Touissant, Meters, Lee Allen, Harold
Battiste, Alvin Robinson, Ronnie Barron, Shirley Goodman, Jessie
Hill; others. If you buy only one by Dr. John, this features classic
songs from *Desitively Bonnaroo, In the Right Place, Gumbo, Gris-
Gris,* and *Remedies.* Warner Special Products 27612-2
Dr. John also is heard on recordings by Professor Longhair, Tommy
Ridgely, Huey Smith (chapter 3); Johnny Adams, Marcia Ball, Aaron

Neville (chapter 4); Bluesiana Triangle, Harry Connick, Jr., Dirty Dozen Brass Band (chapter 6); Donald Harrison (chapter 7).

Jean Knight
Mr. Big Stuff. Recorded in 1972. Stax SCD-855402

Meters   See also anthologies, chapters 3 and 7
Funky Miracle. Recorded ca. 1968–69. "Cissy Strut" and other Josie hits. Charly CD NEV2 (2 CDs)
Good Old Funky Music. Recorded ca. 1968–1970s. Previously unissued material. With Cyril Neville on some numbers. Rounder CD-2104
Look-Ka Py Py. Recorded in 1970. Rounder CD-2103
Meters Jam. Recorded 1968–1970s. Previously unissued material. George Porter has criticized album's quality. Rounder CD 2105
The Meters also are heard on recordings by Allen Toussaint (chapter 3); Dr. John, the Neville Brothers, Robbie Robertson, Wild Tchoupitoulas (chapter 4).

Ziggy (Zigaboo) Modeliste
Modeliste is heard on recordings by Professor Longhair (chapter 3); The Meters (chapter 4).

John Mooney
Late Last Night. With John Cleary, others. Recorded in New Orleans, ca. 1990. Bullseye Blues CDBB-9505
Mooney also is heard on recordings by Champion Jack Dupree (chapter 3).

Aaron Neville   See also anthologies, chapters 3 and 4
Classic Aaron Neville: My Greatest Gift. Recorded 1968–1970s. His Toussaint-era recordings. Rounder CD-2102
Orchid in the Storm. With Art Neville, others. Recorded in New Orleans, 1980s. His first solo album in many years. Rhino R21K-70956
Tell It like It Is. Recorded ca. 1966–67. This reissue of the original 1967 album, along with *The Classic Aaron Neville,* represents the best of Neville's earlier recordings. Curb / CEMA D21S-77491
Warm Your Heart. With Linda Ronstadt, Dr. John; others. Recorded 1990–91. A & M 75021-5354-2
Neville also is heard on recordings by the Neville Brothers, Robbie Robertson, Linda Ronstadt, Wild Tchoupitoulas.

Art Neville   See also anthologies, chapters 3 and 7
Mardi Gras Rock 'n' Roll. Recorded in New Orleans in 1956–58. His

Specialty sessions, including "Rockin' Pneumonia" with Larry Williams, plus some previously unissued cuts. Ace CDCHD-188
Neville also is heard on recordings by the Hawketts (chapter 3); the Meters, Aaron Neville, the Neville Brothers (chapter 4).

Charles Neville See also anthologies, chapter 6
Charles Neville & Diversity. With James Singleton, John Vidacovich; others. Recorded in New Orleans, 1990. Delta Music 15 331
Neville also is heard on recordings by Def Generation, the Neville Brothers, and Wild Tchoupitoulas.

Cyril Neville
Neville is heard on recordings by Def Generation, the Neville Brothers, and Wild Tchoupitoulas.

Ivan Neville
If My Ancestors Could See Me Now. Recorded ca. 1988. Polydor 834896-2
Neville also is heard on recordings by the Neville Brothers and Robbie Robertson.

Neville Brothers See also anthologies, chapters 3 and 4
Brother's Keeper. With Leo Nocentelli, others. A & M 75021-5312-2
Fiyo on the Bayou. Recorded in Bogalusa, La., 1981. A & M 75021-4866-2
History of the Neville Brothers: Legacy. Recorded 1955–72. With the Hawketts, Art Neville, Aaron Neville, the Meters. 50 songs from the pre-Neville Brothers era. Charly (U.K.) NEV1 (2 CDs)
Live Neville-ization and Live at Tipitina's, Vol. 2. With Ivan Neville; others. Recorded in New Orleans, 1982. Spindletop SPT 9108; SPT 9115
Treacherous: History of the Neville Brothers (1955–1985) and Treacherous Too! History of the Neville Brothers, Vol. 2 (1955–1987) With the Hawketts, Art Neville, Aaron Neville, Wild Tchoupitoulas, Neville Brothers, Cyril Neville. Comprehensive anthologies. Vol. 2 contains lesser-known material. Rhino R2 71494 (2 CDs); R2 70776
Uptown. Recorded in Metairie, La., ca. 1987. EMI E21Y-46754
Yellow Moon. A & M 75021-5240-2

Randy Newman
Good Old Boys. Includes title song and "Louisiana 1927." Reprise MS-2193-2
Land of Dreams. Includes title song and "New Orleans Wins the War." Reprise 25773-4

Leo Nocentelli
Nocentelli is heard on recordings by the Meters, the Neville Brothers (chapter 4); Henry Butler (chapter 6).

George Porter, Jr.
Runnin' Partner. Recorded in New Orleans, ca. 1990. Rounder CD-2099
Porter also is heard on recordings by Snooks Eaglin, Earl King (chapter 3); the Meters (chapter 4); Bo Dollis (chapter 7).

Louis Prima
Zooma Zooma: The Best of Louis Prima. With Keely Smith, Sam Butera, and the Witnesses. Recorded 1957–59. Rhino R21S-70225

Radiators
Law of the Fish. Recorded ca. 1987. Epic EK-40888
Total Evaporation. Recorded ca. 1991. Epic EK-46832
Zig-Zaggin' through Ghostland. Recorded ca. 1989. Epic EK-44343

Mac Rebennack (see **Dr. John**)

Robbie Robertson
Storyville. Recorded ca. 1991. With the Meters, Aaron Neville, Ivan Neville, ReBirth Brass Band, Bo Dollis, Zion Harmonizers, Tony Dagradi; others. Geffen GEFD-24303

Alvin Robinson   Robinson is heard on recordings by Dr. John.

Linda Ronstadt
Cry like a Rainstorm, Howl like the Wind. Recorded in 1989. With Aaron Neville. Elektra 60872-2
Ronstadt also is heard on a recording by Aaron Neville.

Mason Ruffner
Gypsy Blood. CBS Associated ZK-40601

Paul Simon
Graceland. With Rocking Dopsie on one number. Warner Bros. 25590-2

Subdudes
Lucky. Recorded ca. 1991. EastWest Records America 91671-2
Subdudes. Recorded ca. 1989. Atlantic 82015-2

Irma Thomas   See also anthologies, chapters 3, 4, and 7
New Rules. Recorded in Slidell, La., 1985. Rounder CD-2046

Ruler of Hearts. Recorded 1960–62 and 1976. Later cuts are live Jazz and Heritage Festival recordings. Also includes two different versions of her signature tune, "It's Raining," recorded many years apart. Charly CD 195

Simply the Best: Live. Recorded in New Orleans and San Francisco, 1990. Rounder CD-2110

Something Good: The Muscle Shoals Sessions. Recorded in 1967. Chess CHD-93004

Soul Queen of New Orleans. Recorded in Baton Rouge and Ville Platte, La., ca. 1977–78. "Swamp-pop"-influenced remakes of older hits. Maison de Soul C-1005 (cassette only)

Way I Feel. Recorded in Metairie, La., 1987. Rounder CD-2058

Wild Tchoupitoulas   See also anthologies, chapters 3 and 4

Wild Tchoupitoulas. With George Landry, the Meters, Cyril Neville, Aaron Neville, Charles Neville. Recorded ca. 1976. Antilles ANCD-7052

Wild Tchoupitoulas also are heard on recordings by the Neville Brothers.

Marva Wright   See anthologies, chapters 3 and 4

Heartbreakin' Woman. Recorded ca. 1991. Tipitina Records 1402

CHAPTER 5: RAGIN' CAJUNS
....

ANTHOLOGIES

Note to Readers: Besides the recordings listed below, many additional anthologies are available on the Rounder, Swallow, Maison de Soul, Mardi Gras, and Arhoolie labels.

Alligator Stomp; Cajun & Zydeco Classics. Vols. 1, 2 and 3. Performances by Rockin' Sidney, Rocking Dopsie, D. L. Menard, Clifton Chenier, Bruce Daigrepont, Johnnie Allan, Jo-El Sonnier, Rusty and Doug Kershaw, Boozoo Chavis, Beausoleil, Queen Ida, Terrance Simien, Balfa Brothers, Fats Domino and Doug Kershaw, Buckwheat Zydeco, Belton Richard, John Delafose, Nathan Abshire, Iry Lejeune, C.J. Chenier, Savoy-Doucet Cajun Band, Eddie Lejeune, John Delafose, Aldus Roger, Nathan and Zydeco Cha-Chas, Cajun Gold, Fernest and the Thunders, File, others. Rhino R21S-70946; R21S-70740; R21S-70312

Cajun Social Music. Performances by Marc Savoy, Sady Courville, Nathan Abshire; others. Recorded in Louisiana, 1975. Smithsonian / Folkways SFCD-40006

Cajun, Vol. 1, 1929–1939: Abbeville Breakdown. Performances by Amédée Breaux with Cleoma Breaux and Ophy Breaux, Joe Falcon with Cleoma Breaux and Ophy Breaux; Joe Falcon, Breaux Frères; others. Columbia CK-46220

Le Gran Mamou: A Cajun Music Anthology. The Historic Victor / Bluebird Sessions, 1928–1941. Performances by Amédée Ardoin and Dennis McGee, Falcon Trio, Nathan Abshire and the Rayne-Bo Ramblers, Hackberry Ramblers, Lawrence Walker; others. Recorded mostly in New Orleans. Country Music Foundation CMF-013-D

J'ai Été au Bal (I Went to the Dance): the Cajun and Zydeco Music of Louisiana. Vols. 1 and 2. Soundtrack from the 1990 film. 1928–89 performances by Michael Doucet, Canray Fontenot, Dennis McGee, Amédée Ardoin and Dennis McGee, Bois Sec Ardoin and Sons, Nathan Abshire, Marc Savoy, Marc and Ann Savoy, Joe Falcon and Cleoma Breaux, Odile Falcon, Solange Falcon, Hackberry Ramblers, Harry Choates, Iry LeJeune, Queen Ida, Beausoleil, Rockin' Sidney, Cajun Gold, Clifton Chenier, D. L. Menard, Belton Richard, Johnny Allan, Dewey Balfa, Balfa Brothers, John Delafose, Boozoo Chavis, Wayne Toups and Zydecajun; others. Arhoolie CD-331; CD-332

Zydeco Live! Direct from Richard's Club, Lawtell, Louisiana. Vols. 1 and 2. 1988 performances by Boozoo Chavis, Nathan and Zydeco Cha-Chas, John Delafose; others. Rounder CD-2069; CD-2070

Zydeco Shootout at El Sid O's. Recent live performances by Lynn August, Zydeco Force; others. Rounder CD-2108

ARTIST LISTINGS

Nathan Abshire   See also anthologies
Good Times are Killing Me / Pine Grove Blues. With the Balfa Brothers. Recorded 1966–1970's. Ace (U.K.) CHD 329

Johnnie Allan   See also anthologies, chapters 3 and 5
Johnnie Allan's Greatest Hits. Jin 9017; C-9017 (LP and cassette only)

Alphonse "Boisec" Ardoin   See also anthologies, chapters 5 and 7
Boisec; La Musique Creole. With Canray Fontenot and the Ardoin Brothers. Recorded near Mamou, La., 1971, 1973. Arhoolie 1070 (LP only)

Amédée Ardoin   See also anthologies
His Original Recordings, 1928–38. Old Timey 124 (LP only)

Ardoin Brothers Band   See anthologies, chapter 7
The Ardoin Brothers Band also are heard on a recording by Alphonse
"Boisec" Ardoin.

Balfa Brothers   See also anthologies, chapters 5 and 7
J'ai Vu le Loup, Le Renard et la Belette. Recorded in 1975. Rounder
   CD-6007
Play Traditional Cajun Music, Vols. 1 & II. With Marc Savoy; others.
   Recorded 1965–66. Swallow SW-CD-6011
The Balfa Brothers also are heard on a recording by Nathan Abshire.

Dewey Balfa   See also anthologies
Dewey Balfa and Friends / Souvenirs. Remastered version of two albums
   from the 1980s. Ace (U.K.) CHD 328
En Bas du Chene Vert (Under A Green Oak Tree). With Marc Savoy,
   D. L. Menard. Recorded in 1976. Contents of LP plus some previ-
   ously unissued material. Arhoolie CD-312.

Beausoleil   See also anthologies, chapters 4, 5, and 7
These are some of Beausoleil's best recordings:
Allons à Lafayette & More with Canray Fontenot. Recorded in Louisi-
   ana ca. 1981. Material from two early albums. Arhoolie CD-308
Bayou Boogie. Recorded in Crowley, La., 1985. One of their first
   recordings to incorporate R&B and rock. Rounder CD-6015
Cajun Conja. Recorded in Metairie, La., 1991. Rhino R21S-70525
Hot Chilli Mama. Recorded in California, 1987. Good mixture of tra-
   ditional and pop-oriented selections. Arhoolie CD-5040
Live! From the Left Coast. Recorded in San Francisco, 1989. Rounder
   CD-6035
Beausoleil also is heard on recordings by David Doucet and Michael
   Doucet.

Bois Sec (*see* Alphonse "Boisec" Ardoin)

Buckwheat Zydeco (Stanley "Buckwheat" Dural, Jr.)   See also
anthologies Chapters 4, 5, and 7
These are some of the best of Dural's numerous recordings:
100% Fortified Zydeco. Recorded in Texas, ca. 1983. Black Top CDBT-
   1024
Buckwheat's Zydeco Party. Recorded in Massachusetts., 1983–1985.

Includes material from two previously-released albums. Rounder CD-11528

On a Night like This. Recorded in Metairie, La. Island 422-842739-2

On Track. Charisma 91822-2

Taking It Home. With Eric Clapton; others. Recorded ca. 1988. Live recording. Island 842603-2

Where There's Smoke There's Fire. Recorded in California. Dwight Yokum plays on one number. Island 422-842925-2

Cajun Brew   See listing under Michael Doucet

Cajun Experience

Cajun Experience. With Paul Daigle, Mike Doucet, Robert Elkins. Recorded in 1984. Swallow 6058; C-6058 (LP and cassette only)

Cajun Gold   See also anthologies

Paul Daigle, Robert Elkins and Cajun Gold. Swallow 6060; C-6060 (LP and cassette only)

Boozoo Chavis   See also anthologies

Boozoo Chavis. Recorded in New Orleans, 1990. American Explorer/ Elektra 61146-2

Lake Charles Atomic Bomb (Original Goldband Recordings). Recorded between mid-1950s-early 1960s. Includes "Paper in My Shoe." Rounder Cd-2097

Zydeco Trail Ride. Maison de Soul MDSCD-1034

C. J. Chenier   See also anthologies

Hot Rod. With Red Hot Louisiana Band. Slash 26263-2

Clifton Chenier   See also anthologies, chapters 5 and 7

These are some of Chenier's best recordings:

Bayou Blues. Specialty SPCD-2139

Bogalusa Boogie. Recorded in Bogalusa, La., 1975. Arhoolie CD-347

Bon Ton Roulet and More. Recorded ca. 1964-73. Contains material from two albums. Arhoolie CD-345

Clifton Chenier and Rockin' Dupsee. Despite the title, not duets. Chenier's sessions recorded 1958-60; Dupsee's recorded 1970-74. Flyright (U.K.) CD 17

I'm Here. Recorded in Bogalusa, La., ca. 1982. Grammy-award winner. Alligator ALCD-4729

Live at St. Mark's. Recorded in California, 1971. If you buy only one live album by Chenier, this is considered one of his best. Arhoolie CD-313

Louisiana Blues & Zydeco. Recorded in Houston and California, 1965, 1967. Material from two albums. Arhoolie CD-329

60 minutes with the King of Zydeco. Material taken from ten Arhoolie LPs. Arhoolie CD-301

Zydeco Legend! Recorded in 1975, 1984. Material from two albums. Maison de Soul CD-105

Harry Choates See also anthologies
Fiddle King of Cajun Swing. Recorded 1946–1949. Arhoolie C-5027 (cassette only)

Sady Courville and Dennis McGee See also anthologies, chapters 5 and 7
La Vieille Musique Acadienne. Swallow 6030 (LP only)

Bruce Daigrepont See also anthologies
Coeur des Cajuns. With David Doucet; others. Recorded in New Orleans. Rounder CD-6026

Stir Up the Roux. Recorded in New Orleans. Rounder CD-6016

John Delafose See also anthologies, chapters 5 and 7
Joe Pete Got Two Women. Recorded in Crowley, La., 1980 and 1982. Contains material from two Arhoolie albums. Arhoolie CD-335

David Doucet
Quand J'ai Parti. With Beausoleil. Recorded in 1989. Rounder CD-6040

Doucet also is heard on recordings by Bruce Daigrepont and Michael Doucet.

Michael Doucet See also anthologies, chapters 5 and 7
Beau Solo. With David Doucet. Arhoolie CD-21

Belizaire the Cajun. Soundtrack from the 1986 film. With Beausoleil. Arhoolie C-5038 (cassette only)

Michael Doucet & Cajun Brew. Recorded in Metairie, La. Rounder CD-6017

Doucet also is heard on recordings by Beausoleil, Cajun Experience, Savoy-Doucet Cajun Band.

Joe Falcon See also anthologies
Live at a Cajun Dance in Scott, Louisiana. Recorded in 1963. Arhoolie C-5005 (cassette only)

Fernest (Arceneaux) and the Thunders See also anthologies
Zydeco Stomp. Recorded in London, 1981. JSP (U.K.) 220

Filé   See also anthologies
Cajun Dance Band. Flying Fish FF-70418
2 Left Feet. Flying Fish FF-70507

Canray Fontenot   See anthologies, chapters 5 and 7
Fontenot also is heard on recordings by Alphonse "Boisec" Ardoin and
   Beausoleil.

Hackberry Ramblers   See also anthologies
Early Recordings, 1935–1948. Recorded mostly in New Orleans. Old
   Timey 127 (cassette only)
Louisiana Cajun Music. Recorded in 1963. Arhoolie 5003 (cassette
   only)

Doug Kershaw   See also anthologies
Best of Doug Kershaw. Recorded 1972–78. Warner Bros. 25964-2

Eddie Lejeune   See also anthologies
Cajun Soul. With D. L. Menard; others. Rounder CD-6013
It's in the Blood. With the Morse Playboys. Rounder CD-6043
Lejeune also is heard on a recording by D. L. Menard.

Iry Lejeune   See anthologies

Mamou
Mamou. Recorded in Austin, ca. 1988. MCA MCAD-10124
Ugly Day. Recorded ca. 1991. Rounder CD-6050

McCauley, Reed & Vidrine
1929 and Back. Swallow C-6090 (cassette only)

Dennis McGee   See Sady Courville and Dennis McGee
See also anthologies

D. L. Menard   See also anthologies, chapters 5 and 7
Cajun Saturday Night. Rounder CD-0918
No Matter Where You At, There You Are. With Eddie LeJeune; others.
   Recorded in Lafayette, La., ca. 1988. Rounder CD-6021
Swallow Recordings. With Marc Savoy; others. Recorded 1960s–1970s.
   Contains original version of "Back Door." Ace (U.K.) CHD 327
Menard also is heard on recordings by Dewey Balfa and Eddie LeJeune.

Nathan (Williams) and the Zydeco Cha Chas   See also anthologies, chapters 5 and 7

Steady Rock. Recorded in Metairie, La., 1988. Rounder CD-2091

Your Mama Don't Know. Rounder CD-2107

Jimmy C. Newman

Alligator Man. Recorded ca. 1991. More "swamp-pop" than his numerous C & W albums, with several songs written by Johnnie Allan. Rounder CD 6039

Queen Ida (Guillory)   See also anthologies

Among her numerous recordings, here are two of the best:

Cookin' with Queen Ida and Her Zydeco Band. Recorded ca. 1989. Cookbook with the same title also available! GNP Crescendo GNPD-2197

Queen Ida and Bon Temps Zydeco Band on Tour. Recorded live in Europe, 1982. GNP Crescendo GNPD-2147

Belton Richard   See also anthologies

Belton Richard and His Musical Aces. Swallow 6010 (LP only)

Zachary Richard   See also anthologies, chapters 4 and 7

Mardi Gras Mambo. Recorded in Scott, La. Rounder CD-6037

Women in the Room. Recorded ca. 1989. With Jimmy Buffett; others. A&M 75021-5302-2

Zack Attack. Recorded in Paris, 1984. If you buy only one of Richard's earlier recordings now available on CD, this is one of the best. Arzéd RZ CD-1009

Zack's Bon Ton. Recorded ca. 1988. Rounder CD-6027

Steve Riley and the Mamou Playboys

Steve Riley and the Mamou Playboys. Recorded in Scott, La., 1989. Rounder CD-6038

Rockin' Dopsie (Dupsee)   See also anthologies, chapters 5 and 7

Louisiana Music. Recorded in New Orleans, 1990. Atlantic 82307-2

Saturday Night Zydeco. Grammy-nominee in 1989. Reissue of previously released album with some additional tracks. Maison de Soul CD-104

Zy-De-Co-In. His first two albums for the Sonet label reissued on one CD. Gazell GCCD-3003

Dopsie also is heard on recordings by Paul Simon (chapter 4); Clifton Chenier (chapter 5).

Rockin' Sidney   See also anthologies, chapters 3 and 5

My Toot Toot. Recorded ca. 1982–84. Selections from two previously released albums. Maison de Soul MdS-CD-1009

Aldus Roger   See anthologies

Savoy-Doucet Cajun Band   See also anthologies
Two-Step D'Amédé. Recorded in Louisiana, 1988. Arhoolie CD-316

Marc Savoy   See anthologies
Savoy also is heard on recordings by the Balfa Brothers, Dewey Balfa, D. L. Menard, Savoy-Doucet Cajun Band.

Terrance Simien   See also anthologies, chapters 4 and 5
Zydeco on the Bayou. Recorded in New Orleans, ca. 1989. Restless 72368-2
Simien also is heard on a recording by Clarence "Gatemouth" Brown (chapter 3).

Jo-El Sonnier   See also anthologies
Cajun Life. Recorded in Crowley, La., and Nashville, ca. 1980. More traditional Cajun than later releases. Rounder CD-3049
Come On Joe. Recorded in Nashville, ca. 1987. RCA 6372-2-R
Have a Little Faith. Recorded ca. 1989. RCA 9718-2-R
Tears of Joy. Recorded ca. 1991. Capitol C21S-95684

Wayne Toups and Zydecajun   See also anthologies
Blast from the Bayou. Recorded in Crowley, La., and Nashville. Mercury 836518-2
Fish Out of Water. Recorded in Crowley, La. Mercury 848289-2
Johnnie Can't Dance. Mercury 846585-2
Zydecajun! Recorded in Crowley, La., ca. 1986. Most traditional album on the Mercury label. Mercury 846584-2

Lawrence Walker   See also anthologies
Legend at Last. Swallow 6051 (LP only)

CHAPTER 6: BACK TO THE FUTURE: CONTEMPORARY JAZZ

ANTHOLOGIES

New New Orleans Music: Jump Jazz. 1985–86 performances by the Ed Frank Quintet, Ramsey Mclean and the Survivors (Ramsey Mclean, Charles Neville, Charmaine Neville, Steve Masakowski; others). Recorded in New Orleans. Rounder CD-2065

New New Orleans Music: New Music Jazz. Performances by the New Orleans Saxophone Ensemble (Tony Dagradi, Earl Turbinton; others); Improvisational Arts Ensemble (Kidd Jordan, Kent Jordan, Clyde Kerr, Jr.; others). Rounder CD-2066

New New Orleans Music: Vocal Jazz. Performances by Germaine Bazzle, Alvin "Red" Tyler, James Black, Lady BJ, Ellis Marsalis Quartet (Victor Goines; others). Rounder CD-2067

New Orleans Brass Bands: Down Yonder. Performances by Dejan's Olympia Brass Band, Chosen Few, Rebirth Marching Band [sic], Dirty Dozen Brass Band. Rounder CD-11562.

ARTIST LISTINGS

Astral Project

Dreams of Love. With Tony Dagradi, Steve Masakowski, James Singleton, David Torkanowsky, John Vidacovich. Recorded in Metairie, La., 1987–88. Rounder CD-2071

Alvin Batiste

Bayou Magic. India Navigation IN-1069-CD

Clarinet Summit, Vols. 1 & 2. Recorded in 1984. Indian Navigation IN-1062-CD

Batiste also is heard on recordings by Ellis Marsalis and Wynton Marsalis.

Germaine Bazzle   See anthologies, chapters 4 and 6

Bazzle also is heard on a recording by Alvin "Red" Tyler.

James Black   See anthologies

Terence Blanchard   See also Donald Harrison and Terence Blanchard

Jungle Fever. Soundtrack from the 1991 film. Score composed by Blanchard. Motown MOTD-6291

Terence Blanchard. With Branford Marsalis; others. Columbia CK-47354

Blanchard also is heard on a recording by Branford Marsalis.

Terence Blanchard and Donald Harrison

Black Pearl. Recorded in NYC, 1988. Columbia CK-44216

Crystal Stair. Recorded ca. 1987. Columbia CK-40830

Discernment. Recorded in NYC, 1984. George Wein Collection CCD-43008

Nascence. Recorded in NYC, 1986. Columbia C-40335 (LP)

New York Second Line. Recorded in NYC, 1983. George Wein Collection CCD-43002

Bluesiana Triangle

Bluesiana Triangle; Bluesiana II. With Dr. John; others. Critics liked this interesting mixture of "New Orleans sounds, blues, instrumental jazz." Windham Hill Jazz WD-0125; Windham Hill Jazz 101133-2

Henry Butler   See also anthologies, chapter 7
Orleans Inspiration. With Leo Nocentelli; others. Recorded live in New Orleans at Tipitina's. Windham Hill Jazz WD-0122.

Harry Connick, Jr.

Blue Light, Red Light. Recorded in NYC, 1991. Columbia CK-48685
Harry Connick, Jr. Recorded in NYC, 1987. Columbia CK-40702
Lofty's Roach Souffle. Harry Connick Trio. Recorded in NYC, 1990. Columbia CK-46223
20. With Dr. John; others. Recorded in NYC, 1988. Columbia CK-44369
We Are in Love. With Branford Marsalis; others. Recorded in NYC and Hollywood, 1990. Columbia CK-46146
When Harry Met Sally. Soundtrack from the 1989 film. Columbia CK-45319

Tony Dagradi   See also anthologies, chapters 4 and 6
Images from the Floating World. With John Vidacovich, James Singleton. Recorded in New Orleans. Core Records (Germany) COCD 9.00727
Sweet Remembrance. Recorded in NYC, 1987. Gramavision 18-8707-2
Dagradi also is heard on recordings by Professor Longhair (chapter 3); Robbie Robertson (chapter 4); Astral Project (chapter 6).

Dirty Dozen Brass Band   See also anthologies, chapters 3, 4, 6, and 7
Live: Mardi Gras in Montreux. Recorded in 1985. Rounder CD-2052
My Feet Can't Fail Me Now. Recorded ca. 1984. George Wein Collection CCD-43005
New Orleans Album. With Danny Barker, Dave Bartholomew, Eddie Bo, Elvis Costello. Recorded in New Orleans, 1989. Columbia CK-45414
Open Up Watcha Gonna Do for the Rest of Your Life. Recent release features many original compositions by band members. Columbia CK-47383

Voodoo. With Dr. John, Branford Marsalis; others. Recorded in NYC and Metairie, La., 1987. If you buy only one by the group, this first Columbia album best captures their distinctive style. Columbia CK-45042

Victor Goines   See also anthologies
Genesis. Recorded in New Orleans, ca. 1991. With Harold Battiste; others. AFO 92-0428-2

Donald Harrison   See also Terence Blanchard and Donald Harrison
See also listing under Donald Harrison in chapter 7
For Art's Sake. With Marlon Jordan; others. Candid CCD-79501

Improvisational Arts Quintet   See anthologies

Edward "Kidd" Jordan   See anthologies

Kent Jordan   See also anthologies
Essence. Recorded ca. 1988. Columbia CK-40868
Night Aire. Recorded ca. 1986. Columbia CK-40386
Jordan also is heard on recordings by Marlon Jordan, Mars, Wynton Marsalis.

Marlon Jordan
For You Only. With Branford Marsalis, Kent Jordan; others. Recorded in New Orleans and NYC 1988. Columbia CK-45200
Learson's Return. Marlon Jordan Quintet. Recorded in Los Angeles, ca. 1991. Columbia CK-46930
Jordan also is heard on a recording by Donald Harrison.

Clyde Kerr, Jr.   See anthologies
Kerr also is heard on recordings by Alvin "Red" Tyler.

Lady BJ (Joanne Crayton)   See anthologies

Rick Margitza
Color. With Steve Masakowski; others. Recorded in NYC, 1989. Blue Note B21S-92279
Hope. With Steve Masakowski; others. Recorded in NYC, 1990. Blue Note B21S-94858
This Is New. Recorded in NYC, 1991. Blue Note B21Z-97196
Margitza also is heard on recordings by Steve Masakowski, David Torkanowsky.

Mars

Mars. With Steve Masakowski, John Vidacovich, James Singleton, Kent Jordan, David Torkanowsky, Ed Black; others. Nebula NU-5004

Branford Marsalis

Note to Readers: In addition to the following listings, Branford has also recorded several classical albums and has appeared as a sideman on many popular and jazz recordings.

Beautyful Ones Are Not Yet Born. With Wynton Marsalis; others. Recorded in England, 1991. Columbia CK-46990.

Crazy People Music. Recorded in NYC, 1990. Columbia CK-46072

Do the Right Thing. Soundtrack of the 1989 film, composed by Bill Lee. With Branford Marsalis; others. Columbia CK-45406.

Mo' Better Blues. Soundtrack from the 1990 film. Branford Marsalis Quartet (with Terence Blanchard; others). Columbia CK-46792

Random Abstract. Recorded in Tokyo, 1987. Columbia CK-44055

Renaissance. Recorded in 1986–87. Columbia CK-40711

Royal Garden Blues. With Ellis Marsalis; others. Recorded in NYC, 1986. Columbia CK-40363

Scenes in the City. Recorded in NYC, 1983. Columbia CK-38951

Trio Jeepy. Recorded in NYC, 1988. Columbia CK-44199

Marsalis also is heard on recordings by Terence Blanchard, Harry Connick, Jr., Dirty Dozen Brass Band, Marlon Jordan, Ellis Marsalis, Wynton Marsalis.

Delfeayo Marsalis

Pontius Pilate's Decision. With Wynton, Branford and Jason Marsalis; others. Recorded in 1991–92. Novus 63134-2

Ellis Marsalis

Note to Readers: In addition to the recordings listed below, Ellis also has appeared as a sideman on albums by Courtney Pine, Nat Adderley; others.

See also anthologies

Classic / Ellis. Reissue of *Monkey Puzzle,* recorded in New Orleans, 1963, plus additional selections from same period. AFO 91-0428-2

Ellis Marsalis Trio. Recorded in NYC, 1990. Blue Note 96107

Fathers and Sons. Recorded ca. 1982. Ellis with Branford and Wynton are featured on half of this recording. Columbia 37972 (cassette only)

Heart of Gold. Trio album recorded ca. 1991. Jason Marsalis appears briefly. Columbia CK-47509

Homecoming. Duets with Eddie Harris, recorded in Dallas, ca. 1984. Spindletop 105

In the Beginning. American Jazz Quintet (Ellis Marsalis, Alvin Batiste, Harold Battiste; others). Recorded 1956, 1958. Selections from the original four-volume LPs. AFO 91-102802

Piano in E. Solo album recorded in New Orleans, 1986. Rounder CD-2100

Marsalis also is heard on recordings by Branford Marsalis, Wynton Marsalis, Steve Masakowski.

Jason Marsalis

Marsalis is heard on recordings by Ellis and Delfeayo Marsalis.

Wynton Marsalis

Note to Readers: In addition to the following listings, Wynton has also recorded several classical albums and has appeared as a sideman on several jazz recordings.

Black Codes (From the Underground). With Branford Marsalis; others. Recorded in NYC, 1985. Columbia CK-4009

Hot House Flowers. With Branford Marsalis, Kent Jordan; others. Recorded in NYC, 1984. Columbia CK-39530

J Mood. Recorded in NYC, 1985. Columbia CK-40308

Majesty of the Blues. Wynton Marsalis Sextet. Also with Michael White, Danny Barker; others. Recorded in 1988. If you buy only one by Marsalis, this is his great tribute to traditional New Orleans jazz. Columbia CK-45091

Soul Gestures in Southern Blue. Vol. I: Thick in the South. Vol. II: Uptown Ruler. Vol. III: Levee Low Moan. Recorded ca. 1987–88. Not strictly a series, but can be considered his blues trilogy. Columbia CK-47977; CK-47976; CK-47975

Standard Time, Vol. 1. Vol. 2: Intimacy Calling. Vol. 3: Resolution of Romance. Recorded 1986–90. The three discs are linked by the series title: most songs are jazz and pop standards. Pianists include Ellis Marsalis; one critic called Vol. 3 Wynton's "homage to Ellis." Columbia CK-40461; CK-47346; CK-46143

Think of One. With Branford Marsalis; others. Recorded in NYC, ca. 1983. Columbia CK-38641

Tune in Tomorrow. Soundtrack from the 1990 film. With Johnny Adams, Alvin Batiste, Michael White; others. Columbia CK-47044

Wynton Marsalis Quartet: Live at Blues Alley. Recorded in Washington, D.C., 1986. Columbia G2K-40675 (2 CDs)

Wynton Marsalis. With Branford Marsalis; others. Recorded in Japan and NYC, ca. 1982. His debut jazz album for Columbia. Columbia CK-37574

Marsalis also is heard on recordings by Michael White (chapter 2); Branford Marsalis, Ellis Marsalis (chapter 6).

Steve Masakowski   See also anthologies
Steve Masakowski and Friends. With Ellis Marsalis, Rick Margitza; others. Recorded in New Orleans, 1984. Nebula NU 5010

Masakowski also is heard on recordings by Astral Project, Rick Margitza, Mars, Alvin "Red" Tyler.

Charmaine Neville   See anthologies

Walter Payton
Payton is heard on recordings by Michael White (chapter 2); Champion Jack Dupree (chapter 3).

ReBirth Brass Band   See also anthologies, chapters 3, 4, 6, and 7
Feel like Funkin' It Up. Recorded in Metairie, La. Rounder CD-2093
ReBirth Kickin' It Live! Recorded during Mardi Gras in New Orleans, 1990. Rounder CD-2106

The group also is heard on recordings by Robbie Robertson (chapter 4); Bo Dollis (chapter 7).

James Singleton
Singleton is heard on recordings by Johnny Adams, James Booker, Charles Neville (chapter 4); Astral Project, Tony Dagradi, Mars, Earl Turbinton, Jr., Alvin "Red" Tyler (chapter 6).

Willie Tee (Turbinton)   See anthologies, chapter 4
Tee also is heard on a recording by Earl Turbinton, Jr.

David Torkanowsky
Steppin' Out. With Rick Margitza; others. Recorded in Metairie, La., 1988. Rounder CD-2090

Torkanowsky also is heard on recordings by Astral Project, Mars, Alvin "Red" Tyler.

Earl Turbinton, Jr.   See also anthologies, chapters 4 and 6
Brothers for Life. With Willie Tee; James Singleton; others. Recorded in Metairie La., 1987. Rounder CD-2064

Alvin "Red" Tyler   See also anthologies, chapters 3, 4, and 6
Graciously. With David Torkanowsky, James Singleton, Steve Masa-

kowski, Clyde Kerr, Jr., John Vidacovich. Recorded in Metairie, La., 1986. Rounder CD-2061

Heritage. With David Torkanowsky, James Singleton, Clyde Kerr, Jr., John Vidacovich, Germaine Bazzle. Recorded in Slidell, La., 1985. Rounder CD-2047

Tyler also is heard on recordings by Clarence "Gatemouth" Brown, Champion Jack Dupree, Tommy Ridgely, Huey Smith (chapter 3); Johnny Adams, James Booker (chapter 4).

John Vidacovich

Vidacovich is heard on recordings by Professor Longhair; (chapter 3); Johnny Adams, James Booker, Charles Neville (chapter 4); Astral Project, Tony Dagradi, Mars, Alvin "Red" Tyler (chapter 6).

CHAPTER 7: WHERE TO HEAR IT— WHERE TO FIND IT

ANTHOLOGIES

Best of Jazz Fest: Live from New Orleans, 1988. Performances by Zachary Richard, Rockin' Dopsie, Olympia Brass Band, Dr. John, Allen Toussaint, Irma Thomas. Mardi Gras Records (New Orleans) MG 1011

Festival de Musique Acadienne '81. Performances by Bois Sec Ardoin, Michael Doucet, Ardoin Brothers Band, D.L. Menard, Zachary Richard, Dennis McGee and Sady Courville, Canray Fontenot, Beausoleil, John Delafose, Balfa Brothers Band; others. Swallow 6048 (LP and cassette only)

Mardi Gras in New Orleans, Vols. 1 and 2. Performances by Professor Longhair, Al Johnson, Hawketts, Bo Dollis and Wild Magnolias, Earl King, Sugar Boy Crawford, Dixie Cups, Olympia Brass Band, Meters; others. The ultimate Mardi Gras anthology, including original versions of "Carnival Time," and all the other songs of the season; some not available on other CDs. Mardi Gras Records (New Orleans) MG1001; MG1005

Mardi Gras Party. 1970s–1990s performances by Bo Dollis and Wild Magnolias, Buckwheat Zydeco, Beausoleil, Professor Longhair, Zachary Richard, James Booker, Marcia Ball, Art Neville, ReBirth Brass Band, Irma Thomas, Nathan and Zydeco Cha Chas, Monk

Boudreaux and Golden Eagles, Dirty Dozen Brass Band, Tuts Washington. Rounder CD-11567

New Orleans Jazz & Heritage Festival, 1976. Performances by Allen Toussaint, Ernie K-Doe, Lee Dorsey, Robert Parker, Irma Thomas, Earl King, Professor Longhair; others. Rhino R2CD-71111 (2 CDs)

New Orleans Jazz & Heritage Festival (10th Anniversary). Ca. 1978 performances by Clifton Chenier, Henry Butler; others. Flying Fish FF-70099

ARTIST LISTINGS

Bo Dollis   See also anthologies

I'm back . . . at Carnival Time! With Wild Magnolias, Golden Eagles, ReBirth Jazz Band, George Porter, Snooks Eaglin. Recorded in Metairie, La. Rounder CD-2094

Dollis also is heard on recordings by Champion Jack Dupree (chapter 3); Robbie Robertson (chapter 4).

Golden Eagles (Mardi Gras Indians)   See also anthologies, chapters 4 and 7

Lightning and Thunder. With Monk Boudreaux. Rounder CD-2073

Golden Eagles also are heard on a recording by Bo Dollis.

Donald Harrison

Indian Blues. Interesting mixture of jazz and Mardi Gras Indian music with Dr. John, Donald Harrison, Sr., and his Mardi Gras Indian tribe. Da Music (Germany) CCD 79514

Magnificent Seventh's Brass Band

Authentic New Orleans Jazz Funeral. Including "wake service, funeral procession, joyous send-off," etc. Mardi Gras Records (New Orleans) MG 1012

VIDEOGRAPHY
••

Note To Readers: The videos listed below are all in VHS format. Good mail-order sources include Glen Pitre's Louisiana Catalog (% Cote Blanche Productions, 3101 West Main, Bayouside, Cut Off, LA 70345-9436) and, for Cajun and zydeco subjects, either Floyd's Record Shop (Post Drawer 10, Ville Platte, LA

70586) or Down-Home Music (6921 Stockton Street, El Cerrito, CA 94530). Ordering information is included for those videos which are difficult to find either through commercial video stores or mail-order sources.

Allons Danser! (Let's Dance!) "A step-by-step approach to Cajun dancing." Dance instruction by Randy Speyrer; music by Dewey Balfa, Michael Doucet, Beausoleil; others. 30 min. Bruce Conque, Inc., 1987.

Always for Pleasure. With Professor Longhair, Olympia Brass Band, Kid Thomas Valentine, Wild Tchoupitoulas with the Neville Brothers; others. Includes footage on jazz funerals / brass bands; Mardi-Gras rituals and Indians. Video version of the 1978 film. Directed by Les Blank. 58 min. Flower Films, 1979.

Belizaire the Cajun. Music by Michael Doucet and Beausoleil. Video version of the 1985 film. Produced, written, directed by Glen Pitre. 113 min. Cote Blanche Feature Films, Ltd. / Key Video, 1987.

Best of Blank. Compilation from films made between 1967 and 1987. Louisiana artists include Clifton Chenier, Mardi Gras Indians; others. Produced and directed by Les Blank. Flower Films & Video, 1988.

Best of the Fest. With performers appearing at the Jazz Fest in the late 1980s: Irma Thomas, Zachary Richard, Greater Macedonia Baptist Church, Dr. John and Professor Longhair, Dirty Dozen Brass Band, Allen Toussaint, Neville Brothers; others. Narrated by Quint Davis. Produced and directed by Ken Ehrlich. 50 min. Ken Ehrlich Productions, 1989.

Big Easy. Music by the Dixie Cups, Professor Longhair, Buckwheat Zydeco, Zachary Richard, Neville Brothers, Beausoleil, Wild Tchoupitoulas; others. Video version of the 1987 film. Directed by Jim McBride. 100 min. HBO Video, 1987.

Blues and Swing. Wynton Marsalis in concert with his quartet and in workshops conducted at Harvard University and Duke Ellington School of the Arts, Washington, D.C. Produced and directed by Stanley Dorfman. 79 min. CMV Enterprises, 1988.

Blues de Balfa, Les. With Dewey Balfa, Balfa Brothers, Rockin' Dopsie, Nathan Abshire; others. Produced and directed by Yasha Aginsky. 28 min. Flower Films, 1983.

Buckwheat Zydeco: Taking It Home. Filmed live at a concert in London. Directed by Bob Portway. 55 min. Island, 1990.

Cajun Country: Don't Drop the Potato. "A taste of Cajun music and culture" which includes a visit to Mardi Gras . . ." Episode from the television series, American Patchwork. 60 min. Pacific Arts Video Publishing, 1990.

Cajun Visits. With Dennis McGee, Canray Fontenot, Dewey Balfa; others. In Cajun French with English subtitles. Produced and directed by Yasha Aginsky. 29 min. Flower Films, 1983.

Cinemax Presents Fats Domino & Friends. With Jerry Lee Lewis; others. Directed by Len Dell'Amico; music director, Paul Shaffer. 60 min. HBO Video, 1986.

Clifton Chenier, King of Zydeco. Includes performances at 1982 San Francisco Blues Festival and 1977 Jazz Fest. Executive director and producer, Chris Strachwitz. 55 min. Arhoolie, 1987.

Clifton Chenier. Produced and directed by Carl Colby. 58 min. Phoenix Films & Video, 1978.

Dedans le Sud de la Louisiane. Interviews and performances; in Cajun French with English subtitles. 43 min. Cote Blanche, 1983.

Do the Right Thing. Music by Bill Lee; performed by Branford Marsalis; others. Video version of the 1989 film. Produced, directed, and written by Spike Lee. 120 min. MCA Home Video, 1990.

Dr. John Teaches New Orleans Piano. "In lesson one Dr. John discusses playing styles of the musicians he heard and worked with . . . in New Orleans. In lesson two [he] discusses styles and techniques of the musicians who have influenced his fabulous New Orleans piano sound." 120 min (two tapes). Homespun Tapes, 1988.

Dr. John with Chris Barber's Jazz and Blues Band. Recorded live in London, 1983. 55 min. Zoetrope Ltd, 1983.

Dry Wood. With "Bois Sec" Ardoin and family; Canray Fontenot. Video version of the 1974 film. Directed by Les Blank. 37 min. Flower Films, 1979.

Fats Domino: Live! At the Universal Amphitheatre. Recorded live in Los Angeles, 1985. Directed by T. V. Grasso. 20 min. MCA Home Video, 1985.

Hot Pepper. With Clifton Chenier; others. Video version of the 1972 film by Les Blank. 54 min. Flower Films, ca. 1979.

I Love to Cajun Dance. "How-to" Cajun dance video. Dance instruction by Betty Cecil; music by Nous Autres. 30 min. Cote Blanche, 1988.

In That Number! The New Orleans Brass Band Festival. With Chosen Few, Dirty Dozen, Danny Barker; others. Directed by Jerry Brock. 60 min. 1985. For ordering information, contact the Louisiana State Museum: (504) 568-6968.

J'ai Été au Bal (I Went to the Dance: the Cajun and Zydeco Music of

Louisiana). With Michael Doucet, Clifton Chenier, Queen Ida, Rockin' Sidney, Marc and Ann Savoy, Dennis McGee, Odile Falcon, Canray Fontenot, Paul Daigle and Cajun Gold; others. Historical sequences about Joe Falcon, Amede [sic] Ardoin, Iry Lejeune, Harry Choates; others. Narrated by Barry Jean Ancelet, Michael Doucet. Produced and directed by Les Blank, Chris Strachwitz. 84 min. Brazos Films, 1989.

Jazz Parades. With Preservation Hall Jazz Band, Dirty Dozen Brass Band; others. Episode from the television series, American Patchwork. Written, directed, and produced by Alan Lomax. 60 min. PBS Video, distributed by Pacific Arts Video, 1991.

Jungle Fever. Score composed by Terence Blanchard. Video version of 1991 movie. Directed by Spike Lee. 131 min. MCA/Universal Home Video, 1992.

Let the Good Times Roll. Filmed at the 1990 Jazz Fest. With Fats Domino, Harry Connick, Jr., Wynton Marsalis, Percy Humphrey, Dirty Dozen Brass Band, Rebirth Brass Band, Aaron Neville and the Zion Harmonizers, Buckwheat Zydeco, Gospel Soul Children, John Mooney, Neville Brothers, Charles Neville and Diversity, Cyril Neville and Uptown All-Stars, Olympia Brass Band, Queen Ida, Zachary Richard, Subdudes, Irma Thomas, Allen Toussaint, Michael White, Wild Magnolias; others. Directed by Paul Justman. 90 min. Island Video / distr. by Polygram, 1992.

Mo' Better Blues. Music performed by Branford Marsalis. Video version of the 1990 film. Directed by Spike Lee. 129 min. MCA Universal Home Video, 1990.

Mystery of the Purple Rose: Creole Jazz Pioneers. Documentary about A.J. Piron and his orchestra. 30 min. 1988. Directed by Peggy Scott Laborde. For ordering information, contact WYES-TV: (504) 486-5511.

Piano Players Rarely Ever Play Together. With Professor Longhair, Allen Toussaint, and Tuts Washington. Produced and directed by Stevenson J. Palfi. 60 min. Stevenson Productions, 1984.

Satchmo in New Orleans: "Red Beans & Ricely Yours." Directed by Peggy Scott Laborde. 60 min. 1990. For ordering information, contact WYES-TV: (504) 486-5511.

Satchmo: Louis Armstrong. Interviews, film clips, and live performances from the 1930s to 1960s. Based on the book by Gary Giddins. Directed by Gary Giddins and Kendrick Simmons. Ca. 86 min. CMV Enterprises, 1989.

Singin' & Swingin.' Harry Connick, Jr. Five music videos and three live performances, plus an interview. Directed by Jeb Brien. 45 min. CBS Music Video Enterprises, 1990.

Spend It All. With Balfa Brothers, Marc Savoy, Nathan Abshire; others. Video version of the 1971 film. Directed by Les Blank, Skip Gerson. 41 min. Flower Films, 1979.

Steep. Branford Marsalis, in concert with his quartet and in workshops at Harvard University and Duke Ellington School of the Arts, Washington, D.C. Also contains interviews with members of his group plus Delfeayo Marsalis; others. Directed by Ken Dennis; music produced by Delfeayo Marsalis. 90 min. CMV Enterprises, 1988.

Swinging Out Live. Harry Connick, Jr. Filmed live at the Majestic Theater in Dallas, 1990. Directed by Jeb Brien. 77 min. Sony Music Video Enterprises, 1991.

Tell It like It Is: Live at Storyville Jazz Hall in New Orleans. Neville Brothers. With Buckwheat Zydeco, Ivan Neville, Dixie Cups, Dirty Dozen Brass Band; others. Music director, Herbie Hancock. 60 min. HBO Video, 1989.

Tribute to Sidney Bechet. With Bob Wilber and the Smithsonian Jazz Repertory Ensemble. Features songs associated with Bechet. Recorded at the Smithsonian Institution, Washington, D.C. Produced and directed by Clark Santee and Delia Gravel Santee. 60 min. Kultur, 1982.

Trumpet Kings. Hosted and performed by Wynton Marsalis. Features 22 jazz trumpeters, including Louis Armstrong. Written, produced, and directed by Burrill Crohn. 72 min. Video Artists International, 1985.

Tune In Tomorrow. Music by Wynton Marsalis. Video version of the 1990 film. Directed by Jon Amiel. 90 min. HBO Video, 1990.

Up from the Cradle of Jazz. Focuses on Lastie and Neville families of New Orleans. Directed by Jason Berry. 30 min. 1980. For ordering information, contact Center for Study of Southern Culture, University of Mississippi: (601) 232-5993.

When Harry Met Sally. With music performed by Harry Connick, Jr.; others. Video version of the 1989 film. Directed by Rob Reiner. 96 min. Nelson Entertainment, 1989.

While We Danced: Music of Mardi Gras. Directed by Peggy Scott Laborde. 30 min. For ordering information, contact WYES-TV: (504) 486-5511.

Zydeco Gumbo. With Clifton Chenier, John Delafose, Boo Zoo Chavis, Terence Semian [sic], Willis Prudhomme. Taped on location in

Southwest Louisiana. Film by Dan Hildebrandt. 28 min. Rhapsody Films, 1990.

Zydeco Nite 'n' Day. With Boo Zoo Chavis, Rocking Dopsie, Buckwheat Zydeco, Terrance Simien, John Delafose, Nathan Williams and Zydeco Cha Chas, Clifton Chenier, Alphonse "Boi Sec" Ardoin and Canray Fontenot; others. Produced by Karen Anderson and Robert Dowling. 70 min. Island Visual Arts, distributed by PolyGram Video, 1991.

Zydeco: Creole Music and Culture in Rural Louisiana. With Amédée Ardoin, Alphonse "Bois Sec" Ardoin; others. Video version of the 1983 film. A film by Nicholas R. Spitzer and Steven Duplanier. 57 min. Flower Films, 1984.

Bibliography

Albertson, Chris. *Bessie*. New York: Stein & Day, 1972.

Allan, Johnnie. *Memories: A Pictorial History of South Louisiana Music, 1920's–1980's*. Lafayette, La.: Jadfel, 1988–.

Ancelet, Barry Jean. *The Makers of Cajun Music*. Austin: U. of Texas, 1984.

Armstrong, Louis. *Satchmo: My Life in New Orleans*. New intro. by Dan Morgenstern. New York: Da Capo, 1986 (repr. of 1954 ed.).

Bane, Michael. *Who's Who in Rock*. New York: Facts on File, 1981.

Barker, Danny. *A Life in Jazz*. New York: Oxford, 1986.

Bechet, Sidney. *Treat It Gentle*. With new preface by Rudi Blesh. New York: Da Capo, 1978 (repr. of 1960 ed.).

Berry, Jason, Jonathon Foose, and Tad Jones. *Up from the Cradle of Jazz: New Orleans Music Since World War II*. New York: Da Capo, 1992 (repr. of 1986 ed.).

Bethel, Tom. *George Lewis: A Jazzman from New Orleans*. Berkeley: U. of California, 1977.

Beyer, Jimmy. *Baton Rouge Blues: A Guide to the Baton Rouge Bluesmen and their Music*. Baton Rouge, La.: Arts & Humanities Council of Greater Baton Rouge, 1980.

Bigard, Barney. *With Louis and the Duke: The Autobiography of a Jazz Clarinetist*. Ed. by Barry Martyn. New York: Oxford, 1986.

Blackwell Guide to Recorded Blues. Rev. ed. with CD suppl. Ed. by Paul Oliver. Cambridge: Blackwell, 1991.

Blackwell Guide to Recorded Jazz. Ed. by Barry Kernfeld. Cambridge, Ma.: Blackwell, 1991.

Blassingame, John W. *Black New Orleans, 1960–1880*. Chicago: U. of Chicago, 1973.

Boulard, Garry. *Just a Gigolo: The Life and Times of Louis Prima.* Lafayette, La.: Center for Louisiana Studies, U. of Southwestern Louisiana, 1989.

Broven, John. *Rhythm & Blues in New Orleans.* Gretna, La.: Pelican, 1978 (repr. of 1974 ed.).

———. *South to Louisiana: The Music of the Cajun Bayous.* Gretna, La.: Pelican, 1983.

Brunn, Harry. *The Story of the Original Dixieland Jazz Band.* New York: Da Capo Press, 1977 (repr. of 1960 ed.).

Buerkle, Jack V., and Danny Barker. *Bourbon Street Black: The New Orleans Black Jazzman.* New York: Oxford, 1973.

Carter, William. *Preservation Hall: Music from the Heart.* New York: Norton, 1991.

Charters, Samuel B. *Jazz: New Orleans, 1885–1963: An Index to the Negro Musicians of New Orleans.* New York: Da Capo, 1983 (repr. of 1963 ed.).

Chilton, John. *Sidney Bechet: The Wizard of Jazz.* New York: Oxford, 1987.

Collier, James Lincoln. *Louis Armstrong, An American Genius.* New York: Oxford, 1983.

———. *The Making of Jazz: A Comprehensive History.* Boston: Houghton Mifflin, 1978.

Cotton, Lee. *Shake, Rattle & Roll: The Golden Age of American Rock 'n Roll.* Ann Arbor: Pierian, 1989.

Crawford, Ralston. *Music in the Streets.* New Orleans: Historic New Orleans Collection, 1983.

Daigle, Pierre V. *Tears, Love, and Laughter: The Story of the Cajuns and Their Music.* Rev. and exp. 4th ed. Ville Platte, La.: Swallow, 1987.

Davis, Francis. *In the Moment: Jazz in the 1980s.* New York: Oxford, 1986.

Davis, Miles, with Quincy Troupe. *Miles, The Autobiography.* New York: Simon & Schuster, 1989.

Draper, David E. *Mardi Gras Indians: The Ethnomusicology of Black Associations in New Orleans.* Ann Arbor, Mich.: University Microfilms, 1978 (photocopy of 1973 Tulane U. thesis).

Fountain, Pete, with Bill Neely. *A Closer Walk: The Pete Fountain Story.* Chicago: Regnery, 1972.

Francois, Raymond E., ed. *Yé Yaille, Chère: Traditional Cajun Dance Music.* Lafayette, La.: Thunderstone, 1990.

George, Nelson. *The Death of Rhythm & Blues.* New York: Pantheon, 1988.

Giddins, Gary. *Rhythm-A-Ning: Jazz Tradition and Innovation in the '80's.* New York: Oxford, 1985.

————. *Riding on a Blue Note: Jazz and American Pop.* New York: Oxford, 1981.

————. *Satchmo.* New York: Doubleday, 1988.

Gillett, Charlie. *The Sound of the City.* Rev. ed. New York: Pantheon, 1984.

Goffin, Robert. *Horn of Plenty: The Story of Louis Armstrong.* Trans. by James F. Bezou. Westport, Conn.: Greenwood, 1978 (repr. of 1947 ed.)

Goreau, Laurraine. *Just Mahalia, Baby: The Mahalia Jackson Story.* Gretna, La.: Pelican, 1984 (repr. of 1975 ed.).

Guralnick, Peter. *Feel Like Going Home: Portraits in Blues & Rock 'n Roll.* New York: Vintage, 1981 (repr. of 1971 ed.).

Hannusch, Jeff. *I Hear You Knockin': The Sound of New Orleans Rhythm and Blues.* Ville Platte, La.: Swallow, 1985.

Heilbut, Anthony. *The Gospel Sound: Good News and Bad Times.* 4th Limelight ed. New York: Limelight, 1992.

Jackson, Jesse. *Make a Joyful Noise unto the Lord: The Life of Mahalia Jackson, Queen of Gospel Singers.* New York: Crowell, 1974.

Jackson, Mahalia, with Evan McLeod Wylie. *Movin' On Up.* New York: Hawthorn, 1966.

Joe, Cousin, and Harriet J. Ottenheimer. *Cousin Joe: Blues from New Orleans.* Chicago: U. of Chicago, 1987.

Jones, Max, and John Chilton. *Louis: The Louis Armstrong Story, 1900–1971.* New York: Da Capo, 1988 (repr. of 1971 ed.).

Lambert, George E. *Johnny Dodds.* New York: Barnes, 1961.

Leadbitter, Mike, ed. *Nothing but the Blues: An Illustrated Documentary.* London: Hanover Books, 1971.

Leavitt, Mel. *A Short History of New Orleans.* San Francisco: Lexikos, 1982.

Levy, Louis H. *Formalization of New Orleans Jazz Musicians: A Case Study of Organizational Change.* Ann Arbor, Mich.: University Microfilms, 1978 (photocopy of Virginia Polytechnic Institute thesis).

Lomax, Alan. *Mister Jelly Roll.* 2nd ed. Berkeley: U. of California, 1973.

Malone, Bill C. *Country Music, U.S.A.* Rev. ed. Austin: U. of Texas, 1985.

Marcus, Greil, ed. *Stranded: Rock & Roll for a Desert Island.* New York: Knopf, 1979.

Marquis, Donald M. *Finding Buddy Bolden, First Man of Jazz: The Journal of a Search.* Rev. ed. Goshen, Ind.: Pinchpenny, 1990.

———. *In Search of Buddy Bolden: First Man of Jazz.* New York: Da Capo, 1980 (repr. of 1978 ed.).

Martinez, Raymond J. *Portraits of New Orleans Jazz: Its Peoples and Places.* New Orleans: Hope, 1971.

Miller, Jim, ed. *Rolling Stone Illustrated History of Rock and Roll.* Rev. ed. New York: Rolling Stone, 1980.

Murray, Albert. *Stomping the Blues.* New York: Da Capo, 1989 (repr. of 1976 ed.).

New Grove Dictionary of American Music, ed. by H. Wiley Hitchcock and Stanley Sadie. 4 vols. New York: Grove's Dictionaries of Music, 1986.

New Grove Dictionary of Jazz, ed. by Barry Kernfeld. 2 vols. New York: Grove's Dictionaries of Music, 1988.

Oakley, Giles. *The Devil's Music: A History of the Blues.* Rev. ed. London: British Broadcasting Corp., 1983.

Oliver, Paul, Max Harrison, and William Bolcom. *The New Grove Gospel, Blues, and Jazz.* New York: Norton, 1986.

Palmer, Robert. *A Tale of Two Cities: Memphis Rock and New Orleans Roll.* Brooklyn: Institute for Studies in American Music, School of Performing Arts, Brooklyn College of the City U. of New York, 1979.

———. *Deep Blues.* New York: Viking, 1981.

Panassie, Hugues. *Louis Armstrong.* New York: Da Capo, 1979 (repr. of 1971 ed.).

Pareles, Jon, and Patricia Romanowski, eds. *Rolling Stone Encyclopedia of Rock and Roll.* New York: Summit, 1983.

Pinford, Mike. *Louis Armstrong, His Life and Times.* New York: Universe, 1987.

Pleasants, Henry. *The Great American Popular Singers.* New York: Simon & Schuster, 1974.

Rockmore, Noel. *Preservation Hall Portraits.* Baton Rouge: Louisiana St. U. Press, 1968.

Rose, Al. *Storyville, New Orleans, Being an Authentic, Illustrated Account of the Notorious Red-light District.* University, Ala.: U. of Alabama, 1974.

Rose, Al, and Edmond Souchon. *New Orleans Jazz: A Family Album.* 3rd ed. Baton Rouge, La.: Louisiana State U., 1984.

Savoy, Ann Allen. *Cajun Music: A Reflection of a People.* Eunice, La.: Bluebird, 1984.

Schafer, William J. *Brass Bands and New Orleans Jazz.* Baton Rouge: Louisiana St. U. Press, 1977.

Scott, Frank, *et al. The Down Home Guide to the Blues.* Pennington, NJ: A Capella Books, 1991.

Shapiro, Nat, and Nat Hentoff, eds. *Hear Me Talkin' to Ya: The Story of Jazz by the Men Who Made It.* New York: Rinehart, 1955.

Shaw, Arnold. *Honkers & Shouters: The Golden Years of Rhythm and Blues.* New York: Macmillan, 1978.

Smith, Michael P. *A Joyful Noise: A Celebration of New Orleans Music.* Dallas: Taylor, 1990.

———. *New Orleans Jazz Fest: A Pictorial History.* With foreword by Ben Sandmel. Gretna, La.: Pelican, 1991.

Sonnier, Austin M. *Second Linin': Jazzmen of Southwest Louisiana, 1900–1950.* Lafayette, La.: Center for Louisiana Studies, U. of Southwestern Louisiana, 1989.

Spedale, Rhodes. *Guide to Jazz in New Orleans.* New Orleans: Hope, 1984.

Stearns, Marshall. *The Story of Jazz.* New York: Oxford, 1956.

Taylor, Joe Gray. *Louisiana: A History.* Rev. ed. New York: Norton, 1984.

Travailler, C'est Trop Dur: The Tools of Cajun Music. Lafayette, La.: Lafayette Natural History Museum Association, 1984 (exhibition catalog).

Turner, Frederick. *Remembering Song: Encounters with the New Orleans Jazz Tradition.* New York: Viking, 1982.

Ward, Ed, Geoffrey Stokes, and Ken Tucker. *Rock of Ages: Rolling Stone History of Rock & Roll.* New York: Summit, 1986.

Whitburn, Joel. *The Billboard Book of Top 40 Hits.* 5th ed. New York: Billboard Books, 1992.

White, Charles. *The Life and Times of Little Richard—The Quasar of Rock.* New York: Harmony, 1984.

Williams, Martin T. *Jazz Masters of New Orleans.* New York: Da Capo, 1979 (repr. of 1967 ed.).

———. *King Oliver.* New York: Barnes, 1961.

Wright, Laurie, *et al. King Oliver.* Rev. ed. Chigwell, England: Storyville, 1987.

Notes

Much of the information in this book came from interviews we conducted with performers, producers, critics, and record company officials. In addition, we relied on books, magazine and newspaper articles, and album liner notes. Most chart positions are from *The Billboard Book of Top 40 Hits* by Joel Whitburn. The following reference books and magazines, which were especially useful, have been abbreviated as shown:

The New Grove Dictionary of Jazz (NGDJ), ed. by Barry Kernfeld. 2 vols. New York: Grove's Dictionaries of Music, 1988

The New Grove Dictionary of American Music (NGDAM), ed. by H. Wiley Hitchcock and Stanley Sadie. 4 vols. New York: Grove's Dictionaries of Music, 1986

Oliver, Paul, Max Harrison, and William Bolcom. *The New Grove Gospel, Blues, and Jazz* (GBJ). New York: Norton, 1986.

Downbeat (DB)

Wavelength (WL)

1: Introduction: Jambalaya, Crawfish Pie, Filé Gumbo (pages 13–24)

The Choctaw . . . Mel Leavitt, *A Short History of New Orleans* (San Francisco: Lexikos, 1982), 10–11.

With the territory . . . Joe Gray Taylor, *Louisiana: A History*. Revised ed. (New York: Norton, 1984), 9–10.

A shortage of women . . . Leavitt, 26, 33–34.

During his 10 years . . . Jack V. Buerkle and Danny Barker, *Bourbon Street Black* (New York, Oxford, 1973), 5.

So it was that music . . . Leavitt, 38. Taylor, 15.

According to historians . . . Taylor, 24.

Where were the newcomers from? . . . Taylor, 24–25.

The haughty French . . . Leavitt, 55–65.

The Code Noir . . . Taylor, 26–27.

As one sociologist notes . . . Buerkle, 8–9.

For simplicity's sake, we use "Creoles" in this book to refer to Creoles of Color, rather than whites of French descent.

During La Belle Epoque . . . Leavitt, 80–89.

"French tendency to parade . . ." Buerkle, 6.

"Every holiday . . ." ibid.

"Visitors seemed to agree . . ." Leavitt, 68.

Urban slaves in New Orleans . . . Taylor, 60–61.

One of the biggest slave markets . . . Taylor, 72.

"Perhaps the most sophisticated . . ." Taylor, 60–61.

Owners were not able . . . John W. Blassingame, *Black New Orleans, 1960–1880* (Chicago: University of Chicago, 1973), 2.

Congo Square information is from Blassingame, 5; Buerkle, 11; and from Martin T. Williams, *Jazz Masters of New Orleans* (New York: Da Capo, 1979) 6–7.

A biographer . . . Henry Edward Durell, quoted in Williams, 6.

Racism and segregation sprang up . . . Taylor, 120–21.

They developed their own form of society . . . Blassingame, 140, 147.

Blacks also formed organizations . . . Donald M. Marquis, *In Search of Buddy Bolden: First Man of Jazz* (New York: Da Capo, 1980), 32; and Alan Lomax, *Mister Jelly Roll*. 2nd ed. (Berkeley: University of California, 1973), 11.

Their members sold their used instruments . . . Buerkle, 14.

Jelly Roll Morton vividly recalled . . . Lomax, 11–12.

"The most miserable feeling . . ." Nat Shapiro and Nat Hentoff, *Hear Me Talkin' to Ya: The Story of Jazz by the Men Who Made It* (New York: Rinehart, 1955), 15.

Sometimes the parades were so long . . . Marquis, 33.

One more key element . . . The information on Storyville is mainly from Al Rose, *Storyville, New Orleans, Being an Authentic, Illustrated Account of the Notorious Red-light District* (University, Alabama: University of Alabama, 1974). Also Buerkle, 19; Lomax, 50–51; Williams, 16–7.

Danny Barker once offered . . . Shapiro, 10–11.

As Sidney Bechet wrote . . . Sidney Bechet, *Treat It Gentle* (New York: Da Capo, 1978), 215.

"Something came along . . ." Lomax, xiv.

2: The Cradle of Jazz Still Rocks

THE BIRTH OF JAZZ (pages 25–33)

A man named Poree . . . Williams, 2.

At the time, popular music . . . NGDJ, 168; Williams, xii–xiii; Smithsonian *Classic Jazz* liner notes.

As critic Martin Williams wrote . . . Williams, xiii.

Born Charles Joseph Bolden . . . Marquis, 4–5.

His biographer, Don Marquis . . . Marquis, 6.

Marquis thinks . . . Marquis, 34–38.

A young Creole . . . Lomax, 60.

"Call the children . . ." Shapiro, 37.

Bolden's rivals . . . Marquis, 79–81.

"Bolden cause all that . . ." Lomax, 86.

By 1906 . . . Marquis, 112–114.

In 1907 . . . Marquis, 122.

Bands would advertise . . . Shapiro, 37.

Among the pretenders . . . Williams, 15.

A powerful cornetist . . . Williams, 20.

Keppard was such a suspicious man . . . Bechet, 112.

Born in 1885 . . . Williams, 79–81.

Another declared Oliver would . . . Shapiro, 42.

Louis Armstrong used to say . . . Williams, 79.

Determined to seize the crown . . . Williams, 84.

"He was the best . . ." Shapiro, 42.

"There was a real excitement . . ." Bechet, 116.

This explanation . . . Smithsonian *Classic Jazz* liner notes.

White groups as well as blacks . . . Williams, 27–28.

LaRocca was the son . . . Williams, 28–32.

THE PIONEER—JELLY ROLL MORTON (pages 33–41)

Duke Ellington once said . . . quoted by Philip W. Payne in introduction to "Giants of Jazz" *Jelly Roll Morton* album, Time-Life Records.

Lomax, on the other hand . . . Lomax, xii.

Born on . . . NGDJ, 136.

"They always had . . ." Lomax, 5–6.

"Considered one of the best . . ." Lomax, 22–23.

"I liked the freedom . . ." ibid.

A musician, she scolded . . . Williams, 44.

As Lomax wrote . . . Lomax, 104.

"The music the whores liked." Shapiro, 55.

"The stomping grounds . . ." Lomax, 42–43.

"All these men . . ." Lomax, 43.

Clarence Williams summed up . . . Shapiro, 55.

"It was only a back room . . ." Lomax, 104.

"When the settled Creole folks . . ." Lomax, 98.

"This peculiar form . . ." quoted by Chris Albertson in liner notes for "Giants of Jazz" *Jelly Roll Morton* album.

"Pretty little waitress . . ." Lomax, 171.

"The piano rocked . . ." Williams, 56.

Still, St. Cyr said . . . Lomax, 193.

"One of the most remarkable . . ." Williams, 58.

"W.C. Handy is a liar." Lomax, 234.

SIDNEY BECHET—REED POET (pages 41–48)

"The first jazz romantic . . ." Whitney Balliett, "Sidney Bechet," *The New Yorker,* March 18, 1991, 80.

"I wasn't ready . . ." Bechet, 69–70.

"What is that?" Lomax, 94.

"I knew I was too young . . ." Bechet, 70–71.

Leonard Bechet remarked . . . Lomax, 96.

Ansermet . . . Bechet, 127.

"You tell it . . ." Bechet, 215.

British critic Max Harison noted . . . in liner notes for "Complete Blue Note Recordings of Sidney Bechet."

Bechet was tickled . . . Bechet, 128.

"Fooling around . . ." quoted by Frank K. Kappler in liner notes for "Giants of Jazz" *Sidney Bechet* album.

"I had a lot of pleasure . . ." Bechet, 181.

According to Martin Williams . . . Williams, 159.

"When he discovered his real instrument . . ." Williams, 138.

SATCHMO (pages 48–58)

The *New Grove Dictionary of Jazz* . . . NGDJ, 27.

One biographer . . . James Lincoln Collier, *Louis Armstrong, An American Genius* (New York: Oxford, 1983) 3.

It may not be overstating . . . Williams, 163.

He was born . . . Tad Jones, in video documentary *Satchmo in New Orleans,* makes a persuasive case for August 4, 1901, judging by baptismal certificate and other evidence.

It was called . . . Louis Armstrong, *Satchmo: My Life in New Orleans* (New York: Da Capo, 1986), 7.

"I did not know . . ." Armstrong, 8.

Perhaps, as one scholar suggests . . . Dr. John Joyce, in video documentary *Satchmo in New Orleans.*

The man played so hard . . . Armstrong, 23.

This was how he described . . . Armstrong, 47–48.

A friend, Cocaine Buddy . . . Williams, 167–68.

"Beat out some of the damnedest . . ." Armstrong, 64.

"He played more blues . . ." Shapiro, 46.

"You still blowing that cornet? . . ." Williams, 171.

"I wanted to do more . . ." Armstrong, 182.

"I rushed home . . ." Armstrong, 227–28.

"Oh, you're the young man . . . Armstrong, 231.

"I had hit . . ." Armstrong, 240.

"America's Florence . . ." Lomax, x.

Here is how Lomax . . . Lomax, 179.

"Oh, those cats were glowing!" Armstrong, 240.

"Doing something he would eventually . . ." Collier, *Louis Armstrong,* 108.

"I'm accepted . . ." Collier, *Louis Armstrong,* 318–19.

"Within Bourbon Street Black . . ." Buerkle, 70.

"All we can do . . ." speech by Marsalis introducing Armstrong films, Lincoln Center, January 16, 1992.

"Americans, unknowingly . . ." Feather quoted by Henry Pleasants in *The Great American Popular Singers* (New York: Simon & Schuster, 1974), 99.

"I'm proud . . ." quoted in Pleasants, 109.

APRÈS LOUIS (pages 58–67)

"A lot of them . . ." Shapiro, 66–68.

"We had only two tempos . . ." Williams, 128.

"They tried to write . . ." Bechet, 95.

"The greatest horn . . ." Leonard Feather refers to album of this name in column in *International Musician,* August 1961.

"What the heck . . ." quoted in *Dixie* magazine, July 20, 1961.

"Roving Dixieland . . ." quoted in *Time,* June 9, 1961.

Critic Leonard Feather . . . in *International Musician,* August 1961.

"We try to satisfy . . ." quoted in *Dixie,* July 30, 1961.

Critic Nat Hentoff . . . in *Holiday,* November 1961.

"Al is no longer a jazz musician . . ." quoted in article in New Orleans *Times-Picayune,* 1968 (no exact date on clipping in vertical files, Hogan Jazz Archives, Tulane University).

"It sure takes all the fun out . . ." quoted in New Orleans *States-Item,* February 9, 1970.

His booking agent . . . conversation with Grace Lichtenstein, February 1, 1991.

Like Hirt, he strayed quite far . . . *DB,* November 23, 1961, 20–21.

"I went to Bourbon Street . . ." Pete Fountain with Bill Neely, *A Closer Walk: The Pete Fountain Story* (Chicago: Regnery, 1972), 32–33.

"Get lost, kid . . ." Fountain, 53.

"It was Faz pushing . . ." Fountain, 59–62.

It was a tight group . . . Fountain, 73–80.

"On the bandstand . . ." Fountain, 108.

The end came . . . Fountain, 155.

"Swinging Dixie . . ." *DB,* November 23, 1961.

He acknowledged . . . Howard Mandel, "Pete Fountain, Crescent City Clarinet," *DB,* January 1985, 61.

The bottom line . . . Bill Esposito in *Second Line,* Winter, 1974, 18–19.

GRAND OLD MEN (pages 67–71)

As guitarist Danny Barker . . . Buerkle, 91.

His aunt, he recalled . . . quoted by Jeff Hannusch in *Dixie* magazine, September 1981.

Washington found a mentor . . . ibid.

Women, he bragged . . . Jeff Hannusch, *I Hear You Knockin': The Sound of New Orleans Rhythm and Blues* (Ville Platte, La.: Swallow, 1985), 8.

Jeff Hannusch, who produced . . . interview with Grace Lichtenstein, March 1992.

Critics heard . . . Vincent Fumar, New Orleans *Times-Picayune,* December 9, 1983; Jim Roberts, *DB,* April 1984.

3: Rebirth: The First Wave of R&B

BEGINNINGS—FESS, FATS, AND THE FIFTIES
(pages 72–79)

As Nelson George wrote . . . Nelson George, *The Death of Rhythm and Blues* (New York: Pantheon, 1988), 25.

"We were jazz musicians . . ." Earl Palmer interview with Grace Lichtenstein, June 1991.

"That wasn't a spiritual . . ." Roy Brown in liner notes for "Saturday Nite" album.

"He had a religious . . ." Rick Coleman, "Happy Birthday Rock 'n' Roll," *WL*, June 1987, 8–9.

"You should have heard . . ." ibid.

According to Mac Rebennack . . . Mac Rebennack interview with Grace Lichtenstein, May 1991.

"I slipped the porter . . ." "Saturday Nite" liner notes.

A northerner and a jazz buff . . . Hannusch, *Knockin'*, 119–26.

" 'Good Rockin' Tonight' was . . ." ibid.

THE LEGEND—PROFESSOR LONGHAIR
(pages 79–89)

"The Bach of rock 'n' roll . . ." Allen Toussaint interview with Grace Lichtenstein, February 1992.

What impressed him most . . . Byrd and Washington in video documentary, *Piano Players Rarely Play Together*.

For more on Mardi Gras Indians at Carnival, see chapter 7.

Byrd told one interviewer . . . Hannusch, *Knockin'*, 18.

He told another . . . Robert Palmer, *A Tale of Two Cities: Memphis Rock and New Orleans Roll* (Brooklyn, N.Y.: Institute for Studies in American Music, Brooklyn College, 1979).

According to Byrd, the year . . . Hannusch, *Knockin'*, 20.

"They said I was ten years ahead . . ." *Piano Players* documentary.

"It really was the most incredible . . ." George W. S. Trow, Jr., "Profile of Ahmet Ertegum," *The New Yorker*, June 5, 1978, 50.

"Plenty money . . ." Hannusch, *Knockin'*, 22.

"Fess stole the show . . ." Palmer interview.

As sax player Red Tyler . . . John Broven, *Rhythm and Blues in New Orleans* (Gretna, La.: Pelican, 1978) 41.

"Big Chief" is credited to Earl King, the prolific New Orleans songwriter and singer, but some local people insist it was actually written by Dr. Gismo, a neighborhood fellow who was not a professional musician.

By the time English blues writer . . . Mike Leadbitter, *Nothing but the Blues: An Illustrated Documentary* (London: Hanover Books, 1973).

"When Fess got up to play . . ." Quint Davis interview with Grace Lichtenstein, November 1990.

He kept referring . . . Allison Miner interview with Grace Lichtenstein, February 1991.

To Allison Miner . . . ibid.

Dagradi recalled . . . Tony Dagradi interview with Grace Lichtenstein, February 1992.

"As jazz funerals go . . ." Jason Berry, Jonathon Foose, and Tad Jones, *Up from the Cradle of Jazz* (Athens, Ga.: University of Georgia Press, 1986), 28.

According to Robert Palmer . . . Palmer, *Tale*, 5.

Gary Giddins wrote . . . Gary Giddins, *Riding on a Blue Note* (New York: Oxford, 1981) 108.

THE STAR—FATS DOMINO (pages 89–99)

"He just about raised . . ." Jason Berry, "The Fat Man Turns Sixty," *New Orleans*, May 1988, 88.

"Just a li'l ole fat boy . . ." Hannùsch, *Knockin'*, 12.

"Played all types . . ." Kalamu Ya Salaam, "Music Legend," *Off-beat*, June 1990, 18.

The drummer . . . Palmer interview.

Fats "was killing them . . ." Salaam, "Music Legend," 19.

As Palmer explained . . . Palmer interview.

Cosimo would yell . . . Palmer interview.

Bartholomew was searching . . . Hannusch, *Knockin'*, 101.

"It took me . . ." liner notes for "Antoine 'Fats' Domino: the Legendary Imperial Recordings, CD boxed set.

"Herbert Hardesty, his tenor-sax companion . . ." Herbert Hardesty interview with Grace Lichtenstein, February 1992.

The singer and the band . . . liner notes for "Legendary Masters" album.

"The police panicked . . ." Hardesty interview.

"Nobody could tell him . . ." ibid.

"Actually, we all cooked . . ." ibid.

"He'd stop . . ." Steve Armbruster, "The J & M Studio Story," *WL*, November 1989, 29.

"Off-the cuff . . ." Lee Cotton, *Shake, Rattle & Roll: The Golden Age of American Rock 'n' Roll* (Ann Arbor: Pierian, 1989), 39.

"Look, just try . . . Salaam, "Music Legend," 20.

"I was a country boy . . ." Berry, "Fat Man," 89.

"Man, that night . . ." "Legendary Imperial" liner notes.

"I am the bank . . ." Berry, "Fat Man," 89.

Quint Davis said . . . conversation with Laura Dankner, April 1991.

As Cosimo Matassa told . . . Peter Guralnick, "Fats Domino," *Rolling Stone Illustrated History of Rock and Roll*. Revised ed., 47.

"I went out and got . . ." Salaam, "Music Legend," 21.

Finally, Rupe told him . . . Broven. *Rhythm and Blues,* 106.

THE FIFTIES CHART-TOPPERS (pages 99–109)

Wrote one historian . . . Cotton, *Shake, Rattle, & Roll,* 152–53.

Critics think . . . especially Robert Palmer, *Deep Blues,* 249.

"Wrapped in a piece of paper . . ." Ed Ward, Geoffrey Stokes, and Ken Tucker, *Rock of Ages: The Rolling Stone History of Rock and Roll* (New York: Summit, 1986), 103.

As Blackwell remembered . . . Ward, *Rock of Ages,* 104.

Pounding on the piano . . . Charles White, *The Life and Times of Little Richard—The Quasar of Rock* (New York: Harmony, 1984).

"It was flat out . . ." Rebennack interview.

Could she clean up . . . White, *Life and Times.*

Palmer recalled . . . Palmer interview.

"This is not about ice cream . . . Rebennack interview.

"A kind of comic madness . . ." Langdon Winner, "Little Richard," *Rolling Stone Illustrated History,* 49.

"An eruption . . ." Robert Palmer, "Rock at the Wop-Boppa-Lu-Bop Crossroads," *New York Times,* April 1, 1990.

"The Big Bang . . ." Rick Coleman, "Little Richard—Make a Joyful Noise!", *WL,* November 1984, 17.

He called Palmer . . . White, *Life and Times.*

"He was playing . . ." Rebennack interview.

"Richard and them used to . . ." Rick Coleman, "Little Richard—The New Orleans Connection," *WL,* November 1984, 23.

Like many older . . . Hannusch, *Knockin',* 210.

Smith claimed . . . Hannusch, *Knockin',* 41.

"Could slide in . . ." Rebennack interview.

"I must have signed . . ." Broven, *Rhythm and Blues.*

THE STARMAKER—ALLEN TOUSSAINT (pages 110–23)

"Down and out . . ." Toussaint interview.

"Enlarged my thoughts . . ." ibid.

"My parents . . ." ibid.

"I always felt . . ." ibid.

"I played precisely . . ." ibid.

The two experiences . . . ibid.

"I'd write a song . . ." ibid.

He paid Toussaint . . . Hannusch, *Knockin',* 145.

Toussaint admitted he didn't like it . . . Toussaint interview.

Toussaint had written it . . . Hannusch, *Knockin'*, 337.

"K-Doe began to want . . ." Toussaint interview.

"Ernie blamed Toussaint and his partner . . ." Hannusch, *Knockin'*, 341.

Not so, Toussaint protested . . . Toussaint interview.

Toussaint remembered the Minit years . . . ibid.

Irma Thomas later described it . . . Irma Thomas interview with Grace Lichtenstein, November 1990.

The label was eager . . . Berry, *Cradle*, 190.

For the only time . . . Toussaint interview.

"Lee Dorsey was a guy . . ." ibid.

He admired the way Motown . . . ibid.

"He wanted to have . . ." ibid.

"I'm a producer, musician . . ." quote from *Piano Players* video documentary.

Stars, he said . . . Toussaint interview.

Even when he was front and center . . . ibid.

"Some of you think . . ." from Toussaint's Jazz Festival performance, May 5, 1991.

GOSPEL AND BLUES (pages 123–36)

Mahalia Jackson material based on information from: Jesse Jackson, *Make a Joyful Noise unto the Lord: The Life of Mahalia Jackson, Queen of Gospel Singers* (New York: Crowell, 1974); Mahalia Jackson with Evan McLeon Wylie, *Movin' On Up* (New York: Hawthorn, 1966); and Antony Heilbut, *The Gospel Sound, Good News and Bad Times.* 4th ed. (New York: Limelight, 1992).

"What's that you're singing?" Jackson, *Joyful Noise.*

Jackson disappointed some fans . . . Heilbut, 69.

According to Sherman Washington . . . Sherman Washington interview with Grace Lichtenstein, May 1991.

Washington said that at first . . . Washington interview.

"If it hadn't been . . ." ibid.

"I have a lot of memories . . ." Champion Jack Dupree interview with Grace Lichtenstein, May 1991.

"We could live . . ." ibid.

"You could get a room . . ." ibid.

As he tells it . . . ibid.

"Blues is life . . ." public interview with Allison Miner, Jazz Festival, 1991.

Material on Cousin Joe is based on: Cousin Joe and Harriet J.

Ottenheimer, *Cousin Joe: Blues from New Orleans* (Chicago: University of Chicago, 1987).

"I played his guitar . . ." Gatemouth Brown public interview with Allison Miner, Jazz Festival, 1991.

The difference between . . . ibid.

"He was crying . . ." Rick Coleman, "Snooks Eaglin," *WL*, September 1987, 23.

Not so, said Toussaint . . . Toussaint interview.

"He wanted me to get some stuff . . ." Coleman, "Snooks," 23.

4: The Second Wave of R&B

RIGHT PLACE, RIGHT TIME (pages 137–43)

"You might say Jelly Roll Morton . . ." quoted in liner notes for "Mr. Mystery" album on Sundown label.

"Probably the first experience . . ." quoted in liner notes of "Classified" album on Rounder.

Allen Toussaint, who knew . . . Toussaint interview.

"He was the first . . ." Rebennack interview.

Rebennack said he would make the rounds . . . Rebennack interview.

An evening with him . . . Bunny Matthews, "James Booker: Music as a Mysterious Art," *WL*, December 1983, 24.

The way Booker told the story . . . Berry, *Cradle*, 177.

"Booker was a very trying guy . . ." Rebennack interview.

One critic . . . Tom McDermott, "No One Ever Played like James Booker," *WL*, February 1986, 23–24.

In a conversation . . . Matthews, "James Booker," 27.

In 1981 . . . Hannusch, *Knockin'*, 45.

THE CONDUIT—DR. JOHN (pages 143–53)

One rock history . . . Jon Pareles and Patricia Romanowski, eds. *Rolling Stone Encyclopedia of Rock and Roll* (New York: Summit, 1983), 156.

"My aunt Andree showed me . . ." Rebennack interview.

"Whether it was Huey . . ." ibid.

"Man, what is that . . ." ibid.

Rebennack developed . . . ibid.

"Producers and arrangers . . ." ibid.

"Okay, kid . . ." ibid.

"When I traveled . . ." ibid.

"It wasn't exactly like . . ." ibid.

Harold Battiste said . . . Berry, *Cradle*, 186.

According to Rebennack . . . Rebennack interview.

"I'd even talked . . ." ibid.

Rock historian . . . Charlie Gillett, *Sounds of the City*, 348–49.

"I knew I wasn't no singer . . ." Rebennack interview.

"Smelled like the original hashish . . ." ibid.

"This album is like a picture . . ." liner notes for "Dr. John's Gumbo" album.

"He was always very consistent . . ." Rebennack interview.

"New Orleans musicians . . ." ibid.

THE METERS AND THE BIRTH OF FUNK (pages 153–60)

According to songwriter Earl King . . . Broven, *Rhythm and Blues*.

To Meters bassist . . . George Porter, Jr., interview with Grace Lichtenstein, May, 1991.

"Man, we're stuck . . ." ibid.

"Was hanging out . . ." ibid.

"We never knew who . . ." ibid.

"We played six nights a week . . ." Steve Pond, "The Neville Brothers," *Rolling Stone*, August 8, 1991, 70.

"In those days . . ." Porter interview.

"McCartney just wanted . . ." ibid.

"Actually, Fess didn't like . . ." ibid.

"Some of the attitudes . . ." Berry, *Cradle*, 198.

"We were probably . . ." Porter interview.

After their torrid . . . Scott Aiges, "The Meters Stage a Triumphant Return," New Orleans *Times-Picayune*, December 8, 1989.

"We've all matured . . ." Louie Ludwig, "Warning: The Meters are Funking Back to Life," *No Cover*, Vol 1, No. 12, 11.

FIRST FAMILY—THE NEVILLE BROTHERS (pages 160–72)

"The essence of our music . . ." quoted by George Varga, "Musical Gumbo," San Diego *Union*, May 21, 1989, E-1.

Art described . . . liner notes for "Treacherous" album on Rhino label.

"When people came to visit . . ." ibid.

"I used to eat . . ." Berry, *Cradle*, 192.

"All the people I knew . . ." Pond, "Neville Brothers," 73.

"Asked when he knew . . ." ibid.

"I got turned on to him . . ." Macon Fry, "Aaron Neville," *WL*, May 1985, 21.

"My favorite song . . ." ibid.

"I always have been big . . ." ibid.

As Cyril described this new permutation . . . Berry, *Cradle*, 232.

According to Charles . . . "New Orleans' Neville Brothers Go for the Gumbo," *People*, July 1989.

As Cyril told one writer . . . Berry, *Cradle*, 234.

One magazine described . . . Pond, "Neville Brothers," 73.

Another magazine declared bluntly . . . John Ed Bradley, "Bards of the Bayou," *GQ*, 182.

"Hey, man, we couldn't help it . . ." Pond, "Neville Brothers," 73.

As Cyril explained . . . Stephen Holden, "The Pop Life," *New York Times*, February 15, 1989.

"My heart is with . . ." Edna Gundersen, "Balladeer of the Bayou Aaron Neville," *USA Today*, June 11, 1991, 2D.

"Success to me . . ." Bradley, "Bards," 182.

"There are things that happen . . ." Steve Stolder, "The Neville Brothers," *BAM*, April 21, 1989, 36.

IRMA THOMAS AND LESSER SOUL QUEENS
(pages 172–94)

"Sang big and charted small . . ." Gerri Hirshey, *Nowhere to Run* (New York: Times Books, 1984), 364.

"The church was a social . . ." Thomas interview.

"My mother said . . ." ibid.

"I was sexually promiscuous . . ." ibid.

"I made two dollars . . ." ibid.

"They were weekend jobs . . ." ibid.

"My throat specialist . . ." ibid.

"Of course, I was a bit excited . . ." ibid.

"I didn't have time . . ." ibid.

"Met another crook . . ." ibid.

"My poor kids . . ." ibid.

Burke, she said, bullied . . . ibid.

"There are stories . . ." ibid.

"She showed me . . ." ibid.

"Wasn't that much older . . ." Bunny Matthews, "Irma's Still the Queen but Tall Texan Marcia Ball Is Heir Apparent to the New Orleans Musical Throne," *WL*, February 1984, 18.

"New Orleans is a piano town . . ." Marcia Ball public interview with Allison Miner, Jazz Festival, 1991.

"No voice coach . . ." Johnny Adams public interview with Allison Miner, Jazz Festival, 1991.

5: Ragin' Cajuns

CHANKY CHANK—FOLK MUSIC OF
SOUTHERN LOUISIANA (pages 195–208)

According to folklorist . . . Barry Jean Ancelet, *The Makers of Cajun Music* (Austin: University of Texas Press, 1984), 22.

Dennis later explained . . . liner notes for "La Vieille Musique Acadienne" album on Swallow label.

"Being French became a stigma . . ." Ancelet, *Cajun Music*, 25.

Darbone had learned . . . Luderin Darbone interview with Grace Lichtenstein, September 1991.

"We didn't know . . ." Darbone interview.

"He was Cajun . . ." Stephen Williams, *Newsday*, July 21, 1989.

As Dewey described it . . . Dewey Balfa interview with Grace Lichtenstein, September 1991.

"I didn't know where I was . . ." Balfa interview.

"I became very disturbed . . ." ibid.

"Preserve this culture . . ." ibid.

"On one occasion . . ." Michael Doucet interview with Grace Lichtenstein, September 1991.

"I think it awakened . . ." Floyd Soileau interview with Grace Lichtenstein, December 1991.

"We could have looked . . ." Ted Fox, "Zydeco Music: Hot as a Pepper," *Audio*, September 1986, 45.

Soileau, for example, continued to issue . . . Soileau interview.

"We said to ourselves . . ." ibid.

Marc Savoy, for instance, blasted . . . Ben Sandmel, "Born on a Bayou," *Musician*, August 1985, 40.

Balfa compared . . . Balfa interview.

His generation, said McCauley . . . Cory McCauley interview with Grace Lichtenstein, September, 1991.

But Trent Anger . . . quoted in "The Cajuns: Still Loving Life," *National Geographic*, October 1990, 57.

TRADITIONALISTS AND PROGRESSIVES
(pages 208–19)

"Plays the radio . . ." Ancelet, *Cajun Music*, 141.

"Accepted Cajun music . . ." ibid.

"Eight fiddlers playing . . ." ibid.

"I began to understand . . ." ibid.

"Incredible amount of energy . . ." Steve Pond, "Michael Doucet: The Art of Cajun Cooking," *Rolling Stone*, June 16, 1988, 21.

"Traded Blake for Balfa . . ." Ancelet, *Cajun Music*, 145.

"We thought, well, this is . . ." Doucet interview.

"the Grateful Dead . . ." Pond, "Michael Doucet," 21.

"Here's this incredible . . ." ibid.

"The Cajun renaissance . . ." Doucet interview.

"All of a sudden . . ." Pond, "Michael Doucet," 21.

"Like none you ever heard . . ." Soileau interview.

"I promise you won't regret it . . ." ibid.

"You can take any song . . ." Doucet interview.

"You can't call it country . . ." Jim and Carlotta Anderson, "The Good Times Are Rolling in Cajun Country," *Smithsonian*, February 1988, 122.

"If you play exactly . . ." Fox, "Zydeco Music," 49.

"Not just the two-step . . ." Doucet interview.

"I'm kind of enamored . . ." ibid.

"The whole Cajun experience . . ." Zachary Richard interview with Grace Lichtenstein, October 1991.

"The Beatles hit . . ." ibid.

"I shlepped it . . ." ibid.

"We played in a duet . . ." ibid.

"Grabbed me by the scruff . . ." ibid.

"Diplomat of the Acadian . . ." ibid.

"I was being a musical pinball . . ." ibid.

"There were no stylistic . . ." ibid.

He viewed it as "schizophrenic . . ." ibid.

"I was at a point . . ." ibid.

He acknowledged that . . . ibid.

He analyzed his work . . . ibid.

"A quintessential Cajun song . . ." ibid.

"One can have a significant . . ." ibid.

LE ROI, CLIFTON CHENIER (pages 219–27)

As he later explained, Faulk . . . Ann Allen Savoy, *Cajun Music: A Reflection of a People* (Eunice, La.: Bluebird, 1984).

"It took a long time . . ." ibid.

"If you can't dance . . ." Sandmel, "Born on a Bayou," 38.

"I like to hear . . ." quoted by Ben Sandmel in Savoy, *Cajun Music.*

"They don't tell a story . . ." ibid.

"I couldn't believe it . . ." Strachwitz interview with Grace Lichtenstein, December 1991.

"He was ambitious . . ." ibid.

Black churches, Strachwitz believed . . . ibid.

Later, according to Strachwitz . . . ibid.

"Old people come to my shows . . ." Sandmel, "Born on a Bayou," 38.

A music writer . . . Ben Sandmel interview with Grace Lichtenstein, December 1991.

"That isn't what the kids . . ." Daniel Wolff, "Clifton Chenier," *Nation,* March 1988, 391.

"That's why all the numbers . . ." Strachwitz interview.

As Strachwitz remarked . . ." ibid.

"I know one thing . . ." Savoy, *Cajun Music.*

"Can I help you . . ." Sandmel, "Born on a Bayou," 39.

According to Sandmel . . . Sandmel interview.

EVERYONE'S TOOT TOOT—ZYDECO ROCK
(pages 227–35)

"I'll gamble on it . . ." Soileau interview.

"It was the weakest . . ." ibid.

"Toot Toot," he believed . . . ibid.

"People could see . . ." Doucet interview.

"Zydeco is rock and French . . ." quoted by Sandmel in Savoy, *Cajun Music.*

"Running away from the accordion . . ." Frances Frank Marcus, "Bringing Buckwheat's Zydeco Sound to America," *New York Times,* May 30, 1987.

"It was my father's . . ." Brooke Wentz, "Reclaiming His Roots," *DB,* August 1990, 29.

Dural claimed he became . . . ibid.

"Now you, Mom, and Dad . . ." ibid.

"Our parents wouldn't speak . . ." Fox, "Zydeco Music," 49.

Cajun was music . . . Marcus, "Bringing Buckwheat's Zydeco Sound."

"There is more attention . . ." Wentz, "Reclaiming His Roots," 29.

"We were brought up . . ." Queen Ida public interview with Allison Miner, Jazz Festival, 1991.

Her brother, she recalled . . . ibid.

"When I finally found . . ." Wayne Toups interview with Grace Lichtenstein, October 1991.

His aim, Toups said . . . ibid.

"Twenty to thirty minutes . . ." ibid.

"I knew he was a songwriter . . ." C.J. Chenier interview with Grace Lichtenstein, December 1991.

"Instead," he recalled . . . ibid.

"All the guys . . ." ibid.

"He didn't say a whole lot . . ." ibid.

"Whoa! Full of energy . . ." ibid.

"I guess everybody . . ." ibid.

6: Back to the Future: Contemporary Jazz

BRASS BANDS REDUX (pages 236–401)

"What we remembered . . ." Victoria Dawson, "Dirty Dozen March to Different Drum," New Orleans *Times-Picayune*, April 29, 1990, A-4.

"We did it and it worked . . ." ibid.

Critiquing it . . . Chris Albertson, "My Feet Can't Fail Me Now," *Stereo Review*, February, 1985, 81.

"We do what people . . ." Jason Berry, "Something Old, Something New," New Orleans *Times-Picayune*, June 16, 1989, 22.

"When we found out . . ." Kermit Ruffins interview with Grace Lichtenstein, September 1991.

"Before you knew it . . ." ibid.

KEEPERS OF THE FLAME—THE MARSALIS FAMILY
(pages 240–57)

"Go down in jazz history . . ." New Orleans *Times-Picayune*, 1989.

"Confirmed bebopper . . ." Berry, *Cradle*, 147.

"I didn't really object . . ." ibid.

"A music that was relatively new . . ." Ellis Marsalis interview with Grace Lichtenstein, February 1992.

"Figure out what . . ." ibid.

"Most of the musicians . . ." Yorke Corbin, "Ellis Marsalis," *WL*, October 1982, 16.

"I was fortunate . . ." Rhodes Spedale, "Ellis Marsalis," *New Orleans,* October 1981.

"Just having the opportunity . . ." quoted in liner notes for "Resolution of Romance" album on Columbia label.

"My father would stay up . . ." Wynton Marsalis interview with Grace Lichtenstein, March 1992.

"I learned everything . . ." Leslie Gourse, "Harry Connick, Jr.," *DB*, April 1988, 48.

"Open to that much . . ." Ellis Marsalis interview.

"It's the same old story . . ." Kalamu Ya Salaam, "The Return of Ellis Marsalis," *WL*, September 1988, 6.

"Every time we played . . ." Victor Goines interview with Grace Lichtenstein, February 1992.

"I heard my father . . ." liner notes for "Resolution of Romance." He was sorry . . . Ellis Marsalis interview.

"Wynton Marsalis is to jazz . . ." Geraldine Wyckoff, "The Chicago Connection, *Gambit,* September 10, 1991, 25.

"A new jazz age . . ." Cover story, *Time,* October 22, 1990.

"I better buy . . ." Ellis Marsalis interview.

"Nobody could go like that . . ." Barbara Rowe, "Whether Classical or Jazz, Wynton Marsalis and his Horn Are at the Top of the Charts," *People,* February 1984, 96.

"The best thing . . ." Howard Mandel, "The Wynton Marsalis Interview" *DB,* July 1984, 17.

"He taught me about the importance . . ." Wynton Marsalis interview.

"Flabbergasted . . ." quoted by Whitney Balliett, "Whiz Kid," *The New Yorker,* June 20, 1983, 79.

"Now don't let me down . . ." *Time,* 67.

"I could always tell . . ." Balliett, "Whiz Kid," 78.

"So many black musicians . . ." ibid.

"I got lost . . ." Francis Davis, *In the Moment: Jazz in the 1980s* (New York: Oxford, 1986).

It is Wynton's firmly held viewpoint . . . Wynton Marsalis interview.

According to Hancock . . . Steve Bloom, "The Hottest Lips in America," *Rolling Stone,* November 8, 1984, 38.

"Who gave an art form . . ." ibid.

"A little harsh . . ." ibid.

"The established cats . . ." quoted in Davis, *In the Moment.*

"Play with or without a vibrato . . ." Balliett, "Whiz Kid," 80.

"It wasn't so much . . ." Wynton Marsalis interview.

"With my brother . . ." ibid.

"I've got every record Miles . . ." Frank Conroy, "Top Brass," *Esquire,* December 1984, 435.

Wynton added, "and I had to listen . . ." Wynton Marsalis interview.

"I heard that music . . ." ibid.

On his own first albums . . . ibid.

"Majesty," Marsalis proclaimed . . . quoted by Stanley Crouch in liner notes for "Majesty of the Blues" album on Columbia label.

"If Wynton has sacrificed . . ." Art Lange, review, *DB,* November 1991.

"Every time I would mess up . . ." Stanley Crouch, "Wynton Marsalis Interview," DB, November 1987, 18.

"We'd play basketball . . ." *Time,* 70.

"Just a down-home guy . . ." Ruffins interview.

"Any amount of money . . ." Gene Seymour, "Got to Deal with the Blues, *Newsday,* August 6, 1991, 51.

Creating something "significant" . . . Wynton Marsalis interview.

Self-styled "lazy . . ." A. James Liska, "Wynton and Branford Marsalis Interview," *DB,* December 1982, 15.

Wynton, he said . . . Salaam, "Return," 6.

Wynton used to keep after me . . . Davis, *In the Moment.*

"I became immersed . . ." ibid.

"Sounded awful . . ." quoted by A. B. Spellman in liner notes for "Scenes from the City" album on Columbia label.

"Look," he said, "we ain't paying you . . ." Davis, *In the Moment.*

"Sitting back . . ." Liska, "Wynton and Branford," 15.

He insisted . . . Spellman, "Scenes" liner notes.

"Didn't have any prejudice . . ." Eric Pooley, "Horn of Plenty," *New York,* October 14, 1991, 60.

In Kirkland's opinion . . . ibid.

"I am a jazz musician . . ." ibid.

"100 percent better . . ." Kevin Whitehead, "The Many Sides of Branford Marsalis," *DB,* March 1987, 17.

"A jam session . . ." "Sax Summit," *DB,* January 1992, 18.

"Of the two brothers . . ." Stephen Fried, "The Holy Goof," *GQ,* May 1991, 201.

"It's too early . . ." Wynton Marsalis interview.

"He's just musically gifted . . ." Ellis Marsalis interview.

IS THE DA's SON THE NEXT SINATRA?—
HARRY CONNICK, JR. (pages 258–65)

"A great shower singer . . ." live performance, New Orleans, 1991.

"That sound generated . . ." Leslie Gourse, "Harry Connick, Jr.," 48.

"I learned a lot . . ." ibid.

"My father came down there . . ." Michael Bourne, "When Harry Met Stardom," DB, March 1990, 16.

"I didn't know what was wrong . . ." Rob Tannenbaum, "The Entertainer," Rolling Stone, March 23, 1989, 34.

A fellow student recalled . . . James Lien, "Harry Connick, Jr.," WL, December 1988, 23.

"So I'd do Stevie Wonder . . ." Bourne, "When Harry Met Stardom," 17.

"As soon as he gets into competition . . ." Ellis Marsalis interview.

"Call me . . ." Gourse, "Harry Connick, Jr.," 48.

"He came in with a rhythm section . . ." Steve Masakowski interview with Grace Lichtenstein, February 1992.

"An oil guy from Zimbabwe . . ." Michael Gross, "Nightlife," New York, September 1990.

Branford Marsalis recalled . . . Chris Albertson, "The New Jazz," Stereo Review, March 1989, 100.

"You were supposed to call . . ." Gourse, "Harry Connick, Jr.," 48.

"We had no rehearsal . . ." Stephen Fried, "The Next Big Thing," GQ, September 1989, 488.

Wynton and Branford both . . . Gourse, "Harry Connick, Jr.," 48.

He said he was forced . . . Bourne, "When Harry Met Stardom," 17.

"I opened up my throat . . ." Camille Barker, "Harry Connick, Jr.," Offbeat, November 1989, 8.

"I sing, and I'm young . . ." Tannenbaum, "The Entertainer," 34.

"I don't want to be a revivalist . . ." ibid.

"I roll my socks . . ." Cathleen McGuigan, "The Bourbon Street Kid Hits His Stride," Newsweek, February 20, 1989, 67.

"Didn't want to be part . . ." Bourne, "When Harry Met Stardom," 18.

"I don't think I'm anything . . ." Tannenbaum, "The Entertainer," 34.

"He's like a god . . ." Mary Ellin Barrett, "Jazzy Harry," *USA Weekend*, July 6–8, 1990, 5.

"He's an idol . . ." quoted by source who was present; wants to remain anonymous.

"There's nothing wrong . . ." James T. Jones IV, "Oh, How Harry Tickles Jazz Piano Fans," *USA Today*, June 13, 1990, 2-D.

"The main difference . . ." Fried, "The Holy Goof," 202.

A *Down Beat* reviewer . . . Bill Milkowski, "Blue Light, Red Light," *DB*, November 1991.

WYNTON'S FLOCK (pages 265–68)

"It is as if someone . . ." Chris Albertson, "Harry Connick, Jr.," *Stereo Review*, November 1988, 130.

"From what I knew . . ." Bob Cataliotti, "The Right Direction," *WL*, January 1988, 23.

What he found, he said . . . Dagradi interview.

"It brings on its own kind . . ." Masakowski interview.

7: Where to Hear it—Where to Find It

JAZZFEST (pages 269–76)

"*The* festival . . ." Peter Nelson, "Jazz by the River," *Esquire*, April 1989, 44.

"The richest, liveliest . . ." Steve Pond, "Crescent City Craziness," *Rolling Stone*, June 19, 1988.

"The world's biggest . . ." David Fricke, "Fun on the Bayou," *Rolling Stone*, June 18, 1987, 20.

"It's like watching . . ." quoted by John Wilson in the New York *Times*, May 16, 1971.

"We pay everyone . . ." Davis interview.

"Part of the charisma . . ." Fricke, "Fun on the Bayou," 15.

"Generic oldies acts . . ." Jon Pareles, "Another Chorus of Nostalgia at the New Orleans Festival," *New York Times*, May 7, 1990, C-11. Another way of looking at these performers, who were fifties favorites like Clarence "Frogman" Henry, is to see them simply as older, rather than "oldies," artists, who naturally draw from what in New Orleans is the "classic" repertoire—the great tunes of the fifties and early sixties such as "Lipstick Traces," "Iko, Iko," and "Big Chief."

According to *Wavelength* . . . "Jazzfest," *WL*, May 1991, 19.

MARDI GRAS AND OTHER PARTIES (pages 276–80)
    A local economics professor . . . identified as James Bobo of University of New Orleans in Leavitt, 150.
    "I feel like I am coming back home . . ." quoted by Festival International press release.

THE CLUB SCENE (pages 280–85)
    "That's how they make . . ." Lomax, 86.
    "The drop-outs . . ." Toussaint interview.
    "We were the only . . ." Charlie Bering interview with Grace Lichtenstein, February 1992.
    "Made me want to be a jazz musician . . ." liner notes for "Live at Blues Alley" album on Columbia label.

Permissions